Cities Going Green

Cities Going Green

A Handbook of Best Practices

Edited by Roger L. Kemp *and*
Carl J. Stephani

McFarland & Company, Inc., Publishers
Jefferson, North Carolina, and London

LIBRARY OF CONGRESS CATALOGUING-IN-PUBLICATION DATA

Cities going green : a handbook of best practices / edited by
Roger L. Kemp and Carl J. Stephani.
p.   cm.
Includes bibliographical references and index.

ISBN 978-0-7864-5968-1
softcover : 50# alkaline paper ∞

1. Urban ecology (Sociology)— United States.   2. Sustainable development —
United States.   I. Kemp, Roger L.   II. Stephani, Carl J.
HT243.U6C577   2011   307.76 — dc22   2011015410

BRITISH LIBRARY CATALOGUING DATA ARE AVAILABLE

Front cover image © 2011 Shutterstock

Manufactured in the United States of America

*McFarland & Company, Inc., Publishers
Box 611, Jefferson, North Carolina 28640
www.mcfarlandpub.com*

To Gabriel, Jonathan, and Matthew:
May this volume help them,
and the community leaders they elect,
appreciate and implement these, and other best practices
to build more wholesome, livable,
and environmentally conscious
communities for generations into the future.

Acknowledgments

Grateful acknowledgment is made to the following organizations and publishers for granting permission to reprint the material in this volume.

American Planning Association
BowTie, Inc.
City of Salt Lake City
e.Republic Inc.
Government Finance Officers Association
Hanley Wood Business Media
The Hartford Courant Company
Institute of Transportation Engineers
Insurance Institute for Highway Safety
International City/County Management Association
League of California Cities
National Association of Realtors
New Jersey State League of Municipalities
Penton Media Inc.
Sierra Club
Urban Land Institute
U.S. Environmental Protection Agency
The Walkable and Livable Communities Institute
Water Environment Research Foundation
World Future Society

Table of Contents

Part III. The Future

Appendices

Preface

Over the past several decades there have been numerous "planning movements" within the United States. They have gone by the titles of Urban Renewal, Garden Cities, Healthy Cities, Smart Growth, Eco-Cities, and Sustainability, to name a few. Citizens, nonprofit organizations, and local public officials in increasing numbers are embracing growth and development management practices as vehicles to facilitate positive planning practices in their downtowns, as well as enhance general planning practices within their respective communities. Public officials especially are learning that they have the municipal power to shape their environment, in their downtowns and suburbs, in a positive manner to enhance the quality of life for the citizens they serve.

Not only can those involved in local government processes renew their downtowns and neighborhoods, they can also have a profound influence on new growth patterns within their political jurisdictions. Contemporary growth management practices are quickly becoming a fact of life in our communities. These emerging planning and development practices generally focus on four aspects of our natural and man-made environments. These areas of attention typically include air quality, water quality, the prudent use and re-use of land, and measures to enhance the existing quality of life for citizens.

The types of modern planning and development practices evolving in our communities include measures that promote planning practices that relate to the creation, protection, preservation, restoration, and enhancement of not only the man-made environment, but also what

is left of our natural environment, too. The "cities going green" movement focuses on ways to create, protect, preserve, enhance and restore the quality of life that individuals and families appreciate in the cities, towns, and suburbs in which they live, especially when it relates to all aspects of their natural environment.

This reference work assembles, for the first time, materials based on a national literature search and makes this information available to citizens, nonprofit organizations, and public officials throughout the nation. The goal is to help educate citizens, as well as public officials, on how to best use these new cities going green planning and development practices to improve their quality of life, as well as to facilitate the restoration of the natural environment within their respective communities.

This volume is divided into three sections for ease of reference. The first section introduces the reader to the rapidly evolving field of cities "going green." The second section, and by design the longest, includes numerous case studies, or best practices, on how cities and towns (as well as nonprofit organizations and public officials) are initiating measures to "go green," which is essential to maintaining the quality of life in the cities and towns throughout the country. The third section focuses on the future of communities relative to the cities going green movement, and relates the positive planning and development practices that will improve our communities during the coming decades. Also, several appendices that have been assembled to promote a greater understanding of this new field, as well as provide resources for those citizens and public officials seeking

1

additional information on the cities going green movement.

Based on this general conceptual schema, the four sections are examined in greater detail below.

Cities Going Green

The first section describes some of the latest and most innovative trends in the cities going green movement in the United States. These chapters provide an overview to this subject and set the foundation for the various best practices that are presented in the following section.

Briefly, these chapters focus on how communities are giving new life to aging neighborhoods, an overview of the evolving best green building practices, how communities are trying to balance commerce with nature, and the need to preserve nature for future generations. The latest trend, green technology, and how it relates to economic development, is also examined.

These chapters provide the framework and background against which the best going green planning and development practices that have emerged in America's cities in recent years are examined.

Best Practices

The various cities, towns, and communities examined in this section, including the states in which they are located, as well as highlights of the evolving best practices in the new discipline of cities going green, are listed in alphabetical order.

These case studies represent an important and significant research effort to obtain a body of knowledge on the best practices available in the dynamic and still evolving field of environment-related planning and development practices in the municipal levels of governments. The best practices section includes over 40 local governments, which are in nearly one-half of the states, plus Washington, D.C.

CITIES

Annapolis	Hartford
Asheville	Huntersville
Atlanta	Ithaca
Austin	Los Angeles
Billings	Memphis
Blackwater	Minneapolis
Central City	North Fair Oaks
Charleston	Oakland
Charlotte	Oregon City
Chattanooga	Philadelphia
Chicago	Portland
Columbus	Salt Lake City
Concord	San Francisco
Dallas	Santa Rosa
Daybreak	Savannah
Denver	Seattle
Detroit	South Amboy
Eugene	Syracuse
Flagstaff	Tacoma
Gaithersburg	Tallahassee
Greensburg	

STATES

Arizona	New Hampshire
California	New Jersey
Colorado	New York
Connecticut	North Carolina
Florida	Ohio
Georgia	Oregon
Illinois	Pennsylvania
Kansas	South Carolina
Maryland	Tennessee
Michigan	Texas
Minnesota	Utah
Montana	Washington

OTHER LOCATIONS

Washington, D.C.

THE BEST PRACTICES

Improvements to the existing water quality.

Redesign of roadways to enhance the environment.

Improvement of conditions in urban heat islands.

Implementation of emerging green government practices.

Encouragement for updating old structures to green building standards.

Protection of our existing natural corridors.

Restoration of our remaining watershed areas.

Preservation of our undeveloped coastlines.

Construction of people-friendly streets.

Public investment for the acquisition of parks and open spaces.

Development of new sustainable streetscape projects.

Combining conservation goals with development standards and practices.

Encouragement of the new discipline of restorative development.

Locating new urban growth around existing transportation hubs.

Balancing new development with preservation standards.

Development of new sustainable neighborhoods.

Participation in the urban "greening" movement.

Creation of new energy efficient buildings.

Development of new walkable communities.

Cleaning our existing rivers and streams.

Establishment of new community and neighborhood eco-districts.

Encouragement of new neighborhood gardens.

Revision of zoning laws to promote desired growth and preservation patterns.

Diversification of our existing urban forest areas.

Reduction of air pollution to improve our environment.

Approval of new sustainable planning guidelines and practices.

Provision of light rail transportation options for citizens.

Consideration of health issues in the planning and development process.

Promotion of smart growth development guidelines, standards, and practices.

Automation of the stream restoration processes.

Encouragement of bicycle commuting for citizens.

Advancement of green stormwater management practices.

Transforming aging and old buildings into new green buildings.

Reduction of air pollution by building new bikeways.

Implementation of build-it-green programs.

Creation of new fused grid street network systems.

Approval of green building design guidelines and standards.

Revitalization of aging municipal waterfront areas.

Encouragement of watershed education and restoration options for citizens.

Redesigning our existing public roadways for people rather than cars.

Approval and enforcement of new clean water quality regulations.

Encouragement and promotion of newly established eco-friendly neighborhoods.

The Future

The final section examines future planning and development trends in cities, changing societal standards that are facilitating these trends, as well as recently approved and evolving urban planning and development practices. Topics examined include an overview of the going green planning and development practices of cities in the future, and how communities are using what is commonly referred to as sustainability as the common quality of life goal for their citizens. Other subjects reviewed include evolving and likely transportation changes in society in the future, the concern with restoring and preserving the natural qualities of cities, and trends that relate to the revitalization of the nation's downtown areas and neighborhoods. All of these subjects relate to the major trends focusing on the future planning, development, and redevelopment growth practices and patterns that have facilitated the development of so-called green communities throughout our nation.

These readings reflect that the various initiatives and best practices described in this book related to the protection, restoration, and enhancement of our urban environment are here to stay. Part of this national focus is on adopting appropriate planning and development practices that will preserve the remaining parks and open spaces in communities throughout America. Modern planning and development practices that achieve these goals are being developed and implemented with greater frequency during the past few years. The various diseconomies associated with past planning and development practices, which have served to deteriorate the natural aspects of our environment, have facilitated these positive going green planning and development practices.

Appendices

This is the first edited reference work of its type on this topic that offers options for communities to consider and use in their going green planning and development practices. To this end, several important reference resources are included as appendices.

Periodical Bibliography. A listing of major periodicals focusing on contemporary planning and development issues in communities, as well as functional disciplines related to the various related issues and problems facing municipal governments today. The website for each publisher is listed to provide immediate access to these periodicals, as well as information on how to acquire them.

Glossary. Because the new field of cities going green relates to existing local government planning and developments laws, regulations, and planning practices, a list of commonly used terms is included. These terms are used in the municipal planning field.

Acronyms and Abbreviations. For the reasons mentioned above, the various acronyms and abbreviations that are used in the municipal planning field are listed. While seasoned planners may have a working knowledge of these letters, other individuals reading this volume may wish to review these common acronyms and abbreviations for their information.

Regional Resource Directory. This appendix includes a listing of all of the community governments included in Part II. Readers wishing to follow up on any of the best practices are provided with immediate access to each government via its online website. In those communities with the council-manager form of government, it is suggested that inquiries and questions be directed to the office of the city manager. In those cities with the strong-mayor form of government, it is recommended that all inquiries and questions be made directly to the office of the mayor.

National Resource Directory. This list includes all major national professional, membership, and research organizations serving public officials, professionals, and concerned citizens. Many of these organizations focus on various issues related to cities, zoning, land-use practices, as well as major issues and subjects related to planning and development topics. The websites are identified for each organization and association.

State Municipal League Directory. Most states have a professional municipal association, which serves as a valuable source of information about the city governments. State leagues typically have copies of municipal laws and policies, as well as model practices, available for public officials in their state to review. The website for each state's municipal league is listed to provide access to these valuable documents and related sources of online information.

State Library Directory. Each state has a central state library, and each one typically contains copies of state laws, proposed and adopted, in an online database. Many state libraries also have copies of the various laws adopted in those cities and towns within their jurisdiction. These libraries serve as an excellent resource. The website for each state library is listed to provide the reader with direct access to this valuable online information.

The editors hope that the information contained in this volume will assist local public officials, citizens, and leaders of municipal organizations as they attempt to make sense out of, and cope with, the existing and emerging going green issues in their communities. The future of America's municipalities depends upon the proper planning and management of our inner-city areas, as well as the many neighborhoods that surround them. Citizens not only expect but demand that prudent measures be adopted and implemented to ensure that future growth will not negatively impact, but help create, protect, preserve, restore, and positively impact our nation's natural environment, as well as its many resources.

PART I : GOING GREEN

CHAPTER 1

Communities Give New Life to Old Neighborhoods

Steve Garman

In the early 1980s, a visionary named Robert Davis took a risk with a radical departure from conventional land use by recreating small-town America as it was in the beginning of the 20th century. Not a Disney model, but a real, living environment with real people in real houses. His setting was unlikely: a beach in Florida.

Davis was not a wealthy Florida land speculator. He had inherited 80 acres in south Walton County in the Florida panhandle — in those days called "The Redneck Riviera" by those who favored more populated areas of Florida. The only enterprise on the property was a shrimp stand. Davis, however, had several things working on his behalf.

His land abutted the white sand beaches and aquamarine surf of the emerald coast, an area whose beaches are superior to those anywhere else in Florida. He had a land-use concept that various local governments and developers had toyed with, with some success, but no one had put it to a large-scale test. Davis also had the advantage of a friendly Florida law that allowed discretionary land use authority for Developments of Regional Impact, or "DRIs."

But Davis's ace in the hole was a memory — a memory of youthful summers, of lounging on porches, listening to stories, catching lightning bugs, walking to the corner market for soda and ice cream, of knowing your neighbors and being known.

Robert Davis and his partner architects, Andreas Duany and Elizabeth Plater-Zabek, drew the 80-acre a community we now know as Seaside Florida. To Davis, the project was a canvas on which every corner, every block, and every lot had to be carefully planned. The finished picture had to work as a total neighborhood concept. It was 1981, and New Urbanism as we know it today was born.

In Washington, D.C., and Decatur, Illinois

Meanwhile, in Washington, D.C., the Department of Housing and Urban Development (HUD) was experimenting with more flexible and innovative designs for federally funded housing developments in America's local governments. HUD wanted to create more livable space at lower prices, replacing high-rise housing projects with comfortable, nurturing neighborhoods. Too many well-meaning HUD housing programs had not produced the desired result, and the agency decided

Originally published as "The Hope and Risk of New Urbanism," *Public Management*, Vol. 84, No. 1, January/February, 2002, published and copyrighted by ICMA (International City/County Management Association), Washington, D.C. Reprinted with permission of the publisher.

that conventional housing programs and regulation were part of the problem.

In 1993, the HOPE Program — Housing Opportunities for People Everywhere — was created. The ideas and concepts being explored by Davis in Florida, and a few other innovators elsewhere, looked to be the neighborhood concept HUD had been seeking, so a marriage was arranged. The Federal Housing Agency became a champion for the New Urbanism through the new and flexible HOPE, program.

In central Illinois, the early 1990s found the city of Decatur embarking on a multiyear neighborhood restoration program in a badly deteriorated area known as the Near North. Adjacent to the central business district, the area contains approximately 10 acres, including a 20-acre public housing project called Longview. Longview has 386 units and is under the jurisdiction of the Decatur Housing Authority (DHA), funded, in part, by HUD.

In the mid 1990s, the DHA applied for a HOPE VI grant to replace the aging Longview. Decatur was already buying and clearing the dilapidated New Near North Neighborhood, so the city and DHA joined to create an innovative HOPE VI grant application that would not just replace Longview, but create a 120-acre mixed-income land use development providing affordable housing and other neighborhood improvements.

DHA was notified in fall 1999 that the grant had been approved and some $35 million in HUD funds could be put into the project

HOPE VI projects (the VI refers to the sixth round of HOPE funding) tend to be highly individual, since they reflect the needs of the community in which the grant is authorized. One common element, however, is that they employ the neighborhood design concepts of the New Urbanism. This coming together of circumstances and events is fortuitous for Decatur and creates an unusual opportunity.

The challenge facing HUD, the DHA, and the city is to create a high quality, pedestrian-friendly, mixed-use development that, in any area of any city, would be considered a desirable living environment. A place of choice, not necessity.

Conversion and Blight, Computers and Suburbia

Turning a deteriorated area into a high-quality living environment is a problem that federal-subsidy money can address, but can it be designed creatively enough to attract lower-, middle-, and higher-income buyers and renters?

The New Urbanism is at once simple and difficult to define. Put most simply, New Urbanism takes the conventional neighborhood designs of pre–World War II America and goes a step further; an entire neighborhood area is designed as a complete environment aimed at enhancing the quality of life of its inhabitants. In short, a safe, complete, "old world" village — an anti-sprawl experience.

Today, most local governments have neighborhoods that are friendlier to cars and trucks than people. The sizes and configurations of streets, garages, cul-de-sacs, driveways, and other neighborhood and property elements were designed to accommodate automobiles and fire trucks rather than people. With escalating use of cars and public transportation, the concept of villages — of people-friendly neighborhoods — began to disappear.

American neighborhoods are becoming islands of gated communities in a sea of urban sprawl. The computer has further polarized neighbors with its intensely personal window on the world, but not on the yard next door. Instant, worldwide communications available on a screen in your den often leaves no time to visit across the backyard fence.

Hope of HOPE

A perfect HOPE VI project is one in which 33 percent of the homes are occupied by conventional "public housing"— annual contributions contract (ACC)— tenants, 33 percent by tenants in tax credit properties, and 33 percent by market rate homeowners and renters — and no one can tell which is which and who is who. A worthy challenge.

In ACC housing, a tenant pays 30 percent of his or her income as rent, regardless of what it cost to build the unit. Market price issues do not come into play in putting ACC tenants into HOPE VI housing. The tenants of such units are encouraged to nudge their lifestyle toward upward mobility, and community support services aimed at facilitating that growth are an integral part of the HOPE VI process.

In tax credit units, a fixed rental rate is established; qualifying tenants must have an income that is less than 60 percent of the median income in the area, both ACC and tax credit units target various segments of the lower-than-average-in-come population. In our economy this can mean health care and civil service workers, teachers, secretaries, reporters, and others who are in careers with greater income potential but who are unable to afford market price housing.

The real challenge in the Decatur project is the for-rent and for-sale housing at "market" prices. Such neighborhoods are commonly referred to as mixed income.

Decatur Housing Inventory

New housing for middle-income individuals and families in Decatur has been virtually nonexistent in recent years. Population decline and a healthy inventory of older homes in good neighborhoods have quashed demand, as construction costs have risen faster than property appreciation. A new 1,200-square-foot house would cost much more than an older home of the same size in a quality neighborhood.

Thus, little middle-income housing has been constructed, which creates a particularly thorny problem: how to market rental and for sale property in the targeted HOPE VI neighborhood.

The answer is not simple, and it must come from a unified attack on the problem by a broad and creative front. Everyone involved in the Decatur housing industry, from zoning administrators to mortgage companies, must be involved in the challenge and committed to the goal.

The HOPE program allows Decatur to become a laboratory of how to make homeownership more affordable. With the HUD grant, an open, innovative nature and a willingness to bring all facets of homeownership into play, Decatur has an exceptional opportunity to become the model for others. Perhaps what sets the Decatur project apart from others are the size and availability of land beyond the old public housing to be demolished. The 20-acre Longview public housing won't merely be replaced with 20 acres of new housing but with 120 acres of neighborhood redevelopment. In most HOPE VI projects, one acre of public housing is replaced with one acre of HOPE VI housing.

The Impact on Community

It would be difficult to overstate the significance of the project on the community of Decatur. One primary goal of every HOPE VI project is spillover benefit, or the positive impact the new neighborhood can have on adjacent neighborhoods. In Decatur, as in many other communities, some of the urban neighborhoods radiating from the central core are more than 100 years old and showing serious signs of distress.

The worst was the 120 acres targeted for redevelopment, but others are approaching the same level of deterioration. A successful project in the Near North can radiate out to other neighborhoods, just as a deteriorating Near North caused a negative radiation. A new downtown redevelopment agenda is especially important relative to the New Near North Neighborhood.

The same suburban phenomenon that led to the deterioration of the Near North neighborhood facilitated the deterioration of downtown Decatur. The market moved away, so the businesses and services of post–World War II downtown Decatur moved with it.

The HOPE VI project hopes to reverse the cycle, by pulling a new market into the inner city. Since new downtown development is critical to the process, the city has initiated and facilitated new development opportunities on an ambitious level.

An entire downtown block has been purchased and is scheduled for demolition by the end of the year. New office buildings are anticipated. The Archer Daniels Midland Company (ADM) recently purchased a 60,000-square-foot building in downtown Decatur, and the food, nutrition, and alternative fuel-processing giant will convert the building to a worldwide training center, housing from 250 to 350 employees.

ADM employees will come from all over the globe and work downtown for four or five days at a time. A mostly unused 600-car parking garage will be renovated through a joint agreement between ADM and the city and made safer and more user-friendly for future downtown employees and shoppers, as well as ADM employees.

New linkages between the New Near North Neighborhood development and downtown will emerge. Managers and planners have learned over the years that inner-city reconstruction efforts necessitate new investment, which encourages more new investment, just as blight encourages blight.

The challenge that faces the city and DHA is daunting. We must borrow from the success of others just as we learn from their failures. We can embrace reality and the success of Robert Davis's New Urbanism and make it ours, adjusted for the Midwestern climate and culture. With the financial help of HUD; the determination and cooperation of the city, the Decatur Housing Authority, and stakeholders; the active advice and intervention of all players in the Decatur housing industry; the investment and courage of our major industrial and financial leaders — and the understanding and patience of the citizens of Decatur — the HOPE VI project has what it takes to succeed.

As with any endeavor where the potential rewards are great, the chance of failure also is great, and this creates risk. As local government managers know, taking risks is not easy in the public sector. But the hope for New Urbanism in the downtown environs is a risk worth taking.

NOTE

The Near North Redevelopment Project received a grant of $2.5 million from HUD for the construction of new streets, utilities, and green space development. (Source: U.S. Department of Housing and Urban Development website, August 13, 2009.)

CHAPTER 2

Evolving Green Building Practices
Jim Heid

Green development — especially, green land-based development that emphasizes the tenets of environmental responsibility or sustainability at the community level — is at a crossroads. The concept of building in an environmentally appropriate manner has stirred a wide response from the development community, ranging from evangelical adoption to raised-eyebrow cynicism, but the majority of land developers could be characterized as cautiously interested. Although the green development movement, which started out addressing a diffuse and broad set of issues, has gained increased focus, large-scale adoption of its principles will remain elusive until those principles are clearly defined and put forth in a way that allows them to achieve universal implementation.

To move beyond theory, an assessment is needed of the challenges faced and the results achieved by today's oft-cited leading-edge projects. To date, much of the research, writing, and financial analysis has surrounded green buildings, which by their very nature represent singular products that allow thorough analysis providing relatively easily quantified results, such as energy savings and product differentiation that may translate into higher leasing rates. While green building is valuable as a step toward fostering better real estate development, greater potential for significant change in the built environment lies in green land development, which has a greater impact on the general population through its role in shaping urban and suburban forms.

Changes in the land development paradigm — or at least creation of new land development trends — often come about because of passionate, visionary developers and patient investors who are willing to test, refine, and rework new ideas in a nonformulaic manner, often requiring a long investment horizon. In the case of green land development, this has meant that the best examples began with greenfield sites where land was easier to assemble, though not necessarily to entitle, and where niche markets — primarily high-end, sophisticated buyers — were targeted. With green concepts developed and tested in this setting, new projects have come forward on more complex infill sites and have been carefully programmed to reach a broader market.

The ten U.S. developments comprising a portfolio of the most noted green land development projects have raised the awareness of green development issues and tested new concepts with varying levels of success. Therefore, they provide the most effective case studies for learning from others' efforts in green development. Anecdotal analysis of and site visits to these projects, as well as discussion with noted planners and developers, have led to creation of a set of ten elements of land development, affording a consistent method for evaluating

Originally published as "Green Reflections," *Urban Land*, Vol. 63, No. 7, July 2004, by the Urban Land Institute, Washington, DC. Reprinted with permission of the publisher.

project success. (See "Ten Elements of Land Development" at the end of this chapter.)

A comparative evaluation of these projects shows how well each addressed the essence of the ten elements of land development. A more detailed assessment and the implications for future developments follows.

First-Generation Projects

Civano, Tucson, Arizona. Civano was the first project that tried to combine new urbanism and green development. Its location on the fringe makes it not particularly appropriate environmentally, but its plan was successfully shaped to respond to natural systems. Civano set ambitious and rigorous performance targets for resource efficiency, water use, waste generation, and job creation. There is some mixing of scales and products. The initial neighborhood center provides an example of how early uses of sales and marketing can be combined with community focus in an architecturally expressive way while the use of new construction materials and techniques is communicated to buyers. Unfortunately, as a pioneer in an unproven market, Civano's value as a case study comes in the many lessons it provides regarding the challenges of public/private partnership when breaking new ground, the difficulties of moving green theory to builder execution, and the challenges of gaining a market that never materialized at a scale or speed consistent with the vision.

Prairie Crossing, Grayslake, Illinois. Although it could be argued that the greenfield location is not appropriate for the project, the community's net density is a significant improvement over that of other development that has taken place in the surrounding area. Because the property was primarily farmland, there was not a significant natural system to shape the site plan; hence, the plan is driven more by housing concepts than any natural systems requirements. Resource efficiency was a significant goal, and it was achieved fairly well through home design and energy efficiency standards, given the state of the industry when the project was developed. Streets do not pro-

vide much of a public realm due to the low density and more rural character of the community. Mixed uses are not particularly strong because the product appealed primarily to people of a fairly high socioeconomic level, but a new, higher-density, mixed-use transit center is expected to provide more diversity in both residential options and some supporting commercial uses. Infrastructure is well conceived: Prairie Crossing's stormwater management system provides a model with measurable financial benefits — $1.2 million in initial infrastructure savings. In terms of cultural connections, the community's focus on agriculture as its essence provides both a unique commercial and social aspect consistent with the mission and ambience of the development.

Dewees Island, Isle of Palms, South Carolina. Given its location and broader barrier island context, the community's site plan reflects careful thinking and planning. The systems-based structure is evident, with the final master plan guided by natural systems and a significant commitment to natural resource conservation. Resource efficiency is high in regard to home design, water, and irrigation requirements. Dewees Island is accessible only by ferry: no motor vehicles are permitted and all community transport is by electric cart only. Art analysis comparing the energy consumption of the island's regularly scheduled ferry service to that of standard automobile trips would provide a means of assessing the community's energy operating characteristics. Streets play an interesting part in the community fabric, both because of their limited scale and their use of crushed shells, a highly permeable surface. The cultural connections, which include a nature center and community outreach educational programs, are well executed and serve as a significant model for other developments.

Spring Island, Beaufort, South Carolina. Sometimes thought of as a Dewees Island with golf, Spring Island is, in fact, very different. While the location is just as remote and appealing, the developer's initial vision to downzone the property to only develop units consistent with the site's carrying capacity yielded a program, character, and feel that are distinct. Consisting of a much more tailored appearance with fewer hard-edge green requirements (i.e., energy and irrigation), the site is planned and developed to have little impact on the environment. The roadways are too rural to be the center of activity, and the buyers are from too narrow of a socioeconomic profile to require a variety of lifestyle products. But the architecture and the nature center are well done and play an important role in creating the character and cachet of the project. As Spring Island incorporates a golf course, it provides a model for how golf can be carefully sited and developed to create both a great game experience and a community asset, while eschewing the conventional wisdom of exploiting every front foot of fairway. The development's sophisticated financial tools for creating and funding long-term conservation and education could be used as a model for future projects.

The Impact and Returns of First-Generation Projects

These four projects represent the initial generation of green land development — those large-tract developments that pioneered many of the ideas viewed today as commonplace. The projects resulted from the vision and environmental commitment of a handful of developers or, in the case of Civano, one city that sought to find a new development model sensitive to the land and the community.

Two of the four projects — Civano and Prairie Crossing — were established as learning models to allow the ideas being discussed among a small circle of thinkers to be tested on the open market. As a result, their financial returns are less than optimal and might even be considered irrelevant in the capital markets. However, the other two projects, Dewees Island and Spring Island, have demonstrated that a market exists for this kind of development — that buyers are willing to pay a premium to belong to such a community, or see the tenets of green development as a compelling point of differentiation that leads them to choose real estate in a green community rather than in a more traditional one.

Second-Generation Projects

Hidden Springs, Boise, Idaho. The initial planning effort looked beyond the project boundary to study the "development shed" of 10,000 acres, evaluating the impacts on and potential development patterns in the area's future if all development as identified in the comprehensive plan were to follow the Hidden Springs model. This shifted development locations and densities across the site. Equally important, the site's features — slopes, a low valley of high-quality land, the road system, and washes — drove the development patterns according to a natural systems structure. Consequently, open space was preserved for habitat, which helped to boost real estate values. Streets take on an important role as the public realm, are well scaled, and form an important part of both the vehicular and pedestrian circulation system. The crossroads mercantile center effectively serves as the town center. The community, which now has about 33 percent of its total 1,035-lot entitlement sold, is maturing well and seeing strong buyer recognition.

Highland Gardens, Denver, Colorado. Though small at 27 acres, Highland Gardens is one of the most complete and thoroughly conceived green land developments of any generation. Starting with a strong infill location — a highly developed urbanized neighborhood — and applying a broad-based set of development principles ranging from diversity to sustainability, the community experienced rapid sales. The project is ambitious in the number of products it delivered, the self-imposed energy and resource efficiency goals it set for itself, its creative use of tax credits, and the socially conscious adaptive use of the site's legacy buildings. In many ways, it excels at incorporating all ten elements of land development and serves as a worthwhile model for developers of product types.

Coffee Creek, Chesterton, Indiana. Coffee Creek emerged as a land development exercise to take advantage of a land asset held by the Lake Erie Land Company. Demonstrating convergence of green development and new urbanism, the community pioneered significant density proposals and unique stormwater management techniques, including the use of "level spreaders" to restore and dissipate stormwater flows into the community's centerpiece, Coffee Creek Preserve. The project envisions 1,200 residential units and more than 1 million square feet of commercial space to create a jobs/housing balance. The preserve has been constructed and receives more than 15,000 visitors annually. Both commercial and residential development is underway, but at a much slower pace than comparable projects.

The Impact and Returns of Second-Generation Projects

These three projects represent the second generation of green land development — an advanced set of communities whose development couples the first generation's aspirations with experience and the savvy of a more market-driven approach. The developers were schooled in the lessons of the first-generation projects and sought to incorporate their benefits and ideas into a more traditionally financed, constructed, and marketed project. Hidden Springs, which set out with ambitious goals and ideals, has delivered on a number of its objectives, but, like other pioneering projects, has required more time than anticipated for the market to catch up to the vision. Coffee Creek, which now is gaining momentum, also started slow, and, in the words of one project executive, developers "have learned that the green and urbanist agenda do not always move forward at the same pace." One of the ironies of Hidden Springs is the success of the community's riskiest product — higher-density, alley-loaded village homes — in a market where the perceived demand was for big lots. Highland Garden Village has experienced significant acceptance and success in the marketplace, and now has built and sold out all but its 65,000-to-90,000-square-foot commercial component.

Current Projects

Stapleton, Denver, Colorado. Stapleton, a significant infill site in a highly urbanized area

of Denver, provides another example of the convergence of green development and new urbanism. Multiple builders are building on multiple parcels, often across the street from one another, to assure diversity in appearance and product. The result is an emerging mixed-use village offering a wide variety of products in a walkable community with a strong open-space component and a restored natural landscape — all reclaimed from a closed public airport.

Baldwin Park, Winter Park, Florida. Baldwin Park is one of the first community development projects to emerge from a decade of military base closures. It combines the principles of new urbanism in the physical plan with green development ideals in its operation and execution. Located on the edge of Winter Park and Orlando, Baldwin Park is providing another significant urban infill community. Mixed uses, walkable neighborhoods, innovative infrastructure, and extensive recycling of site materials — more than 500,000 tons of reconstituted concrete from over 4.5 million square feet of buildings from the former Orlando Naval Training Center — demonstrate how the science and practicality of certain green techniques have matured in the past decade. Baldwin Park is entitled for 3,700 residential units and more than 1.4 million square feet of office/retail space; the developer has written contracts for 620 units following the opening of the sales center in April 2003.

Noisette, North Charleston, South Carolina. Noisette represents the capstone of 13 years of experimentation and application of green development principles. An ambitious development proposal by John Knott and a wide range of consultants and investors, the project seeks to take the lessons learned by greenfield, environmentally friendly developments and apply them to a disinvested, economically challenged inner-city core. Combining the former Charleston Naval Base, city lands, private lands, and public parks, the project envisions a long-term community that demonstrates all aspects of green development and provides a laboratory for evaluating, monitoring, and learning from the experience of regenerating the urban core. The master plan has been adopted by the city of North Charleston, and ground has been broken on 1,000 new residential units and a new riverfront park.

The way land is developed and development's impact on the urban and suburban form cannot be improved overnight. For generations, both the private and public sectors have sought to find better ways to develop residential communities, with varying degrees of success. But land development at its essence is a temporal exercise: communities are developed and sold by developers with an increasingly short-term view, largely due to financing challenges and the uncertainties of the entitlement process. The ten elements of land development, and the case study reviews in light of those elements, provide a first step for creation of a common language and a way of evaluating the success and merits of the past decade's efforts

Ten Elements of Land Development

The following ten elements of land development cut across planning ideologies to provide a litmus test for a development's environmental success. While not a checklist or formula, the ten elements can help create a common vocabulary that planning teams, developers, and policy makers can use to discuss the efficacy of a proposed project and how well the design addresses ideals of high quality land development.

1. **Contextually and Locationally Responsive.** While infill and regeneration sites are the most environmentally friendly; the fact remains that most future development will occur in Greenfield settings. Focusing planning or study efforts outside the parcel boundary to identify affected systems and linkages, as well as potential synergies within an appropriate "development shed" will result in a more responsive and appropriate development plan.

2. **Systems-Based Structure.** Thorough understanding of a site and its carrying capacity is critical to sustainable development. Today, the power of geographic information system (GIS) technology and improved scientific analysis permits much more intelligent assessment and modeling of development alternatives for a given property, and allows development to be shaped by a site's inherent natural systems, which should be identified and set aside before development.

3. **Resource Efficiency.** Resource efficiency is a simple moniker that encompasses a diversity of implementation strategies ranging from the macro scale of transportation — reducing vehicular dependence — to a micro level of efficient use of water or energy for habitable spaces. Balancing consumption and production — especially when dealing with energy — is becoming more viable with the advent of lower-cost photovoltaic cells and increasingly efficient and cost-effective techniques in wind-generated power and distributed energy generation. Finally, the developer can influence the balance in the postdevelopment phase by establishing systems to manage waste streams.

4. **Streets as Public Realm.** What had been banished to the infrastructure column in land development pro formas has reemerged as the cornerstone of a community amenity. Attentive and detailed understanding of the complex interplay of width and scale; pedestrian character; texture, light, and shadow; and architectural arid landscape edge conditions has allowed the conversion of asphalt to agora — a higher plane of public connection and place making.

5. **Fine-Grain Mixed Use.** While many developments of the 1970s and 1980s sought to create the vitality and energy evocative of small villages and towns, their execution reflected a naïveté about market dynamics and a lack of sophistication in physical design. The "build it and they will come" approach to village centers created programmatically correct but locationally deficient struggling retail centers. Today, greater knowledge and practicality has led to finer-grain mixing of both residential products and limited commercial uses to create greater community vitality and richness. A long-term view that establishes flexible codes and building types will ensure that fine-grain mixed use, which may not be viable today, can evolve over time, as it did in many of America's best-loved villages.

6. **Infrastructure as Asset.** Once considered nuisances to be piped away as quickly as possible, stormwater and wastewater, through

enlightened thinking are now recognized as significant resources. Improved science and a sustainable approach on both stormwater management and wastewater treatment issues have produced solutions that are scientifically possible, biologically beneficial, and aesthetically appealing. In arid climates, simply reusing effluent on landscape areas cuts consumption of potable water, reduces piping requirements, and recharges the aquifer. Stormwater retention, detention, and first flush treatment allows creation of new landscape and habitat environments while also reducing initial infrastructure costs.

7. **Conscious Materials Choice.** The art of building ultimately relies on the selection and use of particular materials. While initial environmental efforts focused on use of energy-efficient appliances or construction materials, increasing attention is being paid to all material choices. This attention requires complex and sometimes competing analyses. Selection of the right, truly environmentally responsible materials requires developers and designers to explore where the materials come from (the energy cost of transportation), how it is made (the kind of energy required to make it and any negative production impacts on the environment, employees, or the quality of life), and whether it comes from a renewable source or contains significant amounts of postconsumer materials. Additional considerations include the environmental impacts created during installation, such as the amount of energy required and whether it endangers the installer's health and whether is will generate detrimental effects such as off-gassing after installation. The final issues are how much maintenance the material will require and whether it can be reused or recycled when it becomes obsolete.

8. **Economic Viability.** One of the three components of sustainability along with ecology and social equity, economic sustainability is often lost or its importance diminished during the public approval or entitlement process. It is critically important that citizens and approval agencies recognize that the best way to change the development paradigm is to make sure new forms of development are economically viable. A project that achieves all its environmental goals but does not provide a reasonable return to the investor will also fail so spark genuine interest in creating similar projects, no matter how much legislation is put in place.

9. **Places Not Projects.** Place making is difficult to define, but increasingly a common language is emerging to allow discussion of core components and issues that must be addressed as part of community design. Environments that make places out of projects are carefully woven together through an understanding of program mix and synergy; material, color, light, and transparency; the role of landscape and pedestrian space; and the type and spatial organization of furnishing, signs, art, and soft programming.

10. **Connect People and Culture.** One of the most compelling realizations to emerge from recent land development success stories is that buyers will pay a premium to be part of something authentic. A site that is properly selected and analyzed will yield a wealth of information that not only provides clues for land use and spatial organization, but also the essence of the community — its roots. A carefully developed understanding of the history of both the site and the region will form the soul of the community that connects buyers with shared values. Consideration of how individuals are included in the ultimate evolution of the community — not through a set of dogmatic and aesthetically driven codes, but through a program and a shared set of principles — will allow new residents to develop a sense of authorship and an even higher level of connection to each other, the community, and the region at large.

CHAPTER 3

Ways to Balance Nature and Commerce
Edward T. McMahon

What did you do on your last vacation? Would you recommend the place you visited to a friend? Or were you disappointed? Did dirty air, traffic congestion, crowded beaches, slipshod service, or excessive commercialism leave you feeling frustrated and cheated? Americans spend almost $800 billion a year on travel and recreational pursuits away from home. One out of every 8.4 jobs — or 11 percent of total U.S. employment — is related to the travel/tourism industry. Some 37 states claim it as their leading industry and in 2004 alone it generated over $250 billion in federal, state, and local tax revenues.

Tourism provides American communities with many benefits, including new jobs, an expanded tax base, enhanced infrastructure, improved facilities, and a market for local products, art, and handicrafts. It can also create burdens such as crowding, traffic, noise, more crime, haphazard development, cost-of-living increases, and degraded resources.

Sustainable tourism, on the other hand, helps maximize the benefits of tourism while minimizing the downsides. It differs from the mass-market brand of tourism because tangible benefits are measured rather than sheer heads counted.

American cities and towns spend millions of dollars on tourism marketing to entice visitors. This, in turn, helps create demand or expand a market. This is critical in a competitive marketplace.

Yet, tourism involves much more than marketing. It also involves making destinations more appealing. This means conserving and enhancing a destination's natural tourism assets; in short, protecting the environment. The unique heritage, culture, wildlife, or natural beauty of a community or region is really what attracts visitors in the first place.

In today's tourism marketplace, competition for tourists' dollars can be fierce. If a destination is too crowded, too commercial, or too much like every other place, then why go there? It is for this reason that local planning, land development, and urban design standards are so important to communities with tourism resources. Communities get the message that they are in trouble when new development shapes the character of the community — instead of the character of the community shaping new development.

There are significant differences between tourists' and residents' perceptions of a community. Tourists tend to be open and receptive to everything they see, while residents tend to tune out the familiar environment along the roads they travel day in and day out. This suggests that local tourism officials need to become much more aware of the overall character of their community.

If the character of a destination is at odds with its description in advertising and promotional literature, for example, the tourist will

Originally published as "Sustainable Destinations," *Urban Land*, Vol. 64, No. 8, August 2005, by the Urban Land Institute, Washington, D.C. Reprinted with permission of the publisher.

feel cheated. Creation of a false image — beautifully photographed uncrowded beaches when the more realistic picture is standing room only — can spoil a vacation. What is more, it can reduce the likelihood of repeat visitation: tourists may come once, but they will not come back. Alternatively, fond memories and word of mouth can be a destination's best public relations.

Tourism is a voluntary activity — which means that tourists can choose from a wide range of competing destinations. Given a variety of choices, where will they end up? According to heritage tourism expert Amy Webb, virtually every study of traveler motivations has shown that, along with rest and recreation, visiting scenic areas and historic sites are the top reasons why people travel. In a speech, travel writer Arthur Frommer noted, "Among cities with no particular recreational appeal, those that have preserved their past continue to enjoy tourism. Those that haven't, receive almost no tourism at all. Tourism simply doesn't go to a city that has lost its soul."

So how can a community attract tourists — and their dollars — without losing its soul? First, a community needs to recognize that sustainable tourism is a long-term strategy, not a quick fix. Second, a community needs to understand that people become tourists in order to visit a specific, special place. As economic development expert Don Rypkema says, "Nobody goes anywhere to go down a water-slide or buy a T-shirt. They may do both of these things, but that isn't the reason they went there." People travel to see places, especially those that are special, unusual, and unique. In short, any place can create a tourist attraction, but it is those places that are attractions in and of themselves that people most want to visit.

Preservation-minded cities like Annapolis, Maryland; Savannah, Georgia; Charleston, South Carolina; New Orleans, Louisiana; Santa Fe, New Mexico; Quebec City, Canada; and San Miguel de Allende, Mexico, are among North America's leading tourism destinations precisely because they have protected their unique architectural heritage. By contrast, cities that have obliterated their past attract hardly any tourists at all, except for the highly competitive and notoriously fickle convention business.

Not every community is blessed with a great natural wonder or a rich legacy of historic buildings, but most communities have tourism potential. Realizing this potential begins by inventorying a community's assets — both existing and potential. What natural, cultural, or historic resources does a community have to offer? What features give a community its special character and identity? This is how Lowell, Massachusetts, began its transformation from a gritty, industrial city, with an unemployment rate of 23 percent, to a city that now receives over 800,000 visitors a year, has restored 250 historic buildings, and has seen over $1 billion in new investments. It all began by recognizing the potential that existed in the abandoned mill buildings that characterized the city, and then planning to realize that potential.

Sustainable tourism means preserving and protecting resources. The more a community does to conserve its unique resources, whether natural, architectural, or cultural, the more tourists it will attract. On the other hand, the more a community comes to resemble "Anyplace, U.S.A.," the less reason there is to visit. Make a destination more appealing, and people will stay longer — and spend more.

The following are six recommendations that communities might want to consider:

Focus on authenticity. Communities should make every effort to preserve the authentic aspects of local heritage and culture, including food, handicrafts, art, music, language, architecture, landscape, traditions, and history. Sustainable tourism emphasizes the real over the artificial. It recognizes that the true story of an area is worth telling, even if it is painful or disturbing.

In Birmingham, Alabama, for example, the Civil Rights Museum and the Historic District tell the story of the city's turbulent history during the civil rights era. The authentic representation of the city's past adds value and appeal to Birmingham as a destination and the museum and adjacent historic district have proved popular with visitors from all over the world.

By contrast, many tourist attractions near

the Smoky Mountains National Park portray Cherokee Indians as using teepees and totem poles and wearing feather war bonnets, even though this was never a part of their culture. This commercialized stereotype of a Native American has caused anger toward the tourism industry and devalued the area as a destination.

Ensure that tourism-support facilities — hotels, motels, restaurants, and shops — are architecturally and environmentally compatible with their surroundings. Tourists need places to eat and sleep. They also appreciate the dependable level of service and accommodations usually found in American hotels and motels but tourists also crave integrity of place wherever they go — and homogenous, "off-the-shelf" corporate chain and franchise architecture works against integrity of place. Freeport, Maine, home of the L.L.Bean Company, for example, is a draw for shoppers seeking bargains at the town's many outlets, but the town has also protected its character by ensuring that the likes of McDonald's, Taco Bell, Arby's, and other chains either reuse historic structures or erect one-of-a-kind buildings rather than the cookie-cutter anywhere-in-the-USA type of buildings.

Every tourist development should have a harmonious relationship with its setting. Tourism-support facilities should reflect the broader environmental context of the community and should respect the specific size, character, and functional factors of their site within the surrounding landscape. A community's food and lodging establishments are part of the total tourism package. Motels should reflect a city and not each other. Hotels in Maine, for instance, should be different in style than those in Maryland or Montana. It is this search for something different that has given rise to the booming bed-and-breakfast, adventure travel, and heritage tourism industries.

Interpret the resource. Education and interpretation are keys to sustainable tourism — visitors want information about what they are seeing. Interpretation can also be a powerful storytelling tool that can make an attraction, even an entire community, come alive. It can also result in better-managed resources by explaining why they are important. Interpretation instills respect and fosters stewardship in both visitors and residents. Education about natural and cultural resources can instill community pride and strengthen sense of place. The town of Gettysburg, Pennsylvania, for example, developed a community-wide interpretation program that involves public art, wayside exhibits, and interpretative markers that tell the story of the town and its role in the battle of Gettysburg. Since the program was developed, the number of visitors spending time and money in the town has drastically increased.

Consider aesthetics and ecology. Clean air and water and healthy natural systems are fundamentally important to sustainable tourism, but so is community appearance. Many cities have gotten used to ugliness, accepting it as inevitable to progress. However, other more enlightened communities recognize that the way a community looks affects its image and its economic well-being. Protecting scenic views and vistas, planting trees, landscaping parking lots, and controlling signs are all fundamentally important to the economic health of a community.

For example, Vermont's tourism office touts the fact that it is one of four states that completely prohibits billboards. Likewise, Oregon's marketing slogan is "Oregon, things look different here." Imagine a marketing campaign that touts billboards as an attraction or urges tourists to visit by bragging, "Things look the same here."

Enhance the journey as well as the destination. Tourism is the sum total of the travel experience. It is not just what happens at the destination. It involves everything that people see — and do — from the time they leave home until the vacation is over. Getting there can he half the fun, but frequently it is not.

There are many truly noteworthy destinations in America; however, there are very few truly noteworthy journeys left, which is why it is in the interest of the tourism industry to encourage the development of heritage corridors, bike paths, hiking trails, and other forms of alternative transportation. This is also why local and state governments should designate scenic byways and protect roads with unique scenic or historic character.

Recognize that tourism has limits. Savvy communities always ask how many tourists are too many. Tourism development that exceeds the carrying capacity of the ecosystem or fails to respect a community's sense of place will result in resentment and the eventual destruction of the very attributes that tourists have come to enjoy. Too many cars, boats, tour buses, condominiums — or people — can overwhelm a community and harm fragile resources.

A few communities have managed to balance nature and commerce in ways that benefit both. A popular Gulf Coast resort, Sanibel Island in Florida, is one of the world's premier places to collect seashells and see subtropical birds. To protect its abundant wildlife, white sand beaches, and quiet charm, Sanibel built an extensive network of off-road bike paths and developed a master plan based on an analysis of what was needed to protect the island's natural systems. The plan set a limit on the island population consistent with its drinking water supply, the habitat needs of wildlife, the need to evacuate the island before hurricanes, and other considerations. By establishing development standards based on ecological constants, Sanibel has managed to preserve one of America's most exceptional subtropical environments, while also accommodating a high level of visitation.

In recent years, American tourism has had steadily less to do with America and more to do with mass marketing. As the amount of open land decreases, advertising dollars increase. As historic buildings disappear, theme parks proliferate. Unless the tourism industry thinks it can continue to sell trips to communities clogged with traffic, look-a-like motels, overcrowded beaches, and cluttered commercial strips, it needs to create a plan to protect the natural, cultural, and scenic resources on which it relies. Citizens, elected officials, and developers alike can take a leadership role in promoting — through community education and comprehensive plan policies — a sustainable tourism agenda that will strengthen the local economy by protecting and enhancing the community's tourism assets.

CHAPTER 4

Preserving Nature for Future Generations
Thomas Arrandale

Doris Fischer is just one of a thousand newcomers who've moved to Madison County, Montana, over the past decade.

Like the others, this Pennsylvania native was enticed westward by snow-capped mountains and blue-ribbon trout streams flowing down from Yellowstone National Park. As the county's only full-time planner, Fischer now helps community leaders figure out how to save the area's wide open spaces from being broken apart as more and more tenderfoots settle along secluded Rocky Mountains valleys.

Of all the region's spectacular places, Madison County may well have the best chance to hold onto the Old West's expansive and untamed character. Glitzy ski resort mansions already are cropping up on grizzly bear habitat along the county line. But down in the isolated valleys, pioneer families have begun working to preserve ranching as the county's most enduring way of life, in part by putting valuable rangelands under conservation easements.

Still, as in most rural western communities, Madison County residents hesitate about whether or not county government should step in and try to avert the hasty development that is already ruining other landscapes around old ranching and mining towns up and down the Rockies.

Madison County is still Marlboro Country. Cowboy individualism prevails. "People in urban areas are accustomed to living with lim-

itations set by their governments," Fischer says. "Out here, old-timers still hold to the idea that the neighbors aren't going to do anything to make life more difficult."

That frontier sentiment makes Fischer's job a real challenge. Right now, Madison County has just 7,000 residents occupying 3,500 square miles, an expanse that's larger than Rhode Island and Delaware put together. But rugged mountains and forests take up half the county, and current residents live in far-flung ranches and four tiny towns scattered across sweeping valleys where the Madison and Jefferson rivers and their sparkling tributaries rush down from the wilderness.

The county's population grew more than 14 percent in the 1990s, and now hard economic times are tempting ranching families to cash in by subdividing the pricey acreage they own in a stunningly beautiful landscape. A recently completed build-out analysis suggests that growth will certainly match that rate in the current decade, and could possibly accelerate as more outsiders, who are buying vacation cabins and condominiums, decide to live there year-round.

If Not Now, When?

The county hired Fischer four years ago to help update its comprehensive plan. "We've

Originally published as "Rocky Mountain Revamp," *Planning*, Vol. 70, No. 1, January 2004, by the American Planning Association, Suite 1200, 205 North Michigan Avenue, Chicago, Illinois 60601. Reprinted with permission of the publisher.

been nibbling at it ever since," she says. "We're not doing enough." So far, independent-minded ranchers and small-town residents haven't been ready to let the county government use stricter land-use rules to direct where growth occurs. In the last couple of years, residents gave some thought to setting up zoning districts to protect parts of the Madison and Ruby River valleys, "but they didn't want to do it," says County Commission chairman Dave Schulz. "Not yet."

Fischer and the officials she works for acknowledge they've got to get ready for all the new residents that may be arriving in the county. Just since June 1999, the county has approved 53 new subdivisions that created 835 more lots; two-thirds of available tracts still remain available for new homes.

"The question I have is what are we going to do so growth does not eliminate the things that brought people here in the first place?" says Lane Adamson, a county planning board member who also directs the Madison Valley Ranchlands Group, an association that local ranching families have formed to keep economic change from overwhelming their way of life. The members have begun working with the Nature Conservancy to protect lands through easements, combat invading noxious rangeland weeds, and market local "conservation beef" at premium prices.

Ranchers are also watching uneasily as subdividers eye Madison Valley for potential development of more houses and cabins along one of the country's most prized fly fishing rivers. "At some point you say, okay, we're not going to allow that to happen," Adamson notes.

Helpers

Looking for ways to manage Madison's expected growth, Fischer, Schulz, and Adamson repaired with another county commissioner and two planning board members in October 2003 to Red Lodge, Montana. Along with counterparts from six other Montana, Wyoming, and Idaho counties, they spent three days rethinking how rural communities can accom-modate growth without sacrificing the West's distinctive character. They'd all been invited by the National Association of Counties and the Sonoran Institute, a Tucson-based think tank.

The one-of-a-kind program, called the Western Community Stewardship Forum, brings rural counties together to talk over their options for managing the growth. Five of the counties whose representatives met in 2003 abut Yellowstone National Park, and the two others lie astride critical wildlife habitat that links the park to other Northern Rocky Mountain ecosystems.

They're all going through accelerating economic and social changes as newcomers flock into sparsely settled valleys that help sustain deer, elk, moose, wolves, grizzly bears, cutthroat trout, and the rest of the region's matchless wildlife populations. Yellowstone's threatened grizzly population has begun slowly expanding through mountain ranges and down into the valleys that surround the park, and conflicts between people and bears will inevitably increase if more and more subdivisions are built without regard to the bears' habitat.

The counties that gathered at Red Lodge "all share a commitment to deal with their growth," notes Randy Carpenter, a planner with the Sonoran Institute's northwest office in Bozeman, Montana. If their efforts keep privately owned landholdings from being completely carved up, he adds, "these counties will also play critical roles in linking the wilderness and keeping ecosystems intact."

As it is, the Yellowstone region is one of the last truly wild places in North America. That very wildness is one of the keys to its economic future. Demand for the West's timber, minerals, and beef has faded, but the Yellowstone region's population has grown by 131,000 since 1970 as retirees, engineers, accountants, and other service professionals have arrived. "The region's quality of life, including its natural amenities, is one distinct competitive advantage we have in today's marketplace," says Ben Alexander, the associate director of the Sonoran Institute's socioeconomics program.

About the Institute

The Sonoran Institute has been conducting community stewardships forums since 1999, advising 34 counties in eight Rocky Mountain states on their options for managing growth while maintaining their economic prospects. Planning and economic consultants from the institute's Tucson and Bozeman offices have helped counties build on growth management strategies their teams have crafted at the sessions.

Custer County, Colorado, used Sonoran's support to adopt a master plan, update zoning rules, and embrace privately funded conservation easements on 11,000 acres. Rio Arriba County, New Mexico, got help developing a comprehensive plan and conserving small-scale acequia farmlands along the Rio Grande and Rio Chama valleys.

After attending a previous forum, Sublette County, Wyoming, set up a program that will use oil and gas revenues to buy development rights to agricultural land. In Lemhi County, Idaho, where growth is spreading across private Salmon River ranchlands hemmed in by federally owned lands, the institute is advising a rancher-led working group that is mapping parcels to help county officials determine where development will be least destructive and which lands they want to stay in agriculture.

Founded in 1991, the institute works with communities throughout the Rocky Mountain West, including those in southern Canada and northern Mexico. It operates with a staff of 32 economists, planners, and other experts and a $3 million annual budget with revenue raised from foundations, individual donors, and consulting contracts with the U.S. Department of the Interior.

Instead of providing top-down prescriptions, the institute provides advice and information to local communities. "Our goal is to help key decision-makers make better land-use decisions," says executive director Luther Probst, a former World Wildlife Fund official who founded the institute. "We're unique among environmental organizations because our objectives are not just preserving landscapes but also vibrant economies and livable communities."

Change of Heart?

County officials throughout the rural West are often leery of environmental agendas. But talking over growth management tools with similar counties at the Sonoran forums sits well with ranchers, farmers, and rural townspeople. In parts of Gallatin County, Montana, "if you mentioned the word 'zoning,' two years ago, they'd throw you out of the room," says Joe Skinner, a farmer who serves on the county planning board. "I came to the forum anti-zoning and anti–Sonoran, but when I got out of the forum, we realized that there are all different kinds" of tools for managing growth. "Sonoran is very honest about their goals, but what we want is very similar."

In follow-up work with Gallatin County, the institute helped organize workshops for county and local land trust officials to discuss tools for protecting agricultural lands. Located on Yellowstone's northwestern flank, Gallatin County contains some of Montana's richest farmlands. But in the last 30 years, 40,000 newcomers have moved into the county, and Bozeman, the county seat, began sprawling over the Gallatin River Valley.

Like local governments in places like Santa Fe, New Mexico; Aspen, Colorado; and Jackson, Wyoming, city and county officials are now locked in politically charged debates over banning big-box stores, charging development impact fees, buying development rights, and creating zoning districts to keep productive agricultural lands from being carved up and turned into more weed-choked, 20-acre home sites.

That's the fate that other counties in the Rockies hope to avoid. In organizing the 2003 community stewardship forum, NACO and the Sonoran Institute invited five other counties that border Yellowstone to sit down with two rapidly urbanizing Montana counties. Madison County sent a group to the forum three years ago, but commissioners decided to send Fischer and other leaders back once again to sharpen the focus on expanding the county's growth management options.

Not one of the seven counties yet has 60,000 residents, but they've all experienced the growth that's spread from Denver, Phoenix, and other large cities. Ennis, Madison County's biggest town, still has fewer than 900 residents, but at the Big Sky ski resort on the county's eastern border, developers are now sprinkling what Montana natives scornfully call "starter mansions" on steep forested slopes and Madison Range ridgelines.

The Big Sky complex already generates one-third of the county's tax base, and creates jobs for construction workers who commute 50 or so miles over a mountainous dirt road from Ennis and other towns. Not many will ever afford to live there, but Big Sky is giving Madison County residents a glimpse of how rapidly unplanned growth can occur.

Growth Pressures

All up and down the Rocky Mountains, from Mexico to Canada, retirees and footloose computer-era entrepreneurs are looking for new homes and vacation cabins where they can live under big western skies. In the last decade or so, new development has supplanted the Old West mainstays of boom-and-bust mining, logging, and agriculture as the Yellowstone region's economic workhorse.

Natural resource industries have been declining in the West since 1970. In the Greater Yellowstone region, mining employment has barely grown at all since then, and the region's farm and ranch income has dropped by two-thirds. In 2000, mining, logging, and agriculture provided less than 10 percent of the region's income, down by more than half 30 years earlier.

Meanwhile, the economy has boomed in the communities closest to the Rockies, according to the Sonoran Institute, with newcomers helping to fuel a population growth of 61 percent in the 20 counties surrounding Yellowstone National Park. The region has created 143,000 new jobs in the last three decades, more than 100,000 in the service and professional sectors. But investment and retirement returns are now the most important source of financial support for people in the area, accounting for 38 percent of personal income.

Television entrepreneur Ted Turner has bought two Madison Valley ranches, television network anchor Tom Brokaw and film star Dennis Quaid live part time in Park County, on the other side of the Bridger and Gallatin Mountains from Gallatin County. But not everyone shares in the prosperity. Average annual wages for workers have fallen in constant terms, from $27,262 in 1970 to $23,426 in 2000. In Madison County, 45 percent of the labor force is now self-employed, and those residents earn an average of $13,512 a year as farmhands, part-time construction workers, artists and artisans, and hunting and finishing outfitters. "That's a sign of stress" in the region's economy, Alexander says.

Meanwhile, the median price for a house in Teton County, Wyoming, has jumped to $365,000. One result is that the population of Teton County, Idaho, jumped nearly 75 percent in the 1990s, in part because resort workers began commuting through the sometimes treacherous Snake River Canyon to find affordable housing across the state border.

Moving On

Families who have worked the land for generations no longer make much of a living ranching or farming there. Now many are approaching retirement age, and their children are moving away instead of taking over the family homesteads. Now the pressure is on to sell to wealthy outsiders or to subdivide their holdings for new houses or vacation cabins. In many agricultural families, "they've worked their whole lives on that land, and that land is their whole IRA," says Jim Durgan, a Park County commissioner whose family has ranched along the Yellowstone River since the 1920s.

Durgan lives in the Paradise Valley, where the Yellowstone River flows down from the park through rangelands and irrigated fields lined by jagged mountains. He remembers nights when he could step out his back door and "all the lights you could see were the stars" above Montana's celebrated Big Sky Country. "Now you see lights all around you" up and down the valley from homes that have been built on what used to be nothing but farmland and pastures.

But like Madison County, Park County employs just one full-time planner. For years, politically influential Paradise Valley ranchers have dug in their heels against meaningful planning, contending that limits on how they can take profits from rising property values would unfairly rob them of their birthrights. Two years ago, they raised an uproar when the Park County Environmental Council, a local environmental group, commissioned a build-out study of Paradise Valley.

Ellen Woodbury, the county's planner at the time, joined critics in challenging the study's validity. Back then, notes Jim Barrett, the council's director, county officials "perceived it as if we were singling Park County out as the worst place in the West when it comes to managing growth."

Durgan, who served on the county planning board for 16 years, was elected to the commission a year ago. Woodbury quit last year and was hired to help a Bozeman-based developer win county approval for a 38-unit subdivision on 900 acres of prime irrigated land right on the Yellowstone River.

Last fall, Durgan and fellow commissioner Ed Schilling traveled to the Sonoran forum in Red Lodge to take a fresh look at options for dealing with the consequences of future development pressures. Notably, they invited Barrett to sit on the county's delegation.

"With other counties there, and with a whole range of economic viewpoints represented, we could see that others are desperate for help in figuring out how they can respond to the same issues we're all facing," Barrett says. The way Schilling puts it, conferring with six other counties "shows that we're not the lone ranger here" in finally coming to terms with the challenges that growth creates for rural communities.

Resolutions

The Park County group left the forum last October with plans to conduct a county-wide build-out analysis, then ask the institute for help conducting public discussions on what tools the county could consider for managing development. Madison County officials headed back to the county courthouse in the old mining town of Virginia City with a more ambitious agenda. Along with a right-to-farm ordinance, county officials agreed to draft subdivision design guidelines including wildfire safety rules, outdoor lighting controls, and restrictions on ridgetop construction.

What's more, they agreed to push fees to cover the costs of extending county services. Later this year, the ranchlands group that Adamson heads may once more broach the idea of creating a zoning district to manage housing developments that are beginning to spread onto the Madison Valley.

Madison County remains wary about relying on government regulation. But after thinking the alternatives through at the Red Lodge forums, "we now feel that these are manageable things to accomplish," Fischer says. Working with Sonoran Institute advisers, and just talking with other counties that must deal with the same plight, "gave us a clarity and confidence that we're on the right track."

NOTE

The Sonora Institute has been working continuously with Madison County officials since 1999, offering technical assistance and community outreach to help them address the challenges of growth. Collaboration with the Madison Valley Ranchlands Group and the grassroots, citizen-led Madison Growth Solutions is helping ensure that this area protects its natural assets and sustains its agricultural heritage while adapting to growth opportunities. (Source: Sonora Institute website, October 23, 2010.)

CHAPTER 5

Green Technology and Economic Development

Chad Vander Veen

Traveling east along U.S. Highway 12 from Helena, Montana, it's entirely possible to drive for an hour or more without seeing another human. Windswept plains dotted by curiously named hamlets wait for signs of life to come careening down the mostly empty road.

Past Townsend, a small burg on the southern tip of Canyon Ferry Lake, the deer on the highway far outnumber vehicles; and when dusk settles in, they prove much more dangerous. But the farther east you travel, the more you notice one particular man-made structure — electric transmission towers. Specifically cross-like high-voltage direct current towers, which stand in stark contrast to the empty land that spreads in every direction.

The towers eventually terminate in an area known as Judith Gap, notable for its name and not much else. That is, until recently, when from the waving grasses and grazing cattle rose 90 masts looming hundreds of feet in the air. But here there are no sails whipping, no ropes cracking: rather atop these mammoth masts sit wind turbines, each with three enormous blades that turn gently in Big Sky country.

The wind farm at Judith Gap is one of many that have taken root in the vast expanse of central-eastern Montana. And the seeds are being sown for many more. Montana is part of a "wind belt" that envelopes Wyoming, Col-

orado, New Mexico and northern Texas. These states are in the midst of a wind rush that has driven Montana Gov. Brian Schweitzer and other governors to open their arms and offer incentives to businesses looking to harness the wind, in turn creating jobs and delivering a new kind of green to feed the economy.

In Montana, the abundance of both wind and state incentives have drawn investment from renewable energy companies like Chicago-based Invenergy and Spanish firm NaturEner. These and other companies say they find the state an ideal place to do business.

"What we find in Montana is a very open environment for development, both socially and politically," says Bill Alexander, chief development officer for NaturEner. That's typical of a new market, an emerging market. But we found the legislative body in Montana has been very interested in helping to continue the incentives for development."

In 2007, Montana passed HB 3, "Clean and Green" legislation aimed at attracting renewable energy businesses to the state. The bill created new tax classifications and new. lower property tax rates for renewable energy firms operating in Montana. There are also grants available for renewable energy research, and loan and bond programs. In all, companies will find more than 30 additional state programs for

Originally published as "Can Green Technology Propel Economic Development," *Governing*, Vol. 23, No. 6, March 2010, by e.Republic Inc., Washington, D.C. Reprinted with permission of the publisher.

renewable energy. For example, companies generating wind power would likely qualify for at least seven state tax incentives — not to mention a host of federal renewable energy programs.

"Montana has, according to recent studies, the second-best wind energy resources in the country, some of the best on the planet," says Schweitzer. "We have many energy resources that can be cleaner and greener. We're excited about developing our wind."

Schweitzer is among an emerging group of state leaders who are staking at least a piece of their futures on green technology. With states across the nation looking to kick-start their economic engines, green technology increasingly is viewed as, if not the engine, at least a piston helping drive it.

That's the case in Colorado, where Gov. Bill Ritter ordered his Energy Office, Economic Development Office and state CIO to collaborate on ways to nurture green technology start-ups and create demand among consumers for emerging — and typically more expensive — green products.

Colorado is testing a new Discovery Grant Program designed to help early stage companies, which are often simply groups of researchers attempting to take an idea out of the lab and into the commercial market.

"At that point, there's not a lot of available seed capital. So to give them some small grants at the very beginning really shows great support from the state," says Matt Cheroutes, director of communications and external affairs for the Colorado Governor's Office of Economic Development and International Trade.

Cheroutes, a founding member of the Colorado Cleantech Industry Association, says strong executive support for green technology in Colorado will lead to job growth and economic prosperity. But that won't happen, he says, unless companies can deliver their products to a public that can afford them — a tall order in green tech markets that are often too immature to deliver at affordable economies of scale.

Cheroutes says the state works closely with renewable energy firms to develop incentives for consumers. Take solar power, for example, where the cost of installing solar panels typically doesn't pencil out for the average homeowner.

"We've had a lot of people in our state say they want solar on their homes," Cheroutes says. "But they simply can't afford the initial investment to do it. We've seen estimates anywhere from $8,000 for a very small home to $15,000 for a medium-sized home. These days, not a lot of people have the ability to pay that."

The state worked with two Colorado solar firms — SolarCity and SunRun — to develop a financing model that makes solar installations more affordable. Instead of paying the full installation fee upfront, consumers instead put up a down payment that is a fraction of the total cost. Over the next three or four years, the energy savings the consumer realizes goes back to the solar company to pay the remaining balance. After the company is paid in full, the consumer's energy bill decreases significantly.

The Obama administration expects green technology companies to become important players in the nation's economy. The U.S. Department of Energy (DOE) estimates that the wind industry alone will support a half million jobs in the nation by 2030. In the western United States, this activity also would boost annual property tax revenues by more than $1.5 billion and increase payments to rural landowners to more than $600 million over the same time period, according to the DOE's 20 percent Wind by 2030 report.

The report explores the challenges and implications of generating one-fifth of the nation's electricity needs through wind power. Under that scenario, Montana stands to benefit handsomely from embracing wind power. Given the current and planned wind power capacity for the state, if 20 percent of the nation is in fact using wind power by 2030, Montana could expect 2,875 long-term new jobs, 16,888 short-term jobs, a $78.2 million increase in property tax revenue, and a $230 million annual economic boost over the long term. In addition, data indicates a two-year wind farm construction phase could generate a $900 million short-term economic boost.

But not everyone buys into the rosy predictions. Numerous industry analysts, economists and academics say the green technology sector is too small to drive economic recovery, or that the amount of government subsidies needed to make it successful would effectively cancel out any benefits. Observers also claim wind-power numbers, such as those in the DOE report, are wildly optimistic or simply made up.

"Green jobs estimates include huge numbers of clerical, bureaucratic and administrative positions that do not produce goods and services for consumption," according to the authors of Green Jobs Myths, a March 2009 University of Illinois Law and Economics research paper. Written by a group of business and economics professors, the paper also contends that, "Government interference — such as restricting successful technologies in favor of speculative technologies favored by special interests — will generate stagnation."

One of the authors, Roger Meiners, a professor of economics at the University of Texas at Arlington, went into further detail on the VoiceAmerica Talk Radio Network's Free Market program. "The numbers thrown around about the number of jobs that will be created by these alternative energy programs, primarily wind turbines and solar sources of energy, just range all over the place," he says. "One group will say a million jobs, another will say 3 million, and I think they're really just pulling them out of the air, because when you look for where they come up with these numbers, there's nothing there; they just simply make the assertion that this many jobs will be created."

Green technology may indeed create jobs, but it's worth questioning how much money will be spent upfront to create them, Meiners adds.

"If the administration pours tens of billions of dollars into this program as is built into the budget, then obviously there are going to be a lot of people put to work helping to build wind farms, a smart energy grid, expanded solar grids and so on. It could well be in the hundreds of thousands [of jobs created]. The question is, what's the cost, what's the benefit?"

Still, one California group says its research shows that green jobs are growing while the state's economy suffers. Next 10, a nonprofit focused on building the green economy, found significant expansion of California's green economy in a report released in December 2009. From 1995 to 2008, the Sacramento area saw green tech jobs grow by 87 percent, followed by the San Diego region (57 percent), the Bay Area (51 percent), and Orange County and Inland Empire (50 percent).

"Data shows that green-sector businesses are taking root across every region of California, generating jobs across a wide spectrum of skill levels and earnings potential," says F. Noel Perry, founder of Next 10, following the release of the data. "While green jobs clearly cannot solve the state's current unemployment challenges, over time these jobs could become a growing portion of total jobs in California."

Others add that government agencies can nurture green job growth by being early customers for green technology products.

"Government is a big buyer of products and services," says Gary Simon, co-chair of the Sacramento Area Regional Technology Alliance's CleanTech program. "If one pays attention to buying the cleaner, greener products over the standard, that's what we're trying to show is available. Really you're not paying that much more to be clean, green and sustainable. And if you look at the economics over time, it's actually cheaper to be green and sustainable."

But with the green technology industry still largely in its infancy, it can be difficult to know where to look for, say, a thin-film solar vendor. It wouldn't be surprising to find the staff of a green startup focused on simply trying to keep the lights on, to say nothing of navigating the treacherous waters of government procurement. But Simon says the companies are out there and that it may be on government to find them.

"[State and local governments] simply have to look a little bit harder. For everything they buy and use now, there's going to be a clean, green, sustainable alternative." he says. "Finding where those companies are now is a bit of a hunt because it's a small part of the overall economy in the U.S. But they are there."

In Montana, Schweitzer follows what could be described as a "Field of Dreams" approach to developing the state's green economy. In other words, build wind farms and companies that provide supporting technologies, and jobs will come.

So far, Montana's clean energy incentives appear to be working. NaturEner is spending billions to construct wind farms in the state. Last October, the company opened the state's largest wind farm, a 210-megawatt facility in Glacier County. It's also in planning stages to open a second, even larger 309-megawatt facility a few miles north of the Glacier farm. These wind farms have already created hundreds of temporary and full-time jobs.

NaturEner's wind farms dwarf even the massive Judith Gap wind farm built by Invenergy. That 135-megawatt facility began operation in 2005 and features more than 90 wind turbines. It also generated hundreds of construction jobs and about a dozen full-time jobs, filled primarily by residents of the nearby and remote town of Harlowton.

"We took advantage of [an incentive] for new and emerging businesses for our first two wind projects there in Toole County," says NaturEner's Alexander, adding that the incentive is why the company is pursuing development of a third wind farm in the state. The Rim Rock project is a 309-megawatt project that should go to construction sometime this winter. It will have 206 turbines. The one we just finished was 140 turbines, so this one will be 50 percent larger than that."

Schweitzer hopes this activity will spur technical breakthroughs that make clean power generation more practical. For instance, better storage technology would reduce the need for expensive transmission lines, a key concern for wind power and other renewable energy sources that generate electricity far from population centers.

"We actually have an unlimited supply of energy, whether it be tidal or wind or solar," Schweitzer says. The most important technology of our time, and for the next decade, will be storage technology. If we could build a transmission system that had storage on the other end, so the consumer who had that battery in their car could be buying electricity or selling it back into the grid, we would need less transmission."

These obstacles are exactly what Schweit-

zer is counting on to drive economic progress in Montana, as innovative companies spring up in the state to tackle such issues. If these plans seem overly optimistic, consider the fact that San Diego Gas & Electric, a Southern California utility serving more than 1 million people, is currently a customer of the Glacier Wind Farm. California has also set a goal for 33 percent of the state's energy to come from renewable sources by 2020. That's an enormous business opportunity for Montana, even using traditional transmission lines. If investment in transmission technology results in significantly improved capacity and efficiency, or if a next-generation storage technology is developed, the level of economic opportunity in Montana becomes so sizable as to be difficult to fathom.

To be effective, however, green incentives must be carefully designed to avoid unintended roadblocks. Many businesses, having been promised grants or other financial perks, have opened shop only to discover the crippling disincentives of bureaucracy.

"If I were governor, I would have a full analysis done of the state's incentive programs, as well as certification programs, and look for those things which do serve to support investment in infrastructure, but also identify those things that work against it, like zoning laws," says K.C. Healy, director of Deloitte's Energy & Resources practice. "There are various sorts of structural things governments can do to where they incent one side but then they make it extremely difficult to carry it out on the ground."

Invenergy's Alexander said Montana takes a less "regulatory" approach than other states his company deals with. "The primary approach we get from Montana is how can they help us? How can the local community help us? How can the government help us expedite the permitting process, what do we need to help promote the projects?" he says. "In other areas, the first approach is sometimes for us to disclose everything we want to do, and let them vet that internally so they can decide if we're doing to right thing for the environment, if we're doing the right thing for the cultural and historical sites within the area."

Besides executive leadership, grants, financing packages and tax incentives, green technology's success as an economic engine may hinge on simple evolution. Despite the best efforts of government, it may come down to whether society has reached the point where the traditional economy, driven by fossil fuels, is no longer acceptable.

The culture has changed in Colorado," says Cheroutes. "It's something that everyone in Colorado has sort of agreed to and bought in to. And whether that's out of a desire to protect our mountains or to keep our kids from being sent halfway around the world to fight, or if it's to keep kids who are home employed and working, it's a cultural mind change, and sometimes those are the hardest things to deal with in the beginning. So if you have the will of the people, of industry and of political leaders, you can make anything happen."

Of course, it doesn't hurt to have government leadership shepherding that evolution.

PART II : BEST PRACTICES

CHAPTER 6

Annapolis and Other Cities Improve Their Water Quality

Don Waye

Many government entities are finding ways to reduce residents' use of lawn fertilizers that contain phosphorus. Some governments choose to pass laws or ordinances prohibiting the use of fertilizers that contain phosphorus except in special cases, such as on new lawns or when a soil test indicates that phosphorus is needed. Others are increasing education efforts to help residents better understand that fertilizer with phosphorus is not always necessary. Evidence suggests that these endeavors are making a difference. The City of Ann Arbor, Michigan, for instance, has seen phosphorus levels in the Huron River drop an average of 28 percent after it enacted a phosphorus ordinance in 2006.

Numerous local governments across the country have phosphorus restrictions in place. For example, several counties in Michigan have passed countywide ordinances limiting or banning the use of fertilizer that contains phosphorus. The city of Ann Arbor, Michigan passed a strict phosphorus ordinance in 2006 after a total maximum daily load (TMDL) study on the Huron River showed that the city had to reduce the amount of phosphorus discharged from the city's watershed. Ann Arbor's ordinance prohibits application of phosphorus except when a soil test shows that it is needed, or when planting a new lawn. It prohibits applying fertilizer within 25 feet of any water-body. Ann

Arbor also prohibits any manufactured fertilizer application prior to April 1 or after November 15 unless the soil temperature at a depth of 2 inches has been measured, and is greater than 37 degrees Fahrenheit. Additionally, the city requires all commercial fertilizer applicators to register annually; plus, the applicators must provide at least one copy of a city-published manufactured fertilizer informational pamphlet to each customer.

Similarly, to comply with phosphorus TMDLs requirements, the New Jersey Department of Environmental Protection (NJDEP) is mandating that more than 100 New Jersey municipalities adopt local ordinances prohibiting the use of fertilizers containing phosphorus except under special circumstances (see ordinance details at www.state.NJ.US/DEP/watershed mgt/DOCS/tmdl/fertilizer application model ordinance.pdf). The state is also working to reduce fertilizer application statewide. In April 2008, NJDEP signed a Memorandum of Understanding (MOU) with two major fertilizer producers to address phosphorus use in lawn fertilizers. By signing the MOU, the fertilizer producers agreed to reduce the amount of phosphorus in their lawn fertilizer products, distribute these products in garden centers statewide and work with the New Jersey Department of Environmental Protection to develop strategies

Originally published as "Ordinance Improves Huron River Quality — Restrictions Spread Nationwide," *Nonpoint Source News-Notes*, Issue 88, October 2009, by the U.S. Environmental Protection Agency, Washington, D.C.

to educate the public about proper selection and use of lawn fertilizer. For more information, see "Recent Partnership Limits Phosphorus in New Jersey Fertilizer," on page 12 of *Nonpoint Source News-Notes* issue 86, available at www.epa.gov/NewsNotes/pdf/86issue.pdf.

Annapolis, Maryland, recently became the first municipality in the Chesapeake Bay watershed to adapt an ordinance banning the use of fertilizer that contains phosphorus. Since January 1, 2009, residents have been required to use only phosphorus-free fertilizer, except in gardens, on newly established turf and in cases where a soil test shows a phosphorus deficiency. For more information, see www.annapolis.gov/upload/images/government/council/adopted/ol008.pdf.

Numerous local governments in Florida have passed fertilizer ordinances over the past decade to reduce nutrient pollution of surface waters. Building on the success of these ordinances, Florida passed a statewide law in June 2009 that requires all local governments to adopt a model fertilizer use ordinance as a minimum standard. This ordinance restricts or prohibits the application of fertilizer that contains nitrogen and phosphorus in certain areas and during certain times of the year.

Two other states have also passed laws prohibiting phosphorus in most fertilizer. Minnesota enacted a statewide law in 2005 prohibiting the use of phosphorus lawn fertilizer unless new turf is being established or a soil test shows a need for phosphorus (see www.mda.state.mn.us/protecting/waterprotection/lawncwaterq.htm). In April 2009, Wisconsin Governor Doyle signed the "Clean Lakes" bill (2009 Wisconsin Act 9). The bill established a statewide law prohibiting the display, sale and use of lawn fertilizer containing phosphorus, with certain reasonable exceptions (e.g., when establishing grass or when a soil test shows that phosphorus is needed). The law takes effect in April 2010, which gives retailers time to prepare. Although retailers will not be permitted to display turf fertilizer that is labeled as containing phosphorus, they may post a sign advising customers that turf fertilizer containing phosphorus is available upon request for qualified uses. To read the statute, see www.legis.state.wi.us/2009/data/AB-3.pdf.

Are the Regulations Reducing Phosphorus?

Minnesota has collected retailers' sales numbers since phosphorus laws went into effect in the Minneapolis/St. Paul area in 2003 and statewide in 2005. A 2007 report (see www.mda.state.mn.us/protecting/waterprotection/phoslaw.htm) found that the law substantially reduced phosphorus lawn fertilizer use. The report noted that the use of lawn fertilizers containing phosphorus decreased 38 percent between 2003 and 2006. By 2006 only 18 percent of lawn fertilizer for sale contained phosphorus. Additionally, Minnesota's law has not increased consumers' costs and has successfully provided a focus point for extensive yard care and water quality education.

One study completed in 2007 by the Minnesota Department of Agriculture found that runoff data were too variable in the years following phosphorus lawn fertilizer restrictions to indicate short-term trends in water quality (see www.mda.state.mn.us/protecting/waterprotection/phoslaw.htm). A paired watershed study completed for the Minnesota Water Pollution Control agency between 2004 and 2006 indicates that restricting the use of phosphorus lawn fertilizer reduces the export of phosphorus from urban residential developments by 12 to 15 percent. However, this study was complicated by a number of factors and addressed a limited area (see www.pca.state.mn.us/publications/stormwaterresearch-fertilizer.pdf).

Fortunately, compelling water quality data are now available from the city of Ann Arbor, Michigan, which adopted a phosphorus ordinance in 2006 in an effort to comply with TMDL requirements. A University of Michigan research team looked at a historical data set collected on the Huron River and compared it to data collected after the ordinance went into effect in 2007. Their analysis showed that phosphorus levels in the Huron River dropped an average of 28 percent in just the first year. Other water quality parameters, including nitrate, silica and colored dissolved organic matter, did not change systematically as did phosphorus levels. More details on the study, which was funded through EPA's Science to Achieve

Results (STAR) program, are available at www. umich.edu/~hrstudy. The study's primary author, University of Michigan professor John Lehman, believes that the decline can be attributed to the passage of the ordinance in combination with the public education efforts and general increased environmental awareness among Ann Arbor residents.

Educating People About Fertilizer

Reluctant to prohibit its residents from using fertilizer with phosphorus, Maine instead passed a statewide law that it hopes will raise people's awareness and change their behavior. The law requires all fertilizer retailers to post educational signs. The signs, approved by the Maine Department of Environment, explain the link between phosphorus use and algae growth and discourage people from using phosphorus-containing fertilizer except on new or reseeded lawns. See www.maine.gov/dep/blwq/doclake/fert/phospage.htm for more information on Maine's law.

Some localities still rely completely on education to reduce the use of fertilizers that contain phosphorus. In 2006 the Lake Champlain Basin Program (www.lcbp.org) in Vermont, New York and Quebec began working with several partners in the watershed to pool resources and ideas to create a coordinated outreach message for both fertilizer consumers and retailers. In addition to promoting the use of phosphorus-free fertilizer with a "Don't 'P' on Your Lawn" message, this partnership has created other healthy lawn tips and encouraged local retailers to stock phosphorus-free fertilizers (see www.lawntolake.org).

These educational efforts appear to be making a difference. In Maine, a 2009 followup survey indicates that most fertilizer retailers are complying with the law — 87 percent of surveyed stores had posted the educational signs as required. Plus, 97 percent of stores now offer phosphorus-free products. Anecdotal evidence suggests that more consumers are purchasing phosphorus-free products as a result. For more details on the survey, see the spring 2009 issue of Maine's *Nonpoint Source Times* at www. maine.gov/dep/blwq/newslet/npstimes/spring2009.pdf

The Lake Champlain Basin Program's education efforts are also paying off, notes Nicole Ballinger, the program's communications coordinator. "The amount of non-farm phosphate being sold in Vermont is decreasing and the number of phosphorus-free fertilizer items available for sale is increasing." In 2008, retailers reported 221 phosphorus-free items for sale, compared with 188 in 2007. Many of these retailers ask their salespeople wear "P-free" buttons and have voluntarily posted informational brochures and posters in their stores to help educate consumers. For more information on how the "Don't 'P' on Your Lawn" effort fits into the overall management of the Lake Champlain system, see the 2008 State of the Lake report at www.lcbp.org/PDFs/SOL2008-web.pdf.

Why Is Phosphorus Targeted?

In most freshwater systems (e.g., lakes, rivers and streams), phosphorus is a limiting nutrient. Other nutrients such as nitrogen and potassium are needed for freshwater plant growth, but they usually exist in adequate levels. In such systems, the availability of phosphorus controls the growth of algae, so even small amounts of phosphorus entering a waterbody go a long way toward stimulating runaway growth of algae and other aquatic plants.

When unnaturally high levels of phosphorus reach freshwater systems, plants can grow unchecked. causing a proliferation of algae and aquatic weeds to the detriment of other organisms that share the ecosystem. An overabundance of surface algae prevents sunlight from reaching underwater organisms that depend on this light. Often, this unsustainable growth of algae (called a bloom) reaches a critical mass that triggers a catastrophic die-off of the bloom. As the bloom decays and sinks, it depletes the essential free oxygen from the aquatic habitat, typically resulting in mass kills of desirable organisms. By limiting the amount of phosphorus applied in fertilizer, localities hope to reduce incidences of aquatic plant overgrowth and detrimental ecosystem effects.

CHAPTER 7

Asheville and Other Cities Redesign Their Roadways to Enhance the Environment

Insurance Institute for Highway Safety

Traffic congestion and motor vehicle crashes are widespread problems, especially in urban areas. Roundabouts, used in place of stop signs and traffic signals, are a type of circular intersection that can significantly improve traffic flow and safety. Where roundabouts have been installed, motor vehicle crashes have declined by about 40 percent, and those involving injuries have been reduced by about 80 percent. Crash reductions are accompanied by significant improvements in traffic flow, thus reducing vehicle delays, fuel consumption, and air pollution. Information about roundabouts, how they improve traffic flow and safety, is provided in the following paragraphs.

Modern roundabouts were developed in the United Kingdom in the 1960s and now are widely used in many countries. The modern roundabout is a circular intersection with design features that promote safe and efficient traffic flow. At roundabouts in the United States, vehicles travel counterclockwise around a raised center island, with entering traffic yielding the right-of-way to circulating traffic. In urban settings, entering vehicles negotiate a curve sharp enough to slow speeds to about 15 to 20 mph; in rural settings, entering vehicles may be held to somewhat higher speeds (30 to 35 mph). Within the roundabout and as vehicles exit, slow speeds are maintained by the deflection of traffic around the center island and the relatively tight radius of the roundabout and exit lanes. Slow speeds aid in the smooth movement of vehicles into, around, and out of a roundabout. Drivers approaching a roundabout must reduce their speeds, look for potential conflicts with vehicles already in the circle, and be prepared to stop for pedestrians and bicyclists. Once in the roundabout, drivers proceed to the appropriate exit, following the guidance provided by traffic signs and pavement markings.

Modern roundabouts are much smaller than older traffic circles and rotaries, and roundabouts require vehicles to negotiate a sharper curve to enter. These differences make travel speeds in roundabouts slower than speeds in traffic circles and rotaries. Because of the higher speeds in older circles and rotaries, many were equipped with traffic signals or stop signs to help reduce potential crashes. In addition, some older traffic circles and rotaries operated according to the traditional "yield-to-the-right" rule, with circulating traffic yielding to entering traffic.

Originally published as "Roundabouts," *Research Report*, January 2009, published by the Insurance Institute for Highway Safety, Arlington, VA. Reprinted with permission of the publisher.

How Do Roundabouts Affect Safety?

Several features of roundabouts promote safety. At traditional intersections with stop signs or traffic signals, some of the most common types of crashes are right-angle, left-turn, and head-on collisions. These types of collisions can be severe because vehicles may be traveling through the intersection at high speeds. With roundabouts, these types of potentially serious crashes essentially are eliminated because vehicles travel in the same direction. Installing roundabouts in place of traffic signals can also reduce the likelihood of rear-end crashes and their severity by removing the incentive for drivers to speed up as they approach green lights and by reducing abrupt stops at red lights. The vehicle-to-vehicle conflicts that occur at roundabouts generally involve a vehicle merging into the circular roadway, with both vehicles traveling at low speeds — generally less than 20 mph in urban areas and less than 30 to 35 mph in rural areas.

A 2001 Institute study of 23 intersections in the United States reported that converting intersections from traffic signals or stop signs to roundabouts reduced injury crashes by 80 percent and all crashes by 40 percent.[1] Similar results were reported by Eisenman et al.: a 75 percent decrease in injury crashes and a 37 percent decrease in total crashes at 35 intersections that were converted from traffic signals to roundabouts.[2] Studies of intersections in Europe and Australia that were converted to roundabouts have reported 41 to 61 percent reductions in injury crashes and 45 to 75 percent reductions in severe injury crashes.[3]

Proper design can help to optimize the safety benefits of roundabouts. Centerlines of roads leading to roundabouts should be properly aligned with the central island. Approach roads should be sufficiently curved, far enough in advance of roundabouts, to reduce vehicle speeds of entering drivers. Islands separating the approach and exit lanes, known as splitter islands, should extend far enough from the roundabout to provide pedestrian refuge and to delineate the roundabout. Traffic signs, pavement markings, and lighting should be ade-

quate so that drivers are aware that they are approaching a roundabout and that they should reduce their travel speed. With multi-lane roundabouts, signs and lane markings should help drivers choose the appropriate lane when entering and exiting the roundabout.

Despite the demonstrated safety benefits of roundabouts, some crashes still occur. An Institute study of crashes at 38 roundabouts in Maryland found that four crash types (run-off-road, rear-end, sideswipe, and entering-circulating) accounted for almost all crashes. A common crash type at both single-lane and double-lane roundabouts involved vehicles colliding with the central island. These crashes, which often involved unsafe speeds, accounted for almost half of all single-vehicle run-off-road crashes. Collisions occurred more frequently at entrances to roundabouts rather than within the circulatory roadway or at exits. About three-quarters of the crashes involved property damage. There were no right-angle or head-on collisions, potentially severe crash types that commonly occur at traditional intersections.[4]

In the study of crashes at Maryland roundabouts, Institute researchers concluded that unsafe speeds were an important driver crash factor. Some drivers may not have seen the roundabout in time. Measures to alert drivers of the need to reduce speeds (e.g., speed limit signs well in advance of roundabouts) and increase the conspicuity of roundabouts (e.g., larger roundabout ahead signs and yield signs, enhanced landscaping of center islands, pavement with reflector markings) may help to reduce crashes at roundabouts. Certain design features such as adequate curvature of approach roads also may aid in reducing speeds.

Several studies conducted by the Institute and others have reported significant improvements in traffic flow following conversion of traditional intersections to roundabouts. A study of three intersections in Kansas, Maryland, and Nevada, where roundabouts replaced stop signs, found that vehicle delays were reduced 13 to 23 percent and the proportion of vehicles that stopped was reduced 14 to 37 percent.[5] A study of three locations in New Hampshire, New York, and Washington, where roundabouts replaced traffic signals or stop signs, found an 89 percent average reduction in vehicle delays and a 56 percent average reduction in vehicle stops.[6] A study of 11 intersections in Kansas found a 65 percent average reduction in delays and a 52 percent average reduction in vehicle stops after roundabouts were installed.[7]

A recent Institute study documented missed opportunities to improve traffic flow and safety at 10 urban intersections suitable for roundabouts where either traffic signals were installed or major modifications were made to signalized intersections.[8] It was estimated that the use of roundabouts instead of traffic signals at these 10 intersections would have reduced vehicle delays by 62 to 74 percent. This is equivalent to approximately 325,000 fewer hours of vehicle delay on an annual basis.

Because roundabouts improve the efficiency of traffic flow, they also reduce vehicle emissions and fuel consumption. In one study, replacing a signalized intersection with a roundabout reduced carbon monoxide emissions by 29 percent and nitrous oxide emissions by 21 percent.[9] In another study, replacing traffic signals and stop signs with roundabouts reduced carbon monoxide emissions by 32 percent, nitrous oxide emissions by 34 percent, carbon dioxide emissions by 37 percent, and hydrocarbon emissions by 42 percent.[10] Constructing roundabouts in place of traffic signals can reduce fuel consumption by about 30 percent.[11] At 10 intersections studied in Virginia, this amounted to more than 200,000 gallons of fuel per year.[12] And roundabouts can enhance aesthetics by providing landscaping opportunities.

To accommodate vehicles with large turning radii such as trucks, buses, and tractor-trailers, roundabouts provide an area between the circulatory roadway and the central island, known as a truck apron, over which the rear wheels of these vehicles can safely track. The truck apron generally is composed of a different material texture than the paved surface, such as brick or cobble stones, to discourage routine use by smaller vehicles.

Age-related declines in vision, hearing, and cognitive functions, as well as physical impairments, may affect some older adults' driving ability. Intersections can be especially challenging for older drivers. Relative to other age groups, senior drivers are over-involved in crashes occurring at intersections. In 2006, forty percent of drivers 70 and older in fatal crashes were involved in multiple-vehicle intersection crashes, compared with 22 percent among drivers younger than 70. Older drivers' intersection crashes often are due to their failure to yield the right-of-way.[13] Particular problems for older drivers at traditional intersections include left turns and entering busy thoroughfares from cross streets. Roundabouts eliminate these situations entirely. A recent study in six communities where roundabouts replaced traditional intersections found that about two-thirds of drivers 65 and older supported the roundabouts.[14] Although safety effects of roundabouts specifically for older drivers are unknown, the 2001 Institute study of 23 intersections converted from traffic signals or stop signs to roundabouts reported the average age of crash-involved drivers did not increase following the installation of roundabouts, suggesting roundabouts may not pose a problem for older drivers.[15]

Roundabouts generally are safer for pedestrians than traditional intersections. In a roundabout, pedestrians walk on sidewalks around the perimeter of the circulatory roadway. If it is necessary for pedestrians to cross the roadway. they cross only one direction of traffic at a time. In addition, crossing distances are relatively short, and traffic speeds are lower than at traditional intersections. Studies in Europe indicate that, on average, converting conventional intersections to roundabouts can reduce pedestrian crashes by about 75 percent.[16] Single-lane roundabouts, in particular, have been reported to involve substantially lower pedestrian crash rates than comparable intersections with traffic signals.[17]

Do Drivers Favor Roundabouts?

Drivers may be skeptical, or even opposed, to roundabouts when they are proposed. However, opinions quickly change when drivers become familiar with roundabouts. A 2002 Institute study in three communities where single-lane roundabouts replaced stop sign-controlled intersections found 31 percent of drivers supported the roundabouts before construction compared with 63 percent shortly after.[18] Another study surveyed drivers in three additional communities where single-lane roundabouts replaced stop signs or traffic signals. Overall, 36 percent of drivers supported the roundabouts before construction compared with 50 percent shortly after. Follow-up surveys conducted in these six communities after roundabouts had been in place for more than one year found the level of public support increased to about 70 percent on average.[19]

The additional travel lanes in multi-lane roundabouts increase the complexity of the driving task. Information is not yet available on drivers' attitudes toward multi-lane roundabouts in the United States.

Despite the safety and other benefits of roundabouts, as well as the high levels of public acceptance once they are built, some states and cities have been slow to build roundabouts, and some are even opposed to building them. The principal impediment is the negative perception held by some drivers and elected officials. Transportation agencies also have long been accustomed to installing traffic signals, and it can take time for deeply rooted design practices to change.

The first modern roundabouts in the United States were constructed in Nevada in 1990. Since that time, although the precise number of roundabouts is unknown, approximately 1,000 have been built. By comparison, there are about 20,000 roundabouts in France, 15,000 in Australia, and 10,000 in the United Kingdom. States that have active programs to construct roundabouts include Alaska, California, Colorado, Connecticut, Florida, Hawaii, Indiana, Kansas, Maryland, Michigan, Minnesota, Mississippi, Nevada, New Hampshire, New York, North Carolina, Oregon, South Carolina, Utah, Vermont, Virginia, Washington, and Wisconsin.

Roundabouts do not necessarily require more space than traditional intersections. Geometric design details vary from site to site and must take into account traffic volumes, land use, topography, and other factors. Because they can process traffic more efficiently than traffic signals and stop signs, roundabouts typically require fewer traffic lanes to accommodate the same amount of traffic. In some cases, roundabouts can require more space than stop signs or traffic signals at the actual intersection to accommodate the central island and circulating lanes, but approaches to roundabouts typically require fewer traffic lanes and less right-of-way than those at traditional intersections.

Roundabouts are appropriate at many intersections, including high crash locations and intersections with large traffic delays, complex geometry (more than four approach roads, for example), frequent left-turn movements, and relatively balanced traffic flows. Roundabouts can be constructed along congested arterials, in lieu of road widening, and can be appropriate in lieu of traffic signals at freeway exits and entrances.

Roundabouts are not appropriate everywhere. Intersections that may not be good candidates include those with topographic or site constraints that limit the ability to provide appropriate geometry, those with highly unbalanced traffic flows (that is, very high traffic volumes on the main street and very light traffic on the side street), and isolated intersections in a network of traffic signals.

NOTES

1. B.N. Persaud, R.A. Retting, P.E. Garder and D. Lord, "Safety Effect of Roundabout Conversions in the United States: Empirical Bayes Observational Before-After Study," *Transportation Research Record* 1751 (2001):1–8.

2. S. Eisenman, J. Josselyn, G. List, B. Persaud, C. Lyon, B. Robinson, M. Blogg, E. Waltman, and R. Troutbeck, "Operational and Safety Performance of Modern Roundabouts and Other Intersection Types," Final Report, SPR Project C-01-47 (Albany: New York State Department of Transportation, 2004).

3. Federal Highway Administration, "Roundabouts: An Informational Guide," Report no. RD-00-067 (Washington, DC: U.S. Department of Transportation, 2000).

4. S. Mandavilli, A. McCartt and R.A. Retting, "Crash Patterns and Potential Engineering Countermeasures at Maryland Roundabouts," *Traffic Injury Prevention* 10 (2008): 44–50.

5. R.A. Retting, G. Luttrell and E.R. Russell, "Public Opinion and Traffic Flow Impacts of Newly Installed Modern Roundabouts in the United States," *ITE Journal* 72 (2002): 30–32, 37.

6. R.A. Retting, S. Mandavilli, E.R. Russell and A.T. McCartt, "Roundabouts, Traffic Flow and Public Opinion," *Traffic Engineering and Control* 47 (2006): 268–72.

7. E.R. Russell, S. Mandavilli and M.J. Rys, "Operational Performance of Kansas Roundabouts: Phase II," Report no. K-TRAN KSU-02-04, Final Report 01–04 (Manhattan: Department of Civil Engineering, Kansas State University, 2004).

8. C. Bergh, R.A. Retting and E.J. Myers, "Continued Reliance on Traffic Signals: The Cost of Missed Opportunities to Improve Traffic Flow and Safety at Urban Intersections" (Arlington, VA: Insurance Institute for Highway Safety, 2005).

9. A. Varhelyi, "The Effects of Small Roundabouts on Emissions and Fuel Consumption: A Case Study," *Transportation Research Part D: Transport and Environment* 7 (2002): 65–71.

10. S. Mandavilli, E.R. Russell and M. Rys, "Modern Roundabouts in the United States: An Efficient Intersection Alternative for Reducing Vehicular Emissions," poster presentation at the 83rd annual meeting of the Transportation Research Board, Washington, D.C., 2004.

11. Varhelyi, "The Effects"; J. Niiittymaki and P.G. Hoglund, "Estimating Vehicle Emissions and Air Pollution Related to Driving Patterns and Traffic Calming," presented at the Urban Transport Systems Conference, Lund, Sweden, 1999.

12. Bergh, Retting and Myers, "Continued Reliance."

13. D.R. Mayhew, H.M. Simpson and S.A. Ferguson, "Collisions Involving Senior Drivers: High-Risk Conditions and Locations," *Traffic Injury Prevention* 7 (2006): 117–24.

14. R.A. Retting, S.Y. Kyrychenko and A.T. McCartt, "Long-term Trends in Public Opinion Following Construction of Roundabouts," *Transportation Research Record* 2019 (2007): 219–24.

15. Persaud, Retting, Garder and Lord, "Safety Effect."

16. W. Brilon, B. Stuwe and O. Drews, "Sicherheit und Leistungsfahigkeit von Kreisverkehrsplatzen," FE No. 77359/91 (Bochum, Germany: Lehrstuhl fur Verkehrswesen, Ruhr-Universitat Bochum, 1993), cited by R. Elvik, "Effects on Road Safety of Converting Intersections to Roundabouts: A Review of Evidence from Non-US Studies," *Transportation Research Record* 1847: 1–10; and C. Schoon and J. van Minnen, "The Safety of Roundabouts in the Netherlands," *Traffic Engineering and Control* 35 (1994): 142–48.

17. U. Brude and J. Larsson, "What Roundabout Design Provides the Highest Possible Safety?" *Nordic Road and Transport Research* 2 (2000): 17–21.

18. Retting, Luttrell and Russell, "Public Opinion."

19. Retting, Kyrychenko and McCartt, "Long-term Trends."

CHAPTER 8

Atlanta and Other Cities
Improve Their Urban Heat Islands

Maurice Estes, Jr., Dale Quattrochi *and* Elizabeth Stasiak

Reinvestment in urban centers is breathing new life into neighborhoods that have been languishing as a result of explosive suburban development over the past several decades. In communities all over the United States, adaptive reuse, brownfields redevelopment, relocation of entertainment venues into downtowns, and other infill initiatives are transforming urban landscapes, economies, and quality of life. The way in which this development occurs, however, could exacerbate the urban heat island (UHI) effect, an existing problem in many areas and one that poses a threat to the long-term sustainability and environmental quality of localities.

The UHI phenomenon is rooted in how landcovers respond to solar heating and how the heat from these surfaces affects the local environment. This phenomenon is responsible for urban centers' having higher air temperatures and poorer air quality than suburban or rural areas. The UHI effect also forces the development of meteorological events (increased precipitation), boosts energy demands, poses threats to public health, and potentially contributes to global warming.

While the name of this phenomenon implies that it is solely an urban problem, research has shown that the effects of UHI also are becoming prevalent in suburbs. As suburban areas increasingly develop, using land-covers and building materials common to urban areas, they are inheriting such urban problems as heat islands. For this reason, it may become necessary for nonurban communities to engage in heat island mitigation. The good news is that, through education and planning, the effects of the UHI phenomenon can be mitigated.

Although this theory has not been not scientifically validated as yet, heat islands may be viewed more as products of urban design than of the density of development.[1] Urban sprawl, for example, directly worsens UHI because there is an increase in built-up surfaces (pavement, buildings) and a reduction in natural surfaces (forests). Therefore, localities can continue to grow and develop without aggravating UHI by using sustainable development strategies.

What Is the UHI Phenomenon?

The urban heat island effect results from the way in which urban landcovers (buildings, pavement) respond to solar radiation, particular on extremely warm, sunny days in the summer. While all materials absorb heat from the sun, materials from the built environment, like

Originally published as "The Urban Heat Island Phenomenon: How Its Effects Can Influence Environmental Decision Making in Your Community," *Public Management*, Vol. 85, No. 3, April 2003, published and copyrighted by the ICMA (International City/County Management Association), Washington, D.C. Reprinted with permission of the publisher.

concrete and asphalt, absorb higher levels of solar radiation throughout the day than do natural landcovers.

After sunset, the built environment is no longer subjected to intense solar radiation. Surfaces that compose the urban landscape re-radiate this stored heat energy to the lower atmosphere. The total effect of this thermal energy re-radiation can cause the air temperature in localities to be elevated by three degrees Fahrenheit or more, in contrast to rural areas.

These elevated air temperatures effectively form a dome of higher air temperatures over a community, trapping air pollutants, degrading air quality, and preventing the heat waning as it would under natural conditions.

Conversely, natural landcovers, such as grasses and trees, can help to mitigate the UHI phenomenon. Natural landcovers absorb heat from the sun and use it as energy, via evapo-transpiration, a process by which vegetation actually helps to cool the air. Few local governments or highly developed communities, however, maintain enough greenspace to compensate for all the heat radiated by the built environment. Such natural landcovers as trees can be used to shade materials that, with direct solar radiation, would absorb and radiate high levels of heat.

Another factor that contributes to the development of UHI is the reflectivity of surfaces across the urban landscape. Reflectivity of a surface is known as its albedo. Human-induced surfaces typical of the city landscape, such as rooftops, asphalt, and concrete, have relatively low reflectivity quotients — a low albedo — in comparison with natural surfaces.

Trees, grass, and other vegetated surfaces, therefore, absorb sunlight for use in evapo-transpiration, as opposed to storing it like nonnatural surfaces. The water in them draws heat as it evaporates, cooling the air in the process. Surfaces ubiquitous to the urban landscape like rooftops or pavements, however, can be made more reflective through a number of manufacturing processes, thereby increasing their albedo and reducing their heat storage capacities.

How Is UHI Detected?

Through the science of remote sensing, information-gathering devices on satellites and aircraft can collect data on the state and condition of the land surface. Thermal infrared (TIR) sensors can obtain quantitative information on the amount of heat that is expressed by different surfaces across the landscape. These TIR data are critical for assessing "what's hot and what's not" across the urban landscape and ultimately, for determining the magnitude of UHI over an urban area.

TIR aircraft data was collected during the day over the central business district (CBD) of Atlanta, Georgia, in May 1997. The data depict the amount of surface heat energy detected by the TIR sensor on board the aircraft. The air temperature at the time these data were obtained over Atlanta was barely 80° Fahrenheit.

Temperatures for built-up surfaces across the CBD were in excess of 100° Fahrenheit, with building rooftops having surface temperatures of almost 120° Fahrenheit. In contrast, residential areas adjacent to the CBD, where trees and grass were more extensive, had surface temperatures significantly lower than those seen in the CBD.

Thus, areas with high surface temperatures, such as those in the Atlanta CBD, are likely sources of the high surface thermal radiation that drives the UHI effect and may be viewed as "hot spots" in contrast to cooler, vegetated areas like forests. TIR remote-sensing data, therefore, confirm and communicate the differences in heat absorption, radiation, and albedo between natural and human-made surfaces as they influence the development of UHI.

What Are the Effects of UHI?

The UHI phenomenon affects the environment and population in a number of ways, including through the degradation of air quality, threats to public health, and the triggering of meteorological occurrences. Urban environmental conditions also could threaten the viability of local governments, as fewer people will seek or choose to be in built-up places or downtowns for residential, business, or entertainment purposes. These shifts in lifestyle could reverse the current trend of urban in-migration and could cause an urban exodus similar to that of the mid–1900s, which left many traditional urban centers languishing for years and from which many American communities still are trying to recover.

Air quality. UHI may be a significant contributor to elevated ozone levels by adding excess background thermal radiation to the overall chemical reactions that form ground-level ozone (O_3). Sunlight and elevated heat levels can photochemically "cook" ozone to far more dangerous levels when the air temperature is higher than 90 degrees.[2]

Toxic to humans at ground level, ozone inflames lung tissue and aggravates a range of respiratory ailments, including asthma. Over urban areas, ozone is formed in the presence of calm wind conditions, intense sunlight, and high air temperatures, and as a result of the chemical interactions of two compounds: volatile organic compounds (YOCs) and nitrogen oxides (NOx).

VOCs come from a variety of non–point-source contributors, such as paint cans, gasoline cans, or even biological sources (vegetation). Contributors of NOx are primarily associated with point-source contributors like smokestacks, automobile exhaust systems, and other origins of emissions.

The UHI effect, which under the right conditions can drive up air temperatures by 10° Fahrenheit or more, acts as an additive background effect to solar radiation and may contribute to the formation of ozone. If UHI can be mitigated, scientists hope that significant reductions in ozone levels can result. More important, a greater knowledge of the relationship between UHI and ozone levels can have significant budgetary impacts on state and local governments.

Under the more stringent air-quality guidelines set by the U.S. Environmental Protection Agency in 1997, nearly 300 counties in 34 states will not meet the new air-quality standards for ground-level ozone and will be considered in a condition of nonattainment. This designation carries serious penalties to metropolitan areas. One of the most severe of these is the risk of losing funding for new highway development if plans are not made and enacted to reduce ozone levels to meet EPA standards.

A state containing metropolitan areas not in attainment of EPA ozone levels must develop an implementation plan (SIP) to illustrate the measures it will take to bring these areas into attainment.

Public health. Elevated air temperatures are not only uncomfortable but also can push temperatures from hot to dangerously hot, threatening public health. Poor air quality and high temperatures will be particularly harmful to children, the elderly, and those with chronic and respiratory illnesses. But even for those who are healthy, poor air quality and excessive heat can threaten good health and physical condition.

On the average, 1,500 American city dwellers die each year because of the heat, which is more deaths than those from all other natural disasters combined.[3] The compounding effect of heat waves and UHI could prove to be even deadlier to urban populations.

Global warming. The UHI phenomenon potentially contributes to global warming. The hotter the air temperatures, the higher the demand for electricity to generate air conditioning, which further boosts the sulfur, nitrogen, and particulate matter in the air. The vast quantity of greenhouse gases emitted as a result of excess energy production further contributes to larger-scale climatic effects through the process of global warming.[4]

Meteorological effects. As UHI modifies urban climates, its effects change local meteorology. The UHI phenomenon is a proven mechanism that forces the development of precipitation events either over, or downwind of, communities. Furthermore, naturally occurring storms often intensify as they pass through cities with a UHI; moderate rainstorms may turn into full-blown thunder and lightning storms. Houston, for example, has realized a 40 percent increase in lightning strikes.[5] Researchers have found that this lightning frequency is not seasonal but is rather a result of the urban heat island effect and air pollution.[6]

Addressing the UHI Phenomenon

While no communities have developed comprehensive programs to mitigate the effects of heat islands,[7] localities are recognizing the need to address the urban heat island. In Chicago, for one, several municipal buildings have been designed to accommodate vegetated rooftops.

In addition, a number of cities of all sizes and geographic locations specifically mention mitigation of the UHI phenomenon or climatic relief as a rationale for enacting certain zoning ordinances, like those relating to landscaping standards, tree preservation, and parking lots. Perhaps the most progressive program is an ongoing effort in the Atlanta metropolitan area that seeks to observe, measure, model, and analyze how the rapid growth of greater Atlanta since the early 1970s has affected the region's climate and air quality.

The National Aeronautics and Space Administration (NASA) is using its technological capabilities to assist Atlanta in mitigating the UHI phenomenon through an endeavor called Project ATLANTA (ATlanta Land-use ANalysis: Temperature and Air-quality). Project ATLANTA began as a scientific research effort focused on how urban growth in the Atlanta metropolitan area over approximately the past 25 years has affected the region's meteorology and air quality.

Integral to Project ATLANTA's original research tasks has been the measurement and mapping of the extent of the area's UHI (using TIR remote-sensing data), in relation to the distribution and composition of various urban surface types common to Atlanta's urban landscape. Soon after the start of Project ATLANTA, however, it became obvious that a fundamental driver of the scientific research for the investigation was the goal of gaining accurate information on the characteristics and effects of the metropolitan area's UHI so that urban planners, government officials, and the like could use this information to make sound, rational decisions on the future of Atlanta's overall environment.

As a consequence, Project ATLANTA has been developing some information products for use by decisionmakers and the general public to evaluate possible strategies for mitigating the UHI effect. These have included: (1) TIR remote-sensing data in the form of thermal maps that depict the distribution of surface temperatures over Atlanta as derived from aircraft and satellite data; (2) landcover classification maps (also derived from aircraft and satellite remote-sensing data) that present the distribution of landcovers (vegetation, high-density urban development, pavement) across the Atlanta urban landscape; and (3) an "urban fabric analysis" (again using remote-sensing data) that could quantify both the surface heating differences among urban landcovers and the distribution of thermal hot spots across the landscape.

What Can Be Done?

Communities can mitigate or prevent the UHI phenomenon by employing local planning initiatives and promoting sustainable development. Some common planning practices like the integration of greenspace can actually be crafted and bolstered to become community-wide strategies for mitigating UHI. Strategies can be employed to retrofit currently developed sites (through any renovation or redevelopment process) and integrated into site plans for new construction. Some mitigation strategies include:

- Increasing greenspace and tree planting.
- Increasing the reflectivity (albedo) of urban surfaces by installing highly reflective roofing materials or by "lightening up" the color of pavements with a number of commercially available products and methods.
- Using "green" building materials to improve the albedo of these surfaces and also raise energy efficiency.
- Employing green building designs, such as those that include vegetated rooftops. A number of local governments encourage green building development in their communities through programs that offer such incentives as density and height bonuses.
- Designing site plans that minimize or eliminate expanses of exposed, paved surfaces.

For example, instead of asphalt parking lots, consider underground parking.

- Promoting the use of mass transit and reducing reliance on the automobile, as auto emissions can worsen UHI and its effects.
- Decreasing expanses of impervious surface, which will reduce runoff in general and mitigate pollutant runoff in general into waterways.
- Installing "porous paving" that filters more rainwater into paved surfaces, keeping these surfaces cooler and also helping to lessen water runoff.

Dramatic Benefits

While all the effects and challenges of mitigating the UHI phenomenon may seem insurmountable, research is showing that cooling the air temperature of a city by as little as 5° Fahrenheit can have dramatic benefits.[8] Lower air temperatures could translate into less intensity in the photochemical reactions that create ozone and smog.

Local mitigation efforts can be significant. The Lawrence Berkeley National Laboratory in California estimates that changing the reflexivity of pavements in Los Angeles alone could achieve up to $90 million in energy and smog reduction benefits each year.[9] Successful UHI mitigation strategies can compound in their benefits and can improve urban environments, protect public health, preserve quality of life, and conserve energy resources.

Unchecked, the intensifying effects of the UHI phenomenon could make urbanized areas increasingly unpleasant places. Declining urban environmental conditions and quality of life may essentially encourage sprawl, as citizens try to escape poor air quality and oppressive temperatures. In fact, all the money and other resources that have been or are now dedicated to urban revitalization, sprawl management, greenspace protection, and infill development may come to naught if few people choose to live, work, or recreate in communities plagued by UHI.

By integrating mitigation strategies, communities can be planned to grow in a way that supports and sustains long-term investment, as well as protects citizens and their environment.

NOTES

1. Brian Stone and Michael O. Rodgers, "Urban Form and Thermal Efficiency: How the Design of Cities Influences the Urban Heat Island Effect," *APA Journal*, Vol. 67, No. 2 (Spring 2002): 189.
2. Frances Lyman, "Survival Plan for Urban Heat Islands," MSNBC News, www.msnbc.com/news791658.asp, August 14, 2002.
3. Tara Bahrampour, "Most Deadly of the Natural Disasters: The Heat Wave," *The New York Times*, August 13, 2002, p. 1
4. Stone and Rodgers, 188.
5. Lyman.
6. Texas A&M University, Office of University Relations. "Houston Called 'Lightning Capital of Texas,'" *AggieDaily*, http://rev.tamu.edu/stories/02/071002-12.html, December 12, 2002.
7. Stone and Rodgers, 189.
8. Lyman.
9. Lyman.

WORKS CITED

Bahrampour, Tara. "Most Deadly of the Natural Disasters: The Heat Wave." *The New York Times*, August 13, 2002.

Lyman, Frances. "Survival Plan for Urban Heat Islands." MSNBC News, www.msnbc.com/news/791658.asp, August 14, 2002.

Stone, Brian, and Michael O. Rodgers. "Urban Form and Thermal Efficiency: How the Design of Cities Influences the Urban Heat Island Effect." *APA Journal*, Vol. 67, No. 2 (Spring 2002): 186–198.

Texas A&M University, Office of University Relations. "Houston Called 'Lightning Capital of Texas.'" *AggieDaily*, http://rev.tamu.edu/stories/02/071002-12.html, December 12, 2002.

CHAPTER 9

Austin and Other Cities Implement Green Government Practices

Zach Patton

As the economic crisis deepens for states and localities, many governments are being forced to delay investment in new green IT products and initiatives. Thanks to the upfront costs associated with new technologies, energy efficiency has become a lower-priority issue for public-sector agencies over the past year.

The number of IT professionals who identify energy efficiency as a "very important consideration when purchasing new equipment" dropped from 34 percent in 2008 to 26 percent in 2009, according to a survey conducted last fall by technology and IT services vendor CDW-G. And in a November survey of state technology officers by the National Association of State Chief Information Officers (NASCIO), "budget and cost control" rose to the top of the priority list for 2010. Green IT, which had ranked No. 7 on the list the previous year, has now fallen out of the top 10.

While environmentalism may have ebbed as an IT priority, there's still quite the green tint to state and local technology operations right now. The focus is on finding efficiencies to save money, but many of those cost-saving initiatives also happen to be eco-friendly, says Paul Christman, director of state and local government sales for Quest software. "Right now, public-sector CIOs joke that it's not green because it's environmentally friendly," he says.

"It's green because it saves you money. If you can save money by decreasing your power costs and heating and cooling costs, great. All those things are good, and they can also be tagged as 'green.'"

The push to consolidate multiple, energy-wasting data centers into fewer, more efficient facilities is something states have been talking about for decades. But some real progress has been made in the past few years, as states have redoubled their efforts to increase efficiency. Indiana, a leader in consolidation efforts, has already reduced its data centers from seven sites to one. Michigan, another progressive state in this area, has consolidated some 4,000 servers scattered around the state into just three data centers, saving the state $19 million so far and freeing up 30,000 square feet of office space. Now the state is planning a single, massive "information and technology center." The move will allow Michigan to deliver a broad scope of IT services to all its agencies, with a greatly reduced carbon footprint.

The majority of states are now following suit, according to NASCIO, which reports that most states are either implementing consolidation efforts or planning to do so. Massachusetts, for example, set a goal of consolidating 183 data centers into two, an effort the state hopes will be "substantially complete" by 2012. California

Originally published as "Keeping Government Green," *Governing*, Vol. 23, No. 6, March 2010, published by e.Republic Inc., Washington, D.C. Reprinted with permission of the publisher.

hopes to help stem some of its massive budget deficit by consolidating its 400 data facilities.

There's another facet of consolidation, though, that has less to do with brick-and-mortar buildings. Sharing services across agency lines can reduce a state's energy consumption. E-mail systems are usually one of the first processes states turn to in an effort to share services. States such as Michigan, California and Indiana have streamlined their multiple, agency-specific e-mail units into statewide systems. In late 2007, Missouri completed its transition from 14 agency e-mail systems to just one, resulting in an immediate savings or cost avoidance of more than $2 million, as well as a 70 percent reduction in the infrastructure required.

Consolidating data servers into a single location certainly is more efficient, but boosting the efficiency of the individual servers themselves is really the key to reducing energy consumption. That's why so many states and localities have implemented virtualization initiatives — allowing multiple operations to run on a single physical server. Virtualization is what has allowed Indiana to reduce the number of servers it uses by one-third. And it's how the publicly owned Austin Energy in Texas uses only 150 servers to run applications that otherwise would require 600 servers. "Virtualization is the biggest issue, because it really hits the two components of cost savings and green IT," says Bert Jarreau, CIO of the National Association of Counties. "It allows you to use 70 percent of one system versus 10 percent of 10 systems."

Maximizing servers' potential this way already has some states looking beyond virtualization to cloud computing, in which data may not be stored at state facilities at all. Multiple governments could share one cloud, or a government may store information in a private-sector cloud. The concept itself is no more novel than Web-based e-mail, in which data is stored on the Internet. "The technology of cloud computing has been around for a number of years," says Christman. "But cheap storage, faster servers and higher-speed connection have all made it a real possibility now." Christman adds that cloud storage is really nothing more than large-scale shared services via the Web.

Two of the nation's most technologically progressive states — Michigan and Utah — are moving forward with plans for developing their own clouds, which would host information for state agencies as well as cities, counties and education systems. Colorado and New York also are looking at whether a private cloud — with state agencies as the anchor tenants — would make sense. The great advantage of these state-run clouds is that they mitigate the privacy and cyber-security issues of turning public data over to a third-party company. "With cloud computing, there are lots of concerns about, 'Where's my data going to be residing?'" says Jarreau. "People are very, very concerned about it being hosted outside the state."

Cloud storage and desktop visualization don't just reduce governments' carbon footprint by reducing the need for energy-guzzling data centers. These technologies also help pave the way for another kind of green IT initiative: telecommuting. If employees could accomplish their jobs without needing to come into the office — or not as often — then governments' overall environmental impact could be greatly reduced. Fewer in-office employees means lower energy use and more efficient use of space, as well as fewer cars on the road.

Critical to making telecommuting a truly viable option, though, is investing in high-speed broadband, says Seattle Chief Technology Officer Bill Schrier, who has advocated broadband-to-the-home implementation for years. "Many of us have a high-definition television at home," he said at a recent Governing conference. "Well, slap a high-def camera on there, and what have you got? A two-way, high-def office environment. But you can't do it without broadband. Broadband is the key." Schrier says the city may begin implementing a fiber plan — possibly funded in part by federal stimulus funds — later this year.

Similar to telecommuting, the notion of truncated workweeks seeks to reduce government energy use by shortening the amount of time an employee spends in the office. So far, the government that has most embraced this idea is Utah, which is now 18 months into its plan to close state government on Fridays, eliminating the need to heat or cool many state buildings one day a week. While first-year savings fell far short of the anticipated $3 million, the state nonetheless reduced its energy consumption by 13 percent in the program's first year. Technology was a central part of Utah's decision: Citizens can now access more than 850 state services online, making it much more palatable for agencies to close on Fridays.

Sometimes the best solutions are the most obvious ones. Some state and local governments are achieving tremendous reductions in their energy use simply by encouraging — or mandating — that employees turn off their desktop computers at the end of the day. Minnesota, for example, launched an initiative to get employees to power down, with a predicted cost savings of $50 annually per computer. Other places have gone further. Seattle, for example, now utilizes software that reduces power to desktops when they're not in use. Since putting the new software in place a couple of years ago, the city has reduced the energy consumption of its desktops by more than 35 percent.

CHAPTER 10

Billings and Other Cities Encourage Updating Old Structures to Green Standards

Glen Martin

For those who can afford them, exquisitely designed green dwellings fitted with every kind of energy-saving gewgaw are all the rage. But what about those of us who live in the world of small apartments, cracker-box condominiums, tract houses, and drafty old Victorians? Are we condemned to schlep around our admittedly pedestrian homes, leaving gigantic carbon footprints simply because we can't afford the latest in earth-friendly housing tech?

Not necessarily. Common sense and common materials can go a long way toward making your house or condo more energy efficient and healthier; even apartment dwellers can find buildings remodeled to green specs by enlightened owners or nonprofits. Consider the following examples:

Tract Home

Frank Schiavo bought his San Jose, California, home new in 1978 for $63,500. It was pretty standard — indeed, it was exactly like 500 other houses in the same development. And like them, it was a voracious energy hog. Schiavo, a former high school teacher and retired environmental studies lecturer at San Jose State University, found that intolerable. He was determined to retrofit his home to jibe with his environmentally progressive sensibilities.

"The trouble was that I was a retired educator, so I didn't have a very large budget," Schiavo recalls. "I had to keep things simple."

Schiavo's remodel centers on passive solar heating — in the form of a 40-foot sunroom attached to the back of the house. The room contains exterior windows as well as interior windows on the back wall of the original home — all double paned, of course; the floor is brick. During the winter, Schiavo says, the sun is low in the sky, and most of the thermal energy is directed to the floor. The bricks heat up until the room is positively torrid. "Then it's just a matter of opening up the back windows to the house and letting the hot air flood in," he says.

In the summer, Schiavo notes, the sun is high in the sky, and the floor is shielded from intense rays by the eaves of the house. "It seldom gets all that warm in the sunroom then, and when it does, you just open the windows and let the heat vent," he explains.

Schiavo has installed rigid foam insulation beneath his home's exterior siding, fitted solar hot-water panels over his garage, and installed

Originally published as "Building Better: Stay-at-Home Green," *Sierra Magazine*, January/February 2009, by the Sierra Club, San Francisco, CA. Article appears with permission of *Sierra*, the national magazine of the Sierra Club.

small photovoltaic panels — enough to supply 800 watts when the sun is bright. He also replaced all his incandescent lightbulbs with compact fluorescents, uses a clothesline instead of a dryer, and washes his dishes by hand. Next up: an energy-efficient furnace.

"I'm pretty happy with the results so far," says Schiavo. "In August, my electric bill was $13.70. Of course, it goes up in winter — It may reach $25."

Historic Lodge

In 1994, when Cathie and John Imes bought the Arbor House — an historic building in Madison, Wisconsin — they had visions of an environmentally friendly bed-and-breakfast for eco-conscious travelers.

They got their wish. The Arbor House complex — which includes the original 1853 building and an annex they added — now hosts more than 4,000 guests annually. But it took a lot of work and a fair amount of frustration.

As Cathie recalls, building the annex sustainably was far easier than retrofitting the original structure, a popular watering hole and dance hall for local gentry in the mid–19th century. "Because the Arbor House has national-landmark status, we couldn't just wade in there and start ripping things up," she says. "Every move had to be vetted and approved by an engineer specializing in historic structures."

That wasn't cheap. "Right now we need a new roof, and our engineer was just out here to examine it," Cathie says. "It was expensive just for him to look at it. I almost fell over." Still, she and her husband are businesspeople, and their efforts have penciled out to a profitable bottom line. The inn employs high-efficiency hot-water heaters and radiant in-floor heating systems that are 95 percent energy efficient, says John. The wood used in the renovation was either recycled or from Forest Stewardship Council–certified sources. The windows are triple paned for energy efficiency, the fixtures and faucets are designed for low water use, the floor tiles are fabricated from recycled glass, and the carpeting is 100 percent wool.

Along with sustainability, health is a guiding principle at the Inn. "All our caulking is low toxicity, and we use solvent-free mineral silicate paint," John says. Compact fluorescents, dimmers, and motion-sensor light switches keep electrical consumption to a minimum. Arbor House is also a Wisconsin wind power sponsor — the inn pays a premium on its utility bill to support wind-generated electricity production in the state. "It's in keeping with our philosophy and a good marketing point," Cathie says. The biggest challenge in the greening of Arbor House? "Installing the windows," according to Cathie. "The walls are 12-inch-thick stone. Putting in modern thermopane windows while maintaining the historical integrity was an ordeal."

Apartment Building

It may sound like something out of a Road Runner cartoon, but the Acme Building in downtown Billings, Montana, is real — and a godsend to the city's low-income residents.

Like the Arbor House, the Acme is listed in the National Register of Historic Places. Built in 1911, the former theater and commercial venue was in pretty sad shape when it was acquired by homeWORD, a nonprofit affordable-housing provider.

The group gutted the Acme and rebuilt it with the environment in mind, keeping the lovely brick and cast-stone facade intact. The project was finished in 2004, with 19 apartments on the upper two floors that rent for $250 to $450 monthly. The low-income flats are largely subsidized by ground-floor commercial businesses, which pay fair market value.

"It was a wonderful project because it allowed us to preserve one of the town's most beautiful old buildings and create housing that was both environmentally sound and affordable," says Jennifer Betz, an asset manager for homeWORD.

The Acme has been equipped with an 18,000-watt photovoltaic array — one of the largest in the state — providing much of the apartment dwellers' electrical needs, says Betz. Many of the building's original materials were salvaged and used in the remodel, including wood flooring, trim, doors, and the main stair-way. The heating and cooling systems are energy efficient, and minimal PVC piping was used.

All the plaster removed during remodeling was composted rather than taken to a landfill, and cabinetry, decking, and interior doors are made of composite–waste wood. About 1,700 pounds of copper and brass were removed and recycled; the radiators — totaling ten tons in weight — and more than 40 sinks were removed for reuse.

Roadblocks were predictable — mainly finding the $3.4 million the project required.

Funding was ultimately obtained through federal low-income and historic-landmark tax credits, city housing programs, and various loans and grants. As with the Arbor House, planners had to take pains to preserve the building's historic aspects.

Despite the tribulations, tenants are happy with the results. The building has been booked solid since Its opening. "A lot of times, affordable housing isn't in optimum condition or in the best locale," says Betz. "It's nice to provide our clients with a truly comfortable, healthy place to live."

CHAPTER 11

Blackwater and Other Cities Protect Their Natural Corridors

A. Elizabeth Watson

In 2007, the National Trust for Historic Preservation named "Historic Places in Power Line Corridors" in seven Mid-Atlantic states on its annual list of 11 Most Endangered Places.

The corridors — involving sizeable upgrades to existing power transmission lines or new lines entirely — are part of a fast-tracked program devised by Congress in the Energy Policy Act of 2005. It directed the U.S. Department of Energy to create a process for designating large geographic areas as National Interest Energy Transmission Corridors.

The implication in such a process is that local opposition can be trumped by national interest. One of the projects in the National Trust's list is a proposed new route, with a new crossing under the Chesapeake Bay heading across Maryland's Eastern Shore to Delaware. Although the project has recently been postponed pending further study, there is indeed local opposition, particularly in Dorchester County, one of Maryland's most rural counties.

This is the landscape that gave rise to Harriet Tubman, who led as many as 75 to freedom on the Underground Railroad before the Civil War. The vast Blackwater National Wildlife Refuge is also here, rich with bald eagles, waterfowl, and other birds that once ranged across the entire Chesapeake Bay. Dorchester is also a state-designated heritage area.

The area is so important that the National Park Service is involved. Its 2008 study of ways to commemorate Tubman recommended federal assistance in creating a visitors center near Blackwater.

That site is linked to neighboring Caroline County via the recently designated Harriet Tubman Underground Railroad All-American Road, the ultimate National Scenic Byway designation. The federal study recommended the protection of a 2,700-acre agricultural and natural area in Caroline that is closely associated with important elements of Tubman's life story. Two bills under consideration by Congress would allow the park service to follow through, and Maryland is already designing the visitor center.

In all, the National Park Service has identified at least 55 national parks and 14 heritage areas within this National Interest Energy Transmission Corridor. Numerous scenic rivers, scenic byways, and Civil War battlefields — the nation's greatest concentration, according to the National Trust — are also at risk.

The seven-state Mid-Atlantic NIETC designation is a dramatic example of the collision course between modern demands on the rural landscape and years of work by citizens, nonprofits, and government agencies to identify, protect, and interpret special rural places.

Originally published as "Lasting Landscapes," *Planning*, Vol. 76, No. 2, February 2010, by the American Planning Association, Suite 1200, 205 North Michigan Avenue, Chicago, Illinois 60601. Reprinted with permission of the publisher.

Another major planning challenge is figuring out how to ensure the "cultural transmission" of special rural places from this generation to the next. Maryland's power line struggle illustrates critical questions about how to address many different kinds of conflicting values in the countryside. Just how do planners and their communities save whole rural landscapes that express cultural traditions and exhibit healthy relationships with the ecosystems on which they — and their human populations — must rely?

Recognition for Special Places

In a world that will be largely urban by 2050, it may well be that only a few rural places will survive in a form recognizable to those born in, say, 1950. Most of those places are already identified as special, as "protected landscapes." These are defined geographic regions, generally encompassing multiple jurisdictions and resources, where residents have formally recognized their physical character and intrinsic values — and seek to go beyond standard comprehensive plans and growth management techniques to conserve their unique qualities. By carving out these special places, the idea goes, it is possible to devote extra attention and resources to their care, and require government agencies to consider their character when planning or spending money.

Americans are quite ambitious about conserving special landscapes at the federal level. Since 1968, when the National Wild and Scenic Rivers Program was first established, a rich a la carte selection has gradually emerged. Recognition and protection programs now exist at the federal level for trails, battlefields, scenic byways, coastal resources, and heritage areas. In addition, there is an interesting list of unique protected landscapes. The National Park Service administers not only national parks and national seashores, but a host of such other designations as Ebey's Landing National Historical Reserve (1978, Washington State), the Buffalo National River (1972, Arkansas), and the Shenandoah Valley Battlefields National Historic District (1996, Virginia, administered as a National Heritage Area). The U.S. Forest

Service, the U.S. Environmental Protection Agency, and the National Oceanic and Atmospheric Administration have all identified special landscapes.

State versions of protection programs for designated scenic rivers, byways, and heritage areas also exist, joined by state and local initiatives to protect greenways and farmland. Rarer are special landscapes designated for intensive land management at the state level. New York's Adirondacks Park (1891) and New Jersey's regional planning program for its Highlands (2004) are examples.

As Dorchester County's transmission line controversy implies, however, such recognized landscapes are not universally valued and respected, meaning that conflicts will likely continue to arise.

Sustaining Landscapes

Rural areas have always provided food, fiber, energy, and other resources — including land for various utilities and infrastructure — to the nation's growing population. But as suggested by local headlines across the nation featuring such LULUs (locally unwanted land uses) as rubble or sanitary landfills, cell towers, gas line corridors, mountain-top removal for coal extraction, or confined animal feeding operations, the pace and scale of such demands on rural landscapes are growing.

Even without such conflicts, the qualities that make protected landscapes special in the first place are threatened. The most ubiquitous threats are the wealthy, expanding urban and suburban economies that collide with nearby rural areas whose economies still rely on land-based resources. In other areas, especially the Midwest, population loss is the cause of landscape change.

There are other factors as well. Technology has enabled older Americans to pioneer their earliest retirement phase with a second home and office well beyond metro areas. As baby boomers retire by the millions over the next 15 years, the impacts of this demographic shift will play out in the countryside as well as in the economy at large.

Shifts in consumer tastes and markets have changed historic communities and affected the investments of past generations. Witness the ranchettes carved out of ranchland in the West.

There is, moreover, the interesting problem of scale in identifying trends and addressing rural change. The economic landscape in particular often extends beyond the community's perception of its physical landscape. Maryland's Eastern Shore enjoys a colonial heritage that sprang from wealth that long ago relied on the region's overseas connections to its European markets. Now, instead of selling wheat to Europeans, as they did two centuries ago, the region's farmers grow corn and soybeans for poultry bought by processors who sell to a nationwide market.

The paper and wood products that were long at the center of the economies of communities in the Northern Forest of New England and New York are now supplied by overseas companies. Iowa's premier farm landscape is experiencing competition from Brazil's rapidly growing soybean production. Vermont's farmers have struggled for years to maintain the state's most enduring image: the black-and-white Holstein milk cow grazing the green pastures of its beautiful valleys and hillsides.

And so it goes: American industries change and evolve — and local communities and landscapes change with them.

The natural qualities of a landscape also depend on its much broader context. The three state-designated heritage areas on Maryland's Eastern Shore rely on the entire watershed of the Chesapeake Bay to support their maritime traditions, and the bay's migratory waterfowl come from halfway across the globe. Los Caminos del Rio — "the roads of the river" — owes its remarkable landscape and biodiversity along the border between Mexico and Texas to the life-giving qualities of the Rio Grande.

Other forces involved in creating, sustaining, and changing special places are also invisible. Local planning policies and regulations are obvious, but others remain in the shadows — the multiple tax incentives for growth found at the federal level, or state level policies for water resources management.

Similarly, the hard work of long-term maintenance and improvement of a conserved place's biodiversity or water quality is nearly invisible when compared to such more immediate threats as urbanization or LULUs. The attractiveness of the arts trails of western North Carolina depends in great measure on the beauty of a fragile mountain landscape, one that is threatened by air pollution from coal-burning power plants and the pine bark beetle felling pine stands.

Given so many issues, it is little wonder that protecting rural landscapes remains more of a goal than a reality, a daily challenge to planners charged with the effort.

Protection for These Landscapes

The recognition of protected landscapes is accompanied by levels of planning programmatic resources, and local commitments that vary by program.

Most have some kind of special plan addressing the region's needs. National scenic rivers outside federal public lands require management plans that are endorsed by local governments before final recognition. Heritage areas may be designated before formal plans are adopted but few federal funds can be spent there until locals create — and the Secretary of the Interior approves — a management plan. Such plans are often based on reports from a study phase undertaken by the National Park Service or local advocates before designation by Congress.

As for programmatic resources, national scenic byways are especially well marketed by the Federal Highway Administration, which distributes a national map for drivers and supports a separate website (www.byways.org). The Highlands Conservation Act of 2004 allows the U.S. Forest Service to receive up to $1 million annually to support land conservation in Connecticut, New York, New Jersey, and Pennsylvania.

No matter how much federal recognition and resources are afforded to these places, however, local governments and organizations are still expected to pitch in to protect and manage them. This could be an Achilles heel for protected landscapes.

Local land-use regulations and community design techniques by themselves cannot mitigate the economic and natural forces pressing on rural landscapes and communities—protected or not. These tools can only address symptoms and place barriers in the path of change.

One successful policy approach to change the process of change itself is found in the world of historic preservation. Up until the 1960s, the answer to preserving an old building was often to make it into a museum. The more practical strategy of adaptive reuse arose in the 1970s. By the end of that decade, the federal government had created tax incentives for the rehabilitation of commercial historic structures recognized through the National Register of Historic Places. The federal rehab tax incentives revolutionized the practice of urban design and planning and caused a cascade of other needed changes, from new building products to the revival of old skills. A number of states followed over the years with state-level tax programs

For rural landscapes, a somewhat similar idea involved rules for the tax deductibility of conservation easements. In 1961, the Internal Revenue Service allowed a tax deduction for the value of a conservation easement donated within the view of Mount Vernon. By 1969, easements would be recognized in a congressional statement accompanying tax law changes. It was not until 1979 that they were made deductible as a matter of law. Over the same time frame, state laws ensured that easements would be respected over the long term.

Easements offered a new option to property owners (and executors) seeking economic relief besides selling. The number of land trusts rose almost exponentially after 1979, from some 200 in the mid–1980s to 1,667 in 2005, according to the Land Trust Alliance. From 2000 to 2005, private land under conservation easement rose to 6.24 million acres from 2.5 million. Acreage preserved by private means by local, state, and national groups reached 37 million in 2005. The tax incentives are a way to reward landowners for following altruistic instincts, but many are unable or unwilling to make the financial sacrifice to donate easements. Even with the expansion in recent years of purchases of conservation easements, the level of protection they provide is piece-meal at best.

Landscape Conservation 2.0

Even with the laudable rise in protected land—and in the number of formally recognized landscapes in the same time frame—much more is needed before "lasting landscapes" can exist over the long term outside national parks. What we need today is a comprehensive approach to the adaptive reuse of rural landscapes. A mix of methods—interdisciplinary, backed by public investment—might yield an improved version of present practices.

Sustainable economic development approaches could encourage continuation of cultural traditions and traditional economic pursuits of rural populations. Other tools might be found within historic preservation, environmental programs, and heritage interpretation, which promote public appreciation of special resources. A part of the mix would be to address such structural issues as the division of planning from economic development, or soil and water conservation from farmland preservation. Many heritage areas offer examples of the kinds of organizations needed to achieve cross-disciplinary insights and innovation.

Improvements to local land-use regulatory practices are certainly possible. What about improving local decisions through better information, through fiscal impact reviews, or even, say, agricultural impact reviews? The National Register of Historic Places now has Google Earth downloads (http://nrhp.focus.nps.gov/natreg/docs/Download.html). What other powerful information technologies could help? Recreational linkages, transportation improvements, and other community enhancements are also obvious elements of a larger "tool kit" for landscape conservation.

Lasting Landscapes

In 1968, almost literally at the dawn of the era of American protected landscapes—and just before Ian McHarg's *Design with Nature* was published — William H. Whyte wrote a small, seminal book titled *The Last Landscape*. It used the terms "sprawl" and "greenway," foresaw the usefulness of conservation easements, and advocated other planning techniques.

Fast forward 41 years. In the fall of 2009, filmmaker Ken Burns awed a nationwide audience with the story of America's national parks in America's Greatest Idea. From the reservation of Yellowstone in 1872 to the creation of a National Park System of more than 385 units of astounding variety today, Americans have much to be proud of.

We have made many strides since Whyte's time. But we have a long way to go in working out a process for valuing and protecting traditional landscapes in which Americans continue to work and live as well as play.

In a hundred years, perhaps it will be possible for another talented filmmaker to illustrate another system that has preserved the vitality, beauty, and historic qualities of other important American landscapes, not only "last landscapes," but lasting ones.

RESOURCES

Images: Numerous pictures were presented in the original article on some of the natural corridors that are being protected by local governments. The focus was on the tools for protecting those places that Americans consider special. One of these websites includes the U.S. Department of Agriculture, which is listed below under "On the web."

In print: *The Small Town Planning Handbook* 3d ed. by Thomas L. Daniels, John W. Keller, Mark B. Lapping, Katherine Daniels, and James Segedy (Chicago: APA Planners, 2007).

Historic Preservation: An Introduction to Its History, Principles, and Practice by Norman Tyler (New York: W.W. Norton), 2000; *Saving America's Countryside: A Guide to Rural Conservation* 2d ed. by Samuel N. Stokes, A. Elizabeth Watson, and Shelley S. Mastran (Baltimore: Johns Hopkins University Press with the National Trust for Historic Preservation, 1997).

On the web: *Guidelines for Applying Protected Area Management Categories,* edited by Nigel Dudley, IUCN World Commission on Protected Areas, 2008 (http://data.iucn.org/dbtw-wpd/edocs/PAPS-016.pdf).

U.S. Department of Agriculture reports on rural topics may be found at www.ers.usda.gov/briefing; the list of Historic Places in Transmission Line Corridors is at www.preservationnation.org.

CHAPTER 12

Central City Restores Its Watershed Areas

Sharon Harkcom

Sometimes you need to think big. A partnership in Pennsylvania's Dark Shade Creek Watershed did just that — in 1998 they boldly designated an entire 34-square mile, abandoned mine-scarred watershed as one big contaminated property. The U.S. Environmental Protection Agency (EPA) agreed with their designation and in 1999 awarded the coalition a Brownfields Assessment Pilot grant. The coalition used the pilot grant to launch a number of clean up and ecotourism initiatives. Now, only ten years later, the Dark Shade Creek watershed is beginning to recover.

Mining Left Its Mark

The Borough of Central City and Shade Township (combined population of fewer than 5,000) are located within the Dark Shade Creek watershed, a nine-mile tributary of Shade Creek that empties into Stoneycreek River. Dark Shade valley is located within Pennsylvania's Appalachian coal mining region. The mining industry thrived here in the late 1800s and early 1900s, but declined soon after World War II. In 1950, the Dark Shade region supported more than 20,000 mining jobs, compared to only 1,500 by 1995. The loss of jobs was compounded by the negative environmental impacts the mining industry left in its wake. Piles of coal waste covered acres of land throughout the watershed. Waterways ran orange with acid mine drainage (AMD) and did not support fish or other aquatic life. Potentially contaminated land remained vacant. The area's economy was in crisis.

As the 20th century drew to a close, the communities of Central City and Shade Township struggled to fix the overwhelming mining-related problems that continued to cripple its economy and environment. In the late 1990s, a nonprofit group called "AMD & ART" partnered with these communities to explore innovative ways to restore Dark Shade Creek and promote it as a recreational tourist draw for fishing, white water rafting and ecotourism. Noting how many abandoned mines and mining waste piles were scattered throughout the watershed, the partners decided to designate the entire 34-square-mile watershed as a single large contaminated property. The partners applied for and received a $200,000 Brownfields Assessment Pilot grant in 1999 to address mine-scarred lands.

Grants Help to Transform the Watershed

The group's pilot project objective was to further the Dark Shade area's economic growth and provide areas for recreational activities. The group wanted to install AMD treatment sys-

Originally published as "Reclaiming Appalachian Mining Lands — One Watershed at a Time," *Nonpoint Source News-Notes*, Issue 87, June 2009, by the U.S. Environmental Protection Agency, Washington, D.C.

tems on land that could double as community parks, and transform the Dark Shade valley brownfields into usable land for commercial businesses and recreational trails. The EPA brownfields grant enabled the communities of Central City and Shade Township to work with the U.S. Department of Interior's Office of Surface Mining (OSM), the U.S. Department of Agriculture, Pennsylvania Department of Community Economic Development, AMD & ART, and coal companies to clean up and redevelop numerous sites in the project area. The pilot grant also helped launch the Shade Creek Watershed Association, an organization of local community residents that leads community education and coordinates continuous stream sampling.

Since 1999, the project partners have received more than $1 million in grant funds from the EPA, Pennsylvania's Growing Greener Program, OSM, the Pennsylvania Department of Environmental Protection and others to support a variety of restoration projects in the watershed. For example, the Shade Creek Watershed Association frequently doses small tributaries within the watershed with limestone rock and dust as a temporary measure to help raise the waters' pH levels. On a larger scale, the partners removed a number of coal waste piles and restored the land underneath. At one site, the exposed land became a game feeding plot. At another, the partners transformed the land into a park, complete with a walking trail and volleyball court. The partners have installed numerous passive treatment systems for acid mine drainages, including an anoxic limestone dosing system and a bioreactor treatment system that uses biological matter such as mushroom compost and decomposing vegetation to treat the water as it moves through a series of ponds. The Shade Creek Watershed Association plans to install an interpretive trail at the bioreactor site.

A series of additional treatment system and coal waste pile removal projects is currently underway or in the planning stages. For example, at one site, coal waste covers 3.4 acres and is spilling over directly into Dark Shade Creek. The partners will remove two acres of that waste

(18,183 tons) and sell it to a cogeneration plant (which produces both electricity and heat) for approximately $65,000. The remaining coal waste will be capped. The revenue from the coal sale will help pay for the project.

In the near future, the partners hope to address "the big four" acid mine discharge sites, explains Sharon Harkcom, project manager for the Borough of Central City. These four sites are all within one-half to three-quarters of a mile of each other and include two of the worst discharges in the watershed. "It makes sense to try to address them all at once," notes Harkcom. "Fixing these discharges would significantly improve water quality." However, the project is currently limited by a lack of available land to support a passive treatment system (e.g., limestone-lined trenches, etc.), and a lack of funding to treat it with a costly active treatment system (e.g., a system requiring periodic chemical injections to precipitate metals out of solution).

Making Progress

Water quality in some areas of the Dark Shade Creek Watershed is improving. Monitoring data collected by the Shade Creek Watershed Association have shown that the pH of waterways below several new treatment systems is at acceptable levels. Native trout are appearing again in streams that once ran orange with acid mine drainage. "We are seeing fish in Shingle Run again for the first time in more than 100 years," notes Harkcom. Feed plots for local fauna and community parks now stand where abandoned coal refuse piles once towered. The projects have brought jobs to the watershed, and residents of Central City and Shade Townships arc realizing aesthetic and recreational benefits. "However, much work remains to be done," adds Harkcom. "The problems are so extensive — we are working steadily to address as many as we can." Fortunately, the Dark Shade Creek watershed is home to many determined individuals who are seeking to reclaim their mine-scarred lands.

CHAPTER 13

Charleston Preserves Its Coastline

Josh Murphy

Looking for ways to better manage your coastal community and protect it from future land use change or sea level rise? The free "Digital Coast" information resource (www.csc.noaa.gov/digitalcoast) might have just what you need. Developed by the National Oceanic and Atmospheric Administration (NOAA) in partnership with several other organizations, Digital Coast is a Web-based information delivery system that provides not only data, but also the training, tools and examples needed to turn those data into information that can be used by local planners.

NOAA launched phase one of Digital Coast in 2008 and populated it with data and tools available from the NOAA Coastal Services Center. "We structured the website to serve as an information broker," explained Josh Murphy of the NOAA Coastal Services Center. "We are trying to link people with the resources they need to manage their coastal watersheds."

Phase two is underway and is being led by the Digital Coast Partnership Network. Current partners include the NOAA Coastal Services Center, Association of State Floodplain Managers, Coastal States Organization, National Association of Counties, National States Geographic Information Council, and The Nature Conservancy, with financial support from the Mississippi Coordinating Council on Remote Sensing and GIS. These public and private partners, who are either primary users of the system or content providers, are helping NOAA to identify, prioritize and add new components.

What Does Digital Coast Offer?

The Digital Coast website (www.csc.noaa.gov/digitalcoast) contains a variety of free coastal data sets and tools. Data sets are grouped by type, including orthoimagery (aerial photographs), elevation, benthic (underwater) terrain, land cover, hydrography, marine boundaries and socioeconomic data. Digital Coast also provides numerous tools to help coastal managers use these and other data sets. The Web page for each tool displays a series of tabs that provide visitors with overview information, technical and data requirements for using the tool, examples of the tool in action, user support information and directions explaining how to download the tool. Tools are grouped by type:

Analysis tools. These tools help users generate valuable information by pulling from existing data sources and, in some cases, using a geographical information system (GIS). For example, the Habitat Priority Planner helps to identify priority locations for conservation and restoration planning. Users can turn to the Nonpoint Source Pollution and Erosion

Originally published as "Digital Coast Helps Manage the Present and Plan for the Future," *Nonpoint Source News-Notes*, Issue 90, June 2010, by the U.S. Environmental Protection Agency, Washington, D.C.

Comparison Tool to measure runoff, nonpoint source pollution and erosion. An Impervious Surface Analysis Tool calculates the percentage of impervious surfaces for a selected geographic area. Numerous other tools look at rate of change and impacts of long-term sea level rise, coastal project management, communication of hazard-related data and modeling of benthic terrain.

Informational tools. These tools provide guidance or serve as "how to" manuals. For example, the County Snapshots tool provides local officials with a quick look at a county's demographics, infrastructure and environment within the flood zone. The Practitioner's Toolkit for Marine Conservation Agreements explains how to develop and implement a marine conservation agreement project. Other tools help users process weather data in a GIS and find weather-related Internet resources.

Simulation tools. These tools generate visual products to illustrate concepts or issues to a variety of audiences. For example, the CanVis Visual Simulation Tool enables users to add objects to images for the purpose of visualizing impacts of future management decisions (e.g., house or dock placement) or sea level rise. Similarly, the Sea Level Rise and Coastal Flood Frequency Viewer shows sea level rise scenarios and potential impacts.

Data visualization tools. This set of tools presents dynamic views of spatial data. For example, the Legislative Atlas displays maps of ocean and coastal laws and provides access to summaries of the state and federal laws via an interactive Web application. NOAA's Coastal Change Analysis Program (C-CAP) Land Cover Atlas allows users to view regional C-CAP land cover data and explore land cover changes and trends. Other tools assist with finding topographic and bathymetric data, tracking hurricanes, looking at habitat in shallow coastal Texas waters, and visualizing coastal hazards in Long Island, New York.

Data handling tools. These tools help users manipulate datasets. For example, tools can create soil-based thematic maps, view and use nautical and navigational charts, or handle Light Detection and Ranging (LIDAR) topographic data.

How Can Digital Coast Help You?

People will use the website in different ways, depending on their needs. For example, GIS technicians will directly access the data or tools they need. Others, such as town or watershed group leaders, might browse the resources available to get a sense of how they can use the information. "Coastal managers can read the 'In Action' section of the website to see how other people have put the tools and data to work for them," explains Murphy. "We hope people will discover that some of the tools and data sets that they already use can be connected with other resources that they didn't know existed or didn't realize they could incorporate. Digital Coast can help them find ways to generate more information using information that they already have." Digital Coast also highlights training opportunities available that can teach people how to use the resources they find.

Murphy emphasizes that people living far from the coast can still benefit from Digital Coast's data and tools. "What we consider 'coastal' is much broader than some people might think," he explains. "We recognize the link between uplands and coastal environments." Digital Coast includes information for major coastal watersheds — some extending hundreds of miles from the coast.

To help coastal area managers see how NOAA's Digital Coast can benefit them, the National Association of Counties recently released *Building Resilient Coastal Communities: Counties and the Digital Coast* (www.csc.noaa. gov/digitalcoast/inundation/_pdf/Issue_brief. pdf). This document describes the challenges faced by coastal communities and suggests ways that the various data and tools provided by Digital Coast can be used to overcome these challenges.

The Digital Coast Partnership is continually expanding and improving the Digital Coast website. The partners encourage readers to submit suggestions of other existing tools and data sets (any scale) that might be useful for coastal managers. The Digital Coast team is also developing new Web pages that will help connect people with specific tools and data that might help when managing certain high priority issues such as habitat conservation and marine planning. "We constantly strive to improve what we offer and how we present it," notes Murphy. "When we designed Digital Coast we recognized that you can't just present new data and tools and expect people to use them. It helps if you show how these resources can be applied in the real world."

Pilot Project Helps Links Resources

The Digital Coast Partnership recently completed a pilot project designed to help coastal managers use Digital Coast to address a key issue of concern — coastal inundation from sea level rise and flooding. The Part-

nership developed a Coastal Inundation Toolkit (featured on the Digital Coast website), which can help coastal communities:

- Understand the basics of coastal inundation
- Identify a county's exposure and examine potential impacts
- Map inundation to visualize potential impacts
- Assess a community's risks, vulnerability and resilience
- Communicate risk strategies to initiate change
- Discover how other communities are addressing this issue

The toolkit shows coastal managers how to tie together the different Digital Coast resources, such as the County Snapshots tool and CanVis, to assess flooding risks and begin planning for the future.

CHAPTER 14

Charlotte and Other Cities Construct People Friendly Streets

John N. LaPlante *and* Barbara McCann

A complete street is a road that is designed to be safe for drivers, bicyclists, transit vehicles and users, and pedestrians of all ages and abilities. The complete streets concept focuses not just on individual roads but on changing the decision-making and design process so that all users are routinely considered during the planning, designing, building and operating of all roadways. It is about policy and institutional change.

This may seem simple enough. Over the last 30 years, a lot of planning and engineering energy has gone into learning to create beautiful streets that work well for everyone. Standards from *A Policy on Geometric Design of Highways and Streets* have been changed to reflect a multimodal approach, but many roads continue to be built as if private motor vehicles and freight are the only users.[1] Too many urban arterials feature a well engineered place for cars to travel next to a homemade pedestrian facility — a "goat track" tramped in the grass — with a bus stop that is no more than a pole in the ground uncomfortably close to high-speed traffic.

This stems in large part from entrenched planning and design practices. Transportation projects typically begin with an automobile-oriented problem — increasing average daily traffic or deteriorating level of service (LOS).

The performance of the right of way for bicyclists, pedestrians and transit riders or transit vehicles often is not measured. Roadway classification is similarly oriented toward auto mobility.

Using the standard functional classification system, streets designated as arterials are, by definition, intended primarily to provide mobility, with emphasis placed on operating speed and traffic-carrying capacity. This leads to other design requirements that stress access management, wider lane widths, increased turning radii and minimum interference with traffic movements. This, in turn, often leads to urban roadways dividing neighborhoods, destroying local businesses in established communities and creating sterile, inhospitable streetscapes in developing suburbs.

Context-Sensitive Solutions

As a reaction to this unhealthy trend, context-sensitive design concepts and techniques have developed. Within ITE, a new arterial street design paradigm for urban areas is being adopted in the Recommended Practice entitled Context Sensitive Solutions in Designing Major Urban Thoroughfares for Walkable Communities. The document is being developed in

Originally published as "Complete Streets: We Can Get There from Here," *ITE Journal*, Vol. 78, No. 5, May 2008, by the Institute of Transportation Engineers, Washington, D.C. Reprinted with permission of the publisher.

conjunction with the Congress for New Urbanism and the Federal Highway Administration.[2]

How do complete streets initiatives relate to CSS? CSS is a project-oriented and location-specific process and is aimed at making sure a road project fits into its context. Early projects tended to be large roadway improvements and featured extensive public meetings, stakeholder out-reach and plenty of extra work. More recently, CSS practitioners have recognized that this process can be applied to every public involvement and does not necessarily lead to expensive and time-consuming outreach efforts.

Complete streets focuses more on road users and is about making multimodal accommodation routine so that multimodal roads do not require extra funds or extra time to achieve. The intent is to change the everyday practice of transportation agencies so that every mode should be part of every stage of the design process in just about every road project — whether a minor traffic signal rehabilitation or a major road widening. The ultimate aim is to create a complete and safe transportation network or all modes. CSS and complete streets can be seen as complementary not competitive movements.

National Complete Street Coalition

The National Complete Streets Coalition has been working for three years to promote policy and procedural changes at the federal, state, and local levels. In addition to ITE, the coalition includes the American Public Transportation Association, the American Planning Association, AARP, and many others.[3]

The coalition has succeeded in gaining national media attention and policy adoption across the country. More than 50 jurisdictions, from states to small towns, have adopted some type of complete streets policy, most over the last few years. In 2007, several cities adopted notable policies, including Salt Lake City, UT, through a simple executive order; Seattle, WA, through a comprehensive ordinance; and Charlotte, NC, through adoption of its *Urban Street Design Guidelines.*

At the state level, a new law in Illinois requires the state department of transportation to accommodate bicycle and pedestrian travel on all its roads in urbanized areas. It is effective immediately for project planning and required in construction beginning in August 2008. Other places have been building complete streets for a while, including Oregon; Florida; Arlington, VA; and Boulder, CO.

A new complete streets policy adopted by a legislature or city council is likely to make any engineer nervous. If well written, the impact should be gradual and reasonable. These policies are not prescriptive. Complete streets will look different in different places. They must be appropriate to their context and to the modes expected on that corridor.

A bustling street in an urban area may include features for buses, bicycles and pedestrians as well as private cars; in a more rural area with some walkers, a paved shoulder may suffice. Low-traffic streets need few treatments. Places with existing complete streets policies are successfully building a variety of roads that meet the varied needs of children, commuters and other users while creating an overall network that serves all modes.

Implementation Challenges

In order for complete streets to be truly effective, the following implementation measures should be considered:

- Rewrite and/or refocus agency policies and procedures to serve all modes.
- Rewrite and/or adapt design guidelines
- Train and develop staff skills in serving all modes.
- Collect data on all users and modes for performance improvements.

Policy change should result in an institutionalization of the complete streets approach in all aspects of the transportation agency and beyond and often means a restructuring of everyday procedures, beginning with scoping. For example, in Charlotte, transportation planners are using a new six-step complete streets planning process that systematically evaluates the needs of all modes. The National Complete Streets Coalition is offering a Local Implementation Assistance Program to help jurisdictions with this task.

An effective policy should lead to the re-writing of design manuals. The best example of this in the United States is Massachusetts. A complete streets policy statement became one of three guiding principles for the new award-winning design guide — context-sensitivity is another. The new manual has no chapters for bicycling, walking, transit, or disabled users. Every mode is integrated into every chapter, with new tools to help engineers make decisions about balancing the modes.[4]

The third of the four implementation steps is the need for additional training for planners and engineers. Balancing the needs of all users is a challenge, and doing so with every project requires new tools and skills. For example, South Carolina has used its policy to launch a comprehensive training program.

Complete streets policies also should result in new ways to track the success of the road network in serving all users. Florida; Ft. Collins, CO; and other jurisdictions have adopted multimodal level of service standards to do that.

Speed Matters

Complete streets is about more than simple allocation of street space. One of the major components of this new design paradigm is selecting a design speed that is appropriate to the actual street typology and location and that allows safe movement by all road users, including more vulnerable pedestrians and bicyclists. From a safety and community livability standpoint, speed does matter.

Everyone should be familiar with the chart that shows that a pedestrian hit by a car traveling at 20 miles per hour (mph) (32 kilometers per hour [km/hr]) has an 85-percent survivability rate. That same collision with a car going twice as fast, 40 mph (65 km/hr), will lower the survivability likelihood to 15 percent.

Current practice is to use a design speed based on a somewhat arbitrary functional classification and then post a speed limit based on the 85th percentile of speeds engendered by this artificial street designation. This practice is based on the conventional wisdom that to maintain mobility to and through communities, some arterial streets have to be designated as major traffic carriers or the entire regional economy will grind to a halt. Travel speed has always been equated as a necessary component of this mobility.

Redefining Mobility

Given that speeds much over 30 mph (50 km/hr) in urban areas are incompatible with pedestrians (including transit passengers) and bicyclists, if not downright dangerous, is the only choice to sacrifice mobility for community livability? The answer to this question depends on how mobility is defined. One aspect of mobility is travel speed or, more accurately, total travel time.

For a 5-mile (8 km) trip along an arterial corridor with a 45 mph (70 km/hr) travel speed, the added travel time for a reduced speed of 30 mph (50 km/hr) would be 2.5 minutes. In the overall scheme of things, how important is this potential delay compared to the proven safety benefits and the city livability advantages that come with the slower traffic speeds?

Some will quote the standard benefit-cost travel-time delay litany that multiplies these 2.5 minutes times an average daily traffic of 30,000 vehicles times 365 days per year times $20 per hour in time costs, equaling $600,000 in lost wages to the economy. However, in reality, the loss is still under 3 minutes per individual for this one trip, for which he or she is probably not being paid and which is less than the time he or she willingly will spend in line for morning coffee.

Take this scenario one step further, to the all-too-common suburban arterial traffic experience of driving 45 mph (70 km/hr), stopping for up to 2 minutes at a traffic signal, accelerating back up to 45 mph (70 km/hr), only to stop and wait again one-half-mile (0.8 km) down the road. This uncoordinated signal system wastes time and fuel, and the many stops increase crash rates. If these signals can be coordinated to permit two-way progression at a constant speed of 25 or 30 mph (40 or 50 km/hr.), the total travel time ends up being roughly the same.

The other part of the mobility equation is capacity, with the number of lanes acting as the primary surrogate measurement. It should be recognized by now that LOS D is a reasonable peak period LOS in an urban area, provided the above-mentioned signal progression can be maintained. However, some state departments of transportation or regional planning organizations still recommend LOS C (or even B) in an urban setting whenever possible.

Not only is this a waste of tax dollars constructing unneeded pavement, it also increases pedestrian crossing distances (and thus pedestrian crossing times, which impact negatively on signal timing for vehicular traffic) and encourages faster vehicular speeds during the other 22 hours of the day in each direction.

Arterial Traffic Calming Measures

The remainder of this feature deals with specific design measures that may be used to retrofit urban arterials into complete streets. These roads present one of the biggest challenges to engineers in that they tend to be the most hostile to bicyclists, pedestrians and transit riders, but all of these modes are usually present in significant numbers.

Arterial traffic calming first must deal with controlling vehicular speeds. In addition to timing the traffic signals for a 25 or 30 mph (40 or 50 km/hr) operating speed, other possible speed control measures include:

- Narrower travel lanes: Based on the results of a recent National Cooperative Highway Research Program study, 11-foot (3.3-meter [m]) or 10-foot (3.0-m) lanes in urban areas are just as safe as 12-foot (3.6-m) lanes for posted speeds of 45 mph (70 km/hr) or less.[5]
- Road diets: A four-lane to three-lane diet can work for average daily traffic volumes as high as 20,000. This makes the more prudent driver the "pace" car for that roadway and greatly improves left turning safety.

- Tightening corner curb radii: Selecting the appropriate design vehicle and using the minimum needed to provide the "effective" turning radius from the closest approach lane into any lane in the departure roadway will slow down turning vehicle speeds.
- Elimination of any free-flow right-turn lanes: This specifically includes freeway entry and exit ramp connections. Encouraging freeway speeds onto or off arterial streets is particularly dangerous for both pedestrians and bicyclists.
- Raised medians: Raised medians visually narrow the roadway and provide a median refuge for mid-block crossings.
- Median and parkway landscaping: Appropriate low-maintenance landscaping further visually narrows the roadway and provides a calming effect.
- Curb parking: Retaining curb parking provides for community access while creating a significant traffic calming effect.
- Curb bulb-outs: Where on-street parking exists, curb bulb-outs shorten pedestrian crossing distances, improve sight lines and help control parking.

Pedestrian Crossings

The other important element in creating a pedestrian-friendly arterial street is making pedestrian crossing locations safe, comfortable and more frequent. On any road where there is transit service, a pedestrian will cross wherever there is a transit stop, whether it is provided for or not. In a dense downtown case with signals spaced every 300 to 600 feet (90 to 180 m), crossing at a traffic signal is a reasonable expectation. However, along most urban and suburban arterials, these signals usually are spaced no closer than every one-quarter mile.

Requiring travel just 1,200 feet (360 m) or more out of the way to cross a street will add 3 minutes to the travel time of a pedestrian walking at the average 4.0 feet per second (1.2 m per second) walking speed. If a 3-minute detour for all automobile traffic were suggested, this would be the equivalent of adding a distance of 2.3 miles (4 km) for a car traveling at 30 mph (30 km/hr). The outrage would be loud and instantaneous.

Many of the suggested pedestrian crossing improvements flow directly out of the traffic speed control measures noted above. They include:

- Narrower travel lanes: Shorten the pedestrian crossing distance and roadway exposure time.
- Road diets: Reduce the number of lanes to be crossed.
- Tighter corner curb radii: Shorten pedestrian crossing distances and provide space for perpendicular curb ramps.
- Adding corner "pork chop" islands where design vehicle turning radii do not permit a small corner radius: Also shorten pedestrian crossing distances.
- Raised medians: Provide pedestrian refuge and allow pedestrians to cross half the street at a time.
- Curb bulb-outs: Shorten pedestrian crossing distances, improve sight lines and provide space for curb ramps.
- Continental-style crosswalks and pedestrian crossing warning signs: Effective for lightly-traveled arterials posted for urban speed limits.
- Pedestrian-actuated crosswalk warning signs: For heavier traffic flows.
- Pedestrian-actuated HAWK-style signals: Will be in the new Manual on Uniform Traffic Control Devices (MUTCD).
- Full signalization: All pedestrian signals should now be timed using the new MUTCD pedestrian walking speed of 3.5 feet per second (1.05 m per second) to set the Flashing Don't Walk pedestrian clearance time and 3.0 feet per second (0.9 m per second) to determine the total Walk/ Flashing Don't Walk time.
- Countdown clocks: The new MUTCD will not only require countdown clocks at all new pedestrian signal installations, but there will be a 10-year compliance date for retrofitting all existing pedestrian signal locations, finally correcting the longstanding

confusion surrounding the traditional but counter-intuitive Flashing Don't Walk.

Traffic "Taming"

In conclusion, instead of the concept of traffic calming used in discussing the design of residential streets, the term "traffic taming" should describe the concept of making arterial streets more pedestrian, bicycle and community friendly. This compilation of suggestions for retrofitting arterial streets into complete streets is not meant to be all-inclusive. Many more solutions are available once the task of designing arterial roadways for community livability while retaining a reasonable level of mobility along the most important travel corridors is taken seriously.

Complete streets is both evolutionary and revolutionary. A growing awareness of other transportation modes has led to a trend toward accommodating a wider variety of users. Complete streets is simply the latest evolutionary step in this process. At the same time, stepping beyond how design typically is done today by greatly increasing travel options, flexibility and usability, a revolutionary new network of travel can be created for all modes.

Largely through the work of the transportation industry, the United States has succeeded brilliantly over the last century in building better roads for farmers, national security and economic growth. It is now time to achieve the same success in the challenge of completing U.S. streets for everyone.

Notes

1. *A Policy on Geometric Design of Highways and Streets* (Washington, DC: American Association of State Highway and Transportation Officials, 2001), pp. 1–7.

2. *Context Sensitive Solutions in Designing Major Urban Thoroughfares for Walkable Communities, A Draft Recommended Practice* (Washington, DC: ITE, 2006).

3. To see a complete list of coalition members, visit www.completestreets.org/whoweare.html.

4. *Massachusetts Highway Department Project Development & Design Guide,* www.vhb.com/mhdGuide/mhd_Guide Book.asp.

5. National Cooperative Highway Research Program Project 3–27: *Preliminary Report: Urban and Suburban Lane Widths* (Kansas City, MO: Midwest Research Institute, 2007).

CHAPTER 15

Chattanooga and Other Cities
Invest in Parks and Open Spaces

Margaret C.H. Kelly *and* Matthew Zieper

In the past several years local, county, and state election results have clearly demonstrated that protecting open space is an issue of growing importance to American voters. In fact, voters will not only support land conservation initiatives, they also will authorize public funds to pay for such efforts.

The election returns speak for themselves. In 1999, 102 referenda to commit public funds to protect open space were placed before voters in 22 states. Ninety percent (92 referenda) passed, generating more than $1.8 billion in open space acquisition funds.[1] Voters accomplished this by authorizing new property taxes, sales taxes, real estate excise taxes, and general obligation bonds to protect special or unique landscapes.

These statistics, however, tell only part of the story. State and local governments across the United States also launched open-space initiatives that did not require referenda. For example, Illinois Governor George Ryan signed a bill that gave communities $160 million to buy open space and Montgomery County, Maryland, announced a $100 million program to fund open space.[2]

Development of open space is hardly a new phenomenon; however, it has experienced a renaissance of extraordinary scale in the post–

World War II era. During this period, there has been a trend away from older communities and a demand by the middle class for newer, single-use housing on individual lots. While open space everywhere is being converted to other uses, fast-growing corridors clustered near metropolitan areas perhaps have seen the most pressure for housing and other development. For example, total population of the biggest cities in the United States' 39 largest metropolitan areas has grown by one million over the past 20 years. During this same period, however, total suburban population of these 39 metropolitan areas has grown by 30 million.[3]

These new tracts of suburbia and industry arrive mostly at the expense of an ever-shrinking reserve of public and private open space. Currently, the United States has 400 million acres of land in agricultural production — 20 percent of the total land base. Likewise, 600 million acres — 30 percent of the United States — comprises forests and wetlands.[4] These figures represent significant acreage, but they are dwindling at a rapid and steady pace. According to the American Farmland Trust, between 1982 and 1992, 400,000 acres of prime agricultural land were lost to urban and suburban development. On average, this works out to 45.7 acres per day.[5]

Originally published as "Financing for the Future: The Economic Benefits of Parks and Open Space," *Government Finance Review*, Vol. 16, No. 6, December 2000, by the Government Finance Officers Association, Chicago, IL. Reprinted with permission of the publisher.

The pressure on open space is unprecedented and apparent to a general public that for more than a century has been reluctant to abandon the pioneer-era mentality that American resources are boundless and inexhaustible. The recent groundswell of public opinion that has moved local, regional, and state governments to action on behalf of remaining open space is fueled by the public's desire to have a say in the rate and location of future development.

Arguments for Open Space

Each community, county, or state has its own reason or reasons for deciding to fund open space acquisition or enhance existing open, but unproductive, space (e.g., brownfields). Several of these reasons are discussed in more detail below.

The Costs of New Development Often Exceed Local Tax Revenues. Community leaders generally expect that taxes generated by local growth will pay for the increased costs of development, but in many instances this is not the case. A 1998 study by the Trust for Public Land (TPL) examined the relationship between land conservation and property taxes in Massachusetts. The study found that in the short term, property taxes generally rose after a land conservation project. In the longer term, however, those Massachusetts towns with the most protected land enjoyed, on average, the lowest property tax rates.[6] It is entirely possible for the longer-term costs of development — roads, schools, sewer and water infrastructure, fire and police service — to exceed the revenues from increased property taxes.

The conclusions drawn in the TPL Massachusetts study have been replicated in other parts of the country, as well. In Louden County, Virginia (the fastest growing county in the Washington, D.C., area), the costs to service 1,000 new development units exceeded their tax contribution by $2.3 million.[7] In fact, when long-term costs are considered, towns often conclude that they cannot afford not to buy some of their prime remaining open space.

Other studies done in DuPage County,

Illinois, and Morris County, New Jersey, suggested that even commercial development may cost taxpayers in the final analysis. In addition to making demands on community resources, commercial development often attracts residential sprawl and puts further strain on local services.[8]

To implement smart growth, a community must decide what space needs to be protected for recreation, community character, the conservation of natural resources, and open space. These decisions are unique to each community and are often controversial. After all, few, if any, communities can afford to save every neighborhood field or woodlot. However, making these decisions helps shape growth appropriately and control costs.

Open Space, Parks, and Outdoor Recreation Opportunities Attract New Businesses and Increase Real Estate Values. In a 1995 poll conducted by the Regional Plan Association and the Quinnipac College Polling Institute, respondents cited low crime with safe streets and access to greenery and open space as the major criteria for a satisfactory quality of life.[9]

The parks/open space quality of life factor provides at least two more benefits to communities. First, communities that make parks, open space, and outdoor recreation a priority generally have enhanced property values. This is particularly true of the properties near or adjacent to the open space, parks, or recreation sites. For example, in Oakland, California, a three-mile greenbelt around Lake Merritt added approximately $41 million to surrounding property values.[10] Likewise, in Seattle, Washington, homes bordering the 12-mile Burke Gilman trail sold for 6 percent more than other homes of comparable size.[11]

Second, quality of life and easy access to outdoor recreational opportunities attract new businesses to a community or region. This is evermore true as the United States moves toward a mixed economy based on services, light industry, consumer goods, and new technologies. Businesses and their employees are no longer tied to traditional industrial centers. Instead, businesses look for an appealing location that suits both work and leisure needs. In fact, corporate CEOs say that quality of life for employees is the third most important factor in deciding where to locate a business, behind access to domestic markets and availability of skilled labor.[12]

Chattanooga, Tennessee, is a good example of a city that thrived following a late 1980s collaboration by local government, businesses, and community groups to rebuild deteriorating quality of life and fight rising unemployment and crime. The environmentally progressive redevelopment of Chattanooga's downtown riverfront was funded by $356 million of public and private investment. Between 1988 and 1996 the number of businesses and full-time jobs in the district more than doubled and assessed property values rose by at least $11 million. (127.5 percent). In this same period, the combined city and county property tax revenues grew by $592,000 (99 percent).[13]

Urban Open Space Rejuvenates City Neighborhoods and Attracts Businesses and Tourist Dollars. In the 1850s, famous landscape architect Frederick Law Olmstead argued that the purchase of land for New York City's Central Park would be justified by the increase in value of adjacent properties, and hence increased tax revenues. He was right. By 1864, there was a nearly $60,000 net return in annual taxes beyond what the city was paying in interest on the land and improvements. By 1873 the park — which had cost the city $14 million overall — was responsible for an extra $5.24 million in taxes per year.[14]

Central Park, however, has done more than raise property values and city taxes. The park also draws millions of residents and tourists to its attractions and those of nearby hotels, restaurants, and businesses.

Other cities have similar — and more current — tales of urban rejuvenation. Many involve brownfields — former industrial sites that have some level of contamination from their industrial pasts and will require cleanup before they can be put to new use. Even with the costs of environmental cleanup factored in, a recycled parcel is often less expensive to develop than virgin land because it already is serviced by roads, utilities, and other infrastructure. Brownfield development also reduces the pressure to develop farms and other open space. For example, in North Birmingham, Alabama, an abandoned steel mill has been reclaimed by an industrial byproducts resale business. With 30 employees, this business is the first tenant on the 900-acre brownfield. Eventually, additional new businesses on the site may employ 2000 people in this economically depressed neighborhood.[15]

Not all urban renewal projects involve brownfields. In Boston, Massachusetts, in the early 1980s, a public-private partnership demolished a 500,000-square-foot concrete parking garage in the heart of the financial district and created a privately funded underground parking facility topped with the Park at Post Office Square. This park features a formal garden and lawns, a walk-through sculpture fountain, and café and is visited by as many as 2,000 people each day. Furthermore, the city receives $1 million each year for its ownership interest in the underground garage and another $1 million in annual taxes. After the construction debt is paid off, the ownership of the garage and park will revert to the city.[16]

The American Tourism Industry Is Heavily Dependent On Local, State, and National Parks and Other Open Space of Scenic, Ecological, or Historic Importance. Nationwide, parks, protected rivers, scenic lands, wildlife habitat, and recreational open space contribute to a $502 billion tourism industry. As one of the country's largest employers, tourism supports seven million jobs.[17] Outdoor recreation (hiking, biking, paddling, fishing, etc.) generated at least $40 billion in 1996 and accounted for 768,000 full-time jobs and $13 billion in annual wages.[18] In fact, river rafters on only one of West Virginia's famous white water rivers — the Gauley — pump $20 million per year into the local economy.[19] Similarly, river rafting, and kayaking contribute $50 million per year to the Colorado state coffers, while the state of Arkansas reaps $1.5 billion annually from all types of outdoor recreation.[20]

Many communities recognize that their natural resources have value to outsiders that translates into local economic benefits and are protecting these resources accordingly. In Stowe, Vermont, for example, people come to vacation year round, drawn by the mountains and the traditional rural and agricultural vistas. For these reasons, Stowe requires that developers seeking building permits guarantee the preservation of scenic views and signature landscapes. Many developers have supported these stringent requirements, believing that by preserving the area's character they also are protecting their investments.[21]

Protected Farm and Ranchland Generate Economic Stability for Agricultural Communities and Preserve Historic Open Landscapes. Not only does agricultural open space represent a traditional American way of life, it also provides a steady annual inflow of dollars to host communities. In 1998, the Growth Alternatives Alliance in Fresno County, California, (the nation's top-producing agricultural county) issued a report entitled "A Landscape of Choice: Strategies; for improving Patterns of Community Growth." According to the report, each acre of irrigated land produces between $6,000 and $12,000 per year for the local economy. Thus, each acre lost reduces the local domestic product accordingly.[22]

Of course, development often brings new sources of local revenue in the form of property and other taxes. However, more than 40 studies in 11 states have found that farms often save communities money by contributing more in taxes than they demand in tax-supported services. For example, in Hebron, Connecticut, farms require $0.43 in services for every dollar they generate in taxes. In contrast, residential properties in the same town required an average of $1.06 in services for every tax dollar. Similarly, in Dunn, Wisconsin, farmland required $0.18 in services per tax dollar, and residential development cost taxpayers $1.06 for each tax dollar collected.[23]

To combat the loss of farmland, states and communities are increasingly turning to the purchase of development rights to agricultural land and restricting this land to farm, woodland, or other open space use. Purchase of Development Rights (PDR) programs began in the eastern United States and spread west across the country. Fifteen states and dozens of county and local governments now sponsor PDR programs. State PDR programs have protected more than 470,000 acres. Maryland, alone,

with one of the oldest (state PDR programs (1977), has protected almost 140,000 acres of farmland.[24]

Watershed, Wetland, and Floodplain Open Space Protection Enhance Drinking Water Quality and Minimize Economic Damages from Flooding. According to the U.S. Army Corps of Engineers, flood damages in the United States average $4.3 billion per year.[25] However, protected floodplain contains no property to be damaged and serves as a "safety valve" for flooding by reducing destruction to downstream areas. A 1993 study by the Illinois State Water Survey found that every 1 percent increase in protected wetlands along a stream corridor reduces peak stream flows by 3.7 percent.[26]

Since 1960, floods along California's Napa River have caused an average of $10 million per year in property damages ($500 million total). For years, engineers have attempted to mitigate the damages, with levees and concrete fortified banks yet seasonal floods still risk lives, damage property, and disrupt the valley's, lucrative tourist trade. To break this cycle, in 1998, county voters allocated $160 million to acquire 500 acres of floodplain, raise bridges, lower levees, and purchase and demolish homes, businesses, and a trailer park that lie on the floodplain.[27] This newly created floodplain will provide the additional benefits of open space, wildlife habitat, or even farmland as the community sees fit.

Other Benefits

In addition to the benefits of open space previously discussed, open land enables nature to perform life-sustaining services that alternatively might be provided technologically (at great expense). These service include:

- degradation of organic wastes;
- filtration of pollutants from soil and water;
- buffering of air pollutants;
- moderation of climate change;
- conservation of soil and water;
- provision of medicines, pigments, and spices;
- preservation of genetic diversity; and
- pollination of food crops and other plants.

Many communities are facing issues related to water quantity and/or quality. Widespread development often results in increased coverage by impervious surfaces (e.g., roads and rooftops) that shunt water away from aquifers and into culverts and streams. As communities nationwide face the cost of treating polluted drinking water, or looking to new sources of water for local needs, there is a growing realization that keeping water clean is almost always cheaper than cleaning it post-contamination. Recognizing this, Congress has authorized the use of a portion of federal clean water funds for watershed acquisition.

New York City's resolved water supply crisis is a good example of one of the many ways that protected open space can provide a cost-effective and life-sustaining service. Manhattan's primary sources of drinking water are located upstate. These traditional sources of water, however, were seriously threatened by encroaching development. To protect its clean drinking water, the city agreed to spend $1.5 billion to preserve 80,000 acres of an upstate New York watershed. The alternative to the open space solution involved construction of an $8 billion water filtration plant with an operating budget of $300 million per year.[28]

Conclusion

From New York to New Mexico, California to Connecticut, state and local governments are coping with the challenges of growth—namely, how to balance the need for continued growth with consideration for preserving natural resources and quality of life. Instead of dismissing parks and open space as unaffordable luxuries, savvy government and civic leaders are embracing them as ways to grow smarter, foster economic development, and protect the fiscal bottom line while conserving critical natural resources. This trend has been gaining steam in recent years, with voters across the country approving billions of dollars to protect land for parks and open space. The choice is clear—parks and open space pay big dividends for state and local governments.

Notes

1. *Voters Invest in Open Space, 1999 Referenda Results* (Washington, DC: Land Trust Alliance).

2. *Ibid.*

3. The Smart Growth Network. See http://www.smart-growth.org/ISSUEAREAS/regionalisn.html.

4. The Smart Growth Network. See http://www.smart-growth.org/ISSUEAREAS/landuse.html.

5. *Ibid.*

6. Deb Brighton, "Community Choices: Thinking Through Land Conservation, Development, and Property Taxes in Massachusetts" (Boston, MA: Trust for Public Land, 1998). See also http://www.tpl.org/tech.

7. Parks and Open Space. Original footnote: National Park Service, Rivers, Trails and Conservation Assistance Program, "Economic Impacts of Protecting Rivers, Trails, and Greenway Corridors," 4th ed. (Washington, DC: National Park Service, 1995), p. 8-4

8. Parks and Open Space. Original footnote: Elizabeth Brabec, "On the Value of Open Spaces," *Scenic America*, Technical Information Series, Vol. 1, No. 2 (Washington, DC: Scenic America, 1992), p. 2.

9. Steve Lerner and William Poole, "The Economic Benefits of Parks and Open Space: How Land Conservation Helps Communities Grow Smart and Protect the Bottom Line" (San Francisco, CA: Trust for Public Land, 1999), p. 14.

10. *Ibid.*, p. 13.

11. *Ibid.*.

12. Parks and Open Space. Original footnote: National Park Service, 1995, p. 7-3.

13. *Ibid.* Original footnote: Statistics from Chattanooga News Bureau and Hamilton County, Tennessee, tax assessor.

14. *Ibid.* Original footnote: Tom Fox, "Urban Open Space: An Investment that Pays," A Monograph Series (New York: Neighborhood Open Space Coalition, 1990), pp. 11–12.

15. Lerner and Poole, p. 19.

16. Parks and Open Space. Original footnote: Peter Harnick, "The Park at Post Office Square," in Garvin and Berens, 1997, p. 150.

17. *Ibid.* Original footnote: National Park Service, 1995, p. 3-5.

18. *Ibid.* Original footnote: National Park Outdoor Recreation Coalition of America, "Economic Benefits of Outdoor Recreation," State of the Industry Report (1997), www.outdoorlink.com/orca/research/97SOI.

19. *Ibid.* Original footnote: National Park Service, Rivers, Trails and Conservation Assistance Program, "Economic Impacts of Protecting Rivers, Trails, and Greenway Corridors," 3d ed. (Washington, DC: National Park Service, 1992), p. 5-6.

20. *Ibid.* Original footnote: National Park Service, 1995, p. 2-8.

21. Lerner and Poole, p. 24.

22. Parks and Open Space. Original footnote: The Growth Alternatives Alliance, "A Landscape of Choice: Strategies for Improving Patterns of Community Growth" (Fresno, CA: Growth Alternatives Alliance, April 1998), pp. 7–8.

23. *Ibid.* Original footnote: American Farmland Trust, "Saving American Farmland: What Works" (Washington, DC: American Farmland Trust, 1997), p. 150.

24. *Ibid.* Original footnote: Daniels, pp. 182–183.

25. *Ibid.* Original footnote: U.S. Army Corps of Engineers, Total Damages Suffered in FY 1997. www.usace.army. mil/inet/functions/cw/cecwe/table2.htm.

26. *Ibid.* Original footnote: Misganaw Demissie and Abdul Khan, "Influence of Wetlands on Streamflow in Illinois" (Champaign: Illinois State Water Survey, October 1993).

27. *Ibid.* Original footnote: Timothy Egam, "For a Flood-Weary Napa Valley, a Vote to Let the River Run Wild," *New York Times*, April 25, 1998, p. Al. Statistics updated by Howard Siegel, project planner, Napa River Flood Control Project.

28. *Ibid.* Original footnote: Trust for Public Land, "Watershed Initiatives, Introduction," www.tpl.org.

CHAPTER 16

Chicago Develops Sustainable Streetscape Projects

Jay Womack

Each spring, large quantities of dissolved nutrients (such as nitrogen and phosphorous) are transported from the upper Midwest into what is called the Gulf of Mexico Dead Zone — an oxygen-deficient area that grows to approximately 8,000 square miles each year and cannot support marine life.

In Chicago, the public right of way includes more than 4,000 miles of streets and 2,100 miles of alleys — paved impermeable surfaces that contribute significantly to urban runoff that eventually makes its way to the Gulf.

The Chicago DOT (CDOT) is addressing this problem with a comprehensive sustainable streetscape project that will use several environmentally friendly techniques commonly associated with LEED-certified buildings but not typical in streetscape designs. The department will evaluate the techniques to assess their suitability for future projects and create a model for watershed planning in the combined sewer area.

Construction is scheduled to begin in late 2009. It is funded largely through a tax increment financing district, but it has also received several grants, including nearly $450,000 through the Illinois EPA 319 nonpoint source pollution program (which funds best management practices such as rain gardens, permeable pavers, and bioswales) and $73,200 from the Federal Highway Administration's Ecological Grant Program in addition to in-kind services from the Metropolitan Water Reclamation District of Greater Chicago.

The project, designed and implemented by AEC firms Wight and Co. and Knight E/A is located on the city's near south side along two major arterials — Cermak Road and Blue Island Avenue between Halsted Street and Western Avenue.

Cermak Road is a five-lane truck route with no on-street parking and 10- to 15-foot-wide parkways. It divides the Pilsen neighborhood from an industrial district along the south branch of the Chicago River. Blue Island Avenue is a five-lane truck route with street parking and 20-foot-wide parkways just north of the project area.

The project began when CDOT set out to determine what the equivalent of a platinum-rated streetscape might look like and what environmental, cultural, and economic benefits it may provide. The platinum rating is the highest level of achievement awarded by the U.S. Green Building Council (USGBC) for a project's level of commitment to sustainability. Wight and Knight developed a series of environmental categories and identified goals similar to a LEED scorecard:

Originally published as "The Greenest Street in Chicago," *Public Works*, Vol. 5, No. 11, November 2009, by Hanley Wood Business Media, Chicago, IL. Reprinted with permission of the publisher.

Recycled Content. Recycle at least 90 percent of construction waste (excluding landscape debris) based on total weight or volume similar to the USGBC's LEED-NC criteria. The sum of post-consumer recycled content plus one-half of the pre-consumer content must constitute at least 20 percent (based on cost) of the total value of the materials in the project.

Energy Conservation. Reduce energy use by a minimum of 40 percent below the streetscape baseline typical of new construction; use reflective surfaces on sidewalks/roadways; use dark-sky-friendly fixtures. Use materials or products that have been extracted, harvested, or recovered, as well as manufactured, within 500 miles of the project site for a minimum of 40 percent (based on cost) of the total materials value similar to LEED-NC criteria.

Stormwater Management. Divert 80 percent of the typical average annual rainfall and at least two thirds of the rainwater that falls within the catchment area into stormwater best management practices that promote infiltration, provide water for new landscape, improve water quality, and reduce stormwater that enters the combined sewer system.

Urban Heat Island Mitigation. Reduce ambient summer temperatures on streets and sidewalks through the use of high-albedo pavements and coatings on roadways and sidewalks, use trees for shading, increase landscape, and incorporate permeable pavements.

Alternative Transportation. Improve bus stops with signage, shelters, and lighting where possible; facilitate use of bikes with new bike lanes. Improve pedestrian mobility with new fully accessible sidewalks and improved crosswalks.

Beauty and Community. Create attractive places that celebrate the community, provide gathering space, and allow for interaction and observation of both people and the natural world.

Water Efficiency. Eliminate use of potable water sources for irrigation. Specify native or climate-adapted, drought-tolerant plants for all landscape material.

Education. Provide public outreach materials/self-guided tour brochures to highlight innovative, sustainable design features of the streetscape.

Commissioning. CDOT, in partnership with the water reclamation district, will model and monitor various aspects of the project, including stormwater initiatives and air quality. Both pre- and post-construction data will be gathered to determine the efficacy and long-term performance of these initiatives.

When complete, the 1.5-mile-long streetscape project is expected to be one of the most environmentally friendly stretches of roadway in Chicago. The project team has designed several simple and cost-effective best management practices to collect and infiltrate street runoff.

On the north side of Cermak Road, runoff will be collected in sidewalk storm-water planters connected to large expanses of engineered soil below the sidewalk. Engineered soil (¾-inch limestone rock coated with soil) is used to both encourage tree growth and provide stormwater detention. When it begins to rain, initial stormwater flow will bypass existing city infrastructure, enter the stormwater planters, migrate into the engineered soil, and be infiltrated or absorbed by tree roots.

This strategy allows for maximum infiltration while taking advantage of existing infrastructure and provides a cost-effective solution within the existing urban fabric. In addition, curb extensions on many of the side streets will be equipped with rain garden planters that interrupt the gutters' flow line to redirect water into the planters.

Street runoff will enter the bioswale through perforated curb sections on either side of existing stormwater inlets. The bioswales will be interconnected beneath cross streets when possible and have one raised overflow structure per block. The existing sewer infrastructure will remain to accommodate large storm events that may overflow into the street.

To intercept the "first flush" pollutants and improve the quality of street runoff before it enters landscape areas along Cermak Road, a layer of zeolite will be incorporated into the stone infiltration zones of both best management practices. Zeolite is a unique type of microporous volcanic mineral that will trade positive ions with those of phosphorous, nitrogen, calcium, and other water-borne pollutants.

For stormwater management along a half-mile stretch of Blue Island Avenue, new dedicated bike lanes and on-street parking lanes will feature permeable pavers. A 3-foot-deep catchment of stone below the pavers will act as detention with overflow pipes connected to existing infrastructure. In addition, infiltration planters, similar to those proposed on the north side of Cermak Road, will catch stormwater that flows over the permeable pavers and will redirect it back into the stone storage layer below.

Sidewalk planters hydrologically connected to the stone catchment areas below the street will provide long-term access to water and encourage deep root growth in the native and drought-tolerant plant species being specified. The permeable pavers themselves will be topped with high-albedo photocatalytic cement (smog-eating concrete). The photocatalytic cement also resists pollutants that gather on its surface, thus keeping its light color and ability to reflect light back up to help achieve uniform light levels. This technique contributed to a lighting design that specifies a white light source in the street fixtures and achieves an anticipated 49 percent energy savings below the streetscape baseline.

Finally, a stormwater plaza at Western and Blue Island avenues will take advantage of an empty city-owned lot that has a slight drop in elevation. With cascading planter beds and a backdrop of trees in an area with little vegetation, the storm-water plaza will create a place for people to sit and provide a location for an educational identifier and future community art installation.

Stormwater from Western Avenue will be directed into the highest planter via a tunnel. Water will build up 2 inches in the first planter and then cascade into lower planters, repeating the movement with each planter. The lowest planter will be equipped with an overflow-connected existing sewer system.

These stormwater best management practices work in combination with the city's goals and initiatives to redefine the role that urban infrastructure can play to improve a city's vitality and quality of life. Daylighting stormwater highlights a natural resource — water — that is often ignored in dense urban areas, and not only helps to educate the public but helps make the city more attractive.

EDITORS' NOTE

The U.S. Environmental Protection Agency has been working with the city of Chicago on an ongoing project titled "Chicago's Sustainable Streets Pilot Project," which is a part of the EPA's national Heat Island Reduction Program. The streetscape project described in this article is included in the Chicago's ongoing Sustainable Streetscape Program. (Source: U.S. Environmental Protection Agency website, November 2, 2010.)

CHAPTER 17

Columbus Combines Conservation with Development

Erin Sherer, Anthony Sasson *and* Tracy Hatmaker

Big Darby Creek — Ecological Background

Big Darby Creek is a high quality stream in central Ohio designated a National and State Scenic River because of its outstanding aquatic biodiversity. It harbors a nationally-recognized diverse population of mussels, fish, and macro-invertebrates, with many state and federally endangered species. It is a prime source for water recreation and natural resource education in Ohio. The watershed is located in central Ohio and covers an area of about 555 square miles (388,000 acres). A biologically important portion is in close proximity to the City of Columbus and surrounding suburbs, making it very attractive for commercial and residential development.

Big Darby Creek flows over 80 miles from its source near Bellefontaine in Logan County to the Scioto River near Circleville in Pickaway County. The Big Darby and tributaries flow over gravel and clay-based glacial till underlain by the limestone bedrock, forming a mostly flat landscape along with gravel substrates along streams and hydric soils in much of the uplands.

Because Big and Little Darby Creeks are among the best quality streams in Ohio and

the Midwest, they are recognized as National (1994) and State (1984) Scenic Rivers. Both Big and Little Darby Creeks are classified under the Clean Water Act as Outstanding State Waters (the highest level of antidegradation in Ohio) by the Ohio Environmental Protection Agency (Ohio EPA) based on exceptional ecological values. Hellbranch Run is classified as Superior High Quality Waters. Most of the mainstem of these streams meet Exceptional Warmwater Habitat goals, the highest Clean Water Act use attainment designation for Ohio aquatic life; some portions of the Big Darby Creek's headwaters are also classified as Coldwater Habitat. Many aquatic biodiversity monitoring sites within the watershed have scored within the top one to twelve percent of Ohio streams. Extensive ODNR Natural Heritage data, Ohio EPA stream monitoring data and The Ohio State University Museum of Biological Diversity records are maintained.

Over 100 species of fish have been recorded as living in the Big Darby watershed. Fifteen of the Big Darby's species are state or federal-listed species, such as spotted darter, bluebreast darter, and tippecanoe darter.

Forty-four mussel species have been recorded, and about 38 species may still be found in the watershed. Twenty-three of these 44

Originally published as "The Big Darby Accord — A Model for TMDL Implementation in an Urbanizing Watershed," *Conference Paper*, National Nonpoint Source Monitoring Workshop, September 2008, Columbus, Ohio, by the U.S. Environmental Protection Agency, Washington, DC.

mussel species are state or federal-listed species, such as northern riffleshell, clubshell and rayed bean. The kidneyshell, limited in range in the rest of Ohio, is relatively common in the Big Darby Creek.

The Big Darby Creek near and downstream of the Big Darby Accord area in Franklin County includes some of the more species-rich and diverse sections. Considerable conservation efforts have taken place since at least the 1970s. While over 8,000 acres have been conserved as parkland, threats from development and agricultural storm water runoff still exist. Despite its recorded biodiversity and species richness, some species are threatened, declining or reduced in range, such as many mussel species (Watters and Flaute, 2004). Phosphorus, sediment and altered riparian habitat are the leading stresses identified by Ohio EPA in the Total Maximum Daily Load (TMDL) Report (Ohio EPA, 2006).

Establishment of the Big Darby Accord

The Big Darby Accord is a local government multi-jurisdictional effort to balance development interests with conservation interests in the Franklin County portion of the Big Darby watershed. The Accord is the product of a series of efforts to address water quality issues in the Big Darby watershed. Without the evolution in thinking about Big Darby Creek and cooperation among jurisdictions that occurred during the course of this series of efforts, it would not have been possible to undertake the Accord.

The Ohio EPA's January 22, 2003, plan, known as the Central Scioto Water Quality Management Plan (CSPU) (Ohio EPA, 2006b), was the step that immediately preceded the Big Darby Accord in this evolution. The Ohio EPA established a moratorium on the extension of central sewers and stated it would not approve permits within the Franklin County portion of the Big Darby Watershed, designated the Environmentally Sensitive Development Area (ESDA), until the plan was updated to include additional environmental protections (Ohio

EPA, 2004). As part of these protections, the plan established conditions for development related to four categories: riparian buffer restrictions; comprehensive storm water management; conservation development restrictions: and adequate public facilities. An External Advisory Group (EAG) was appointed to make recommendations regarding these conditions. The EAG included a broad range of stakeholders from the local jurisdictions to conservation to building industry interests.

As the EAG was finishing its work, many in the group felt that more than a set of best practices would be required to meet their water quality goals. In 2002, the Columbus City Council adopted a moratorium prohibiting extension of Columbus sewers into the Big Darby Creek watershed. In July 2004, City of Columbus officials invited western Franklin County jurisdictions to meet to discuss the possibility of a planning process that would address Big Darby development in a comprehensive manner. This effort would build on the process and relationships built during the EAG meetings and would rely on unprecedented cooperation between the jurisdictions and other stakeholders.

The Big Darby Accord Process

Project Partners and Organization. The Big Darby Accord plan was prepared by a consultant team, led by EDAW, under the oversight of ten participating jurisdictions. The jurisdictions included Columbus, Franklin County, three suburban municipalities (Hilliard, Grove City and Harrisburg) and five townships (Brown, Norwich, Pleasant, Prairie and Washington). These jurisdictions were represented by their elected officials. A working group including one elected official from each jurisdiction was the primary oversight body. Given the volume and complexity of effort required in implementing this project, the working group appointed a four-member team, eventually nicknamed the G4, to work with the consultant team on a day-to-day basis. This team included one representative of area townships, one representative of Columbus, one representative of Franklin

County and one representative of suburban municipalities.

The jurisdictions incorporated the efforts of a range of stakeholders into this planning process. EAG partners such as the Darby Creek Association, The Nature Conservancy, the Ohio Environmental Protection Agency, the Ohio Department of Natural Resources Scenic Rivers program, Columbus Metro Parks and the Franklin Soil and Water Conservation District were joined by representatives of the Building Industry Association of Central Ohio and affordable housing advocates in a group with which the jurisdictions conferred before moving forward with important planning concepts or policies. In addition to meeting as a group, jurisdiction representatives met with representatives of these organizations regularly throughout the process. A series of public meetings, panel discussions and jurisdiction level discussions ensured the incorporation of input from the general public. A landowner's input committee was one important outcome of public meetings held in the early and middle part of the process.

Work Outline. This team of consultants, jurisdictions and stakeholders completed the Big Darby Accord planning process in sixteen months. This process followed a basic planning model including data gathering, formulating alternative plans, analyzing the alternatives and selecting a recommended plan and drafting and adopting a planning document. In moving from data gathering to formulating alternatives, the consultant team performed water quality models. Using the Soil and Water Assessment Tool (SWAT) and the Generalized Watershed Loading Functions (GWLF) model established by Ohio EPA, the Accord model made comparisons to the Ohio EPA's TMDL targets. This compared pollutant loadings for Total Nitrogen, Total Phosphorus and Total Suspended Solids, and resulted in a Big Darby Accord land use plan based on water quality targets. The model compared three basic land use patterns: one based on a continuation of suburban expansion and conventional rural development; one based upon concentrating development in corridors; and one based on concentrating development in nodes. This modeling effort suggested that a cluster-based pattern should be

the basis for land use patterns included in the Big Darby Accord plan.

The Big Darby Accord Strategy

Land Use and Development. The final land use and development strategy included in the Big Darby Accord accommodates approximately 12,000-plus additional dwelling units in a cluster-based pattern. This number of units, or, in some cases, their non-residential equivalents, is based on the amount of development that current zoning would allow in the area. Sanitary sewer conveyance capacity was also a limiting factor. Since the current zoning distributes development in a pattern that is not consistent with the plan, or the conclusions of the water quality modeling results, a mechanism for rearranging development was required. Given legal and political concerns raised about using regulatory tools such as transfer of development rights, a fee-simple/land easement purchase system is recommended.

The cluster pattern features a Town Center that is to be designed to include at least 5,000 equivalent units. This development will be served by the regional water and sewer system. The other primary development areas include those designated for rural open space development, which will include 5,000 equivalent units and featuring at least 50 percent open space. This development type will have a gross density of up to 0.5 units per acre within each development and are to be served by alternative waste water treatment facilities. A development area west of the City of Hilliard, including 2,000 units, also calls for 50 percent open space, but is to include 1.0 unit per acre densities and is to be served by the regional waste water treatment facility. Other units already in the development process, totaling about 3,000 or more in all. are to be completed on the suburban edge of the planning area.

Conservation. Conservation policies in the plan are based on significant open space preservation, stream restoration and best management practices for storm water management. The preservation of approximately 25,000 acres, or 45 percent, of the planning area, as natural open space is the primary water quality protection element in the plan. Of this area, 7,000 acres are already under the control of conservation agencies, primarily Columbus and Franklin County Metro Parks. This leaves about 18,000 acres to be acquired or otherwise protected. The Big Darby Accord also recommends that the partners undertake stream restoration projects focusing on the upper reaches of the Hellbranch Run sub-watershed. Storm water best management practices and groundwater infiltration are tied into Ohio EPA storm water permit requirements. Storm water management recommendations include policies calling for a regional storm water collection and treatment system in the Town Center.

Revenue. As stated above, the Big Darby Accord land use policies stress purchase of land and development rights, as opposed to using a regulatory system such as zoning based transfer of development rights, to provide natural open space. These purchases, along with the cost of stream restoration and provision of other planned land use and conservation measures, will, in large part, be funded be development activity. Future development activity in the planning area will generate revenue streams in three ways: through community authority millage; through tax increment financing mechanisms; and through developer contributions. A new community authority will be formed as development occurs in the area which will contribute at least 5 mills in property assessments to Big Darby Accord purposes. The tax increment financing will be based on the added value of developing areas and will hold the schools

and fire levies harmless, along with making some provisions for county-wide agencies and local government expenses. Finally, developer contributions of $2,500.00 per dwelling will be used mainly for regional infrastructure needed to implement the plan.

These revenues are proposed as the main base of land acquisition funding. At the same time, it is expected that funding sources already relied on, such as the State of Ohio's Water Resource Restoration Sponsor Program or local park levies, will provide additional land acquisition needs.

REFERENCES

Ohio EPA, 2004. "Darby at the Crossroads: A Summary of Ohio EPA's Work and Collaboration to Protect and Restore an Important Water Resource" (Columbus: Division of Surface Water), www.epa.state.oh.us/dsw/documents/DarbyCrossroads_june04.pdf.

Ohio EPA, 2004b. "Biological and Water Quality Study of the Big Darby Creek Watershed, June 2004," www.epa.state.oh.us/dsw/documents/BigDarbyTSD2004_A_0_front.pdf.

Ohio EPA, 2006. "Total Maximum Daily Loads for the Big Darby Creek Watershed, January 2006," www.epa.state.oh.us/dsw/Tmdl/BigDarbyCreekTMDL.html.

Ohio EPA, 2006b. Appendix 9-3, "208 Plan Prescriptions for Water Quality Protection within the Big Darby Creek Watershed Applicable to Portions of: Champaign County, Franklin County, Logan County, Madison County, Pickaway County, Union County" (Columbus: Ohio Environmental Protection Agency), www.epa.state.oh.us/dsw/mgmtplans/Final2006Plan/Final208_Aug06_Append_9-3_DarbyRx.pdf.

Watters, G. T., and C. J. M. Flaute. 2004. "Trends in Freshwater Mussel Populations in the Big Darby Creek and Grand River Systems (OH): A GIS Approach, Part 1: The Big Darby Creek System," Department of Evolution, Ecology and Organismal Biology, The Ohio State University.

CHAPTER 18

Concord and Other Cities Encourage Restorative Development

Storm Cunningham

At last, some good economic news: There's a mushrooming new global economic sector that already exceeds a trillion dollars per year — and even restores natural resources. It's called restorative development, defined as socio-economic revitalization based on the restoration of our natural and built environments. And it will dramatically reshape our economies, communities, and, environments throughout the twenty-first century.

Turning an old-growth forest into a farm, or demolishing a historic building for a shopping mall, is the kind of development we're most familiar with: new development. Decontaminating abandoned industrial property and turning old factories into apartments and stores is another kind of development, one that builds without destroying: restorative development. Returning a distressed old farm to productivity by rebuilding topsoil, removing accumulated salts, and restoring surrounding watersheds is another example of restorative development.

Nations around the globe have accumulated backlogs of needed restoration projects worth trillions of dollars. Meanwhile, hundreds of billions of dollars of new restoration needs are added annually, creating perhaps the largest new growth sector of the world economy. What's more, most of the other so-called "new economies," such as hydrogen, biotech, nano-tech, and digital, are either a direct outgrowth of the restoration economy, or will find their greatest markets in restorative development.

Restoration Industries

Our current restoration economy comprises eight industries. Four involve the natural environment: ecosystem restoration, fisheries restoration, watershed restoration, and agricultural restoration/rural development. The other four industries, which restore the built environment, are:

Brownfields Remediation and Redevelopment. Brownfields are lands that are not being used productively as a result of real or perceived contamination. The U.S. Environmental Protection Agency's Brownfields Initiative has awarded more than $140 million in nationwide grants to help communities clean up abandoned, lightly contaminated sites and restore them to productive community use. For example, in Concord, New Hampshire, officials are working to identify contamination in a 440-acre (178-hectare) industrial corridor and develop a remediation and redevelopment plan with the potential to create more than 2,500 new jobs — or 8 percent of the city's total unemployment.

Originally published as "Restorative Development: Economic Growth without Destruction," *The Futurist*, Vol. 37, No. 4, July/August 2003. Used with permission from the World Future Society, www.wfs.org.

The Money in Restoration

The following selected initiatives come with a hefty — and worthy — price tag, author Cunningham notes. Total projects exceed $1 trillion in expenditures to revive environments, economies, and aesthetics. Here are ten current (or recently completed) restorative projects worldwide.

1. $100 million in dam restoration or removal worldwide.
2. $225 million to restore site around Stonehenge.
3. $450 million to restore Reagan National Airport in Washington, D.C.
4. $500 million to restore Istanbul's Golden Horn Waterfront.
5. $700 million rebuilding of a single highway interchange in Springfield, Virginia.
6. $2.5 billion to replace the Washington, D.C., area's Wilson Bridge.
7. $3.1 billion to launch first phase of Russian railway rehabilitation.
8. $12 billion restoration of a single watershed in China.
9. $15 billion to rebuild and restore Afghanistan.
10. $52 billion per year to restore natural disasters, *not* including human-caused disasters or terrorism.

Infrastructure Refurbishment and Reconstruction. This aspect of restorative development deals with the flows that connect our built environment: power, sewerage; traffic, water, even garbage. One major infrastructure refurbishment project is the London Underground, with an estimated budget of $42 million (£27 million).

Heritage Restoration. A community's physical heritage comprises aspects of the built environment that lasted long enough to be a source of community attachment — or where an event occurred that the community considers intrinsic to its identity. Heritage can also be environmental (fisheries) or cultural (indigenous languages).

Disaster/War Restoration and Rebuilding. Three categories of disasters makes up this restoration industry: war, manmade disasters (such as oil spills, nuclear power accidents, and even mudslides due to deforestation), and natural disasters (such as volcanic eruptions and earthquakes), The cost of rebuilding war-torn Afghanistan is estimated at $15 billion. The cost of restoring worldwide disasters is roughly $52 billion per year.

Some of these industries, such as disaster and war restoration, have been around for millennia. Others, such as brownfields restoration, just appeared in the past decade. New regulations in 1990 made it possible for business people buy contaminated lands. The sudden growth of restorative development and its emergence as a collective economic force can be traced to the convergence of three global crises:

- **The Constraint Crisis:** We are out of room. This doesn't mean there are no more wide-open spaces fit to develop, but rather that virtually every developable acre of land — whether it's a farm, a historic battlefield, or a recreational greenspace — already serves a vital purpose that people will fight to protect from developers.
- **The Contamination Crisis:** Chemical, organic, and radiological contamination from industrial, agricultural, and military activities have affected ecosystems and supplies of water, food, and air.
- **The Corrosion Crisis.** We've been building practically nonstop since the beginning of the Industrial Revolution, and many of the world's cities are getting very old. In the United States, much of the infrastructure is decrepit: The American Society of Civil Engineers has documented a $1.3 trillion backlog for restoring infrastructure.

These are the same three crises that have brought down civilizations throughout history — and that have sometimes triggered their renaissance. However, we now face all three crises simultaneously on a global scale.

Beyond Sustainability

Restorative development, while benefiting the environment, is not an "environmental message" per se. Rather, restorative development is a strategic path for leaders of businesses, nonprofits, and government agencies that wish to grow economically, or that want to revitalize themselves.

Since the beginning of the Industrial Revolution, our growth assumptions have been based on exploring new geographic frontiers and exploiting new natural resources. Now that the greatest new growth frontier is behind us, we need to reexamine what developed in the past three centuries — and all the natural places we've damaged in the process.

For instance, many cities have no remaining green field areas (i.e., land that has never been developed) that they can use for expansion. Some cities, such as Niagara Falls, New York, have discovered that 100 percent of the buildable land they still possess is contaminated. Meanwhile, cities that do have green fields are finding increasing resistance to developing them. To grow economically, both types of architecturally challenged cities must redevelop their brownfields instead.

In fact, some of the largest opportunities for restoration industries involve revitalizing the cities we've created during the past 300 years of unfettered growth. That's why developers worldwide are shifting their focus to restorative development. Now when they proposed to restore ugly, abandoned property that generates no tax revenues; the same citizens' groups, historic preservation societies, and environmental agencies that used to fight their new developments are instead supporting them.

However, restorative development should not be confused with sustainable development. Sustainable development — which has yet to be properly defined or measured — usually requires a decade or more to produce an attractive bottom line. Restorative development pays off big, and pays off now.

What's more, the field of sustainable development emerged in reaction to uncontrolled new development, but it doesn't solve the problem. Sustainable development is simply a greener form of new development; it can't repair the accumulated corrosion and contamination, which will only exacerbate the Constraint Crisis. Sustainability is a great concept, but the world needs restoration first. After all, who really wants to sustain the mess we're living in now?

Restorative development should also not be confused with the maintenance/conservation mode of development. Though highly essential, conservation has largely lost the battle against new development. This is why most of the largest conservation groups, such as The Nature Conservancy, have embraced ecological restoration. They're not just preserving our last few pristine ecosystems; they're buying and restoring the damaged land around them so they can actually *expand*.

We've moved from an unsuccessful attempt to slow the decrease of wildlife habitat to a successful strategy of *increasing* wildlife habitat. That's a very different, and much more hopeful, dynamic. Of course, as with any new field, standards are still being set, and not all early attempts are successful. But that, too, is part of the opportunity for academics, engineers, and scientists..

Tomorrow's Restoration Economy

Restorative development is fully capable of replacing new development as the dominant economic growth mode. It's every bit as profitable as new development (often more so), so it offers an attractive path, a natural evolution, away from the old model. In a corporate world that demands dramatic. quarterly profits, and a political world that demands results during an election cycle, only restorative development can deliver the goods with bipartisan support.

Integrated partnerships among the public sector, private industry, and nongovernmental organizations may be the best long-term vehicles for complex, large-scale restoration projects. They will also likely be the entities that restore nations in decades to come.

With a new economic sector that delivers strong economic, aesthetic, and environmental returns, many new legal tools and investment products will emerge. This will likely include a broad spectrum of restorative real estate investment trusts (REITs) What's more, the opportunities for inventors, entrepreneurs, programmers, and consultants are virtually unlimited: Almost any industry or profession that existed in the dying new development economy will have its analog in the restoration economy.

This is the greatest new frontier for hardware, software, the sciences, economics,, art, philosophy, architecture, engineering, academia, and policy makers: Nothing is more urgent, nothing is more important, and nothing is more economically productive than restoring our world. Virtually every major trend and discipline of this century either will be rooted in restorative development or will converge with it in a way that will transform and revitalize it.

Every city that is currently being touted as a model of rebirth, sustainability, or economic health has already embraced restorative development projects in their new model. For most of them, this was an intuitive, emergent transition: Until recently, they didn't possess the terminology or theoretical structure to talk about or plan for restorative development in a coherent manner.

Now, the dialogue has begun, and this first phase of the restoration economy is about to enter a period of maturation. The concepts and lessons of the past decade must start to be formally incorporated into public policy, university curricula, and business strategies.

Restorative development has already reversed several trends that are taken as gospel by many futurists. Desertification is a good example: We all know that the Sahara has been expanding for decades right? Wrong. Recent analysis of satellite images shows it's been shrinking for about 15 years. Why? The primary mechanism has been restorative agriculture, which was taught to farmers 15 to 20 years ago in about a dozen nations on the edge of the Sahara.

Restorative development already accounts for a major portion of the good economic news on the planet, yet it seldom gets the credit, because we don't measure it. Within the next five to 10 years, it will dominate most development budgets, and will continue to do so for the rest of the twenty-first century.

The Truth About Brownfields

In the early 1990s, few people had heard of brownfields. Now they're in the dictionary — and already widely misunderstood. Here is the truth about five common brownfield misconceptions:

The Purpose of Brownfields Remediation is *not* Simply to Clean the Environment. Unlike Superfund sites — the largest, most contaminated sites in the United States selected for cleanup by the Environmental Protection Agency to keep the public safe — the chief goal of brownfields remediation is turning a profit.

Brownfields Comprise More Than Just Ground and Groundwater. Buildings can also be highly toxic with contaminants such as lead paint, asbestos insulation and mercury that fall under the "hard costs" of brownfields clean up.

Most Brownfields are not Heavily Contaminated. Contamination is often minimal, yet perceived as serious. Abandoned industrial sites, for example, have sat idle for decades because the public falsely assumes they're toxic.

Most Brownfields are not Abandoned. Many contaminated sites are in use, but their contamination has not been assessed. When 30 percent of industrial acreage in Hartford, Connecticut, was abandoned between 1986 and 1997 much of it was found to be contaminated — which means workers. toiled in toxic environs.

Brownfields are not Restricted to Large Industrial Sites in Urban Locations. Many are small and rural, such as rural gas stations (abandoned, and operational) with leaky underground storage tanks. Further, in 27 states, the EPA cannot prevent a company from putting fuel or chemicals into underground storage tanks that are known to be leaking.

CHAPTER 19

Dallas and Other Cities Focus Growth Around Transit Hubs

G.M. Filisko

From Los Angeles to Philadelphia and at a growing number of points in between, developers are jumping aboard the movement to cluster real estate projects near transit hubs.

"There's a growing number of developers who really get transit-oriented development," says Jud Pankey, chief executive officer of Dallas-based Prescott Realty Group. Prescott is currently developing the Lake Highlands Town Center, a nearly 2-million-square-foot, mixed-use project that will include a Dallas Area Rapid Transit (DART) light rail station. "It's a shift because it's a whole new way of doing business, and it's a challenging form of development."

Development clustered near light rail stations, at subway stations and near streetcars — called transit-oriented development, or TOD — is indeed changing the way developers operate. And those who've mastered TOD say the phenomenon will only expand. "In five years, properties along transit routes will have increased in value because people will pay a premium to live where they can walk to a transit station, even if they're not using it every day," says Carl Dranoff, president of Dranoff Properties in Philadelphia and developer of a $180-million project to revitalize the train station and business district in Ardmore, Pa. "Those will be the most sought-after locations, and developers will want

to develop where customers will be — its that simple."

The Forces Behind TOD

Mass transit has had a stop-and-go history in the United States. In cities like New York and Chicago, systems are long entrenched. However, Americans' attachment to their cars has made the penetration of new transit throughout the country a harder sell.

But attitudes may be changing. There's been a shift toward a "green" lifestyle, caused in part by increasingly volatile gas prices. Add to that today's weakened economy, which is forcing Americans to scrutinize every penny they spend on housing and commuting. Ever-worsening traffic gridlock may also be converting nonbelievers into transit evangelists. When asked the best approach to solving traffic problems, 47 percent of respondents to a 2009 National Association of Realtors and Transportation for America poll favored improving public transportation, 25 percent preferred building communities that make it possible for people not to drive, and only 20 percent advocated building new roads.

That strong support has been driving TOD.

Originally published as "Spurring Growth with Transit-Oriented Development," *On Common Ground*, Summer 2009, published by the Community and Political Affairs Division, National Association of Realtors, Washington, DC. Reprinted with permission of the publisher.

"Transit has definitely grown," says Allison Brooks, managing director of Reconnecting America, an Oakland, Calif., nonprofit transit advocacy organization. "There's a demand for more easy living where you don't have to rely on your car. That's caused a real boom in cities and regions investing in new transit systems."

Brooks rattles off just a few cities building new or expanding existing transit systems. "In Denver, voters agreed to tax themselves to pay for a regional light rail system," she says. "Minneapolis–St. Paul is investing in a new light rail system. In Los Angeles, voters approved a tax to pay for the expansion of the current system." Charlotte, N.C., and Phoenix are also investing in transit.

"Transit has been gradually growing since the early 1990s," says G.B. Arrington, vice president and principal practice leader for PB Place-Making, a Portland, Ore., design and planning firm specializing in TOD. "I've been doing TOD since the late 1990s, and I continue to ask myself whether it's going to go away. But the interest and demand in both the public and private sectors continues to grow because developers who follow the principles of TOD will create places that are more resilient in the face of gas prices and climate change."

Federal policy-makers seem to agree. In March, the U.S. Department of Housing and Urban Development (HUD) and the U.S. Department of Transportation (DOT) announced a joint "livable communities" initiative to help Americans better access affordable housing, more transportation options and lower transportation costs. According to the two agencies, the average working American family spends nearly 60 percent of its budget on housing and transportation. They've united to cut those costs by creating affordable, sustainable communities that rely heavily on transit. DOT also announced in March $100 million in federal funding for transit projects that reduce energy consumption or greenhouse gases.

"In the last six months, we've seen national interest at the policy level that we haven't seen before," says Abby Thorne-Lyman, a principal at Strategic Economics, an economic and real estate consulting firm, and a staff member for the Center for Transit-Oriented Development,

a nonprofit research and advocacy group in Berkeley, Calif. "It's become a national movement, not just of developers but also of policymakers realizing they have a role to play and that transit has large benefits in terms of greenhouse gas reduction and economic development."

Increased government commitment to transit should be music to the ears of the NARTFA poll respondents. Fifty-six percent said the federal government isn't paying enough attention to trains and light rail systems, and 75 percent said the government should improve intercity rail and transit.

Challenges and Opportunities

To give consumers what they want, developers must change the way they operate. "TODs are definitely a total pain in the neck," jokes Dranoff. "They're complex projects that require great skills to execute."

Why so complicated? Land assemblage can be difficult. Zoning and permitting restrictions can make the approval process a maze. Lenders often don't understand the large and intricate projects. And local residents often lay down early opposition to the density-rich developments. Handling all those challenges simultaneously requires formidable development and political acumen.

"You've got multiple public entities and public constituencies you really have to work with," says Pankey. "You have not only the transit authority, but other public improvements may also have to be done, and that could mean working with the city, county and a tax increment financing (TIF) district. Those members represent various constituencies, and you have to be able to navigate that process and articulate the benefit of transit living."

Take financing, which typically requires developers to work with both public and private funding. "It's been suggested that TODs need patient money," says Rich von Luhrte, president of RNL, an architecture and urban design firm in Denver, who's worked on TOD since the 1970s. "The funders take a developer who's willing to make a long-term investment in property and go through tremendous effort to do a redevelopment project. The patient money often requires acquiring the property and holding it until the transit service matures and the demand is such that it can support the development."

Not-in-my-backyard (NIMBY) concerns are nothing new to developers, but TOD offers added complications. "Often, neighborhoods impacted by transit stations aren't ready to accept the increased density," explains von Luhrte. "Developers need to generate a tremendous amount of community and city support for TOD to be successful. Too many projects get stalled because NIMBYism stops them or makes them extremely difficult."

Dan Johnson, deputy city manager and chief operating officer for Richardson, Texas, which is adding four stations to the DART rail line that runs through the city, says early planning helped his city avert major NIMBY sentiments. "Several years before the rail was developed, we were active with our city council and speaking in public sessions," he says. "We were also selected by the Urban Land Institute for a panel study in which a task force of professionals conducted planning and visioning sessions. That was very effective in allowing us to get an overall vision and commentary from across the country and to frame our TOD. A lot of problems were circumvented by having that session early on."

Phil Kushlan has had a slightly different experience. The executive director for Capital City Development Corp., a quasi-public urban renewal agency for Boise, Idaho, has had to address public pushback on a $60-million down-

town streetcar redevelopment to be completed in 2011. The project will be financed through a TIF and tax-exempt bonds, but the numbers have raised concern. "The primary issue we've had to deal with is the cost," he says. "People say, 'It's going to cost a fortune!' But we've been able to demonstrate that $60 million is less than the cost of a new freeway interchange and the community benefits over time are much greater than with each new freeway interchange. This isn't a project that withstands a 10-year test; it's a 100-year, transformative community design project. We think it's a much better investment."

Dranoff also believes the value of TOD is worth the extra work. Though the Ardmore project is still in the planning stages, the bulk of Dranoff's developments have been near transit, and that proximity has paid off. Take Symphony House, a 163-unit condo development in Philadelphia's cultural hub. "You can walk out the front door and be within steps of the Kimmel Center, our major performing arts center," explains Dranoff. "You can walk 60 or 70 steps and be at the subway entrance."

Today, Symphony House is 90 percent sold. "We were able to hold our prices, and our fall-out ratio of people who cancelled contracts while waiting for their unit to be finished was only 7 percent," says Dranoff. "We were able to go against the grain because sales on projects near transit are better than those further away."

With those results, Dranoff feels confident taking on the Ardmore TOD. "We're putting our money on it," he says. "Walkability has become a very significant driver for consumers. People don't want to be tethered to their cars."

CHAPTER 20

Daybreak and Other Communities Balance Development and Preservation

Sam Newberg

Daybreak, a 4,100-acre master-planned community in the southwest Salt Lake City metropolitan area, is the first of numerous projects being developed by Kennecott Land that over the next 75 years will add more than 150,000 housing units and 58 million square feet of commercial space to the region.

The community is set apart in many ways from other master-planned developments nationwide: a mining company with a long history in the area is acting as the developer of its land holdings; a substantial amount of attention is being paid to making the development sustainable and environmentally friendly; and the project closely follows the principles of the Envision Utah regional planning framework laid out in the late 1990s.

As development pressure pushed west across the Salt Lake City valley, Rio Tinto, the parent company of mining company Kennecott Utah Copper, realized it could take advantage of an opportunity to reuse portions of its mining land for housing and commercial growth rather than just remediate the sites. Rio Tinto owns 93,000 acres of land along the Oquirrh Mountains on the west side of the Salt Lake valley, making it the largest owner of a contiguous parcel of land in an urban area in the United States. Although less than half of the land will ever be actively developed, Rio Tinto's holdings represent 50 percent of all developable land in the valley.

In 2001, Rio Tinto formed a subsidiary, Kennecott Land, to be the master developer of its property. A 4,100-acre site in South Jordan was chosen for the first development, Daybreak.

Envision Utah Begets Daybreak

Envision Utah is a regional planning body created in the late 1990s by a broad coalition of elected officials, environmental advocates, and business, civic, and religious communities to address the substantial growth expected in the Salt Lake City region. Daybreak in many ways is an embodiment of the principles of Envision Utah and represents what many in the region hope will be the type of development seen in the future.

"Daybreak is a very important story," says Peter Calthorpe, principal of Berkeley, California-based Calthorpe Associates, a planning firm that worked on both Envision Utah and Daybreak. He calls Daybreak a successful example of regional planning and growth management, especially in the context of Envision Utah. "Envision Utah plowed the field, and Daybreak is planting the field," says Robert Grow, founding

Originally published as "Humans/Nature," *Urban Land*, Vol. 65, No. 4, April 2006, by the Urban Land Institute, Washington, D.C. Reprinted with permission of the publisher.

chair emeritus of Envision Utah. However, Peter McMahon, president of Kennecott Land, insists that the company would have developed Daybreak in much the same way whether or not Envision Utah existed. Still, he acknowledges that the public understanding of Envision Utah made it much easier for area residents to accept Daybreak in the context of regional planning.

Alan Matheson, executive director of Envision Utah, agrees. "Envision Utah's extensive visioning process paved the way for public acceptance of the new ideas reflected at Daybreak," he says. "Conversely, Daybreak demonstrates that Envision Utah's principles pass the ultimate test-market success."

Kennecott Land hired Calthorpe Associates to design Daybreak, citing the firm's past work on Envision Utah. "It was a convenient alignment of interests because the things they cared about were pretty consistent with a lot of our core values," explains McMahon.

Development

Daybreak, which began marketing its 1,100-home first phase Founders village in 2004, focuses on the principles of new urbanism, including sustainability, a mix of uses, walkability, and transit connections. In order to create the sales momentum required to eventually sell 14,000 homes at Daybreak, Kennecott Land invested heavily in design and amenities, including open space, which are tangible and evident to buyers, and in careful marketing to sell homes in the early phases of development. Homes follow strict design guidelines, and a new school/community center was built to help attract families.

A major amenity and environmental feature is 85-acre Oquirrh Lake, which is being created in three phases, the first of which will open this summer. When completed in 2010, the lake will have a marina, be open to non-motorized boats, and include trails around its five-mile circumference.

The community design and architecture of homes are based on Salt Lake City neighborhoods of the early 20th century. Streets are generally narrower than their suburban counterparts, with no culs-de-sac, and are lined with sidewalks. Homes are located on smaller lots than those in standard suburbs and have smaller setbacks. Front porches are common, and garages are recessed or located on alleys.

Kennecott Land negotiated with builders to change their product types to suit the design and planning principles used at Daybreak, a move met with skepticism by some firms, which questioned the need to change what was already successful. That argument did not faze Kennecott, says Ty McCutcheon, director of residential real estate. "I'd liken it to Ford rolling out one car in one color and saying that that must be what buyers want because they are buying it," he explains.

To increase architectural diversity in the neighborhood, builders in the first phase of development were restricted from building more than one type of the same home on any particular block. Buyers were also provided a wide color palette from which to choose. In fact, one street at Daybreak has been nicknamed "Crayola Street" by neighbors due to the variety of bold paint colors used on homes.

Ultimately, Kennecott is trying to take buyers beyond the decision to purchase a lot and home, and get them to buy into the community. The tradeoffs are smaller lots and garages than those in traditional suburbs, but benefits are an attractive streetscape and a substantial amount of open space. An active homeowners association organizes events in parks and at the community center, but buyers attribute the development's sense of community to the design of streets and the abundance of open space and parks that provide places where people can meet other residents. "That comes back to design issues," says McMahon. "Design drives behavior. If you create those things, people like it."

Lifelong Learning

Most of the first phase of development has been single-family homes targeted at families with children. Market research conducted by Kennecott indicated that schools are one of the top attractions for families, which is why Daybreak Elementary was built in Founders Village. It opened last fall and has a current enrollment of 1,100 children. Although not all the children enrolled at the school live in Daybreak, many of those who do are able to walk to school.

What sets Daybreak Elementary apart from most other schools is that it shares a building with the Daybreak Community Center. This concentrates activity in one building, allowing the gymnasium and sports fields to be used by the school on weekdays and by the community at large on evenings and weekends. The community center also features exercise equipment, a running track, and meeting rooms, and it has been certified as environmentally friendly through the U.S. Green Building Council's Leadership in Energy and Environmental Design program. Calthorpe calls the shared facility an important innovation, not only because of the cost savings provided by shared facilities, but also because of its ability to engage such a large proportion of the community.

Sustainability

The corporate culture of Rio Tinto emphasizes sustainability. The firm does not believe in the old style of mining, "which was get in, dig it up, and get the hell out of there," says McMahon. "Companies like us really needed to convince local communities that we could behave in a way that was responsible."

Daybreak is itself a brownfield site, part of which was used for mining evaporation ponds before its remediation in the early 1990s. Thirty percent of the land is preserved as open space, construction waste materials are reused on site, the need for irrigation is reduced, stormwater runoff is managed on site, and walkability and transit options encourage reduced automobile use. Also, Daybreak homes meet Energy Star efficiency standards, set through a U.S. Environmental Protection Agency–backed program that evaluates windows, insulation, heating and cooling systems, and other components. When built out, Daybreak will produce an estimated 63 million pounds less in greenhouse gas emissions per year than would a conventional development of the same size, and homeowners will save $200 to $400 per year in heating and cooling costs.

More than 1 million cubic feet of earth will be excavated for Oquirrh Lake, with much of the material to be used for construction of roadbeds or in paving. Thousands of tons of mine rock are being used to line the lake's edge in order to provide habitat for fish, plants, and birds, and all stormwater is being filtered in adjacent wetlands before it is released into the lake. Oquirrh Lake is not just a symbol of sustainability for the developer, but a major recreational amenity for residents of and visitors to Daybreak.

The Future of Daybreak

Daybreak has been highly successful, with Founders Village being nearly sold out. About 500 families moved into their homes in 2005, and another 800 will do so this year, as marketing and construction of the second phase of homes begin.

Kennecott expects to receive approvals and begin construction this year of a village center, the first of several in Daybreak that will provide retail space, office space, and housing. The design of the village center includes a one-way roadway couplet that will separate traffic on two narrower streets rather than having vehicles use a single, wide street. This will allow sufficient traffic to support retail businesses, but also help the center maintain a high-quality pedestrian environment.

A larger town center is planned for Daybreak with a concentration of retail, office, and dense residential development. Kennecott expects most of the nearly 9 million square feet of commercial space planned for Daybreak to be located in this town center, which is intended to be a major employment center.

Two light-rail lines are currently operating in the Salt Lake City region, and a commuter rail line is under construction. The Utah Transit Authority is planning to construct a third line to the southwest metropolitan area by the end of the decade, terminating at Daybreak. Two stations are planned in the town center, providing a link to the commercial development and employment planned there. A freeway is planned nearby as well.

Although Kennecott seeks to provide housing for residents with a broad range of ages and incomes, the success of Daybreak has pushed prices up, creating a shortage of affordable housing. "Through simple market forces, we are having difficulty meeting a variety of housing needs," explains McCutcheon. Kennecott is looking to team up with affordable housing providers such as the Utah Housing Corporation, whose Credits to Own (Crown) Homes program buys residences and passes them on to low-income buyers for tax credits. Future phases of development will include rental housing, as well as home styles more suited to the elderly, although it is not certain what percentage of new units will be affordable.

Kennecott plans to sell about 1,000 homes per year until buildout of Daybreak is complete, expected to be sometime in the next ten to 15 years.

Looking Ahead

Last fall, Kennecott Land held a series of planning sessions with public officials and stakeholders to create a master plan for its entire holdings. Their size is staggering: 75,000 of the 93,000 acres are in Salt Lake County, and 41,000 acres are developable, with 34,000 to remain as open space. The resulting development, which will take 50 to 75 years to complete, is estimated to encompass 150,000 homes, 58 million square feet of commercial space, 100,000 jobs, and 87 schools.

The land plan shows a string of village centers and town centers along the base of the Oquirrh Mountains, connected by roads and transit, with residential development radiating from each center. Daybreak is the model for all this growth and provides a built example of what the future of development in the region could look like.

Matheson is encouraged by the efforts of Kennecott. "Growth is coming to Salt Lake County," he says. "Kennecott's planning along the West Bench [the western half of the Salt Lake City valley] will ensure that much of that growth is accommodated in a way that promotes transportation efficiency, economic development, social cohesion, and environmental values."

Time will tell whether Daybreak is making a difference. Greg Schindler, a city planner for South Jordan, thinks Daybreak has raised the bar for development quality. For example, other developers have seen the success of Daybreak and are starting to build on smaller lots, he says. Also, the city has focused a lot of recent effort on the design of its commercial areas and is working to ensure that they become more walkable.

Calthorpe contends that the principles of Envision Utah have proved successful at a built project such as Daybreak primarily because Envision Utah was a civic-led process, as opposed to being legislated by elected officials. Because civic groups, the Mormon church, business leaders, and environmental advocates agreed on the growth principles of Envision Utah, it can survive the terms of elected officials, and a place like Daybreak can be realized as a model for future growth in the Salt Lake City region, he says.

"Envision Utah is not really subject to changing winds. It is based on people's values," Calthorpe explains. Matheson agrees. "I hope Daybreak's greatest contribution will be to inspire other developers and jurisdictions to take a long-term view and recognize the regional impacts of their decisions."

McMahon sees a lot of promise in the success of Daybreak. "We wanted to build something that we were going to be proud of 30 years later," he says. "It sounds a bit simplistic, but I think it is important." Still, Kennecott is focused on the long term. "They obviously did it right then, and we think we are doing it right now," McMahon says, acknowledging the popular early 20th-century Salt Lake City neighborhoods on which Daybreak is modeled. "We are prepared to be patient about it."

CHAPTER 21

Denver and Other Cities
Develop Sustainable Neighborhoods

Miriam Landman

Across the country, communities increasingly are feeling the ill effects of suburban development patterns, in the form of long commutes to jobs, traffic congestion, air pollution, obesity and poor health due to a lack of regular exercise, loss of community character or identity, and loss of open space and access to natural areas. In response to these stresses, the notions of smart growth, new urbanism, transit-oriented development, and conservation planning have emerged.

As green building proponents begin to recognize that the sustainability of a building or home is determined as much by its location as by its design, they are broadening their perspective to include the goals of smart growth and sustainable land development. In addition to the common call to avoid sensitive habitat, wetlands, viable farmland, and other areas of ecological significance, they emphasize the importance of considering the broader context when a development site is selected. For example, how will the site's surrounding land uses and existing infrastructure and transportation systems (or lack thereof) affect the new residents' travel patterns and lifestyle?

In 2001, staff from the New York City-based Natural Resources Defense Council (NRDG) and members of the U.S. Green Building Council (USGBC) began to discuss how the influence and imagination of the Leadership in Energy and Environmental Design (LEED) rating system could be expanded beyond its focus on the impacts of individual buildings and homes, to the broader-scale impacts of residential and mixed-use developments, master-planned neighborhoods, and communities. As a result, the USGBC, the NRDC, and the Chicago-based Congress for the New Urbanism formed a partnership to develop consensus-based standards for a LEED for Neighborhood Developments (LEED-ND) rating system. Those organizations invited other groups to participate, including the Urban Land Institute. Michael Pawlukiewicz, ULI's director of environmental policy and education, is an active member of the committee and invites input from developers, who will be the primary users of the LEED-ND rating system. The LEED-ND committee aims to make a pilot version of the rating system available by early 2006.

Model Developments, Visionary Developers

In the meantime, without the benefit of a comprehensive national standard for sustainable neighborhood development, many successful

Originally published as "Better Places to Live," *GreenTech*, Vol. 1, No. 1, Fall 2005, published by the Urban Land Institute, Washington, D.C. Reprinted with permission of the publisher.

developments have already been built Through-out the country, there now are hundreds of examples of mixed-use neighborhood develop-ments that incorporate sustainable design prin-ciples in cities and in the countryside — from Battery Park City in Manhattan to a rural com-munity in Indiana.

They represent every type of project: new and redeveloped projects, with custom and pro-duction homes and multifamily residences in a variety of sizes and prices, ranging from high end to market rate to affordable. Sustainability also comes in many styles. While many of the new developments described below feature neo-traditional architecture, sustainability is not represented by any one aesthetic or architectural period. The most innovative sustainable proj-ects embody a combination of the best ideas and practices from the past and the present to create a better future.

Haymount: A Traditional New Town, Caroline County, Virginia

A new urbanist town is emerging on the banks of Virginia's Rappahannock River, 55 miles south of Washington, D.C. The neotra-ditional town of Haymount has been designed to resemble the architecture and layout of early American towns in the area, such as historic Williamsburg, but it will be a showcase for a comprehensive array of modern technologies and innovative, sustainable planning strategies.

The project has broken ground and the first 500 residences are expected to be ready for occupancy around March of next year. Over the next eight years, one-third of the almost 1,800-acre site will be built out with 4,000 homes to accommodate approximately 12,000 residents, along with 500,000 square feet of commercial space and 250,000 square feet of retail. The remaining two-thirds of the site will be left undeveloped as forests, wetlands, and farms.

Haymount developer John Clark of the John A. Clark Company, based in Rappahan-nock, Virginia, started to plan the project over 15 years ago, inspired in part by the wildly suc-cessful Village Homes development in Davis,

California, which he described as "way before its time" and "a project for the record books."

Designed by Miami-based Duany Plater-Zyberk & Company, Haymount will include civic and religious buildings, schools, and a col-lege campus, as well as every housing type. A central plaza will be used for a local farmers' market, which will feature produce from the town's four-acre organic farm and garden. The town also will have a 15-acre vineyard; some of the vines have already been planted.

Of the many sustainable features planned for inclusion in the development, its transporta-tion and wastewater treatment strategies are some of the most noteworthy. Construction is underway on a biological wastewater plant that will be powered by solar photovoltaics and hy-drogen fuel cells. Haymount's design guidelines incorporate green standards for all site work and buildings, and Clark expects that the water facilities will attain a LEED gold or platinum rating.

In addition to being a pedestrian-friendly community, the town plans include the provi-sion of on-site electric minicars for each neigh-borhood, mountain bike trails and road bike loops, and — as a special amenity — two free bi-cycles with every house. As for their transporta-tion options into the wider world, residents will be able to take commuter shuttles into D.C. and Richmond and the town is close to the metropolitan railway.

While it is too soon to tell how the devel-opment will pan out, early signs are positive. As of this summer, more than 1,500 home lots had been presold, months before construction started. Clark says that the marketplace has "proven that this is no longer just a fad. It is simply about people wanting to live in a differ-ent way. Consumers are voting with their pock-etbooks." Furthermore, the developer says that he has been contacted by many national and regional builders who want to participate in building the community.

This is not to say there have not been challenges along the way. As is the case with many innovative developments, the developer found that initially the "building community and the financial community were resistant" to some of the new ideas being proposed. But after

Haymount was approved, Caroline County added language to its comprehensive plan encouraging the use of new urbanist design principles, and two recently approved large-scale projects feature new urbanist designs. Because of changes like these, Clark believes that "the guys who come after us will have a far easier process" to go through to get their projects approved.

Highlands' Garden Village: Reuse of a Historic Urban Site, Denver, Colorado

Highlands' Garden Village (HGV) is a built example of a smaller mixed-use neighborhood development. A 27-acre urban infill development located three miles from downtown Denver, it was designed to blend into the transitional neighborhood that surrounds it

HGV was developed by Perry Rose LLC, a partnership of Chuck Perry and Jonathan Rose. Both partners say they have a strong commitment to affordable housing, urban revitalization, and social responsibility, as well as to environmental sustainability. Perry and Rose hired Berkeley, California-based Calthorpe Associates to do the master planning and schematic design for the Highlands project.

The village was constructed on the site of the vacated Elitch Gardens amusement park and botanical gardens, built in 1890. Having decided to let some of the historic and natural features guide the design, the team retained the original entry and preserved the mature trees and tulip bulbs throughout the site. The team also restored the octagonal theater, recruiting a nonprofit organization to run a regional performance arts center there, and rehabilitated the carousel pavilion and greenhouse, turning them into civic features.

All 306 homes and housing units have been built and sold. The first homes were constructed in 1999 and the final live/work condominiums were completed in 2003. All of the homes were built by Lafayette, Colorado-based Wonderland Homes, which was selected in part because of its extensive green building experience. The homes exceed the green requirements of the Colorado Built Green and federal ENERGY STAR programs. Construction is underway on 70,000 square feet of commercial and retail space, which is expected to be completed next year.

Intended to be diverse the development includes every type of housing, accommodating residents with incomes as low as 30 percent of median up to market rate. HGV's "granny flat" carriage units were the first such units to be approved by the city. The Hearthstone cohousing component was also developed (by another company, Wonderland Hill Development) as a community within the community. Echoing a philosophy espoused by Peter Calthorpe, Perry says, "Communities are like biosystems. Biosystems that are monocultures are less healthy and less sustainable than biosystems that are diverse."

As for the popularity of HGV, Perry reports, "The homes sold more quickly than we had anticipated. They sold at a higher sales price and have appreciated in value more than those in the neighborhood in general, which have appreciated about 10 percent per year; the Highlands' homes have appreciated 14 percent per year."

As for the rental units, "our occupancy rate tends to be higher than [that of] comparable properties, and we have less turnover in both the rentals and in the home sales. People do make the choice to live in areas where there's a sense of community and a value for sustainability."

However, the process to get the project approved was not an easy or short one. The developers ended up preparing a 200-page planned unit development (PUD) ordinance that took two years to get approved. But after that, the city used many features of its PUD as a model for creating a mixed-use zoning district that has been used for other Denver developments.

The developers of Highlands' Garden Village took advantage of available tax credits and incentives, such as Fannie Mae's green mortgages. Perry recommends that future projects make use of the Columbia, Maryland-based Enterprise Foundation's new Green Communities initiative, which is a large investment fund for grants, loans, and equity, and offers green affordable housing and neighborhood standards as well as technical assistance for developers.

Coffee Creek Center: A Restorative, Rural-Urbanist Community, Chesterton, Indiana

Coffee Creek Center combines new urbanist, pedestrian-oriented design with other sustainable design and planning strategies. The development is located in Chesterton, a small town in northern Indiana, 50 miles from Chicago and only a couple of miles from the shores of Lake Michigan. It is being developed on 645 acres, 167 of which are permanently protected via a conservation easement This greenbelt preserve includes a native prairie, a restored stream, and five miles of walking trails.

The development is now five years into its 15-year buildout period. When fully built out, Coffee Creek Center will comprise 2,000 homes and 3 million square feet of commercial space. Many homes and apartments have already been built and four of the six buildings in the retail center are completed, as well as a health care center and a restaurant. The homes were designed according to ENERGY STAR standards.

The community is being developed by the Lake Erie Land Company, based in Chesterton, Indiana. Making ecological restoration a part of all of its projects, the company wanted to make Coffee Creek Center its most environmentally responsible development yet. To make that happen, the Lake Erie Land Company hired sustainability leaders; master land planning was provided by Charlottesville, Virginia-based William McDonough + Partners and ecological and landscape planning was provided by the Elmhurst, Illinois–based Conservation Design Forum (CDF).

CDF restored the native prairie and the creek. The improved water quality allowed salmon to spawn there for the first time in many years. The creek is now a thriving amenity; an amphitheater and pavilion are located near it in the center of the development, and the area has become a hub for many local and community gatherings and activities.

Kelle Mobley, director of operations at the Lake Erie Land Company, says that the company had some difficulty with the approvals process because zoning did not accommodate this type of plan. "With any innovative development, especially when you have different ways of planning development and walkable communities, you have to educate the people with whom you're working and the towns with which you're working." But the company persevered. While sales were slow at first, they have started to pick up. Mobley is seeing "a lot of demand and interest from national and local builders" and businesses are interested in opening there. She reports that the people who have bought homes in Coffee Creek "say that this is the way they want to live. They want to walk to retail. They want natural green space. They want to live in a responsible development"

A listing of other neighborhood developments and new towns with major sustainable development projects located in them within the United States is provided in the next paragraph. Many other case studies are available on the U. S. Department of Energy website (www. sustainable.doe.gov/greendev/stories.shtml).

Neighborhood Developments and New Towns with Sustainable Elements

Aggie Village, Davis, California (University of California at Davis)
Blair Towns, Silver Spring, Maryland (The Tower Companies)
Brewery Blocks, Portland, Oregon (Gerdling Edlen Development)
Civano, Tucson, Arizona (Community of Civano LLC/Case Enterprises)
Coffee Creek Center, Chesterton, Indiana (Lake Erie Land Company)
Daybreak, South Jordan, Utah (Kennecott Land)
Duneland Village, Gary, Gary Indiana (McCormack Baron Salazar)
Ecovillage of Loudoun County Virginia
Haymount, Caroline County, Virginia (John A. Clark Company)

Hidden Springs, Boise, Idaho (Residential Financial Corporation)

Highlands' Garden Village, Denver, Colorado (Perry Rose LLC)

Issaquah Highlands, Issaquah, Washington (Port Blakely Communities)

Jackson Meadow, St. Croix, Minnesota (Jackson Meadow Company)

Laguna West, Elk Grove, Sacramento County, California (Phil Angelides)

Mashpee Commons, Cape Cod, Massachusetts (Mashpee Commons LP)

Mesa del Sol, Albuquerque, New Mexico (Forest City Covington LLC)

Noisette, North Charleston Redevelopment/ Restoration, South Carolina (Noisette Company)

Seaside, Florida (Robert Davis, Seaside Development Company)

Southside Neighborhood Redevelopment, Greensboro, North Carolina (Robert "Nate" Bowman)

Stapleton, Denver, Colorado (Forest City Stapleton)

The Solaire (and other Battery Park City developments), New York City (Albanese Organization)

Terramor Village, Ladera Ranch, Orange County, California (Rancho Mission Viejo)

Vickery, Cumming, Georgia (Hedgewood Properties)

Village Homes, Davis, California (Michael and Judy Corbett)

WaterColor, Seagrove Beach, Florida (Arvida)

West Garfield Park, Chicago, Illinois (Bethel New Life)

Beyond the Neighborhood

Many principles of neighborhood sustainability can be (and are being) integrated into larger-scale policy efforts to create sustainable towns, cities, and regions. In a recent talk, Peter Calthorpe stressed the need for long-term regional visions and planning efforts. He said, "Our economic opportunities are bounded by our region. Our social life tends to be regional. Most of our environmental issues go to the regional scale: the air basin, water quality, transportation, and congestion." He called for a big-picture outlook, saying, "We need to see urban design as a series of networks that expand right to the global scale and overlap one another. There are riparian networks, ecological networks, watershed networks, circulation networks, economic networks."

The United States is witnessing a gradual transformation of the development industry and the landscape. As more communities are developed using sustainable practices and more people see the very real possibilities demonstrated by these life-size models, demand for them is growing and so is developers' interest. Moreover, it seems that once developers — or builders or planners or architects or even towns — have tried out a sustainable approach on one project, they almost always make it a part of their standard practice, seeing no point in turning back.

OTHER RESOURCES

Other resources for information on sustainable communities and developments are shown below.

Organizations and Websites

Center for Neighborhood Technology: http://www.cnt.org

Congress for the New Urbanism: www.cnu.org

Enterprise Foundation's Green Communities initiative: www.enterprisefoundation.org/resources/green/

Funders' Network for Smart Growth and Livable Communities: http://www.fundersnetwork.org

Growth Management Leadership Alliance: www.gmla.org

Livable Places: www.livableplaces.org

Local Government Commission, Center for Livable Communities: www.lgc.org

Natural Resource Defense Council, Smart Growth program: www.nrdc.org/cities/smartGrowth/

NewUrbanism.org: www.newurbanism.org

Rocky Mountain Institute: http://www.rmi.org

Smart Growth America: http://www.smartgrowthamerica.org

Smart Growth Leadership Institute: http://www.sgli.org

Smart Growth Network: http://www.smartgrowth.org

Sprawl Watch Clearinghouse: http://www.sprawlwatch.org

Urban Ecology: http://www.urbanecology.org

Urban Land Institute: http://www.uli.org

U.S. Green Building Council: http://www.sugbc.org

U.S. Environmental Protection Agency's Smart Growth information: http://www.epa.gov/smartgrowth

Books

Arendt, Randall. *Crossroads, Hamlet, Village, Town: Design Characteristics of Traditional Neighborhoods, Old and New.* Chicago: American Planning Association, Planning Advisory Service, 2004.

Calthorpe, Peter, and William Fulton. *The Regional City.* Washington, DC: Island, 2001.

Duany, Andres, Elizabeth Plater-Zyberk and Jeff Speck. *Sub-

urban Nation: The Rise of Sprawl and the Decline of the American Dream. New York: North Point, 2001.

Gause, Jo Allen. *Great Planned Communities*. Washington, DC: Urban Land Institute, 2002.

Jacobs, Jane. *The Death and Life of Great American Cities*. New York: Random House, 1992.

Kay, Jane Holtz. *Asphalt Nation: How the Automobile Took Over America, and How We Can Take It Back*. New York: Crown, 1997.

McHarg, Ian. *Design with Nature*. New York: Wiley, 1995.

Spirn, Anne Whiston. *The Granite Garden: Urban Nature and Human Design*. New York: Basic, 1984.

Van der Ryn, Sim, and Stuart Cowan. *Ecological Design*. Washington, DC: Island, 1995.

Wilson, Alex, Jenifer L. Seal, Lisa McManigal, L. Hunter Lovins, Maureen Cureton and William D. Browning. *Green Development: Integrating Ecology and Real Estate*. New York: Wiley, 1998. (Also see the *Green Development* CD v2.0, 2002, featuring more than 200 case studies.)

CHAPTER 22

Detroit and Other Cities Join the Urban Greening Movement

Cherie Langlois

I promise not to terrify you with the tale of a comet or meteor hurtling through space to strike Earth. (That scenario has been played to death anyway.) Being partial to happily-ever-after stories myself, I would much rather share what happens when something big, green and good hits a city, slamming into it deep and hard enough to reverberate through the lives of residents, the social fabrics of communities, the city's economy, the environment and more. And don't think this story concerns just one mythical city. Detroit, Portland, Philadelphia and many other real cities have been impacted by this (literally) growing phenomenon — most likely even the city where you live.

I'm referring, of course, to the urban-agriculture renaissance — without which you wouldn't be holding this magazine in your hands — and its close ally, the green-space movement. Backyard farms where chickens chuckle and scratch, community gardens brimming with broccoli and beans, wooded parks beckoning families for picnics and bicycle rides — such simple, wholesome places do a city good in some not-so-simple ways. We asked city officials, planners and urban-agriculture leaders to give us the dirt on how these burgeoning movements have bettered their cities.

Portland: City of Green Spaces and Gardens

Portland, the City of Roses, is also a city of soul-soothing green spaces and bountiful vegetable gardens. Take a summer stroll along a tree-lined lane in an older neighborhood, and sure, you see (and smell) roses galore, but you'll also glimpse gardens rich with herbs, fruit trees and vegetables. Walk farther, and you're bound to bump into a lovely park frequented by playing children and strolling couples. Indeed, this vibrant city teems with growing things.

"Portland Parks and Recreation cares for over 10,000 acres of parks and natural areas within the city," confirms Nick Fish, Portland commissioner in charge of parks. "The parks system includes 33 community gardens, with many more in the works, and over 1,500 people are on the waiting list for community garden plots. And the list is growing!"

Working to find creative ways to meet the demand, Fish has launched an initiative to give community gardening a boost in the city. Another sustainability goal aims to create "20-minute neighborhoods," where "a resident can access all of the important things one needs to lead a high quality of life within a 20-minute walk," he explains. These necessities include a

Originally published as "Deep Impact: Brace Yourself," *Urban Farm*, Vol. 2, No. 2, Summer 2010, by BowTie, Inc., Los Angeles, CA. Reprinted with permission of the publisher.

grocery store, park, community center and —
naturally — a place to garden.

Why are Portlanders so hungry to grow
food? While many, no doubt, embrace urban
agriculture for pure enjoyment, for too many
residents, the tragic answer may involve real
hunger — a growing problem plaguing more
than 50,000 Oregonians, according to Fish.
And at their most basic level, urban farms and
community gardens help people in Portland
feed themselves and others, in both good times
and bad.

Increasing food security, lowering grocery
bills and helping people adopt more nutritious
diets rank as some of the most important ways
urban agriculture benefits a city's residents.
They also happen to be stated mission goals of
Growing, Gardens, a Portland urban-ag nonprofit organization that harnesses volunteer
power to build raised-bed organic vegetable
gardens in the yards of low-income residents.
"Each participating family enrolls in a three-
year program," explains Rodney Bender, the
group's garden programs manager. "We provide
them with seeds, compost bins, tools and pretty
much everything else you need for a successful
garden. We also host gardening workshops and
connect each family with a volunteer mentor
to teach them the basics of food gardening."

With some 700 home gardens and about
75 percent of their home gardeners sticking
with their gardens after three years, you could
safely call the program a success. Bender cites
the following results from their 2009 home-
gardener survey as evidence of the positive impact these gardens make in the lives of low-income residents:

- 78 percent of the families reported saving
  money on food.
- 90 percent shared extra produce with someone outside of their household.
- 71 percent increased their daily fruit and vegetable consumption.
- Of the gardeners who regularly used emer-
  gency food boxes, 61 percent reported decreasing the number of boxes they used.

Producing food and sharing it with others,
as many of their home gardeners do, grows a
sense of personal empowerment and commu-

nity, stresses Bender. "We encourage people to
put their vegetable gardens in the front yard,"
he says. "When people see someone gardening
and see how beautiful the garden is, they want
to garden, too. It brings people together, because it's something we all have in common:
We all need to eat. A lot of community building
comes from something as simple as a vegetable
garden."

Fish agrees that the benefits of urban gardens extend well beyond simply eating the
healthy food you grow. "Gardens serve as important outdoor community centers," he says.
"They can help older adults stay active and provide learning opportunities for children. A garden might provide an opportunity for a recent
immigrant to share cultural traditions, or it
could serve as a platform for residents to get to
know each other and organize around an issue
they care about. Gardens not only improve our
self-sufficiency, but also the livability of our
communities."

Philadelphia: Growing from Emptiness

We've all seen tracts of vacant land in cities:
ugly, lifeless places where garbage and glass litter
the ground, graffiti mars every surface, and drug
dealers and homeless souls haunt the night.
Contrast this to a green, growing, blooming
place like Mill Creek Farm, an urban farm built
on old housing sites in west Philadelphia, where
gardeners tend okra, corn and other crops. Or
to an empty lot transformed to verdant grass and
graceful trees, thanks to Philadelphia Green, an
urban revitalization program of the Pennsylvania Horticultural Society. Which place would
you prefer to live near — trashed lot or garden
oasis?

Located in a low-income area, Mill Creek
Farm provides residents with sustainably grown
organic produce at affordable prices, educates
school groups and other visitors about the
basics of growing food, and employs teens
through a summer job-training program. The
farm sits next to a flourishing, long-standing
community garden where elders come to socialize as they grow and share good food — a

vibrant scene that replays itself throughout a city plagued by decades of declining industry and population, says Katherine Gajewski, director of the Mayor's Office of Sustainability in Philadelphia.

"We believe we have the second-largest amount of acreage devoted to agriculture in a U.S. urban area," explains Gajewski, adding that the city has set a goal to bring local food to within 10 minutes of every resident. "You can go to so many parts of Philadelphia and find people growing food in one of the largest cities in the country. It feels really essential to the Philadelphia experience and character."

With 25 percent of Philadelphia's population at or below the poverty line, Gajewski says community gardens like the one at Mill Creek Farm play a critical role in providing nutritious food to people of underserved communities — areas notoriously devoid of supermarkets — and in energizing the community itself. "They've been a way for people to take their neighborhoods back from blight and fill a sense of emptiness."

One way Philadelphia Green combats this pervasive problem of urban blight involves vacant-land stabilization projects, which entail grading over empty lots and planting them with grass and trees, enclosed by a signature post-and-rail fence. Along with sponging up water run-off and giving the community a property-value-boosting facelift, these projects provide training and employment for low-income residents and for people transitioning through rehabilitation programs, says Eileen Gallagher, project manager of community gardens for Philadelphia Green.

"The work gives people skills they can use in other jobs and creates a venue for reentry back into their community for those who need it."

Through another exciting program called City Harvest, Philadelphia Green has joined forces with the prison, inviting inmates to become part of a horticultural project growing greenhouse seedlings for their 45 community gardens. "The inmates grow the seedlings, which are distributed among our gardens four times during the growing season, and then the gardeners grow the seedlings to harvest," says

Gallagher. "At least once a week, they donate part of their harvest to a specific food pantry. Over four years, the gardeners have donated more than 55,000 pounds of fresh produce to their local food cupboards."

The program profoundly impacts inmate participants — people who will one day find themselves on the outside again — by teaching them new skills. Working with the men and women at the prison, Gallagher has observed how growing a carrot or potato switches on the metaphorical light bulb. "A woman will be like, 'Wow! This is where my French fries come from!' or she'll say, 'When I get out, I'm going to have a garden and show my kids how to grow food.' The program exposes them to this whole component of living they've had no experience with — growing vegetables, finding out how delicious stir-fried kale tastes — and they're so jazzed."

Detroit— Planting Seeds to Bring People Back

Like Portland and Philadelphia, recession-ravaged Detroit has found itself enriched by the urban-agriculture and greening movements in ways that are difficult to quantify, but are nonetheless important. Here, where the home-foreclosure rate soars higher than anywhere else in the country and 30 percent of the land lays vacant, increasing numbers of community, school and backyard vegetable gardens have put wasted spaces back into productive use, bringing diverse groups of people together in the bargain. And that's just for starters.

In six years, we've grown from around 80 gardens to 875," says Ashley Atkinson, director of urban agriculture at Greening of Detroit, a partner in the Garden Resource Program Collaborative. This initiative works to improve the quality of life in Detroit by providing resources, education and support to urban gardeners and farmers. "We estimate there are more than 11,000 gardeners in Detroit, which means one in 100 Detroit residents are active in urban agriculture. It's a very thriving community at this moment in time. And since we have so much vacant land here in Detroit, we have really large garden sites and a lot of cool educational programs."

One such program is SEED Wayne, which oversees two campus community gardens and a farmers' market at Wayne State University. Dedicating themselves to building sustainable food systems on and off campus, SEED Wayne student volunteers learn valuable skills, from horticulture to leadership, as they grow herbs and vegetables for campus cafeterias, host workshops, and distribute produce to a local soup kitchen. The students also recycle organic wastes through their on-campus composting facility, steering this nutrient-rich resource away from landfills and into gardens.

"We want to communicate the story of the multiple benefits these gardens provide," says Kami Pothukuchi, associate professor of urban planning at Detroit's Wayne State University and director of the SEED Wayne program. "It's so easy to focus on only one benefit, such as economic — which won't be as large as, for example, what a manufacturing plant offers. But that's not the way to look at gardens. You have to look at the multiple benefits and the interconnections between them."

Many gardeners now produce vegetables for sale, notes Pothukuchi; indeed, once they've developed a set of skills, urban farmers can supplement their incomes effectively with their gardens. "[But] gardens also provide ways for people to be active outside, not cooped up in front of the TV. They bring multiple generations together in a non-threatening way and help connect neighbors. They make a neighborhood look lived in. For us here in Detroit, where many neighborhoods are distressed, that's a big benefit."

"The urban-agriculture movement here has been very powerful in uniting people around music, art and alternative modes of transportation — all of the things that attract people to communities," adds Atkinson. She points to the Detroit Agriculture Network's annual garden tour, which lures some 600 people every year, to illustrate this fact. When the group decided to incorporate a bicycle route a few years ago, they reached out to local cycling groups to help with the event. A partnership blossomed, and an exchange of passions ensued: Some garden-

ers rode bicycles for the first time at the tour, and cyclists who had never wielded a trowel before became food-garden enthusiasts. "We're now seeing more people interested in Detroit and moving here. When you've watched so many people leave, it's heartening to see them moving back."

Growing Up to the Challenge

Like all grassroots crusades, the urban-agriculture and greening movements face challenges, a few of which include:

Access to Land and Utilities. "There's so much vacant land in Detroit, but actually getting access to it, and not having to pay expensive taxes because of the way it's zoned, poses a challenge," says Kami Pothukuchi, associate professor of urban planning at Detroit's Wayne State University. Another access issue: bringing utilities — i.e., water — to the site.

City Codes, Regulations and Restrictions. Many cities and suburbs prohibit keeping backyard chickens or even growing vegetables for sale. (See "Pushing City Limits" in the Spring 2010 issue of *Urban Farm*.) Zoning and land-use rules need to change to make urban agriculture legal, Pothukuchi says.

Funding. It takes money to create and maintain programs that nurture green spaces, community gardens and backyard farms. When funding cuts hit its community-garden program, Philadelphia Green had to substantially slash the number of gardens it assisted. For these programs to get off the ground, "you need at least three years of funding to create a model and sustain the movement and to help people become invested in it and understand how it all works," says Eileen Gallagher, community-garden project manager at Philadelphia Green.

Accessibility. Making the urban-agriculture movement accessible to everyone poses a significant challenge, stresses Rodney Bender, programs manager of Growing Gardens. "Gardening is very popular here in Portland, but many people lack the skills and knowledge, or the resources, to participate."

Balancing Green Space and Gardens with Growth. "Our success as a city depends on growing our revenue and population and getting people back to work," explains Katherine Gajewski, director of the Mayor's Office of Sustainability in

Philadelphia. "It's a delicate balance to work with and around, [but] open space and agricultural lands don't need to be at odds with a growth plan."

Outsiders out for Profit. Large outside commercial interests — bent on buying up huge tracts of land for conventional farming — loom on the horizon as a potential threat to community-based urban farming in Detroit, warns Pothukuchi.

Land Tenure and Preservation. Urban farmers and community gardeners growing on land they don't own risk losing their investment of money, hard work and infrastructure when leases expire or development threatens. Land trusts and conservation easements can help preserve green spaces and gardens for the long-term, Gallagher says.

Soil Contamination. "It might be great for you to use a vacant lot to grow your garden, but if the land could be contaminated with lead, that's a problem," says Gajewski. "We want to keep everyone healthy, so it's important to us where and how these gardens grow."

Marketing and Distribution. Urban farmers and community gardeners can have a tough time accessing markets to sell produce and competing with supermarkets stuffed with cheap, mass-produced food products.

But happily, the buy-local and slow-food campaigns are turning more shoppers and chefs to farmers' markets, CSAs and other urban agriculture outlets. One delicious example: "We have a local brand here called 'Grown in Detroit,' made up of 90 different growers who combine their produce to sell at farmers' markets and restaurants," says Ashley Atkinson, director of urban agriculture at Greening of Detroit. "Some of our community gardeners are making up to $8,000 a year."

CHAPTER 23

Eugene and Other Cities
Create Energy Efficient Buildings
Matt Stansberry

Local governments face a host of challenges — from interdepartmental wrangling to budgetary restrictions — when applying green building practices across their communities. Nonetheless, cities such as Austin, Texas; Eugene, Ore.; and Chicago have pursued green initiatives using the Leadership in Energy and Environmental Design (LEED) green building rating system developed by the Washington-based U.S. Green Building Council (USGBC) and are helping set the standards for municipal construction projects.

Public officials can take a variety of actions to bring their green building goals to fruition, including using cool or green roofs, photovoltaics (solar power), daylighting, energy management and cogeneration. Also, local governments can use a community-owned electric utility to encourage green building projects.

For example, Austin Energy, a city department, began its energy conservation programs — energy efficiency, renewable energy and distributed generation — in the early 1980s. "Austin is a progressive city, so we're a progressive utility," says Richard Morgan, manager of, the city's green building program. In June 2000, Austin's City Council required all municipal buildings built with city funds to meet LEED criteria.

According to Morgan, the city has completed two green projects. City Hall opened in

November 2004, and a $50 million mixed-use emergency services facility — the Combined Transportation Emergency and Communications Center — opened in October.

Working with the Salvation Army, the city also constructed the Austin Resource Center for the Homeless, a $5 million, 26,820-square-foot, three-story building with a parking area. The facility was designed using LEED guidelines to maximize natural light, ventilation and views through openings in the building, courtyards and terraces.

One major challenge for Morgan was educating the public about the lifecycle cost of green buildings vs. traditional construction. According to Morgan, too many public officials over-emphasize the initial cost of a project and overlook the building's total cost of ownership.

Even when a city wants to build green, implementing those practices across local government agencies can be difficult. In Austin, each city department is considered the building's owner and allocates the budget for its building project. Construction costs are a frequent target of cuts.

"Each department has its own project manager," Morgan says. "Some do an exceptional job [executing projects under green guidelines], and some don't; That's why we went to the. city council [to develop a green

Originally published as "It's Not Easy Being Green," *American City & County*, Vol. 120, No. 3, March 2005, published by Penton Media. Reprinted with permission of the publisher.

standard], because we were getting mixed results from project managers. By imposing an outside standard, it is easier to enforce, and it puts interdepartmental wrangling aside. Since [the city's] resolution, standards are defined by the USCBC, and project managers can't say that Austin Energy is being unreasonable."

A Consolidated Approach

In the early 1990s, every department in Eugene had its own design and operation standards. But that did not work very well, according to Ron Sutton, the city's facility operations and maintenance manager. By the mid 1990s, Eugene had created a consolidated facility department. "We have a set of [green building] standards that everyone in the organization works towards," Sutton says. "Individual departments are focused on their programs, not the buildings, which is why a consolidated facility unit is important. It lets departments focus on their core missions."

Eugene uses LEED standards for its construction and major remodeling projects and for existing buildings (LEED-EB) to evaluate its overall operations program. "Eugene [has] about 100 buildings, ranging from park restrooms to performing arts centers, [each presenting] its own set of challenges in cleaning chemicals, operation policies and procedures," Sutton says.

Using LEED-EB gives the city a consistent, third-party way to evaluate Eugene's operations and maintenance program. "We summarized all that we had done and learned [using the green building guidelines] into a presentation to our city council, which was very well received," he says.

As a result of the emphasis on green buildings, Eugene expanded its recycling program, increased indoor air quality diagnostics, improved refrigerant monitoring/reporting, adopted standards for cleaning chemicals created by Washington-based Green Seal, reviewed service contracts and added sustainable procedures. "If you're putting the money in the building, you need to know what you're getting for your money," Sutton says. "The only way

to see if that performance is following through is to certify the building. [While many] private companies have the resources to pursue LEED, there are ways people in the public sector can do this within their budgets." Sutton says that building green could initially cost more, but "if it is truly an organizational priority, there may be opportunities to request additional funding, over and above your baseline budget for the LEED certification process."

A Mayor with a Plan

Chicago has a clear rationale for building green, according to Sadhu Johnston, assistant to Chicago's mayor for green initiatives. "Over the total lifecycle of a building, operating the facility is 80 percent to 90 percent of the total cost of ownership. People ask how we can afford to construct buildings in this way. I ask how we can afford not to," Johnston says.

According to Johnston, Mayor Richard Daley is committed to making Chicago one of the greenest cities in the country in terms of sustainable design. In 2001, the city began its first green building project: a major renovation on a brownfield site. The site previously had served a variety of purposes but most recently was used by a construction and demolition debris recycler.

Completed in January 2003, the facility was named the Chicago Center for Green Technology. The 40,000-square-foot building uses solar and geothermal energy, and includes a rooftop garden and a natural habitat to filter stormwater. The city invested $9 million in cleanup costs and another $5.4 million toward construction and renovation.

Today, the city uses the facility to test sustainable design processes and gauge costs for green construction, and to teach the public about green buildings. The facility's Green Building Resource Center is designed for builders, developers, architects and homeowners looking to incorporate sustainable design practices and green materials into their next building projects.

The center's resources include green building standards and construction guides; reference books; recycled, reused and renewable building material samples; a public-access workstation with links to green technology websites; and staff and volunteers to guide visitors through the research process. Workshops are conducted on topics such as solar electricity, native landscaping and green roots. The center also hosts seminars designed specifically for building industry professionals that address issues such as boiler efficiency.

"Following that project, the city [built more green buildings]— three libraries and a police station — and with each successive project we saw costs going down," Johnston says. He says the first certified building had a 6 percent construction premium. As project managers, engineers and architects learned to optimize green construction practices, by 2004 the city's police station premium was less than 2 percent.

"In June 2004, the city mandated all new buildings would be certified under LEED-NC [for new construction], and we have 12 projects under way. We also require all projects that receive any city funding to pursue green initia-

tives," Johnston says. Target is building two stores in Chicago, and it is receiving tax increment financing from the city because of its commitment to build green.

Securing the commitment from city officials, private companies and construction professionals to build green has been the city's biggest challenge, Johnston says. Learning new techniques and strategies to make the entire process more efficient is a large part of the effort, and the city conducts extensive training in the private sector.

"Chicago is learning the processes and then reaching out to the private sector through these types of incentives," Johnston says. "We're also creating a green building permit process and a green building code which will expedite green building projects."

And if towns the size of Eugene, Austin and Chicago can go green, other local governments can as well. Though different methods, municipal structures and philosophies exist, the local governments can have one goal: to achieve sustainability in the built environment.

CHAPTER 24

Flagstaff and Other Cities Develop Walkable Communities

Dan Burden

How can I find and help build a walkable community? This is one of the most important and necessary questions anyone should ask before settling down in a permanent location. Many corporate leaders looking to expand or move locations are now looking for towns offering appropriate start up breaks, but also where they and their middle managers want to live many years, raise a family and retire. Our organization has a 12-step program for defining and achieving or strengthening community walkability.

But finding a walkable town is a different task. So, I have built a list of the 12 most important things to rate when searching for a Walkable Community. Note that there are many walkable communities in America that are declining, due to poor politics, staffing or a lost vision. And there are some communities on the cusp of becoming walkable that have strong leadership and direction. Given a choice, I would move to the community that is up and coming.

You can, of course, move into a new Walkable Community, such as Seaside, Celebration, Abacoa, Florida; Kentlands, Maryland, The Crossings, Mountain View, California; Fairview Village, Orenco Station, Oregon; Northwest Landing, Washington; and now hundreds of others. I know these places well. I return to them often, photographing, walking and measuring their essences. The paint, the grass, everything is fresh and new there. Some of these new urban villages are rather complete, and fit well into the fabric of the greater town or region they share.

But if you don't want to wait for these places to become organic, go for the real towns of America... they are abundant, old, tried and proven, and they need many defenders of their greatness. This article is mostly on how to find existing Walkable Communities. They are way too numerous to list more than a fraction.

This article is also a little bit on how to protect these delicate real places of the heart. As I write this, I am sitting in East Lansing, one of my favorite Walkable Communities. I am eager to go out for a walk. But I am also 100 miles from Holland, Michigan. I am torn — I'd like to go there, right now, take in the color of the tulips, walk its streets and listen to the outward pride and laughter of its people.

You can either be a passenger on the train to change, or get up in the engine helping stoke the fire, taking in the gusty winds of change feeling the sting and smell of hot cinders burning the hair off the nape of your neck. These up and coming communities may be more affordable, and are likely to be fun places to place your energies. But before you move, truly check out the politics of change.

Originally published as "How Can I Find and Help Build a Walkable Community," *Resource Report*, December 2009, by Walkable and Livable Communities Institute, Inc., Port Townsend, WA. Reprinted with permission of the publisher.

Good towns come in all regions of the country. The best are often small places like Keene, New Hampshire; Winter Park, Florida; Flagstaff, Arizona; Crested Butte, Colorado or Los Gatos, California... or they include big cities like Seattle, Washington; Chicago, Illinois; Milwaukee, Wisconsin; Minneapolis and St Paul, Minnesota; Portland, Oregon; or San Diego, California that have many small, well designed compact, intact neighborhoods, each with a village center and a character and personality of its own.

In some of these villages, strong enclaves of Hispanic, Jewish, Polish, German, Asian, African American or gay cultures are found, taking pride in building or maintaining their communities. Other villages are fully mixed, rich in diversity of people, age, abilities and wealth. You can live in a town that is sprawling itself to death, and still lead a healthy life in several great neighborhoods. Note that top rated towns in this listing either already have or are now developing many villages in their city.

Finding the Great Walkable Community

My wife, Lys, and I left Central Ohio the day after we got married in June, 1970 and moved west in search of a great place to live. We struck gold, almost by accident, in our first search for a town. We settled into and lived in Missoula, Montana without a car for nearly ten years, very happy, healthy, and highly engaged with every level of community life. We knew, felt ownership and took pride in the many good places. We walked and watched over green, canopied streets almost everywhere. We felt the courtesies of drivers who watched out for us. We knew each park, each of the five valley neighborhoods and other places in the pre-sprawl portions of town.

It seems we came to know everyone, and everyone knew us. We had many dozens of friends and hundreds, if not thousands of associates. During our evenings we bicycled into and up the Rattlesnake Creek, Grant Creek, Pattee Canyon, the Hells Gate or, when we had the time, out to French Town or Lolo. Our first

child, Jodi, who maintains our website, was born there. Our small company, Bikecentennial (now Adventure Cycling), was started there 25 years ago, and is still a small but healthy addition to the local economy.

Missoula has a healthy downtown. In the summer a weekly farmers market is held on Saturdays. Many hundreds of people walk or bicycle in to buy their fruit filled pastries, breads, fresh fruits, and organic vegetables. Others come for coffee, listen to music, watch people dance, or just visit. Missoula also has a Friday noon gathering on the rebuilt Clark's Fork River front. People come almost like a weekly pilgrimage for more food, more music and more fun. And just across the street from our little red ginger bread house at 317 Beverly, in Bonner Park, people came on Wednesday nights to hear the small but good community band. Some who bring their cars to these events park them blocks away, some too embarrassed to be seen arriving by car, but not knowing the beauty of walking there.

One immigrant, poor in money, rich in pride of being an American, conceived and built with his own hands, along with the 50 to 60 volunteers he and former Mayor Daniel Kemmis brought together, the newest and best post–World War II carousel in the nation. Missoula also boasts a variety of pricing and sizing of housing stock, great waterfront and trails and a pleasant college campus.

Like many Walkable Communities, today Missoula is also a hearty sprawl place. One only has to look to the down slopes of the mountains to see the ugly brutality of unregulated, unwalkable growth patterns. But Missoula, like all vision directed towns, has and continues to build upon its walkability, while other parts of the same town and county hold contempt for walkability, watering down, isolating and making more distant healthy lifestyles in order to cash into the hungry car culture, complete with all of its demands and droppings.

Like many good places, Missoula is a town highly conflicted, ever in balance. Goodness is not always understood by all people living in a place. There are many short-term investors milking and robbing from long-term accomplishments. It is all too easy for decision makers to close down good, well located and sized schools, healthy and vital local parks, and well located small churches, grocery stores or other retail in order to build big. It always appears to be cheaper to provide the same function on the bigger and cheaper parcel farther out. These farther out places are locations where cars appear to be happy. These outward parcels are cheaper yes, but as we destroy the essences of a good neighborhood, forcing ourselves into a car to have what we need we whittle away the many reasons we came to invest here in the first place. If you move to a walkable community, you must understand its value then learn the skills of building and defending its goodness.

Places more abandoned of walkability, health and vitality have few conflicts. Their sense of place, pride, community values have been lost, or chased away.

All towns in our nation have some degree of walkability. Some hold less than 5 percent, where microscopes are needed to find the remaining shredded and often buried fragments. Some, such as Littleton, New Hampshire, where they are too poor to afford sprawl, have nearly 98 percent walkable scale and features. When you find a town with good walkable features, such as Keene, New Hampshire, you keep returning to recharge. I know I do. I go back often, settle into a nice center town hotel, hang out at local eateries, listen to the town chatter, walk the main street day and night, over and over 2–4 days at a time.

Walkability Items to be rated are always on a scale. A 1–10 scale can be personalized and applied to each of the below twelve categories. Common sense and powers of observation are used to make these determinations. The categories are in no particular order. Never pick a town that you have not visited. Always ask for second and third opinions.

If I were making a commitment to move to a town I would want the town to have high scores on 6 or more of the following 12 categories:

What Walkable Communities Have

1. **Intact Town Centers.** This center includes a quiet, pleasant main street with a hearty, healthy set of stores. These stores are open for business a minimum of 8 hours a day. The stores include things like barbers/beauticians, hardware, druggist, small grocery/deli, sets of good restaurants, clothing, variety store, ice cream shop, stores that attract children, many youth and senior services, places to conduct civic and personal business, library, all within a ¼ mile walk (5 minutes) of the absolute center. If this is a county seat, the county buildings are downtown. If this is an incorporated town the town hall is in the town center. The library is open for business at least 10 hours a day 6–7 days a week. There is still a post office downtown.

2. **Residential Densities, Mixed Income, Mixed Use.** Near the town center, and in a large town at appropriate transit locations there will be true neighborhoods. Higher densities are toward the town center and in appropriate concentrations further out. Housing includes mixed income and mixed use. A truly walkable community does not force lots of people to drive to where they work. Aspen, for example, is a great place to shop and play... but fails to provide housing for anyone who works there. Granny flats, design studios and other affordable housing are part of the mix in even the wealthiest neighborhoods.

3. **Public Space.** There are many places for people to assemble, play and associate with others within their neighborhood. The best neighborhoods have welcoming public space within ⅛ mile (700 feet) of all homes. These spaces are easily accessed by all people.

4. **Universal Design.** The community has a healthy respect for people of all abilities, and has appropriate ramps, medians, refuges, crossings of driveways, sidewalks on all streets where needed, benches, shade and other basic amenities to make walking feasible and enjoyable for everyone.

5. **Key Streets Are Speed Controlled.** Traffic moves on main street and in neighborhoods at safe, pleasant, courteous speeds. Most streets are designed to keep speeds low. Many of these streets are tree lined, have on-street parking and use other methods that are affordable means to keep traffic speeds under control. There is an absence of one-way couplets de-

signed to flush downtown of its traffic in a rush or flight to the suburbs. In most parts of the nation the streets are also green, or have other pleasant landscaping schemes in dry climates.

6. **Streets, Trails Are Well Linked.** The town has good block form, often in a grid or other highly connected pattern. Although hilly terrain calls for slightly different patterns, the linkages are still frequent. Some of the newer neighborhoods that were built to cul-de-sac or other fractured patterns are now being repaired for walking by putting in trail connectors in many places. These links are well designed so that there are many eyes on these places. Code for new streets no longer permits long streets that are disconnected.

7. **Design Is Properly Scaled to ⅛, ¼ and ½ Mile Radius Segments.** From most homes it is possible to get to most services in ¼ mile (actual walked distance). Neighborhood elementary schools are within a ¼ mile walking radius of most homes, while high schools are accessible to most children (1 mile radius). Most important features (parks) are within ⅛ mile, and a good, well designed place to wait for a high frequency (10 to 20 minutes) bus is within ¼ to ½ mile. Note that most of these details can be seen on a good local planning map, and even many can be downloaded from the web.

8. **Town Is Designed for People.** Look for clues that decisions are being made for people first, cars second. Does the town have a lot of open parking lots downtown? Are a lot of streets plagued with multiple commercial driveways, limited on-street parking, fast turning radii on corners. Towns designed for people have many investments being made in plazas, parks, walkways… rarely are they investing in decongesting intersections on the far reaches of town. Towns designed for people are tearing down old, non-historic dwellings, shopping plazas and such and converting them to compact, mixed use, mixed income properties. Ask to review the past year of building permits by category. Much is told about what percentage of construction that is infill and independent small builder stock versus big builder single price range housing or retail stock.

9. **Town Is Thinking Small.** The most walkable towns are boldly stepping forward re-quiring maximum parking allowed, versus minimum required. Groceries and other important stores are not permitted to build above a reasonable square footage, must place the foot print of the structure to the street, etc. Palo Alto, for instance, caps their groceries at 20,000 square feet. This assures that groceries, drug stores and other important items are competitive at a size that is neighborhood friendly. Neighborhood schools are community centers. Older buildings are rebuilt in place, or converted to modern needs. Most parking is on-street.

10. **In Walkable Communities There Are Many People Walking.** This sounds like a silly statement at first… but think again. Often there are places that look walkable, but no one walks. Why? There is always a reason. Is it crime? Is it that there is no place to walk to, even though the streets and walkways are pleasant? Are the downtown stores not open convenient hours? You should be able to see a great diversity of those walking and bicycling. Some will be very young, some very old. People with disabilities will be common. Another clue, where people walk in great abundance virtually all motorists are courteous to pedestrians. It is true.

11. **The Town and Neighborhoods Have a Vision.** Seattle, Washington, Portland, Oregon and Austin, Texas are just three examples where neighborhood master plans have been developed. Honolulu sets aside about $1M per year of funds to be spent by each neighborhood. Visionary, master plans provide direction, build ownership of citizens, engage diverse people, and create opportunities for implementation, to get past sticky issues, and deal with the most basic, fundamental, necessary decisions and commitment. There are budgets set aside for neighborhoods, for sidewalks, trails, links, parks. The community no longer talks about where they will get the money, but how they will change their priorities.

12. **Decision Makers Are Visionary, Communicative, and Forward Thinking.** The town has a strong majority of leaders who "get it." Leaders know that they are not to do all the work… but to listen and respond to the most engaged, involved, broad minded citizens. They rarely are swayed by the anti-group, they

seek the opinions and involvement big brush citizens and retailers. They are purposefully changing and building policies, practices, codes and decisions to make their towns pleasant places for people... reinvesting in the town center, disinfesting in sprawl. These people know the difference between a green field, brown field and grey field. They know what Active Living by Design is all about. The regional government understands and supports the building of a town center, and is not attempting to take funds from the people at the center to induce or support sprawl. Often there is a charismatic leader on the town board, chamber of commerce, planning board, there is an architectural review team, a historic preservation effort, and overall good public process. Check out the website of the town... if they focus on their golf courses, tax breaks, great medical services, scenic majestic mountains, or proximity to the sea... fail to emphasize their neighborhood schools, world class library, lively downtown, focus on citizen participation... they are lost, bewitched and bewildered in their own lust and lure of Walt Disney's Pleasure Island.

Finding walkable communities is a great quest we should all make together. I have many personal favorites. They come in all sizes. Each must be tested out using the above criteria before investing in these places. All are in various stages of healing or becoming more diseased, often at the same time.

Generally, I like a town to be on the small side, but larger towns are on my list if they have many good neighborhoods and villages. Some highly favored towns (Crested Butte, Colorado) have as few as 1,400 people; and many, (such as Littleton, New Hampshire, population 7,000) have 5–15,000. A good size town that is complete can provide good services when populated by 30–50,000 people. When towns get up to 100,000 or more, many added services, like efficient transit, are a must to remain walkable and fun.

My Own Search

Having worked in over 1200 communities in North America I am often asked "What is your favorite Walkable Community?" Easy. In North America it is Victoria, British Columbia. It is the one good great place. Since we cannot all live there, it is better that I list many places, and show a range of quality and completeness. At the risk of leaving out towns that I have not visited, taken a liking to, yet have forgot to include in the short moment I had to prepare this piece, I provide a partial list below of good places to live that are Walkable Communities. Many of these places are not affordable, many are. Many people find it essential to downsize their homes, sell one or all cars in order to rebuild their quality of life and health.

In some states, such as Michigan or California, there are so many towns it is difficult to decide which to include, which to leave out. In a few states (New Mexico or Arizona) it is so hard to find a single listing that I find a need to make a more comprehensive search there at a later point in time. Example Walkable Communities (or portions thereof) I have discovered and returned to more than once include:

Walkable Communities by Region

CANADA

Victoria, Vancouver, Toronto, Montreal, Ottawa, Quebec City, Halifax

NORTHEASTERN STATES AND THE DISTRICT

Maine — Portland, Kennebunkport

Maryland — Annapolis, Kentlands, Bethesda

Massachusetts — Boston, Cambridge, Salem

New Hampshire — Keene, Littleton, Portsmouth, Meredith and Exeter

New Jersey — Princeton

New York — New York City, Albany, Saratoga Springs, East Aurora, Huntington, Ithaca, Hamburg, Port Jefferson

Pennsylvania — Philadelphia, Pittsburgh, State College

Vermont — Burlington, Brattleboro, Montpelier

Virginia — Alexandria, Charlottesville, Virginia Washington, D.C.

SOUTHERN STATES

Alabama — Fairhope

Florida — St Augustine, Winter Park, South Beach, West Palm Beach, South Beach, South Miami, Coconut Grove, Coral Gables, Naples, Celebration, Seaside, Pensacola, Key West

Georgia — Savannah

Louisiana — New Orleans

North Carolina — Asheville, Chapel Hill, Charlotte, Hendersonville

South Carolina — Charleston

Tennessee — Franklin

MIDWESTERN STATES

Illinois — Chicago, Naperville

Michigan — Brighton, Holland, Milford, Birmingham, Traverse City, Kalamazoo, East Lansing, Mackinac Island, Marquette

Minnesota — Minneapolis, St Paul

Ohio — Westerville

Wisconsin — Milwaukee, Madison, Cedarburg

SOUTHWESTERN STATES

Arizona — Flagstaff

New Mexico — Santa Fe

Texas — Austin, San Antonio

ROCKY MOUNTAIN STATES

Colorado — Golden, Ft Collins, Crested Butte, Boulder

Montana — Missoula, Big Fork, Livingston, Bozeman

Wyoming — Jackson

PACIFIC COAST STATES

Alaska — Juneau

California — San Diego, Coronado, La Jolla, Santa Monica, Beverly Hills, Pasadena, Brea, Whittier, Claremont, Valencia, Carpenteria, Santa Barbara, Arcata, Chico, Mountain View, Santa Cruz, Monterey, Carmel-by-the-Sea, San Luis Obispo, Los Gatos, San Francisco, Oakland, Berkeley, Sacramento, Davis, Sonoma, Cotati, Petaluma, Healdsburg

Hawaii — Honolulu

Oregon — Portland, Ashland, Corvallis, Eugene

Washington — Seattle, Kirkland, Redmond, Bellevue, Olympia, Bellingham, Gig Harbor, Bainbridge Island, Port Townsend, Everett, University Place, Langley, Issaquah, Ellensburg

Finally, asked to name the two towns in America most deserving of praise for Herculean tasks they are now performing to overcome the ills of sprawl... Sacramento, California, and Charlotte, North Carolina, deserve special recognition and observation.

CHAPTER 25

Gaithersburg Cleans
Its Rivers and Streams

Leah Miller

The summer of 1969 proved to be a pivotal season for water. Environmental awareness had been on the rise, fueled by decades of visible pollution problems and books such as Rachel Carson's *Silent Spring*, which chronicled the ongoing indiscriminate use of pesticides. On June 22, Ohio's Cuyahoga River attracted national media attention when oil slicks and debris on the river caught fire. Although not the first fire seen on this or other U.S. rivers, the Cuyahoga River fire sparked national disgust and outrage. The public clamored for action. Within a few years, the federal government created the Environmental Protection Agency and passed groundbreaking laws such as the Clean Water Act. That summer also marked the start of another significant, far-reaching national water quality protection program — the Izaak Walton League's (League's) Save Our Streams program, which gave people a way to personally take action and make a difference. Save Our Streams pioneered citizen-based stream monitoring and provided individuals with a simple, reliable tool to assess, restore and protect their local streams. Forty years later, Save Our Streams remains one of the League's most successful conservation programs.

What Is Save Our Streams?

The original Save Our Streams effort began in Maryland as a stream adoption program modeled after the state's adopt-a-highway program. League members and others checked streams regularly for siltation and barriers to fish passage. They reported water pollution problems to the appropriate local and state authorities, removed trash and debris and educated the public about how to prevent water pollution. The League expanded the program nationwide in 1974. In the 1980s Save Our Streams became one of the first programs to successfully train volunteers to assess water quality using a simple, accurate method based on the presence and diversity of stream insects and crustaceans (often referred to as "aquatic bugs"). By examining the number and variety of aquatic bugs, volunteers can determine if a waterway is in trouble.

In 1990, the Save Our Streams stream biological monitoring method became one of the first to be approved by the U.S. Environmental Protection Agency as a method to collect useful and scientifically valid information about water quality. Approximately 300 League chapters are active across the country, many with Save Our Streams programs. Thousands of volunteers across the country now use the Save Our

Originally published as "Forty Years Later — and Still Saving Our Streams," *Nonpoint Source News-Notes*, Issue 87, June 2009, by the U.S. Environmental Protection Agency, Washington, DC.

Streams method and other League resources to determine water quality and protect streams in trouble. Dozens of states have adopted volunteer monitoring programs based on the Save Our Streams method.

Kids (and Adults) Love Bugs

Over the years the Save Our Streams program has grown into a national watershed education and outreach program. League members across the country engage children and adults in monitoring and restoration efforts, raising interest and awareness in water quality issues. "The Save Our Streams monitoring method is real-world science," explains Leah Miller, the League's Director of Clean Water Programs. "Kids and adults both love capturing and identifying aquatic bugs. Plus, you get your water quality rating results on the spot — no waiting for data from the laboratory." This low-tech, hands-on approach to water quality monitoring makes it ideal for schools and watershed groups with limited budgets.

Successful programs continue to grow and expand. For example, the League's Project Watershed in central New York uses Save Our Streams to engage students in hands-on science (www.Projectwatershed.org). Project Watershed partners, including the League's Central New York Chapter and other organizations, schools and agencies have worked with approximately 30 area high schools in recent years to monitor streams. Next year the consortium will bring an additional 30 high schools and middle schools into the program. "The students are inspired to apply what they've learned in the real world," notes Miller. "One group recently went to the local government and advocated protecting a high quality stream." The students used their monitoring data to convince local zoning officials not to permit new development that could degrade water quality.

Monitors Watch for Changes

Once introduced to the Save Our Streams method, volunteers across the country are able to keep a close eye on local waters. "Volunteer monitors can monitor streams frequently and often identify problems that might otherwise go unnoticed for a while," explains Miller. For example, Save Our Stream monitors have found and helped to correct problems caused by sewer leaks, chemical spills, polluted runoff from parking lots and roads, sediment pollution from developments, and runoff of airport de-icing chemicals, among other sources. "In fact, we identified a problem near our headquarters office during a workshop," adds Miller. "We found almost no aquatic bugs when assessing a local stream that was usually healthy. We walked up the stream and discovered oil seeping from the streambank — apparently someone's home heating oil tank had sprung a leak. Our monitoring efforts allowed the problem to be identified and corrected quickly."

Many Save Our Streams volunteer programs across the country work closely with state and local environmental agencies to share data. New York's Onondaga County, for example, uses data collected by the Central New York Project Watershed to inform many of its watershed decisions. Many localities rely on volunteer data to help target restoration efforts or identify areas that need additional monitoring by state or local agencies. Virginia's Save Our Streams program (www.vasos.org) trains and certifies volunteer water monitors throughout the state to ensure they comply with the state's quality assurance and quality control requirements. Once certified, monitors can submit their data to the state agencies for use in statewide water quality assessments.

Program Evolution

Over the years, the League's Save Our Streams program has expanded. League staff can help local groups assess watersheds, restore streams, forge partnerships, advocate for clean water and educate the public. "Our members and volunteer monitors became frustrated because the state or local agencies did not always have the resources to help address water quality problems in a timely manner," explained Miller. "Volunteer monitors, on the other hand, can often take immediate action to solve the problems they identify through monitoring. We can help get them started in their restoration efforts."

Want to learn more? The League offers several workshops, books, and videos focused on monitoring and restoring streams. For example, the League's "Watershed Stewardship Action Kit" offers a series of fact sheets about watershed surveys, water conservation, wetland and stream ecology, and the instructions and data forms for water quality monitoring. The League's "Field Guide to Aquatic Macroinvertebrates" is a laminated guide that includes line drawings and identifying characteristics of the insects and crustaceans that live in stream bottoms. The League's "Guide to Aquatic Insects and Crustaceans" is a more detailed key to aquatic bug identification. The "Save Our Streams for America's Streams — A Guide to Water Quality Monitoring" video demonstrates monitoring techniques. The League also offers workshops on monitoring and assessment, stream restoration, wetland ecology and watershed conservation policies upon request. More information about these resources is available on the League's website at www.iwla.org (click on "Stream and Wetland Publications"). For information about Save Our Streams programs in your state, see www.iwla.org/chapters/Division_021509.pdf.

Save Our Streams Biological Stream Monitoring

Although Save Our Streams programs might differ slightly from state to state, the overall biological monitoring approach and structure is essentially the same. The League relies on the presence of benthic macroinvertebrates to assess water quality. Macroinvertebrates are large enough to see with the naked eye (macro) and have no backbone (invertebrate). Benthic macroinvertebrates live in the benthos, or stream bottom, and include insect larvae, adult insects and crustaceans.

Stream-bottom macroinvertebrates are good indicators of water quality because they differ in their sensitivity to stress in the waterway. Some benthic macroinvertebrates are very sensitive to pollutants in the water. Others are less sensitive to pollution and can be found in almost any stream. Benthic macroinvertebrates usually live in the same area of a stream for most of their lives. Sampling these macroinvertebrates in a stream is a good indication of what the water quality has been for the past few months. If the water quality is generally poor, or if a polluting event occurred within the past several months, it will be reflected in the macroinvertebrate population.

The Save Our Streams program identifies three groups of macroinvertebrate taxa based on their sensitivity to pollution: pollution sensitive, somewhat pollution tolerant and pollution tolerant. The Save Our Streams method involves collecting a sample of macroinvertebrates from the stream, identifying the organisms and rating the water quality. Water quality ratings of excellent, good, fair and poor are based on the tolerance levels of the organisms found and the diversity of organisms in the sample. A stream with excellent water quality should support organisms from all three pollution tolerance groups.

NOTE

The information in the last section of this chapter was excerpted with permission from the Izaak Walton League of America's website (http://www.iwla.org/sos) under the *Save Our Steams* link.

CHAPTER 26

Greensburg and Other Cities Establish Eco-Districts

Johanna Brickman

With the emergence of carbon neutrality as a rapidly approaching target for many communities, paired with evidence that now-occupied green buildings are not consistently demonstrating significant energy performance improvements, eyes are opening to a new approach: an approach that views buildings not as individual entities but as interconnected structures capable of producing and sharing resources such as water and energy. Enter eco-districts, a visioning and investment strategy to manage growth and development in major redevelopment areas and existing neighborhoods. The objective is to test, accelerate, and establish the next generation of best practices in green development and civic infrastructure that can be scaled to create areas with low environmental impact and high economic and social resiliency.

The problem is that a building-by-building approach has long ruled, with individual structures viewed separately for certification, even in campus settings with contiguous ownership. For a variety of reasons — whether cost, complexity, or political will — it has been a challenge to engage the industry in an effort to look at the larger whole in any substantive way. The key is to set and pursue sustainability goals in shared and connective efforts at the neighborhood, district, or campus scale. It is only through such interconnectedness that a truly self-sufficient design will be possible in an economically viable and socially equitable manner.

As is so often the case, nature provides a blueprint of what an interconnected system of buildings might look like. In an ecosystem, all plants, animals, and microorganisms in an area function together with the nonliving physical factors of the environment, to create a unit of interdependent organisms that share the same habitat. According to the author of Biomimicry, Janine Benyus, in the case of mature forests, this interconnectedness manifests itself in canopy trees sharing CO_2 underground with the root systems of shaded undergrowth, or plants using roots of differing depth to store and share water as needed seasonally.

Similarly, buildings can be viewed together as an eco-district, creating a system in which the whole is able to outperform the individual. An eco-district, explains Rob Bennett, founding executive director of the Portland + Oregon Sustainability Institute and a former policy manager for the Clinton Climate Initiative, is "a neighborhood that generates all its energy from on-site renewables, collects and recycles rainwater and waste, and prioritizes pedestrian, bike, and transit access. It combines mixed-use, mixed-income development; neighborhood-scale parks; schools, community centers, and services; and enhanced IT infrastructure." In

Originally published as "Renewable Neighborhoods," *Urban Land*, Vol. 69, No. 1/2, January/February 2010, by the Urban Land Institute, Washington, D.C. Reprinted with permission of the publisher.

many respects, eco-districts can be viewed as the next iteration of the urban renewal districts that are now so common in many American communities.

Examples of such neighborhoods include the Pearl District in Portland, Oregon; LoDo (Lower Downtown) in Denver, and City Creek in Salt Lake City. Urban renewal efforts in these neighborhoods have spawned a slew of Leadership in Energy and Environmental Design (LEED)–certified mixed-use buildings and other positive developments, including expanded retail opportunities, new mass transit, and the development of parks and cultural venues. However, these neighborhoods do not yet produce their own power or treat their water in a closed loop. Eco-districts intend to do just that — leveraging new technology and research as well as growing political and economic will to push the boundaries of sustainable design.

One example of a community-scaled approach to sustainable design is Greensburg, Kansas, a town that was all but destroyed by a category 5 tornado in 2007. After the tornado, the city council passed a resolution stating that all municipal buildings would be built to LEED Platinum standards, making it the first municipality in America to do so. This foresight led Greensburg to be one of the few places where "starting over"— however unfortunate the circumstances that prompted it — became an opportunity to envision and make manifest a new future.

For existing communities, eco-districts provide a similar opportunity to improve the performance of shared services and infrastructure and offer an otherwise unfeasible degree of performance for the buildings within the district. Eco-districts are being considered in a variety of contexts, from college campuses to medical centers to dense urban neighborhoods. In many cases, a single building project has served as the catalyst for exploring a systemic approach to sustainable design.

In Portland, Oregon, for instance, the development of a hotel adjacent to the city's convention center ignited the exploration of transforming the surrounding Lloyd District into an eco-district. The neighborhood is home to a variety of development: commercial office, multifamily housing, two sports stadiums, limited greenways, and a number of public transportation options including light rail, bus, and streetcar. This variety leads to opportunities to trade resources between properties and occupancies, with synergies to be found between the demands and wastes of each.

The state of Oregon and the city of Portland have created entities to help foster both cross-jurisdictional development efforts and broader sustainable initiatives. For example, Oregon Solutions was formed to help address issues that require collaborative community governance, including efforts like eco-districts that require buy-in from governments, private landowners, developers, and business — transcending political boundaries for shared benefit.

The hope is that eco-districts will fuel further economic and physical renewal, coupled with true environmental benefits, including the following:

Improved Waste Management: reducing landfill volumes and minimizing waste collection by using waste to generate electricity and heat and contribute valuable nutrients.

Reduced Carbon Footprint: district thermal systems minimize distributed use of natural gas to generate heating and cooling; decreased vehicle miles traveled due to 24/7 uses and services in the district with inter-modal transit; increased vegetation and wetland conditions sequester more CO_2 from the atmosphere.

Energy Efficiency: reduced energy consumption achieves cost savings for district occupants; renewable energy used effectively to meet limited loads.

Water Efficiency: drinking water not used for any use for which potable water is not required.

Stormwater Management and Pollution Reduction: 100 percent of stormwater filtered within the district, and either reused or infiltrated so as to recharge natural waterways and aquifers; wastewater treated 100 percent within the district, eliminating spills of untreated sewage to waterways.

Habitat: open space planted with plant species providing shelter and food for avian and riparian species; creating connections across the district via habitat corridors to natural areas.

Many municipalities and organizations are now mandating carbon neutrality. But it is not possible unless the built environment as a whole contributes to the solution. Available technology simply will not allow all individual buildings in a city to support themselves completely in a cost-effective manner. While further research and development on the individual building level will likely improve results, these efforts need to be coupled with systemic approaches to sustainable design.

Eco-districts provide a framework for such an approach and, in many communities, policies are leading to their consideration and adoption. What such a district will look like, or how exactly it will operate, is still being debated and considered on a case-by-case basis. What is more certain is that such districts are critical to achieving significant environmental change in the built environment.

Components of Eco-Districts

The following paragraphs highlight the typical, and most common, components of Eco-Districts.

On-Site Energy Generation. On-site renewable energy generation has, to date, proven to be a significant hurdle to achieving carbon-neutral design, especially in dense urban environments where surface area constraints limit effective solar collection and urban wind energy generation is not yet viable. In light of these constraints architects and engineers have begun to look to alternative power-generation resources, including food waste.

Food waste constitutes a land use burden and results in greenhouse gas emissions. With the dense concentration of restaurants, residences, and offices in cities, food waste represents both an available and a relatively easy waste stream to source, separate, and use on site. As a result, many proposals for eco-districts have included waste-to-energy as part of an integrated system, whereby technology could capture either food waste in an anaerobic digestion cogeneration system or all municipal solid waste in a biogasification system to produce both electricity and heat.

Both systems operate on the same principle, whereby microorganisms break down biodegradable material in the absence of oxygen, producing both methane and carbon dioxide-rich biogas suitable for energy production. That energy, in turn, would be distributed throughout the eco-district via a smart grid, a system capable of not only augmenting the electricity produced via biogasification with electricity generated by privately owned or third party-owned photovoltaics, but, a system that can also respond to varying user demand.

Of note, the biogasification system significantly reduces the volume and mass of the input materials, and the remaining solids (at least from anaerobic digestion) can be used as a nutrient-rich fertilizer, greatly reducing transportation needs and landfill waste.

District Thermal Energy. Waste heat generated by the composting and energy generation processes is also of use. Captured as an energy source, that heat can be used to generate hot water for the district, which in turn could be used in heat pumps throughout the eco-district. Depending upon the demands of the district, heat transfer could be achieved for cooling as well through district chilled water.

Alternatively, an ambient loop could serve as either a heat source or heat sink, and additional heat could also be generated either via solar thermal panels or via waste heat mined from the sewer treatment process.

On-site wastewater treatment. To date, on-site wastewater treatment has proven to be expensive and ineffective, requiring both significant initial investments and high maintenance costs to produce more treated, nonpotable water than most buildings create demand for.

An eco-district, however, makes on site wastewater treatment scalable, spreading the cost of the system across more users and using treated water for more uses. For example, excess nonpotable water generated by the treatment facility could be used for functions such as park irrigation or facilities that do not themselves generate sufficient volumes of wastewater to be self-sufficient Moreover, by using just one or two systems for wastewater treatment, an eco-district also significantly reduces the energy necessary to support the pumping and redistribution of water, thus reducing energy demand.

Eco-districts also help address water quality and water quantity with respect to runoff, issues that are especially challenging in dense urban environments that have large, impervious developed areas and significant pollution challenges.

Green infrastructure makes sense for tackling both problems. Codes and policies that encourage green roofs, pervious landscape, and on-site reuse and/or infiltration work hand in hand with strategies to distribute the filtration burden for street runoff to green streets. With stormwater reuse, a similar benefit could be achieved by sharing the cost of storage, filtration, and pumping over a wide swath of occupants while maintaining the efficiency of providing such services to a smaller area.

In fact, there is already precedent for seeking to control water pollution and for placing the burden on developers to minimize pollutant contributions to waterways. An eco-district would simply make meeting those targets easier by providing the tools necessary to store and clean the water used in the development before it is infiltrated, reused or returned to rivers. Moreover, in communities facing water rights challenges, it is important to note that while the water used in an eco-district is used more than once, it does ultimately return to the water table or waterways, preserving downstream flow. The goal is to use water efficiently and less frequently, not prevent it from flowing.

Transportation. Transportation accounts for 30.2 percent of the carbon emissions of a conventional existing building, and 137 percent of a structure designed to meet ASHRAE 90.1-2004, but locating green edifices in dense, urban locations where residents can access a variety of services within close proximity reduces those transportation impacts significantly.

As a result, it follows that any eco-district needs to provide for a divers mix of uses, and ideally it would also support a strong intermodal transportation system that links pedestrian, bicycle, bus, streetcar, and/or light rail to achieve ease of transportation within the district.

Community. The same business/user diversity that reduces the need for transportation also tends to support a socially diverse community with workforce housing and places for all residents to gather and share community space. Without this physical manifestation of community, residents are either not attracted to living in the district, or they are driven to leave their neighborhood to visit places that provide those needs. Ultimately, any district is viable only when social systems are supported and vibrant — and that is what drives successful development and the ongoing improvement of shared systems.

CHAPTER 27

Hartford Encourages
Neighborhood Gardens

Theresa Barger

For three years, at the end of her day working as a mental health counselor, Nicola Allen would go driving through suburban neighborhoods rather than head immediately home to Burton Street in Hartford's North End.

"I just drove around because I hated to come home," she said. Drug dealers roamed her street, residents kept to themselves and people littered with impunity.

She tried talking her husband, Aldwin Allen, into moving to the suburbs. But the young couple who grew up in Hartford had agreed to live in the city for 20 years and try to improve it.

He suggested she find a way to fix what she didn't like. She began to notice that the historic homes on Burton Street had much of the same architectural detailing and character as the suburban homes.

She said she thought to herself, "It's not the houses; it's the people." Suburban home-owners took pride in their homes and land-scapes. She decided to make her property look more like the landscapes she admired.

In the beginning, Allen didn't know a pansy from a petunia.

She bought two gardening books and haunted garden shops, not buying, at first, but asking endless questions. When she saw some-thing she liked in a suburban garden, she'd try to figure out what it was in her book or at the garden store.

It took her about six years of planting, she said, before her garden looked good. She moved burning bushes from the front to the side prop-erty line. She added daffodils, rhododendrons, hyacinths, an ornamental pear tree, day lilies, purple asters, salvia, alliums, azaleas, tulips and roses.

Once her plants were established three years ago, she and her husband decided to take down the chain-link fence in front of their house.

"People came from across the street and told me I was nuts," she said. People will steal the plants, they warned.

"I said, 'I don't think they will.' Everyone on the street said, 'You don't know where you live.'"

The fences trapped litter and created bar-riers.

"There are lovely people living on this street," Allen said. "The homes here, the people here don't match the reputation of here.... My neighbor made soup for me every time I had a baby."

Since removing her fence, Allen, 37, has persuaded many of her neighbors to take their fences down, too, and they've planted or allowed her to plant flowers, shrubs and ornamental trees in their yards. She and her husband, who have lived on Burton Street for 12 years, have three children, ages 8, 6 and 4. Allen gave up her job when their first child was born but always made time for gardening.

One year, she spent $182 to buy 12,740 bulbs on clearance, which she planted throughout the neighborhood. She has planted 20 gardens on Burton and Sigourney streets and helped more than 20 homeowners in other city neighborhoods and at her children's school. The owner of three apartment buildings on Homestead Avenue hired her to plant gardens there.

On Burton Street, the gardens of six houses in a row are now unobstructed by fences. The Allens bought one of those houses as an investment property so they could take down the fence.

"Buying houses wasn't in the plan, but we believe in what we're doing," Allen said. By making the house look good inside and out, she said, they've been able to attract desirable tenants. "You're able to change a street by having the right people in a home."

Allen refuses to plant a garden at any home with a fence. One neighbor said she'd like a garden but wouldn't take down her fence. So Allen planted roses in abundance in the yard across the street.

The following year, the neighbor took out her fence, and together with Allen, they planted a garden full of roses. They also removed two rows of tall hedges bordering a walkway, and the following spring, long-dormant tulips broke through the soil.

Strangers Become Friends

Early on, the Allens held block meetings on their porch, where neighbors who had lived near each other for more than 30 years met for the first time.

"We didn't know each other, and we've become good friends," Frances Skeete said of another retired widow on her block.

Later, the Allens organized a neighborhood painting party. Friends, neighbors, and volunteers from the Village for Families and Children — where Aldwin Allen works as senior director of community programs — painted Skeete's Victorian house, next door to the Allens. (Grant money from the city's former Rising Star Pride Blocks program paid for the paint.) Some neighbors brought ladders. Another brought coffee and doughnuts. Some who couldn't paint stopped by to offer encouragement.

Rod Powell lived in a three-family house he owns on neighboring Magnolia Street for 19 years before moving to West Hartford three years ago.

"I have seen Burton Street go from what was without question the roughest street in the North End because of the drug sales — 10 years ago — to what now is actually a model street of how streets could be," Powell said. The area used to be so drug-infested that the cops were usually on the street five or six times a day, he said.

The transformation wasn't immediate or easy. The neighborhood received a $10,000 grant for plants through the Pride Blocks program, and after convincing skeptical neighbors that there were no strings attached, Nicola Allen used the money to buy shrubs, trees, bulbs and perennials for them.

Over the years, the Allens have bought three investment houses on the street, renovated them, rented them out and planted gardens.

But there have been some steps back along the way.

Some of the children have no experience with flowers. One tenant's kids cut two boltonias that were about to bloom and shredded the buds to pieces, and they cut a silver king euonymus down to the ground.

"I was so hurt, I literally felt like crying," Allen said. "I said to my husband, 'Why am I living here? I could be playing with my children.'"

He reminded her of their 20-year commitment. "If it wasn't for my husband, I would have quit."

Weeding at Midnight

Allen's mother-in-law, who lives one street over on Magnolia Street, was her first teacher.

Allen's in-laws grow geraniums in pots on their balcony and front steps each year but didn't have the variety of perennials that their son and daughter-in-law had amassed.

"As I started to do the planting, they wanted to sell their house on Sigourney and buy here. I said, 'What we need is for you to anchor your street.' 'I'll plant a garden there,'" Nicola Allen said. Now, from April to November, there is always something blooming in her in-laws' front gardens. Allen made a point of creating flower beds close to the sidewalk to catch the eye of passers-by.

"I couldn't do the garden because of my back," mother-in-law Sarah Allen said. "She planted, and she toiled. I looked out at 12 at night; Nicky was down in the garden."

Another time when Nicola Allen was out working in her in-laws' garden, a neighbor stopped by and said, "I'm going to take my fence down." She asked Allen to help her plant a garden at her home on Magnolia Street, and the gardens continued to spread.

Allen says sowing gardens has reaped friendships, not just for her but among many of the neighbors. "We all share with each other," she said. "Giving, you get back."

When she walks down her street, nearly everyone passing on foot or in a car says hello, and several neighbors credit her with being the catalyst to turning their street into an oasis. "I am more than blessed to have them as my neighbor," Skeete said. "She is truly a neighbor in every sense of the word."

CHAPTER 28

Huntersville Revises Its Zoning Laws to Control Growth

Tucker Mitchell

A little less than 10 years ago, the sleepy burg of Huntersville, North Carolina, looked up and saw them coming. "They" were the developers of the booming city of Charlotte, 15 miles to the south.

Having cleared, graded, and covered most of Mecklenburg County, the boys were headed north along Interstate 77 to the rolling fields and pristine woods of Huntersville. It was a scary sight, so the Huntersvillians sounded the alarm.

"We didn't want to get run over by that sprawl everybody talks about," says Randy Quillen, who finished four terms as the town's mayor in November. "We had to do something."

The town did. In 1994 it placed a one-year moratorium on new construction, and used that breathing space to completely rewrite its zoning ordinance. Out went the conventional standards in use since before World War II. In came a one-of-a-kind, cul-de-sac-killing code that embraced the design-oriented principles of New Urbanism and Traditional Neighborhood Development.

Because Huntersville swallowed these principles whole, the new code forced local developers to retool their building machines. However, the town put enough options into the code to avoid legal problems, and the politi-cians of the time were solidly behind the concept. The new code passed in 1996.

Mixed Bag, Not Mixed Use

Smart growth was begun. The town was saved! At least that's what folks thought at the time. Five years later, the view is not as certain or sanguine. The code, written from scratch by former town planner Ann Hammond and David Walters of the College of Architecture at the University of North Carolina–Charlotte, has revealed a loophole or two.

Thanks to the code, the town almost certainly will have a well-connected street grid, says the town's new planning director, Jack Simoneaux. And there are several promising projects under way, including a residential development called Vermillion — acclaimed by New Urbanist organizations and the Sierra Club — and Birkdale Village, a mixed-use "town center" where apartments, stores, a movie theater, and restaurants come together in an architectural mix that conjures up images of a New England fishing village or perhaps a Hollywood set.

The growing legion of Huntersvillians — the town grew from 4,000 to 30,000 in the 1990s, and is expected to top 60,000 before the next decade is through — have a considerably

Originally published as "Going Whole Hog for New Urbanism," *Planning*, Vol. 68, No. 2, February 2002, by the American Planning Association, Chicago, IL. Reprinted with permission of the publisher.

wider range of housing and lifestyle choices than they did before. But being adaptable, the development community quickly figured out how to navigate the new regulations, and there are plenty of anomalies. Development is still haphazard in the ever-growing town, and, aside from the road network, it's still a disconnected mish-mash that may or may not produce a cohesive urban structure some day.

What's more, having figured out what will be approved — and what will sell — builders are creating copycat projects across the booming Huntersville market. The town is awash in a sea of narrow, bungalow-lined streets interspersed with the odd row of townhouses.

They're all the same," says ex-mayor Quillen. "What we really need now are some good old-fashioned cul-de-sac neighborhoods, just to break up the monotony."

Kim Phillips, the town's newly elected mayor and a town commissioner when the code was put in place, adds this: "I'm not sure this came out exactly the way we intended. In fact, I'm pretty sure it did not."

Although the majority of the newly elected board sides with Phillips in favor of the new code and its original, growth-controlling intent, Phillips says a review and revamping of the code is on the agenda in the year ahead. Some "tweaking" is in order, she says.

The Time Is Ripe

At first, developers predicted the Huntersville sky would fall. The town's growth would grind to a halt, they warned, as they turned to other, friendlier climes.

Reality has not matched the predictions. Since the code went into effect, plans that would bring more than 8,500 new housing units into Huntersville — double the number on hand when the code was installed — have been approved, along with four major shopping centers and assorted other development. "It's a good thing the code slowed them down," planning director Jack Simoneaux says tongue in cheek.

All the developers say that the new codes are more difficult to deal with, but they also say that the Huntersville market is too ripe to pass up. The town is on the edge of the prestigious "Lake area" — Duke Energy's Lake Norman, north of Charlotte. Huntersville isn't right on the lake, so it had to wait while some other communities boomed first. The creation of a new interstate exit, complete with a four-lane highway and a major commercial development, helped open up the Huntersville market beginning in 1997.

"It was just our time," says long-time Huntersville builder Roger Cathey. "We could have built shacks around here and done all right."

Tom Tucker, vice-president for Charlotte builder Robert Rhein Homes, more or less agrees. His company did the last major residential project approved before the new code went into place, a 900-home golf course community called Northstone, and recently opened MacAulay, a 600-plus residential community built to new code specifications.

"Huntersville is just a great location right now," says Tucker. "I'd rather do Northstone, which was a huge success for us. But we're doing well at MacAulay, too. We'll be out of there ahead of schedule. People are buying it."

Jim Burbank, president of Saussy-Burbank Homes, which has also developed projects under both codes, says, "I think our projects would have worked under either code. There are elements you have to rework, things you have to get used to, but it can be done."

On the other hand, Russell Ranson, a vice-president for the Crosland Companies Land Division, says the new code may not be as benign as some think. "The rules are more complex and the interpretations are more subjective, and it's more costly to develop," he says. "You're also cutting out part of the market. These homes with small yards in semi-urban settings have a certain appeal, but there remains a demographic out there that wants a big yard or a place to park three or four cars."

Ranson's company completed a 900-unit residential project in the late 1990s and set sales records there. It's a classic subdivision. And it's also home, he notes drily, to most of the commissioners who voted to install the new, anti-cul-de-sac codes.

Tom Low, principal in the Mecklenburg office of Duany Plater-Zybek, the Miami-based New Urbanist firm, marvels at the ability of developers to engineer around the code. He notes that some projects on Huntersville's west side have even used the more cost-effective slab (as opposed to crawl space) construction.

"The problem with slabs is that they put the [New Urbanist] porches down in a sort of hole, especially if there is any negative grade on the lot," says Low. "Basically, it just doesn't fit with the roads. But what [the builders have] done is simply drop the roads two-and-a-half feet. And it does work. Builders can be really brilliant. They've found a way to hit a different price point."

Room for Everyone?

On the down side, it appears that developers are taking advantage of every loophole they can find. A curious phenomenon in some new Huntersville subdivisions is the proliferation of lots that are 60.25 feet wide. Why such precision? The code requires lots of 60 feet or less to have a detached rear garage serviced by an alley. Above 60 feet and the garage can be a front loader.

Developers in the open space district — a planning designation that takes in most of the town's 60 square miles — also have gone to extremes. Clumps of trees and piles of rock allow a project to conform to the open space requirements (15 percent of every project must be open space, and open space must be within 1,300 feet of every building lot).

Jack Simoneaux thinks the original idea was to link up open space across developments, but he's not sure that will ever happen. Builder Jim Burbank says that the very strictures of the open space requirement prevent that from happening. They all but force clear cutting of tracts, he says, except when a site is almost perfectly flat.

Vermillion developer Nate Bowman, a New Urbanist purist, shakes his head at some of the silly designs the code has fostered." Okay, so you put in an alleyway or two and a couple of bungalows," says Bowman. "That does not make it a New Urbanist development."

Bowman's development has drawn some fire for its "high" density (4.5 units per acre) and its unusual design features. He has built small, two-story "doll houses" in several nooks of the neighborhood, and plans for five-story "tower houses" are in the works. But he brushes off his critics and questions their motives.

"People ought to be rooting for us," he says. "We're not saying you have to live here. But if everyone just does what they have been doing, we'll clog up all the roads, pollute the air, and make a real mess. Let us be a tourist attraction, but other than that, just leave us alone." Bowman's development drew more than 300 visitors last year, mostly planners and builders.

Dancing in the Parking Lots

If the housing of Huntersville has taken an unpredictable turn, just the opposite is true for prime commercial projects. Town planners and politicians are uniformly happy with the two largest projects now under way, Birkdale Village and the Rosedale-Market Square shopping centers on Gilead Road just west of I-77.

Birkdale Village, which is nearing completion, was designed as a town center for the immense Birkdale development on both sides of the newly created Sam Furr Road, Huntersville's new exit off I-77. On one side of the four-lane road is a large subdivision built around a golf course — it was approved just before the new code went into effect. On the other side is a mixture of apartments, condos, and single-family houses.

Trying to connect the two is Birkdale Village, with housing above the shops and a huge parking deck hidden inside two rectangles of multi-story buildings. It is an innovative project created by Charlotte development star Peter Pappas to take advantage of the new Huntersville code, rather than battle it. And it appears to be quite successful. David Ravin, a vice-president with the Crosland Companies, the actual developer of the project, says the "Main Street area had to be expanded to accommodate retailer demand.

"Everyone we showed the project to liked

it," says Ravin. "What surprised us is the amount of national retail that was interested." Among those already signed up: Starbucks, Gap Clothing, a national book retailer, and a high-end clothier.

Rosedale-Market Square is more conventional in appearance. Under the old code, it would have been a standard strip center, or centers. Under the new code it consists of several rectangles of low brick buildings with parking on the interior. Major grocery chains anchor both centers. Apartments, townhouses, and offices sit behind the two grocery stores. It is certainly less obtrusive than the standard strip center and echoes the brick wall of an upscale business park across the street.

Robert "Tex" Small, president of AvTex, Inc., the Greenville, South Carolina, firm that developed Market Square, the first of the two side-by-side projects, says working under the new code wasn't bad, but adds that his company was used as a "guinea pig." His biggest complaint is that town staff rejected certain features, then turned around and permitted the same features at the Rosedale center next door.

Ravin says he encountered similar problems at Birkdale Village, but notes that the town worked to find creative solutions. "We don't like the fact that some buildings wound up with four front doors," says Ravin. "And it was hard work. We spent three years on design. But we understood from the start this was something new. We think it's going to turn out to be an excellent project."

A Good Start

Although opinions on Huntersville's code vary widely, the consensus is that it was a fairly good idea. Most of the new projects are attractive and have higher design values than conventional work in neighboring jurisdictions, transportation has been enhanced by the connected street grid, and the town's boom has continued unabated.

The new town board will almost certainly direct staff to review and revamp the code sometime soon. And there are lots of opinions about what to change. Town politicians are worried about open space and copycat designs. Builders would like more of the code set in stone. Other interested parties want to see the code tilted even more towards New Urbanism.

For his part, Simoneaux thinks the key points are the road grid in the open space area, the possibilities offered for high density (not yet tested, he says), and a general discussion of open space.

"The challenges," says Simoneaux, "will be getting a variety of housing choices, across the price spectrum. If we can do that and preserve some open space, we'll have done well because a lot of good things are already in place. Believe me, there are a lot of places that wish they'd done what was done here."

Resources

Here are Huntersville's basic planning policies:

- Growth is coming. The town must guide the development in a sustainable and efficient way.
- Each new development should be viewed in a larger context.
- There are economic as well as aesthetic reasons for adopting traditional town planning.
- Streets are the building blocks of the community.
- Higher density development will be concentrated near highways and rail lines.
- Huntersville should be a distinct and beautiful community.

Find out more about the Huntersville planning philosophy at www.huntersville.org/planning/philos.htm.

Read more about Huntersville planning by visiting http://www.huntersville.org and clicking on "Town Planning."

CHAPTER 29

Ithaca and Other Cities
Diversify Their Urban Forests

Jill Mazullo

The stately American elm was once considered the perfect urban tree. We planted elms with abandon along our boulevards, shading our streets with their pleasing canopy. Until the 1970s, 90 percent of the street trees in Minneapolis were elms, with similarly high figures in many cities around the country.

Early horticulturalists preferred the elm for good reasons, wrote Frank Santamour of the U.S. National Arboretum in 1990 in the Proceedings of the 7th Conference of the Metropolitan Tree Improvement Alliance: their high, full canopy and their ability to tolerate the ravages of urban life, including root compaction, salt, smog, drought, heat, and cold. Our local identity was entwined with the stately trees, with Elm Street becoming one of the most popular street names in America.

But in 1930 a shipment of logs from France brought Dutch elm disease to the U.S. The fungus traveled through the roots of communities of elms, and the movement of firewood and the sale of infected trees spread the disease further. We had lost more than 77 million mature elm trees in the U.S. by the late 1990s.

Minneapolis and St. Paul mourned the loss of elms in the 1960s and 70s, and then turned to a few tree species that could survive boulevard life and shade the streets. One of the most popular of the replacement trees was the green ash. This year, the latest tree pest has arrived in our trees, our media, and our consciousness. The pest has been moving outward from the Great Lakes since its arrival in the 1990s, and last May evidence of the emerald ash borer was discovered in a St. Paul neighborhood.

The predictions are dire. Minnesota could potentially lose all of its ash trees in the next five to 10 years. The emerald ash borer can be stopped with an annual chemical treatment to each ash tree, but cities typically can't afford to treat every tree.

New Tactic

Are we learning from our mistakes? The answer is yes: Urban forests are slowly being diversified. Minneapolis and St. Paul, the largest cities in Minnesota, planted a variety of trees after the elms were devastated, 20 to 25 percent of them green ash.

Both cities have a policy of planting a diverse variety of trees across the city, but on a block-by-block basis. That's why we might live on an all-maple street, or all-ash, but the next block is likely to be all linden, hackberry, or some other species. The downside of the block-by-block diversity plan is that if a pest likes the

Originally published as "Diversifying the Urban Forest," *Planning*, Vol. 76, No. 2, February 2010, by the American Planning Association, Chicago, IL. Reprinted with permission of the publisher.

taste of your block's species, you might have to replace all the trees on your block at the same time.

"The irony is that from an urban forest management perspective, it's easier and more economical to cut down and replant a whole block of trees at one time," says Ralph Sievert, director of forestry for the Minneapolis Park and Recreation Board. "But it doesn't work best for the people who live there."

Minneapolis has found ways to balance economies of scale with emotional or aesthetic considerations by offering residents a choice of species when their boulevard tree is cut down due to disease or hazardous conditions. Recently a Minneapolis block of hold-out elms suddenly succumbed to Dutch elm disease. Sievert helped the home owners choose five different species for their boulevard; Princeton elm (a disease-resistant variety), gingko, American linden, Autumn Blaze maple, and Norway maple. This system will cost a little more to implement, but it will protect residents from a total loss in the future.

What's Diverse?

"Arguably, you could say Dutch elm disease gave rise to the urban forestry movement," says Nina Bassuk, Cornell University professor of urban horticulture. If monoculture is at one extreme, then total diversity is at the other. In a completely diverse system, every house would have a different tree species in front of it; one block with 25 street trees would boast 25 varieties.

So says Jacob Ryg, city forester in Rochester, Minnesota. But he acknowledges that the total diversity plan is merely an ideal; it's not realistic to think a community would embrace such variety. While total diversity would ensure minimal losses on any given street, it is rarely a popular option among residents.

"People like uniformity," says Gary Johnson, professor of forest resources at the University of Minnesota. "Many think a mix of tree species on the same street is chaotic. Tall trees, short trees, fat trees: They may add up to a healthier mix, but it's not acceptable to residents."

Johnson says a colleague made the observation that managing an urban forest is not based on what is scientifically appropriate, but what is politically acceptable. Although arborists know about the benefits of diversity, they haven't always been successful at conveying that message to residents.

Johnson and landscape architect Ken Simons wrote *The Road to a Thoughtful Street Tree Master Plan*, a 100-page manual geared toward communities planning their street tree infrastructure. The manual hews to the accepted guideline of allowing no more than 10 percent of any one species of tree. It also promotes the block-by-block approach.

Frank Santamour of the National Arboretum believes that a fair approach to tree diversity is to plant no more than 10 percent of any one species in any given community, and no more than 20 percent of any genus. Cornell's Nina Bassuk would take that a little further; she says she prefers no more than five percent of any one species.

As chair of Ithaca's Shade Tree Advisory Committee, she has helped to broaden the spectrum of trees planted in her community, with a stunning 430 variants now represented there. She is also the coauthor of a study called "Visual Similarity and Biological Diversity," released in 2006, which encourages communities to consider shade characteristics, leaf shapes, and branching habits of potential tree species and to choose a mixture for their community.

Who Decides?

In larger cities, the parks department or the department of public works may maintain and plant the trees, but a city forester is likely to oversee the assessment of the tree stock in the urban forest, and that person is responsible for developing an appropriate plan for planting open spots, maintaining current trees, and replacing dead or dying trees. There is also likely to be a strong existing urban tree infrastructure.

In smaller cities, the public works department may oversee the urban forest without the benefit of a city forester, in addition to handling plowing and all other official duties. Ryg says the public works people are sometimes referred to as "tree morticians" because, lacking training in long-term tree care, they may remove good limbs or make other bad cuts, "taking a tree on a path to disaster down the road."

Newer subdivisions are often planted for a uniform look. The Minneapolis Star Tribune reported that new subdivisions in the Twin Cities are overplanting Autumn Blaze maple because it grows well where new sod is being watered, and it is readily available at nurseries. But heavy reliance on one species could spell trouble later.

Johnson encourages developers to first lay out a 10-tree palette, knowing that it will take five to 10 years to complete the plantings. While there may be only three trees to choose from at local nurseries in a given year, developers can draw up a contract with a nursery and establish a good working relationship. "Nurseries are hesitant to expand their palette, but with contracts in place for large deliveries, there's less risk," he says. "All the trees don't have to be planted at the same time."

There is no end to the opportunities to improve the urban forest. Bassuk occasionally takes a SWAT team — that is, a student weekend arborist team — to small upstate New York communities to plot out a town's trees with a global positioning system: "You can't plan unless you know what you have already," says Bassuk. She encourages small communities to contact their state's land grant school to see if similar resources exist, or to connect with their state's department of environmental conservation or urban forestry council.

WORKS CITED

Planning the Urban Forest: Ecology. Economy, and Community Development, Planning Advisory Report 555. American Planning Association, www.planning.org, 2010.

Nina Bassuk's "Visual Similarity and Biological Diversity" (2006) is available at www.hort.cornell.edu/uhi/outreach. She is coauthor of "Recommended Urban Trees: Site Assessment and Tree Selection for Stress Tolerance," published in 2009 by the Urban Horticulture Institute at Cornell University: http://www.hort.cornell.edu/uhi/out reach/recurbtree.

"The Road to a Thoughtful Street Tree Master Plan," by Ken Simons and Gary Johnson, is available from www. unri.org.

CHAPTER 30

Los Angeles and Other Cities Explore Measures to Reduce Air Pollution

Paul Tullis

As we approach the Grand Canyon from the south at 22,000 feet, the three 775-foot towers of the Navajo Generating Station loom from the horizon. The stacks, which have been spewing smoke almost constantly since the plant opened in 1974, are among Arizona's tallest structures. The copilot says that the first thing passengers usually notice is Lake Powell, the shrinking 254-square-mile reservoir from which Navajo draws 8 billion gallons of water a year for cooling. But when the light is right and the sky is clear, this mammoth coal-fired power plant on the Navajo Nation rivals one of the most significant geologic features on the face of the earth.

Navajo's smokestacks spew mercury, sulfur dioxide, nitrous oxide, and other substances that poison rivers and crops and developing fetuses throughout the Four Corners region. Threatening the entire globe, however, are the 20 million tons of carbon dioxide they pump into the atmosphere each year — equivalent to the emissions from 3 million cars. That makes Navajo the nation's fifth-largest power plant source of the greenhouse gas. The CO_2 is the inevitable byproduct of burning coal to generate enough electricity for 2 million homes. Twenty-one percent of that electricity is transmitted via 500-kilovolt wires to Los Angeles, 430 miles to the west

L.A. mayor Antonio Villaraigosa vows to change all that. As a member of California's state assembly in the 1990s, Villaraigosa had a commendable environmental record, but global warming didn't really hit home for him until May 2007, the year L.A.'s Griffith Park — one of the largest urban parks in the country — burned for three days at the end of Southern California's rainy season. "Los Angeles was undeniably feeling the impact of climate change," the mayor said. "That was my 'Aha!' moment." (Climate-change models predict increased wildfires in semiarid areas.) So last year, in his second inaugural address, Villaraigosa announced that by 2020 Angelenos would "permanently break our addiction to coal."

At the time, Los Angeles got 8 percent of its electricity from renewable sources and 42 percent from coal — not only from Navajo but from the Intermountain Generating Station in Utah as well. If all goes according to plan, sometime in 2010 the city's proportion of renewable power will grow to 20 percent. Villaraigosa has committed to boosting that number to 40 percent by 2020 and to 60 percent by 2030. This mandate has set the Los Angeles Department of Water and Power (DWP) racing to find more energy from renewables for its nearly 4 million customers.

Villaraigosa's quest raises a striking possi-

Originally published as "The West Without Coal," *Sierra Magazine,* January/February 2010, by the Sierra Club, San Francisco, CA. Article appears with the permission of *Sierra,* the national magazine of the Sierra Club.

bility: Through a combination of geographical accident, citizen activism, and political leadership, the Pacific coast states could wean themselves from coal. The coastal cities in particular are intent on establishing a modern vision of "ecotopia." Already, Seattle gets less than 1 percent of its power from coal and recently sold its ownership interest in a coal plant; its new mayor, Mike McGinn, is the former chair of the Sierra Club's Cascade Chapter and an activist in the Club's Cool Cities program who made it a point to bicycle to campaign events. Portland, Oregon, has a draft "climate action plan" that calls for reducing carbon emissions by 80 percent from 1990 levels by 2050.

To that end, Mayor Sam Adams has called on Portland General Electric (PGE), one of two utilities serving the city, to phase out coal. The other major Oregon utility, Pacific Power, has had a moratorium on power from new coal-fired plants for the last two years. Pacific Gas and Electric Company, which serves 15 million people in the San Francisco Bay Area and throughout northern and central California, is snatching up power-purchase agreements from solar farms before they're even built. San Diego Gas and Electric Company, which serves 3.4 million people, gets half as much coal power today as it did five years ago and says it doesn't plan to renew its last coal contract, which expires in 2013.

Then there's Los Angeles. "We've got an influential and high-profile city and leadership, the nation's largest municipal utility, and some of the most ambitious goals anywhere for transforming our energy supply," said Martin Schlageter, campaign director for the Coalition for Clean Air, a statewide advocacy group. But should L.A. stumble, he warned, everyone will say, "That's what happens when you set ambitious goals," instead of, "If you can put the second-largest city in the country on the path toward a more sustainable future, then I guess we can do it too."

Some may view L.A.'s efforts as ironic, and therefore its commitment as suspect. Los Angeles, after all, is the birthplace of sprawl and smog, the thief that stole water from the Owens River for its burgeoning suburbs, the butt of many a New Yorker's jokes. Yet despite its rep-

utation for shallowness, Los Angeles is leading the fight against global warming. One of its congressional representatives, Henry Waxman, shepherded climate-change legislation through the U.S. House. It has the highest recycling rate (65 percent) of the nation's largest cities and is home to a remarkably successful coalition of wilderness preservationists and green-energy champions.

Among these is David Freeman, recently named — for the second time in his long career — head of L.A.'s fabled Department of Water and Power. Now 83, Freeman has been at the center of U.S. energy policy since before the United States had an energy policy. He drafted the first speech on energy delivered by a president to Congress (for Richard Nixon, in 1971) and was instrumental in establishing the EPA and passing the Clean Air and Clean Water Acts. When he headed the DWP from 1997 to 2001, the agency sold its interest in the coal-burning Mojave Generating Station, near Laughlin, Nevada. Freeman ruefully told me how his successor bought it back — only to see the $90 million investment evaporate after a judge ordered the plant closed for violating the Clean Air Act 40,000 times in less than a decade.

When I met Freeman at his City Hall office, it was 91 degrees outside, and L.A. was pulling down 5,382 megawatts of power. (The department's all-time high is 6,102 megawatts, an amount greater than the total electrical generating capacity of Nigeria.) In an effort to lower that number, Freeman has overseen the distribution of 1.4 million compact fluorescent bulbs to DWP customers and converted 140,000 streetlights, as well as every traffic light in the city, to low-power light-emitting diodes (LEDs).

But efficiency measures will only take you so far, and L.A. is urgently seeking renewable-energy sources. Freeman noted that his boss. Mayor Villaraigosa, is "determined that we get things sufficiently in place or under construction so that by the end of his term [in 2013] no one can reverse it." Freeman's portfolio includes the new Pine Tree wind farm in the Mojave Desert (its 120 megawatts from 80 General Electric turbines make it the largest city-owned wind farm in the country); a facility in Playa del Rey that extracts methane from sewage and turns it into energy; and a 400-megawatt geothermal project near the Salton Sea, a barren lake 130 miles southeast of the city. "We're cooking a lot of meals in the kitchen that we're just not ready to talk about yet," Freeman said, promising a major announcement by the end of 2009. "We have a lot of big ideas."

One thing he is ready to talk about is a plan to take advantage of Los Angeles' 276 annual days of sunshine. In the late '90s, Freeman put into place a rebate program that absorbs about half the installation price for home solar arrays. But even with government tax credits piled onto the rebate, solar has never contributed more than 2 percent to L.A.'s energy mix. Freeman plans to dramatically increase that figure, in part by selling the concept to ordinary citizens at workshops like the one I attended near my house in Los Feliz.

A crowd of 100 listened as moderator Randy Howard described plans to build new solar arrays in the desert, buy power from solar farms, and help pay for homes and businesses to put panels on their roofs. Even renters and the less well-capitalized will be able to purchase "virtual" solar panels through a program dubbed SunShares, so they can get in on the fun. The solar initiatives are going to be expensive, but, as Howard pointed out, when you're building renewables facilities, you're essentially buying 30 or 40 years' worth of fuel, so the cost is all on the front end.

"We've taken polls," Freeman told me a few days later. "People are willing to see their health bill reduced while their energy bill goes up a little. They understand the connection."

Whatever solar and other renewables projects Freeman is or isn't able to bring on line, his Department of Water and Power owns no coal plants. Should L.A. cancel its coal-power contracts, the plants' energy may well be sold elsewhere. But in the Pacific Northwest, another strategy is taking shape: to shut down the coal plants altogether.

In Portland, this strategy is unfolding on two fronts: promoting alternatives and ratcheting up the cost of business as usual. Straddling both is Bruce Nilles, director of the Sierra Club's Beyond Coal Campaign, which since 2005 has succeeded in closing or canceling plans for 107 existing or proposed coal-fired plants.

"The Northwest and California are two places where coal has never had to defend itself," chiefly because coal is not mined there, Nilles said. "People have never had to ask, 'Do we want coal here?'" Nilles and I spoke at the Club's Portland office, halfway between a medical marijuana dispensary and a worker-owned bicycle shop. Afterward, in a highly unscientific survey at the Citybikes co-op, Portland's most committed fossil-fuel shunners were asked where the city gets its electricity. Coal was cited only once. In fact, the 585-megawatt Boardman coal plant, 160 miles to the east in the Columbia River Gorge, is the source of 15 percent of Portland's power; other coal plants provide an additional 25 percent.

In a city as proud of its light rail and smart-growth policy as Portland, that should be a point of shame. And to people like Michael Armstrong, the city's senior sustainability manager, it is. As his title suggests, Armstrong focuses on promoting alternative energy and conservation. We met in his boss's conference room overlooking the stormwater-filtering green roof of the newly constructed Cyan/PDX apartments and the green office building at 200 Market Street, which just switched out its conventional lightbulbs for LEDs. Just out of sight is an office building partly powered by windmills. Armstrong is under orders to dramatically reduce Portland's energy consumption, and it's happening all around us.

"What we want to put ourselves on the hook for," he said, "is to reduce energy use such that we don't need that coal. If we can reduce by 40 percent, we can have a viable conversation about shutting that coal plant down."

Finding that efficiency is Armstrong's Job. He described a program his Bureau of Planning and Sustainability runs in conjunction with Green for All (a national group working to build a green economy) that retrofits older homes in the city for energy efficiency. Paid for in part by federal stimulus dollars, the 500-home pilot program upgrades insulation, windows, and other features. The cost is tacked on to the utility bill but spread out over 15 years;

the energy savings typically mean the net cost doesn't go up even with the extra charge. The program, coming at a time when the housing and credit markets are reeling, has proved popular beyond the usual crunchy crowd.

"It used to be that the energy nerds came to the table to talk about what kind of incentives we could offer to get people to switch out their lightbulbs," Armstrong said. "Now the unions are at the table saying, 'Put my people to work — we want to save energy too.' Everybody sees this as the model, and we've got 100,000 homes that need insulation. That's the kind of scale where we can have a serious conversation about attaining 40 percent [energy savings]" — and getting off coal.

The second front against the plant is a legal one — to make utilities pay the full cost of coal power. As is, Boardman makes electricity at about two cents per kilowatt-hour, an incredibly cheap rate. The strategy is being executed by Aubrey Baldwin, a lawyer with the Pacific Environmental Advocacy Center at Lewis and Clark College's law school, which filed a complaint in federal court against Portland General Electric for allegedly violating the Clean Air Act at Boardman for many years.

"Boardman has had thousands of violations over five years, at $37,500 per violation," explained Baldwin over breakfast on a cool Portland morning last fall. PGE denies any violations. In addition, a Sierra Club analysis claims it would be cheaper for the utility to shut the plant than to spend the up to $600 million it would take for it to meet new federal emissions rules. Yet another potential cost, said Doug Howell of the Club's Beyond Coal Campaign, would be Boardman's "carbon liability" from the climate bill Congress ultimately passes. The House version, approved in June, prices carbon dioxide emissions at $20 per ton, which could put Boardman on the hook for $80 million annually. Put together, Howell said, these charges "dwarf the modest cost increase from getting rid of It." PGE could, of course, pass the costs on to ratepayers, but Oregon customers are accustomed to cheap electricity (about half what Angelenos pay), and PGE is legally required to provide power at the lowest possible rate.

PGE spokesperson Patrick Stupek hastened to point out that the utility has invested $1 billion in the 275-megawatt Biglow Canyon Wind Farm and is progressing toward a goal of having 25 percent renewables by 2025. But after modeling various planning options — including shutting the coal plant — he said, the utility concluded that "the portfolio that offers our customers the best mixture of cost and risk includes continued operation of Boardman with aggressive new emissions controls."

Getting off coal, said Stephanie Pincetl, director of the UCLA Urban Center for People and the Environment, "Is going to be really hard." Utilities like PGE and DWP are under a lot of constraints. Indeed, almost palpable in my discussions with utility representatives was frustration with the pressure they get from environmentalists who don't appreciate their obligations — paramount among which is providing nonstop power.

For example, said Art Sasse, spokesperson for Oregon's Pacific Power, "the wind doesn't blow all the time, and when it does, it tends to be during off-peak times. So if you're replacing coal with wind, you need to add natural gas." Gas from the best new plants has a carbon footprint about half that of coal, but the plants cost $200 million. In Los Angeles, a DWP commissioner, speaking anonymously, grimaced as he explained that his agency is "almost compelled to have natural gas" for reliability reasons. "The most important job we have, besides doing it safely, is to keep the lights on," he said.

In addition to the practical concerns, Pincetl said, "there's a whole set of political constraints." Environmentalists are keen to establish a new energy order, but they don't have a whole lot of allies. At the DWP solar workshop, for instance, the only other identifiable constituency was workers from the union halls who wanted to make sure they got in on the action of building all that solar infrastructure. But labor is far from unified on the issue. In March 2009 a bond measure for solar projects was defeated after other unions opposed the monopoly on jobs it would have given to the International Brotherhood of Electrical Workers. Getting the West off coal this decade is an enormous undertaking. It will require politicians following up on their lofty pronouncements; relentless, informed organizing by grassroots activists; constant legal pressure; and (two words not often seen together) bureaucratic creativity. But first, it may take L.A. to lead the way — which new DWP boss David Freeman is determined to do.

"I'm not in the habit of recommending things to my boss unless they can be done," he said. "We're going to be the agency that people point to and say, Yes — it can be done."

CHAPTER 31

Memphis and Other Cities Approve Sustainable Planning Guidelines

Joe McElroy

Roof-top gardens, permeable parking lots, organic farms — all fine ideas — and just a few of the techniques that enhance, modern master planned communities. But public-sector planners reviewing these large-scale developments must determine what's real and what's just hype. And when the words "green" and "sustainable" are used to tout everything from cars to carbon-neutral weddings to kitty litter, that's no small matter.

"Some developers really are doing better. Unfortunately, others are using the buzzwords but not really following the principles," says Robin Green, the aptly named developer of Hidden Creek at the Darby, a highly praised, 600-acre master planned community near Columbus, Ohio.

Do They Measure Up?

One way to evaluate today's proposals for tomorrow's master planned communities is through the prism of past success stories.

One example is The Woodlands, north of Houston. Designed by Ian McHarg, among others, The Woodlands has been an economic and environmental success, according to Frederick Steiner, dean of architecture and planning at the University of Texas in Austin.

"I haven't seen anything better," he says, pointing to the success of The Woodlands' drainage patterns and protection of environmental resources, which were inspired by McHarg's *Design with Nature*, first published in 1969.

Started in 1974 ,and now in its eighth phase, The Woodlands encompasses 28,000 acres. It is home to approximately 80,000 residents, who can enjoy its 108 forested parks and 150 miles of hiking and bike trails. The development's 1,300 businesses provide 40,000 jobs.

Today's developers echo McHarg's message of building within the parameters dictated by a site's natural features, that is, adjusting to the land instead of forcing the land to adjust to the developer's pro forma.

"Begin with the land; let the environment — including water, woods, and topography — show you where to put the road pattern and how to handle storm water drainage," advises Green. At Hidden Creek — where storm water is filtered through a series of wetlands — 230 acres along Little Darby Creek have been preserved in perpetuity.

The development's roads are also narrower than usual, although Green says that wasn't easy to achieve. "Anything that reduces the amount of impervious surface is good," she says, "but the typical zoning ordinance calls for roads that are often too wide."

Originally published as "Green is the New Granite," Planning, Vol. 73, No. 7, July 2007, by the American Planning Association, Chicago, IL. Reprinted with permission of the publisher.

Madison County, Ohio, ordinances called for 30-foot-wide roads with curbs and gutters. By working closely with the county to address concerns about drainage, layout, and other issues, Green eventually was allowed to build curving 18-foot-wide roads that flow with the land, not to mention 12-foot cul-de-sacs with green space in the middle. She also convinced fire department and school officials that their vehicles could navigate the narrow roads.

Green, former executive director of the Ohio Chapter of The Nature Conservancy, also notes that developers who truly want to do sustainable development — and the planners who encourage them — must learn how to respond to skeptics.

Hidden Creek is now well accepted, but early on, she says, "I used to joke that the word 'no' was the starting point for most of my negotiations." She says she would respond by "taking apart what their reason is for the 'no'" and then arguing out the best way to protect the environment, with both sides still getting most of what they want.

Roadblocks

In an economy where managers often are hired and fired based upon quarterly earnings reports, it can be difficult to obtain financing for sustainable developments, which tend to start slowly but build momentum over time.

Christopher Leinberger, a developer who now leads the real estate program at the University of Michigan, views compact, walkable development as a form of sustainability. He notes that neither Harbor Town in Memphis nor Seaside in the Florida Panhandle — both new urbanist meccas — set the world on fire when lot sales began in 1984. In fact, the developer sold just 20 lots, at $15,000 each, during the first two years.

"However, when a fully built out, human-scale street system emerged, potential buyers could see the value of what was being created," Leinberger says. By 2000, lots were fetching well over $1 million, according to Leinberger.

Investors and developers also worry about the potential for excessive construction costs if they go green. "Sometimes people assume it's expensive to do sustainable development," says Robin Green. "But it's really not, because moving dirt is one of the most expensive things developers do. They could save money if they would lay out their roads and drainage systems to fit with the land."

Green and Urban

Many developers complain that typical post–World War II zoning codes, which emphasize separating land uses, prevent them from producing more imaginative and more sustainable urban developments. But most master planned developments are reviewed as planned unit developments, a zoning classification that provides some regulatory relief. Leinberger says that today it's neighbors, not city hall, who are likely to object to higher density, mixed use projects.

Leinberger believes that the "walkable urbanity" that he espouses offers an improved quality of life that can help defuse opposition. Given half a chance, he believes, many people enjoy walking through interesting, well-designed, safe urban spaces. Walkable urbanity is a key to the success of areas such as Boston's Back Bay and Chicago's North Michigan Avenue, he notes.

As a developer. Leinberger played a major role in the revitalization of downtown Albuquerque. where green techniques have been used to help create a de facto master planned community — a redeveloped downtown complete with housing, office, retail, and entertainment.

"A lot of the best work is being done in existing cities," says Fritz Steiner. He points out that urban master planned communities, which reuse land instead of paving over rural areas, have a leg up in terms of sustainability compared to cornfield subdivisions.

One example is SouthSide Works, a mixed use urban village developed on a 37-acre former steel mill site less than two miles from downtown Pittsburgh. It includes retail, restaurants, a movie theater, office space, and 83 apartments. A central square provides a focal point for these uses. The developer, Pittsburgh's Soffer Organization, has plans for a hotel, more multifamily housing, and an outdoor performance space.

In-town redevelopment efforts like this one get sustainability points for cleaning up brownfield sites, restoring historic structures, and reducing the need to drive.

The past several years have seen greater cooperation between environmentalists and new urbanists, who've had their differences in the past. Some new urbanists dismiss "green" advocates for thinking plants are more important than people. The greens respond by saying new urbanists are willing to allow natural areas to be destroyed for the sake of maintaining urbanist design principles.

Steiner notes that some West Coast new urbanists, notably Peter Calthorpe, tend to be greener than their East Coast counterparts, who are more grounded in older, dense cities.

Steiner promises, with a smile, to "green them all up a bit" next spring when the Congress for the New Urbanism holds its annual conference in Austin.

"Blank Slate"

Of course, developers of "blank slate" master planned communities have more elbow room to try cutting-edge green techniques. Prairie Crossing, a 677-acre "conservation community" north of Chicago, includes an organic farm that provides produce to community residents as well as area customers.

In Lee and Collier counties, Florida, Sid Kitson, the developer of the 17,000-acre Babcock Ranch, has been quoted as saying, "When we started this, we wanted to create the most environmentally sustainable community in the state of Florida." Similarly, in unincorporated southern Orange County, California, the developers of Ladera Ranch have vowed to keep 1,200 acres as open space. The 4,000-acre master planned community, which was started in 1999, is divided into six neighborhoods.

The greenest is the 406-acre Terramor neighborhood, whose single-family houses feature rooftop solar panels. Houses in this neighborhood also include hookups for electric cars

and floors made from recycled tires. Water-based paint covers the exterior walls. The storm water drainage system is based on a series of manmade wetlands, eliminating the need for pipes or culverts. According to the developer, residents are willing to pay $1.50 to $3.50 more per square foot for the neighborhood's green features.

Now look at Noisette, a 3,000-acre "city with in a city" in North Charleston, South Carolina. Local developer John Knott has billed it as a sustainable community ever since he teamed with the city in 1995 to buy the soon-to-close, 400-acre U.S. Navy base that forms the heart of the development.

Like the developers of Ladera, Knott believes that a key element of a green, master planned community is an environmentally friendly storm management system. Noisette includes bioswales — landscaped road medians and backyard rain gardens that allow surface runoff to be filtered through soils and native vegetation. Pervious pavement steers storm water into recycled concrete basins below the sidewalks, where it is treated before flowing toward the Cooper River.

As one might imagine, the Noisette property had plenty of environmental problems after 100 years as a military base. Agricultural use had further degraded the environment. Early research showed that large areas of urbanized watershed that once absorbed 85 percent of rainfall had been destroyed. Storm water runoff from pipes and ditches was causing flooding and drastic seasonal differences in water table levels.

To address these issues, the developer is implementing an eco-restoration effort. During the three- to five-year remediation phase, exotic plants are being replaced by native species. A nature preserve surrounding Noisette Creek. along with conservation and drainage easements, all help to protect wild areas.

Checklist

Whether the project is in the Midwest (Hidden Creek), on the West Coast (Ladera Ranch), or in the South (Noisette), green-minded developers say a proposal touted as sustainable should answer "yes" to the following questions:

- Is the development in a location that makes sense, or is it in the middle of nowhere?
- Is there a commitment to solar access? A topic that received a lot of attention following the 1973 oil embargo, it now has been largely forgotten. Most homes should have a north-south orientation to reduce heating and cooling bills. There's a reason that farmhouses usually have evergreens to the north and deciduous trees to the south.
- Is there an effort to make the homes energy-efficient through effective use of insulation and other techniques? Energy Star designation is a plus.
- Does the development include low-impact design features such as porous paving?
- Is the community walkable, or does it provide some sort of public transit?

Both developer Chris Leinberger and dean Fritz Steiner suggest that planners seek guidance from the new LEED for Neighborhood Development (LEED-ND) rating system, which integrates green building, smart growth, and urbanism into a national standard for neighborhood design.

The original LEED (Leadership in Energy and Environmental Design) standards applied to the design and construction of individual buildings, no matter where they were built. But that didn't go far enough, says Leinberger. "It's not just the green architecture," he says. "It's where the green architecture is placed."

RESOURCES

On the web: The new LEED-ND standard — a collaboration of the U.S. Green Building Council, the Congress for the New Urbanism, and the Natural Resources Defense Council — awards points for addressing planning issues such as compact development, reduced auto dependence, and proximity to schools and jobs.

CHAPTER 32

Minneapolis and Other Cities Provide Light Rail Transportation Options

John Van Gieson

When public transportation analyst Art Guzzetti earned his graduate degree at the University of Pittsburgh in 1979, there were zero light rail systems in the United States.

Thirty years later, 34 light rail systems are serving communities from coast to coast, including Pittsburgh. Many of them are involved in major expansions of their lines, and three dozen more communities are in various stages of planning and developing light rail.

"It started sort of as a way to do the heavy rail in a less expensive way," said Guzzetti, vice president of policy at the American Public Transportation Association (APTA). "It's son of a hybrid in a way. It's a little bit streetcar, and it's a little bit heavy rail, so its in the middle."

Of all the cities where light rail is winning public transportation converts pulling people out of their cars, none has bigger ambitions than Denver. The RTD, the regional transportation agency that serves the Mile High City and all or part of eight adjacent counties, is planning to expand its existing 34-mile light rail system to 122 miles by 2017.

The Cost Factor

There is a major hurdle to overcome, however, and a recession isn't helping. The cost of the expansion is pegged at $6.9 billion — $2.3 billion more than voters were told it would cost in 2004 when they passed, for the second time, a sales tax increase to help pay for light rail. Denver residents and visitors now pay a one percent sales tax to support light rail.

A majority of the 15 members of the RTD Board of Directors favor asking the voters to double the portion of the sales tax dedicated to the FasTracks expansion, as the proposed system is called, to eight-tenths of a percent.

"The consensus was, essentially, we will vote to ask the voters for a tax increase, but we don't know whether it will be in '09 or '10," said Matt Cohen, a Denver realtor who serves on the RTD Board. Unlike most other systems, board members in the Denver area are elected.

"The best case scenario is the voters will approve a four-tenths of one percent increase in the FasTracks sales tax, and the feds will approve $1 billion in funding as we explore public-private partnerships," he said. "If the tax is approved and the feds approve $1 billion in funding, we build out the system by 2017."

Without the additional local and federal funding, it will likely take until 2034 to complete FasTracks, Cohen said. The board has not decided when it will vote on taking the tax increase to the voters, he said.

Originally published as "Light Rail Adds to Transportation Choices: Climb on Board!" *On Common Ground*, Summer 2009, by the Community and Political Affairs Division, National Association of Realtors, Washington, D.C. Reprinted with permission of the publisher.

RTD General Manager Cal Marsella said polls show that 62 percent of Denver area voters support the proposed sales tax increase.

Light rail has been a big hit in cities all over the country that have built new systems in recent years. Denver is already exceeding its ridership projections for 2020.

Light rail and streetcars (including trolleys) comprise a small part of the public transportation market across the country but are growing faster than other modes. APTA reported that light rail and streetcar ridership increased by 8.3 percent in 2008, highest among all modes of public transportation. Total ridership for the year was 465.1 million.

APTA reported double-digit increases in light rail ridership last year in Charlotte, Buffalo, Philadelphia, Sacramento, Baltimore, Minneapolis, Salt Lake City, New Jersey, Denver and Dallas.

"I think that why it works is it gives people an excellent alternative to driving and they like rail," Marsella said. "It's very dependable and runs on a regular schedule, rain or shine."

"One of the reasons light rail is so popular is you can drive a couple of miles to a Park and Ride lot, get on a train and sit there and watch all the traffic congestion as you whiz by," he said.

To put things in perspective, light rail ridership pales beside the major public transportation modes — buses and commuter rail — accounting for less than 1 percent of total transit trips last year. Most Americans, meanwhile, still hop in their cars to commute to work, go shopping, take in a movie or haul the kids to soccer practice.

The transportation environment is changing rapidly, however. Light rail's success in Denver and elsewhere is leading transportation planners and local government officials across the country to propose new systems for their communities.

There's even a proposal by a group called Vision 42 to build a river-to-river light rail system on 42nd Street through the heart of Times Square in New York. That would be New York, the Big Apple, where the city's famous subways haul 2.5 billion riders a year.

Even as light rail is growing in popularity and ridership, however, the global recession is creating funding issues that could put expansion plans on hold, or scaled back, until the economy recovers.

"They're struggling, and they need some help," Guzzetti said. "Many systems are looking at fare increases, service cuts and layoffs."

Light rail construction is financed largely by local tax increases and federal construction grants with other federal, state and local funds added into the mix. Fares comprise a small portion of revenue — just 19 percent of operating expenses for Denver's RTD.

"It's not a money-making proposition," Cohen said. "It's not going to pay for itself in the present model that's currently in place."

"We're always seeking federal grant sources," Marsella said. "We've cut costs here in every way we can. We're always looking at the state budget. So the only place you can look to really is federal grants, if they're there, and raising the sales tax."

But the sales tax increases approved by local voters in referendums are producing less revenue because of the recession.

Charlotte's LYNX light rail system is funded in part with a half-cent sales tax approved by voters in 1998 with 57 percent of the vote. Last year, 70 percent of the voters rejected a ballot issue pushed by light rail opponents to repeal the sales tax.

"We are anticipating this year being down around 10 percent at the end of our fiscal year, which is June," said Olaf Kinard, director of marketing and communications at the Charlotte Area Transit System. He said the shortfall has been projected at $260 million over 10 years. "It is affecting what we look at as to what we're going to do in the future and when."

The federal government has provided major support for construction of light rail systems, coming up with 50 percent of the cost in many instances. Guzzetti noted, however, that the feds pay 80 percent of the cost of highway construction. He said federal support has been increasing, but the government needs to do a lot more.

"I would look at it another way and say they have been underfunding," Guzzetti said. "There are a lot of good projects out there, and there should be a higher level of investment."

The federal economic stimulus plan will help, providing $1 billion in capital investment grants for light rail, heavy rail, commuter rail and high occupancy vehicle projects. Phoenix, New Jersey and Charlotte have received light rail stimulus grants.

Light Rail and Its Link to Community Vitality

Light rail has proven to be a major stimulus to the economies of communities that have built new systems in recent years. Transit-oriented development (TOD) is built into the planning for some systems, but is not a consistent factor in the growth of light rail.

One that actively promoted TOD was Dallas Area Rapid Transit (DART), which currently operates two lines on 45 miles of track in Dallas and its suburbs and is planning to add a third, 28-mile line by December 2010.

In November 2007, the Center for Economic Development and Research at the University of North Texas issued a report on the potential fiscal impacts of TOD in the DART service area. The report came to this startling conclusion: "The total value of projects that are attributable to the presence of a DART Rail station since 1999 is $4.26 billion."

The study reported that homes near rail stations increased in value by 39 percent more than homes not served by light rail.

In Charlotte, transit officials say that more than $291 million in new development has been built near stations on a 10-mile rail line that opened last year. They say an additional $1.6 billion in development has been announced for the rail corridor.

Denver transit officials say 8.4 million square feet of new retail, office and government space has been built along its existing 35-mile rail network. There have been 11,000 residential units built near the rail line.

In Seattle, a U.S. Department of Commerce model estimates that economic activity generated by the University Link, a 3.7-mile connection from downtown to the University of Washington, will be the equivalent of 22,800 direct and indirect jobs.

Light Rail Through the Decades

The light rail movement began in San Diego, which opened the first system in the country in 1981. The San Diego Trolley — a misnomer — operates fire engine red trains on three lines serving 53 stations on 51 miles of track and has the fourth highest light rail ridership in the country. Pittsburgh's Port Authority of Allegheny County started construction of its light rail system in 1981. The term "light rail" is commonly applied to trains that operate on rights-of-way off the streets or on urban-area streets, have several cars and are lighter and shorter than commuter rail trains or heavy rail systems. There is generally some distance between light rail stations, perhaps as much as a mile, except in urban centers. Streetcars, also known as trolleys, usually share city streets with cars, trucks and buses, have one or two cars and stop every few blocks. In most cases, light rail and streetcars run on electricity delivered by overhead power lines. The newest light rail system in the United States is the METRO in Phoenix. Before the METRO opened in December 2008, sprawling, congested Phoenix, the nation's fifth largest city, was the largest American city with no passenger rail service of any kind. Amtrak didn't even stop there. In the first two days of operation, 200,000 rail-starved people rode METRO'S 20-mile starter line.

Next on line later this year is Sound Transit's 15.6-mile Central Link in Seattle. Nearly 62 percent of the voters approved an extension of Seattle's system in the 2008 election. "The fact that people who have these systems want to make them bigger and more expansive tells you something right there," Guzzetti said. "If it wasn't working, you wouldn't want more."

Funding the Light Rail Systems

Like a tasty gumbo, many ingredients can go into the making of a light rail system, but the most important by far are a strong, dedicated local revenue source, usually a sales tax increase, and federal funding.

The starting point, the funding source that turns many light rail dreams into reality, is a local sales tax increase approved by voters. Existing transit sales taxes range from four-tenths to one percent. In some cases, voters have approved sales tax increases on two different occasions.

Light rail is popular in the communities that have it — 93 percent of Denver-area riders rated the trains good or excellent in a poll earlier this year — and voters have shown a remarkable willingness to raise their taxes to pay for a form of transportation they may use rarely, if ever.

Valley Metro, the light rail system in Phoenix, links the city with three suburbs: Tempe, Mesa and Glendale. Tempe voters approved a half-cent tax for public transportation in 1996. In 2000, Phoenix voters passed a four-tenths cent sales tax for public transportation, and in 2004, Maricopa County voters passed Proposition 400, a four-tenths cent sales tax increase that provides funding for additional transportation improvements, including a 27.7-mile light rail extension.

Other areas where voters have approved sales tax increases to support light rail include Charlotte, Salt Lake City, Dallas, Denver, Seattle and Kansas City. Charlotte voters approved, by 57 to 47 percent, a sales tax increase in 1998. Last year, they emphatically rejected, 70 to 30 percent, an attempt to repeal the tax.

Seattle voters rejected a sales tax increase in 2007, then passed a scaled-down increase last year to provide funding for light rail and other projects.

The U.S. Department of Transportation's New Starts program has been providing roughly half the funding for light rail construction. The agency awarded $8.3 billion in 29 grants to light rail systems from 1992 to 2007. Those grants amount to nearly half of the total cost to build those systems, $16.7 billion.

New Starts grants ranged in size from $53.6 million for the Medical Center Extension of the TRAX system in Salt Lake City to $700 million for the Northwest/Southeast extension of the DART system in the Dallas area. Several light rail systems received more than one grant.

The cost of the Salt Lake City extension is $89.4 million. The Utah Transit Authority (UTA) has built three lines totaling 20 miles using a mix of 80 percent local and 20 percent federal funding, according to spokesperson Carrie Bohnsack-Ware. Voters approved a sales tax hike in 2006 with the rate ranging from eleven-sixteenths of a cent in Salt Lake County to one-fourth cent in outlying cities and counties.

The UTA is planning to complete its Front Line 2015 expansion project, four new light rail lines and a commuter rail line to Provo, Utah, a total of 70 miles of track, by 2015.

Total cost of the DART extension in Dallas is $1.4 billion. Morgan Lyons, DART's director of media relations, said the agency gets 75 percent of its funding from a 1 percent sales tax approved by voters in 1988. Fares account for 12 percent of funding, he said, with the remainder coming from interest and federal grants.

DART has 42 miles of new lines under construction and plans to double the size of its system to 93 miles by 2013.

Art Guzzetti, vice president of policy of the American Public Transportation Association, said the feds have not been providing enough support for light rail, but the new administration has made it clear that more funding is on the way.

"There should be a higher level of investment," Guzzetti said.

Some areas have come up with creative finance schemes to raise the money they needed to build their light rail and streetcar systems from a variety of sources beyond sales taxes and federal grants.

When the Hiawatha light rail line in Minneapolis, a 12-mile route linking downtown Minneapolis with the Mall of America and the Minneapolis/St. Paul International Airport, was built at a cost of $715.3 million, local officials relied on a total of seven different sources of funds:

- Federal grant, $334.3 million
- State of Minnesota, $100 million
- Metropolitan Airports Commission, $87 million
- Hennepin County, $84.2 million
- Federal Congestion Mitigation/Air Quality grant, $49.8 million
- Transit capital grant, $39.9 million
- Minnesota Department of Transportation, $20.1 million

The Portland Streetcar, running a four-mile stretch through the center of the city, drew on nearly 20 different sources of funds. The major ones were city parking bonds, $28.6 million; tax increment funds, $21.5 million; local improvement district, $19.5 million; and regional transportation funds, $10 million. The system cost $103.2 million.

"Local businesses volunteered to be taxed by a special district," said Kay Dannen, community relations director for the Portland Streetcar. "The assessment is levied within three blocks of the tracks and varies by type of use. Residential uses are exempt."

Sound Transit, which operates the South Lake Union Streetcar in Seattle, also created an assessment on property owners near the tracks. It contributed $26 million through the Local Improvement District, nearly half the $52.1 million cost. The rest came from federal, state and local government funds.

A Modern Transportation System or an American Heritage

For many years, the best way to get around in American cities and small towns was the streetcar, pulled initially by horses and later powered by overhead electric wires. Starting in the 1930s, about 100 years after the first streetcar lines opened in cities like New York and New Orleans, the industry collapsed and all but disappeared by the mid–1950s.

Now, however, a streetcar revival is sweeping the country, featuring sleek modern cars built in Europe and learning lessons from the success of streetcars there and "heritage" trolleys here, which are modern versions of the cars seen on city streets around the turn of the last century.

Public transportation advocates prefer to call them streetcars, but they are still known in some quarters as trolleys or trams.

Portland, Ore., launched its streetcars in 2001, the first modern streetcar system in North America. Projected ridership of 3,000 persons a day was doubled in the first month.

The line, a four-mile tract that connects downtown with Northwest Portland, the gen-trified Pearl District, Portland State University and the South Waterfront, has been a smashing success. Portland Streetcar reports that more than 10,000 residential units have been built and $3.5 billion has been invested in property within two blocks of the line.

"My husband is a realtor, and he sells a lot of condos," said Kay Dannen, community relations manager for Portland Streetcars. "For most people the primary question is, 'What kind of transit connections are there?'"

Seattle, which is Portland's rival for Coolest City in the Pacific Northwest, opened its South Union Lake street car line, a 2.6-mile loop from downtown south to the high-tech South Lake Union neighborhood. Officials deny that they ever intended to call the line a trolley instead of a streetcar, but local wits dubbed it the South Lake Union Trolley, SLUT for short.

Kapow!, a defunct coffee shop on the trolley, er, street car's route, sold "I Ride the S.L.U.T." T-shirts and had a photograph of Robin Williams wearing one on its website.

Whatever locals call the line, they obviously love it. More than 500,000 riders used the streetcars in the first year, prompting Seattle Mayor Greg Nickels to celebrate by offering free rides for two weeks late last year. The city is planning four additional streetcar lines.

"A half million riders on just the first line reflects the tremendous potential of streetcars," said Nickels. "A Seattle streetcar network will be an important part of our future, offering a climate-friendly transportation choice that helps attract employers and encourages more job creation."

The major booster of a streetcar line in Seattle was Microsoft co-founder Paul Allen, who proposed a line serving a Seattle neighborhood where his venture capital company, Vulcan, Inc., has major investments. The streetcar has helped to trigger a biotech and biomed development boom in the neighborhood, and Amazon.com has announced it will move its headquarters there.

There are about two dozen active streetcar lines in the U.S., mostly "heritage" trolleys, with about 80 others in development or being considered by local officials.

Tennessee Williams fans will be disappointed to learn there is no longer a Streetcar Named Desire, but the St. Charles streetcar in New Orleans has been running since 1834 with some time off to repair Hurricane Katrina damages. Cities as small as Tallahassee, Fla., with a population less than 3,000 at the time, launched streetcar service in the late 1800s. All that remains is a street called Tram Road.

The demise of the streetcar lines that once dominated the public transportation landscape is known by some advocates as the Great American Streetcar Scandal. They accuse General Motors and other companies of setting up a shell company in the 1920s to buy streetcar lines, most of which were privately owned, and put them out of business. The motive: Sell more GM cars and buses.

Nine corporations and seven individuals were indicted on conspiracy charges in 1947, convicted and fined for their role in the scheme.

"The United States still bears untold scars from the American streetcar swindle," author Al Mankoff wrote in an article for a North Jersey Transportation Planning Authority publication. "The once profitable system of privately held independent electric-powered urban transit was destroyed, giving cities the choice between government-subsidized transit or no service at all. An economical, efficient, and non-polluting transit system has been replaced with one that is more expensive, less-efficient and highly polluting. The American taxpayer has paid the price ever since."

Just as the streetcar lines went out of business, so did a once-thriving American streetcar manufacturing industry. That is about to change. United Streetcar, a subsidiary of Oregon Iron Works in Portland, is building prototype streetcars under license to the Czech company Skoda.

"We saw how kind of beloved the Portland Streetcar was and how well it was doing," said Chandra Brown, president of United Streetcar. "I guess we were kind of surprised there were no modern streetcars being built in the United States."

The company has a prototype American-made streetcar ready for testing and is in discussions with Portland Streetcars about selling it six or seven cars when the line is expanded. It is one of two finalists to sell streetcars to a line being planned in Tucson.

"We've got literally tens of other cities that are coming out here to see the cars being built and ride the Portland system," Brown said. "There are more than 80 cities that are looking at streetcars."

CHAPTER 33

North Fair Oaks and Other Cities Consider Health Issues in Their Planning

Heather Wooten

In North Fair Oaks, California, a small unincorporated community in San Mateo County, near the San Francisco Bay, a planning process that aims to maximize transit and infill development to improve health and quality of life is just beginning.

In many ways, North Fair Oaks (pop. 15,000) is similar to communities across the country: It is a built out suburban area within a larger urban region that needs to retool in the face of a changing population and shifting resident needs.

A diverse, working class community, North Fair Oaks struggles to provide affordable housing and access to daily goods and services, especially given the Bay Area's high cost of living.

As planners address these challenges, they are also thinking seriously about how the North Fair Oaks specific plan, which is currently in the works, can improve the community's health.

San Mateo County is not alone in its efforts to yoke planning and health together. Over the last few years, a growing body of research and a small but vocal core of public health advocates and experts have argued that public health should be expressly addressed through planning and the community design processes. In California alone, the last two years have seen more than double the number of general plans that include health-related policies (from about 14 in 2008 to more than 30 today).

Now places as diverse as San Francisco and South Gate;(in Los Angeles County) have taken up the challenge. Richmond, Riverside County, and Delano also are including separate health elements in their general plans, while Shasta County public health staffers are participating in development review.

The big question in San Mateo and elsewhere is, How do we do it? What are the practices, strategies, and programs that actually support this work?

First of all, this effort requires a deep commitment to new partnerships between public agencies and the communities they serve. It also means rethinking each stage of the planning process, from the initial concept to project implementation. The North Fair Oaks approach offers a set of strategies to begin routine integration of health considerations into planning practice.

Originally published as "Healthy Planning in Action," Planning, Vol. 76, No. 2, February 2010, by the American Planning Association, Chicago, IL. Reprinted with permission of the publisher.

Share Information and Build Partnerships

In San Mateo County, early efforts by the health department to work on issues involving the built environment were focused on raising awareness among various agencies (including city and county planning agencies, the parks and recreation departments, housing agencies, and regional transportation planning agencies) about the impact that each had on residents' health. "We used to go and talk about immunizations or H1N1—but we started talking about land use and health, or the connection between food access and health," says Sara T. Mayer, the director of health policy and planning for San Mateo County Health System.

In looking for other opportunities to further their impact, the health department identified planning processes that were beginning or under way and began to attend planning and community engagement meetings.

The first project, begun in 2006, was the Grand Boulevard Initiative for El Camino Real, the corridor that links cities throughout San Mateo County. Department staff came to discussions armed with public health data and priorities that had not been considered in previous transportation projects: mapping all food outlets along El Cainino Real and addressing pedestrian and bicycle access from a physical activity perspective (as opposed to focusing only on the environmental benefits of getting people out of cars). The health department also passed along information heard from residents, namely that the road divided the community and that heavy traffic affected the mental health of nearby residents.

The health department wasn't always sure what its role would be. "It is a learning process that we're in the midst of," Mayer says. "We realized that what we needed was to build staff capacity," to help health professionals and planners understand each other and their jobs, she says. "We needed to be more sophisticated about data analysts and mapping. Planners don't always relate to traditional public health data analysis, like age pyramids. And the health department didn't even know at what stage in the process to participate."

Now, the health department is focused on plugging into policy development as a way to maximize resources and impact. "We need to be able to engage in the conversation and contribute something to it, but not create parallel processes," Mayer says.

An interdepartmental working group grew out of that first corridor project and continues to collaborate today. The working group, which includes the county's parks, planning, public works, and housing departments, as well as SamTrans—San Mateo County's regional transportation district—meets every other month to identify opportunities to work together. The North Fair Oaks specific plan is one of three similar plans in the works throughout the county, where health-promoting policies are a central component of planning.

Often one of the biggest challenges to working together is budgetary. A handful of communities around the country, including Hennepin County, Minnesota; Alexandria, Virginia; and Shasta County, California, add planners to health department staffs or public health professionals to planning. But most partnership efforts carve out of "extra" staff time in both departments, making them vulnerable to cuts when new funding or work priorities pop up. Sharing the funding for interagency staff positions can be an important step in institutionalizing partnerships.

On the flip side of the budgetary coin, an advantage to an interdisciplinary approach is access to additional funding opportunities. In San Mateo County, the interagency working group successfully applied for a planning grant from the Metropolitan Transportation Commission, which allocates federal funding for transit-oriented, infill, and mixed use planning and development.

Assess Conditions That Impact Public Health

Using health data and analyses, public health staff can help identify a community's most critical health concerns and work with planners to address them through planning policies. San Mateo County's Community Health

Profiles provide key health indicators at the city level, including leading causes of death, average life expectancy, childhood obesity by school district, healthy food availability, and park access maps. This easy-to-digest snapshot approach lets planners, elected officials, and other non-health experts understand and identify important health issues that can be affected by planning and development decisions.

In San Mateo County, addressing the needs of an aging population is a major issue for both planners and public health practitioners. To help focus strategies for transportation, housing, and other needs, the health system has developed a demographic projection model called Aging 2020–2030. The county's population over the age of 85 is projected to grow by 148 percent by 2030, and surveys have found important preference differences in housing and transportation choices between today's and tomorrow's seniors.

One of the biggest areas of difference was respondents' reported use of transit now versus their desire to use transit in the future. Many aging San Mateo residents expressed interest, even an expectation, that they would have accessible, high-quality transit service to rely on when they could not drive themselves. This contrasts starkly with the lack of existing transit services in many of the communities surveyed.

Seniors also expressed a strong interest in being able to walk to meet their daily needs, with safe and convenient access to restaurants, services, and entertainment. In many ways, this represents a new retirement model, Mayer says. Armed with this information, planners are realizing that the autocentric patterns that dominate San Mateo County will not serve their community in the next 20 years. The North Fair Oaks plans focus on transit-oriented development and infill is a reflection of the fact it is much more cost-effective to create higher density, compact development along corridors than it is to operate senior buses and other mobility programs.

Two other tools for measuring the effect of the built environment on health are health impact assessments (which look at a range of health indicators and the potential impact of a policy or project) and community food assess-

ments (which examine the availability of groceries, farmers markets, urban agriculture, and other healthy food resources).

In doing these assessments, planners and health practitioners found they have complementary skills. Training and fluency in mapping and geographic analysis are critical for taking stock of existing conditions (such as a lack of pedestrian connectivity or full-service grocery stores) and identifying underserved communities. Analyzing local health data (such as asthma hospitalization rates for children living near freeways) can spur new planning policies that will help protect communities and reduce negative health impacts.

The health department introduced planners to an index called the "social gradient," which shows that people with higher wealth and income are more likely to live longer than people with less wealth. The social gradient pattern applies to neighborhoods as well as to individuals. The index shows that Fair Oaks has the low in the county. That fact has been a motivating factor in getting the resources and investment in this community.

Health impact assessments are now being used in planning processes in many places around the U.S., including a rezoning of the Eastern neighborhoods of San Francisco, the general plan for Humboldt County, California, a bridge expansion in the Seattle area, and the Atlanta Beltline project (a plan to bring transit, trails, parks, and redevelopment to a 22-mile loop of largely abandoned freight rail line circling the city center).

Take Public Health Into Account

Public health staff can play an important role in every stage of plan development, especially in reaching out to the community and in drafting plan language. Even before the North Fair Oaks planning process began, San Mateo County public health staff shared sample health-supportive land-use policies with local planners and decision makers. They also helped develop the project scope, ensuring that the plan would address issues such as park access; access to healthy food options; public transit, walking, and bicycling; public spaces for events (like farmers markets); and access to affordable housing, economic opportunity, and living wage jobs that align with residents' skills and training.

When it came time to pick a consultant to lead the planning effort, Mayer represented the health system on the interviewing team — a first. The entire process was eye-opening, Mayer says, noting that she was struck by the level of detail and the amount of research consultants provided even at the proposal stage. She, in turn, made sure that the consultants understood the public health issues the plan would address.

As the North Fair Oaks plan moves into the plan-making phase (so far, the county has identified the consultants who will carry out the work), the health system will continue to provide guidance and input in two key areas: technical expertise and outreach and engagement. Mayer notes that the health department's role and relationships in the community can make for a more comprehensive process.

"Planning is not just regulation," says Steve Monowitz, a long-range planner with the San Mateo County and Building Department,. "When the community understands the connection between land-use decisions and their health and their children's, they'll see those links and want to play a role in helping the county develop better plans."

Implement Healthy Planning Goals

Of course, getting health-promoting policies into plans is a critical step, but it doesn't mean that what gets built actually reflects those policies. It's vital to ensure that implementation strategies — zoning, subdivision regulations, and design guidelines — translate a broad policy mandate ("promote neighborhood walkability") into specific standards, regulations, and incentives.

Communities such as Los Angeles, Cleveland, and Minneapolis are pioneering a variety of new uses for traditional planning tools, including using conditional use permits for fast

food or drive-through restaurants, defining and allowing community gardens as of right in designated zones, and requiring pedestrian and bicycle infrastructure in new developments.

Some public health agencies such as San Francisco's and Denver's tri-county health department are also creating and using "healthy development" checklists that provide users with a framework for evaluating projects from a public health perspective. They look at issues such as street design, wastewater management, and air quality, among others.

San Mateo County has developed a Healthy Housing checklist that evaluates access to food, public safety, housing density, and transportation and transit. It recognizes the different development patterns across the county, and includes criteria tailored to rural, suburban, and urban neighborhoods. For example, access to healthy food, the checklist asks, "For residential uses, is the project within ___ mile of a supermarket?" Standards call for a half mile in urban communities, one mile for small cities, and two miles in rural areas.

Although the North Fair Oaks plan is not yet in place, the process of moving from policy to implementation may be more efficient and effective with a healthy planning approach. The benefits to planners are obvious to Monowitz, who urges planners and public health staff to take advantage of the opportunity to work together.

"Health departments are staffed with people who can be a great resource to the planning department," he says. "We can only solve these public health problems if we collaborate. And local governments can't do this all on their own. The more we work together and with our community members on plan development and implementation, the more successful we'll be."

RESOURCES

Centers for Disease Control, "Recommended Community Strategies and Measurements to Prevent Obesity in the United States": www.cdc.gov/obesity/downloads/community_strategies_guide.pdf.
Leadership for Healthy Communities, "Action Strategies Toolkit": www.leadershipforhealthycommunities.org/content/view/352/154.

The National Association of City and County Health Officials' "Public Health in Land Use Health policy and planning in San Mateo County: www.smhealth.org/hpp.

Partnership funding opportunity: CDC's American Recovery and Reinvestment Act of 2009, "Communities Putting Prevention to Work": www.cdc.gov/nccdphp/re covery.

Planning and Community Design" checklist: www.naccho.

org/topics/environmental/landuseplanning/toolbox. cfm.

Planning and Community Health Research Center: www. planning.org/nationalcenters/health.

Planning for Healthy Places, a project of Public Health Law and Policy: www.healthyplanning.org.

San Francisco Department of Public Health's "Healthy Development Measurement Tool": http://thehdmt.org.

CHAPTER 34

Oakland and Other Cities Promote Smart Growth Development Practices

Gary Binger *and* Paul Sedway

A diverse region of nearly 7 million people, the San Francisco Bay Area comprises nine counties, three major cities (San Francisco, Oakland, and San Jose), and more than 100 incorporated cities. Most of these jurisdictions are struggling thoughtfully with the challenges of housing supply and affordability, traffic congestion, community opposition to more sustainable growth patterns, preservation of critical open space, redevelopment of underused sites, infrastructure financing, and maintaining strong economies during the current economic downturn.

In the public policy arena, local government officials are exploring ways to respond to pressure from their constituents (including economic, environmental, and social equity leaders) to do a better job of managing growth. And on the ground, from suburban enclaves to inner cities, a new pattern of development seems to be taking shape.

Throughout the Bay Area, faceless strip malls are giving way to attractive mixed-use plazas that invite walking and social interaction. Where uninterrupted tracts of single-family homes have long prevailed, pockets of more compact housing patterns are appearing, often near transit stations. Jurisdictions that once embraced development at any cost are drawing the line on limitless growth, setting aside open

space for future generations. And, here and there, city streets teetering on the edge of urban decay are getting a facelift and an infusion of investment.

In particular, two initiatives now underway are reinforcing and significantly expanding smart growth in the region. One initiative focuses on identifying and providing effective local implementation techniques and other tools to local policy makers. The other centers on creating a regional smart growth vision linked to long-term transportation investments.

The Local Approach

In light of the challenges, the need for political leadership, and the evidence of growing interest from the development community, the Urban Land Institute's San Francisco District Council recently prepared a guidebook designed to help implement effective local smart growth practices. Titled *Smart Growth in the San Francisco Bay Area: Effective Local Approaches*, this resource includes techniques for implementing various smart growth strategies, cites 25 specific local case studies, and provides model procedures and ordinances.

The process of creating the guidebook began with input from local public sector de-

Originally published as "Partnering for Smart Growth Success," *Urban Land*, Vol. 62, No. 9. September 2003, by the Urban Land Institute, Washington, D.C. Reprinted with permission of the publisher.

velopment professionals — those who stand on the front lines of conservation and development policies and programs. Based on their input, the district council focused its research on techniques for implementing compact, infill, transit-oriented, mixed-use, and adaptive use development — as well as on strategies dealing with the jobs/housing balance and inclusionary housing. Investigation into effective community acceptance techniques and infrastructure financing methods, due to the important role they play in the implementation of smart growth strategies, also topped the list.

Findings

Compact Development. Compact growth patterns can be pursued locally through a number of different, yet complementary approaches. One compact development tool used in various communities throughout the Bay Area today is the urban growth boundary. A second approach is the adoption of zoning regulations and incentives for higher-density development in urbanized areas. Successful compact development strategies emerge from localities that amend general plans, neighborhood or district plans, and zoning to support increased density within urban growth boundaries to accommodate expected growth in a way that reflects local values and market conditions. Requiring new development to be established at a minimum intensity promotes the efficient use of available land. City leaders help promote compact development by providing regulatory and fiscal incentives to encourage the redesign of parking capacity in a way that frees up land for other uses, rather than tying up large parcels of valuable land with surface lots.

Infill Development. This strategy works well in older, developed communities that have pockets of unused or underused land. It is especially effective in areas where new development can connect easily to existing transportation and public services infrastructure. Localities committed to making the most of underused properties frequently start by undertaking an inventory of land available for infill development throughout the community. They then establish regulations and policies that explicitly encourage such development in certain areas, occasionally using local redevelopment powers. The use of neighborhood or district plans, overlay zones, and a minimum (rather than a maximum) level of development intensity is particularly beneficial in certain areas. Focusing local capital improvement spending on upgrading infrastructure or on making other public improvements to enhance infill is often critical to success.

Transit-Oriented Development. Transit-oriented development, defined as moderate- to high-density activities located within an easy walk of a major transit stop, generally includes a mix of residential, employment, and shopping opportunities. A number of localities have replanned and rezoned land to transit-supportive densities, and have established the highest-density range permitted in the community in these areas. The funding of drainage, water systems, utilities, pedestrian plazas and parks, and street lighting is particularly effective in making station areas more attractive to private sector investment. Positive local regulations for development near transit often apply urban rather than suburban design standards, and call for the concentration of open space in public areas rather than requiring open space and setbacks for individual projects.

Mixed-Use Development. In contrast to the traditional practice of separating land uses, mixed-use development incorporates several different land uses, such as residential, retail, employment, and entertainment, within a reasonable walking distance of each other. Often, more than one type of mixed-use district will be necessary or appropriate in a community. For example, there may be a need for a mixed-use district that is primarily residential in nature, with only limited commercial development permitted in some areas, while other locations in the community may call for a mixed-use district that is mainly commercial with higher-density multifamily uses mixed in.

To encourage mixed-use development, incentives may be offered including density bonuses, relaxed parking requirements, or expedited processing of permit applications.

Zoning that allows extra height can be particularly effective in encouraging mixed use, e.g., where zoning ordinarily allows three stories of commercial development, it permits four stories if the upper-story use is residential.

Adaptive Use. Adaptive use is the conversion of outmoded structures to new uses. Such use is often coupled with the preservation of historic and architecturally significant buildings. Localities committed to adaptive use frequently clarify rehabilitation code requirements in order to encourage owners and developers to upgrade buildings. By eliminating arbitrary requirements, well-drafted rehabilitation codes limit the need to negotiate variances and make the implementation of code requirements more even-handed. Local agency loans and other financial assistance can play a key role in making adaptive use financially feasible. Local ordinances establishing a system of transferable development rights (TDRs) can facilitate and create private market subsidies and incentives for the preservation of historically significant structures.

Jobs/Housing Balance. Achieving a regionwide jobs/housing balance can help resolve the mismatch in the supply and location of jobs and housing, a key factor in the Bay Area's ongoing struggle with traffic congestion. At the local or subregional level, effecting a jobs/housing balance helps to address challenges faced by employers in suburban job centers who find it difficult to attract skilled workers, and those in urban centers seeking service or unskilled workers.

The relationship between the types of jobs and housing located in a community is often a more important factor in obtaining a greater degree of "self-containment" than simply achieving a numerical balance. Local governments can work to attract jobs that match the employment skills of local residents, and/or support and encourage housing that is affordable or attractive to local workers. Cities and counties can encourage employers to hire workers locally to reduce unnecessary work trips. Programs that bring together employers and vocational and educational providers help residents develop the skills necessary to participate in the local job market.

Inclusionary Housing. Local inclusionary housing provisions expand the supply of affordable housing for low- and moderate-income households and integrate such housing into the community. Successful approaches include getting early input from both for-profit and nonprofit developers to sort out opportunities and constraints in implementing a local program. Incentives such as increased densities and other land use changes enhance residential development capacity and help to offset costs relating to mandated inclusionary housing. Some localities vary requirements by district; for example, infill housing in downtown areas may have a lower inclusionary requirement because infill housing is desired there and/or significant affordable housing may already exist downtown.

ULI's San Francisco District Council is in the process of distributing its smart growth guidebook and sharing its findings with local public officials through direct mailings, interactive workshops, as well as other outreach activities. (Free downloadable copies are available on the San Francisco District Council website at http://sfbayarea.uli.org.)

A Regional Vision

In the waning months of the 20th century, a number of visionary Bay Area leaders began looking ahead to what life would be like in the coming decades when an expected million residents and jobs would be added to the region. Given the growing pains currently facing the Bay Area, these leaders asked if it would be possible to change the course of current growth; to find ways to accommodate the Bay Area's expanding population, provide adequate housing, improve transportation, and protect the environment and open space at the same time. Challenged by the need for action and excited by new forms of development, a number of committed Bay Area citizens and organizations joined with regional government agencies to investigate if and how the Bay Area could grow smarter.

The investigation began in earnest in 1999, when the Bay Area's five regional agencies — those responsible for transportation planning, environmental protection, and regional planning — came together to nurture the buds of smart growth that were cropping up throughout the region. At the same time, the Bay Area Alliance for Sustainable Development — a coalition of 40 organizations representing business, the environment, social equity, and government — embarked on developing public consensus and support for a "regional livability footprint," a preferred land use pattern that could direct the Bay Area toward a more sustainable future.

In 2000, the regional agencies and the Bay Area Alliance combined their outreach efforts and created the Smart Growth Strategy/Regional Livability Footprint Project. From the outset, the project identified three goals: create a smart growth land use vision for the Bay Area to minimize sprawl, provide adequate and affordable housing, improve mobility, protect environmental quality, and preserve open space; develop 20-year land use and transportation projections based on the vision that would, in turn, guide the infrastructure investment decisions of the Metropolitan Transportation Commission (MTC) and other regional partners; and identify and obtain regulatory changes and incentives needed to accomplish these objectives,

For two years, elected officials, business and community leaders, environmentalists, social equity advocates, and interested citizens devoted thousands of hours to the project. They organized, met, planned, debated, generated ideas, drew maps, made projections, and analyzed outcomes. More than 2,000 residents from throughout the region attended daylong Saturday workshops held in each of the Bay Area's nine counties. At these workshops, participants conceptualized how future growth should occur in their individual communities. and in the region as a whole.

Following these workshops, the nine countywide alternatives were stitched together into a single regionwide smart growth land use vision. This preferred alternative would allow more than half of all new housing units and jobs to be located near bus and tail service, compared to just 25 percent of housing and 35 percent of jobs today. It also would permit more households to live within a 30-minute commute to work and would consume 82 percent less undeveloped land.

The process has now advanced to implement the agreed-upon vision. Historically, the Association of Bay Area Governments (ABAG), the region's council of governments, has issued 20-year, trends-based population. employment, and land use projections every two years. These projections were given to the MTC as input into the region's long-range transportation plan and investment strategy. Earlier this year, ABAG's executive board agreed to move away from adopting trends-based projections and, instead, approved a set of policy-based projections reflecting the principles of the regional smart growth strategy. This critical decision elevated the vision from an interesting concept to something that affected regional transportation investments. Now that they have been adopted, these policy-based projections provide input into the modeling of MTC's 2004 Regional Transportation Plan, the document that will guide transportation investments in the region for years to come.

Much, however, remains to be done to ensure that regional smart growth is achieved. Efforts are continuing to increase cooperation among the regional agencies, particularly MTC and ABAG, with one effort seeking a merger of the two. Others are encouraging the formulation of a comprehensive plan that, through incentives and disincentives, may induce local governments to adhere to broad planning policies. The successes in implementing local smart growth approaches have served to heighten public awareness of the value of sound planning at all governmental levels.

The aforementioned elected officials, business and community leaders, environmentalists, social equity advocates, and interested citizens who have led and participated in this effort are now identifying policy changes and incentives needed to accomplish these objectives. More information on this regional effort is available on ABAG's website at www.abag.ca. gov.

It is also important to note that ULI's California Smart Growth Initiative convened a cross section of diverse leaders who agreed on a package of specific state economic incentives and regulatory reforms for promoting smart growth throughout the state. These actions, if pursued by the state, would provide significant support to the Bay Area's local and regional smart growth activities. Information on this statewide initiative, and its recommended actions, is available at www.smartgrowthcalifornia.uli.org.

CHAPTER 35

Oregon City and Other Cities Streamline Their Stream Restoration Process

Alan Horton

Is your stream restoration project mired in paperwork, held up by permits, or stymied by a lack of funding? Does it take years to complete a relatively simple project? These and other similar problems prompted Oregon's Freshwater Trust to develop StreamBank, a Web-based platform that streamlines the stream restoration process. The nonprofit group created software that helps users access funding, identify and acquire necessary permits, and conduct follow-up monitoring and reporting for simple stream restoration projects. By automating the process, StreamBank saves time and money while accelerating environmental improvements. Although currently applicable only for the state of Oregon, The Freshwater Trust is working to expand StreamBank's reach—first through the Pacific Northwest, and then into other regions of the United States.

StreamBank Assesses Proposed Projects

The Freshwater Trust is a statewide nonprofit organization headquartered in Portland, Oregon. Using private grant funds, the group developed StreamBank in 2007 as an automated, interactive Web-based decision program to help people increase the number of stream restoration projects funded and implemented while reducing the workload required to do so.

"StreamBank is like Turbo Tax for stream restoration," explains Alan Horton, Managing Director of The Freshwater Trust. "People input the necessary information and then the program largely takes over."

How does it work? StreamBank leads a restoration project representative—often a staff member of a watershed group or local soil and water conservation district—through a series of Web screens.

First, the representative enters basic information about the proposed project, including the location (using Google Earth to pinpoint it) and type of project (riparian planting, invasive weed removal, etc.). At this point, StreamBank begins working behind the scenes. StreamBank checks data contained in numerous customized Geographic Information System (GIS) layers. These layers include information such as:

- Location of the state's impaired waters
- Areas where funding is available (including any restrictions)
- Endangered species habitat
- Areas that are subject to existing watershed or ecosystem recovery plans.

Originally published as "Stream Bank Tool Offers Promising Approach to Restoring Streams," *Nonpoint Source News-Notes,* Issue 90, June 2010, published by the U.S. Environmental Protection Agency, Washington, D.C.

The program refers to these layers as it assesses and scores proposed projects using a number of computer algorithms. The score helps determine if the project can be matched with existing funding sources. If so, the project is automatically accepted into the Streambank system and moves ahead into the funding matching stage.

"StreamBank is ideal for simple, straightforward restoration projects," explains Horton. "The tool's prioritization matrix automatically determines if a proposed project meets necessary requirements for funding — saving people from having to spend time conducting reviews. If StreamBank's analysis gives a project the green light, the project can be moved on through the process."

StreamBank Overcomes Funding Obstacles

StreamBank removes one of the largest obstacles to stream restoration — acquiring funding in a timely manner. Typically, funding agencies and organizations carry out their own separate processes for awarding funds, with different timeframes and requirements for submitting proposals, awarding grants and reporting. Because restoration professionals have to look to numerous funding sources and balance different requirements and timeframes, projects can be delayed significantly.

StreamBank makes the funding process much easier for funders and project representatives. "StreamBank is designed to function as a sole funder for restoration projects, with the intent of having multiple pots of money from different sources available that, together, can automate matching requirements and meet the full funding needs of a project," explains Suzanne Greene, StreamBank Manager. The goal of The Freshwater Trust is to engage multiple government agencies, foundations, and private companies who will provide funds and be assured that the funds will be used to support stream restoration projects that meet specific biological, administrative and project design criteria. The funders save time and effort, and are assured that they are supporting projects that make a difference and meet their requirements. Qualified projects processed through StreamBank are matched directly to available funding sources that support all stages of the project, including planning, implementation, monitoring and reporting.

The Freshwater Trust has spent the past few years building its case that StreamBank is an ideal way to identify and fund simple restoration projects. In 2007, several private funding sources (The Freshwater Trust members, the Jubitz Family Foundation and Meyer Memorial Trust) supported the software development and initial testing on three stream restoration projects. In 2008, these and other private sources (including Bandon Dunes Golf Resort and the Bella Vista Foundation) provided another $569,000 to support a large-scale pilot StreamBank project. These funds supported 17 successful stream restoration projects processed through StreamBank. Information about each of these projects is included in *StreamBank Case Study 2008*, available at www.Thefreshwater trust.org/publications.

"Our pilot program allowed us to show potential funding sources that StreamBank can be applied successfully and efficiently," notes Horton. In fact, The Freshwater Trust found that using Stream-Bank to complete the pilot projects required, on average, 70 percent less time than if they had been implemented through a traditional grant and permitting cycle.

In 2009, the U.S. Environmental Protection Agency (EPA) agreed to allow the Oregon Department of Environmental Quality (ODEQ) to funnel $60,000 of its Clean Water Act section 319 funds through StreamBank. The Freshwater Trust matched the award 1:1 with private foundation grant money. The combination of funds supported three restoration projects. Pleased with the results, EPA has committed a comparable amount for 2010. Based on past success, The Freshwater Trust anticipates that, over the long-term, ODEQ will consider distributing more of its section 319 funding through StreamBank. The Freshwater Trust is currently working with the Oregon Watershed Enhancement Board and the U.S. Department of Agriculture to secure additional public funding for StreamBank.

StreamBank Eases Reporting

StreamBank reduces the paperwork trail, saving time and ensuring greater consistency between projects. It populates and automatically forwards necessary permit applications to the relevant agencies. "We designed Stream-Bank to make traversing the regulatory process as easy as possible," explains Horton. Ultimately, The Freshwater Trust hopes to work with federal and state agencies to develop "general permits" that will bypass some of the usual required paperwork for simple restoration projects that meet pre-established criteria. "Government agencies establish rules to keep bad things from happening, not to keep good things from happening," Horton adds. "We are exploring ways to make it easier to implement simple projects that will benefit ecosystem health."

StreamBank simplifies the reporting process by synthesizing funder requirements and project outcomes into a reporting template. StreamBank also establishes a project budget, creates a request for proposals (RFPs) for contractors, and generates a schedule for reporting, monitoring and data input (which will vary depending on the requirements outlined by the funding organization). The system remains in contact with the project representative over time, sending emails with reminders about deadlines for data and reports. Moreover, because StreamBank ensures funding for all stages of the approved project, the restoration project representative will receive adequate compensation for time spent on monitoring, reporting and entering data — long after the on-the-ground portion of the project has been completed.

StreamBank Provides for Data Gathering

As noted earlier, StreamBank requires that all projects include monitoring for project effectiveness — and includes the funding to do so. Depending on the type of project and the requirements outlined by the funding organization, long-term monitoring requirements might range from three to ten years after the project is implemented. Data collection and reporting will be standardized across all Stream-Bank projects, allowing users to compare water quality between waterbodies as well as within one waterbody. All data will be submitted through StreamBank and stored in a database that will be made available to agencies, restoration professionals and possibly the general public in the future. The Freshwater Trust is still considering a number of data access methods, and expects to have something in place by 2012.

StreamBank Offers a Glimpse of the Future

The Freshwater Trust is very pleased with the results of the pilot projects and is looking forward to expanding the program's reach. "We are getting better at knowing where to find the data we need as we expand into new areas," explains Horton. "Plus, government agencies are releasing more and more shapefiles [data layers for GIS use]. We have completed StreamBank coverage for most of Oregon and expect to have StreamBank ready to operate throughout the Pacific Northwest by 2012."

StreamBank is designed for use with projects in rural areas where eight common types of restoration practices are usually implemented: riparian fencing, riparian replanting, removing invasive weeds, off-channel watering, restoring fish passage, restoring side channels, installing large woody debris and adding engineered log jams. "We may incorporate more complex practices over time as we expand the program's applicability," adds Horton. The Freshwater Trust is currently adding a stormwater module into StreamBank to apply in areas with more impervious surfaces present. The group has also been working with the Willamette Partnership to see if StreamBank can be used to quantify ecosystem improvements, or "uplift," as credits that could be traded on the open market.

The Freshwater Trust is also creating a platform to allow people to use StreamBank as a watershed planning and project priority tool. "Using this platform, a landowner or restoration professional can identify a potential project site and view the priorities for that area, as well as funding available to complete projects," notes Greene. "The planning platform will provide the user with up-to-date information, such as priority management actions and the balance of funding available for specific project types from various private and public sources." Greene anticipates that the platform will be in place by summer 2011.

As StreamBank becomes more widely used, Horton expects to see projects translate into water quality improvements. "Individually, these simple restoration projects don't have big impacts. But, if you implement numerous projects the cumulative benefit can be huge — especially if you do so across a single watershed." For that reason, Horton hopes to one day be able to expand StreamBank to other regions of the United States that already have large-scale coordinated restoration efforts underway, particularly the Mississippi River, Chesapeake Bay and Long Island Sound watersheds.

RESOURCES

The following details concerning the Freshwater Trust and the StreamBank are provided to give the reader additional information on these two nonprofit organizations.

The Freshwater Trust was established in 2009 through a merger of Oregon Trout and Oregon Water Trust. Founded in 1983 by a group of fly fishing conservationists, Oregon Trout's goal was to work to protect and restore native fish and their ecosystems. Oregon Water Trust was founded in 1993 to work cooperatively with water users to keep more water in landowners' rivers and streams. The Freshwater Trust continues to support these efforts along with the StreamBank program and environmental education. See www.thefreshwatertrust.org.

In 2009, the Willamette Partnership gathered non-government organizations, state and federal regulatory agencies, and others to develop accounting methodologies for salmonid habitat, water quality (temperature), wetlands function and upland prairie function that translate ecological uplift from restoration projects into units of measure that could be traded in an ecosystem services marketplace. The Freshwater Trust participated in this process and applied methodologies for salmonid habitat and temperature to three of its StreamBank pilot projects. The process showed that StreamBank could be modified with an operational calculator to allow a stream restoration project manager to assess the potential ecological uplift and credit generation prior to implementing the project. The project could then be adjusted to achieve the maximum possible uplift and credits. See willamettepartnership.org.

CHAPTER 36

Philadelphia and Other Cities Encourage Bicycle Commuting

Lawrence Houstoun

Amsterdam's Central Station reveals one of the positive and one of the negative aspects of bicycles as a popular form of urban transportation. Bikes, moving and parked, are everywhere, unbelievably so. At each of several adjacent locations are at least a half acre of parked wheels and seats and handlebars and locks ready to transport their owners departing or arriving by train for work or shopping — a veritable sea of bikes, closely packed. A concrete, four-deck parking structure stuffed with hundreds more bikes is nearby for the exclusive use of commuting cyclists

Beyond the station, bikes are parked in places small and large, planned and unplanned, legal and illegal. The sheer visibility of the unridden bikes underscores the enormous success of public planning and investment intended to replace private automobiles; it is an utterly successful civic endeavor.

No one knows how many of those bikes occupying so much scarce urban land are actively owned by anyone. On the rare occasion when a block or so needs to be cleared for construction, a substantial share of the bikes remains unclaimed. Orphan bikes clutter the pedestrian domain. The annual report on biking in the Netherlands reveals without comment that there are 1.1 bikes per capita in that nation of 6 million.

Biking is receiving new attention in the United States as a potential means of reducing journeys to work by car in urban centers. This article compares the current situation here with four recently examined European centers where bikes have been made important resources for commuters. It treats bicycles as economic, not recreational, tools. It is intended to sharpen American vision regarding some practical concerns that will need to be faced should a significant effort be made to increase bike use in order to achieve various social goals, including reducing petroleum consumption, air degradation, and global warming while improving individual health and the urban environment. Thirty years of European infrastructure investments and education have produced a successful transition from automobiles to bicycles.

Who Bikes to Work?

Some generalizations will help illustrate the current U.S. experience. Why do people use bikes for commuting? Users see this mode as one that saves time and money — thousands of dollars a year in fuel, insurance, depreciation, and storage if it replaces a car. Many count the associated physical exercise as a motivating

Originally published as "Where Bikes Rule: A Cautionary Report," Public *Management, Vol. 92, No. 6*, July 2010, published and copyrighted by ICMA (International City/County Management Association), Washington, DC. Reprinted with permission of the publisher.

factor. Commuters may use bikes for the entire trip to work or school or for the trip to transit or from transit (or both).

Typical American workday users of bikes are under 25 years of age and male, and they use equipment more expensive than the common one-speed European urban bikes. Commuting cyclists are often traveling to and from educational institutions and sometimes job sites; some are messengers. Speed is important; bikers often proceed the wrong way on one-way streets, ignore stop signs and traffic lights, and weave among pedestrians on sidewalks. Enforcement of rules is infrequent. Bike lanes painted on pavements seem irrelevant and sometimes dangerous; few bikers (or drivers) pay them any attention. Cyclists appear to be moving at three times the speed of pedestrians.

Portland, Oregon, is probably Bike City USA, as it claims. Decades of traffic improvements in downtown Portland substantially improved biking conditions, contributing to the relatively high proportion of commuters who regularly bike to work. Advocates say, "It's part of the culture, it's what people do here." But biking in Portland is not without its costs. Portland reported six biker deaths in 2007. One blogger wrote, "It's scary." A Portland attorney advertises his success representing injured bikers and will not charge "if there is no monetary recovery."

The Philadelphia Biking Coalition notes that 3.2 percent of downtown workers commute by bike at least once weekly, more than the 1.2 percent of all Philadelphia commuters and substantially higher than the 0.4 percent of commuting cyclists in the multicounty metro region where origins and destinations are scattered. Center City is fairly flat, favoring bikers, but most of those who live and work in downtown walk or use transit. A high share of regular bikers appears to be students. A third of surveyed cyclists report they wear protective helmets (required by law in nearby New Jersey), and users complain of the lack of bike lanes, unsafe road conditions, and the speed and volume of auto traffic. In surveys, the growing downtown residential population complains of the city's failure to enforce bike and auto rules. In response to a January 22, 2009, *Miami Her-*

ald article on government plans to improve biking conditions, bicyclists enthused while others, who don't ride bikes, complained about public funds devoted to this small population group. One noncyclist said, "I'd like to see just once a cyclist stop for a STOP sign."

In contrast, European urban bikers in rush hours evidence a balance of male and female users and a substantial share of middle-aged riders and retirees. They proceed at about 10 miles an hour, comparable with auto speeds and perhaps two or three times the speed of pedestrians. They appear more inclined to obey traffic controls than their American counterparts. As evidence of the extent to which city biking is considered safe, many parents transport their offspring to day care using various carrying devices. Some bikes are fitted with ample capacity for shopping. Some stores make deliveries by bike. The sampled cities all have somewhat more precipitation than is common in the United States, but appropriate clothing appears to overcome most adverse weather concerns.

What appears to limit U.S. urban biking to work? For those older than 25, fear of losing in a potential bike-auto conflict is probably the most important reason; adverse weather is another. Few who bike to work do so every day. Bad weather requires a backup plan for getting to work. Convenient storage facilities are rare in city apartments, and there is a justifiable fear of theft. The American commuting pattern has for so long meant single-occupancy cars that the mind-set is doubtless hard to break. Americans have grown accustomed to the $8,000 annual cost of auto ownership (which includes depreciation), so saving money is a less pressing concern. American streets are designed and refined to facilitate automobile traffic at speeds of 30 miles per hour or more; they are not designed for safe bike traffic.

Copenhagen

Decades of investment in bike infrastructure have produced an impressive record in modal shift from cars to bikes in the Danish capital; 36 percent of travel in Copenhagen is already by bike, and added investments in parking, green biking routes, more bike lanes, and increased safety are designed to improve that record further. Recent city statistics record an 18 to 20 percent increase in bike use and a 9 to 10 percent decline in car traffic. Most of these gains are the result of the "bicycle tracks" that are separated from other traffic by their own curbs, as distinguished from the less expensive "bicycle lanes" that are only marked with white stripes.

Although bikes are not allowed on the famous pedestrian linear facility, the Strøget, they are allowed on the adjacent street. Most subway trains and many buses have bike storage capacity. Special traffic lights at most major intersections control and protect bikers. Round signs with a blue background and a white bicycle indicate bike lanes or routes. Bikes are instructed to give way to trams from any direction.

The Danes are enthusiastic about their success in shifting from streets once jammed with cars and the frustration of searching for parking spaces. Copenhagen looks forward to being designated as the world's top bike city based on usage. Cycling is so important in Danish transportation that authorities invest in research into accidents and injuries associated with the street arrangements mentioned above, plus circumstances where bikes and autos are mixed. Sixty-two percent of cyclists reported that they feel secure in Copenhagen's traffic, up from 58 percent in the 2004 survey. The cycle tracks, where bikers feel most comfortable, have produced an 18 percent increase in cyclists and a 9 percent decrease in car traffic, although accidents have increased with the greater volumes.

The Netherlands

The Dutch work hard to make biking safe, in part through public education. Amsterdam warns visitors not to imitate abuses by some local bikers. Don't, for example, ignore red lights, carry a passenger, ride on sidewalks, forget to use warning bell when passing, or fail to use lights at night. Don't chat on phones while biking. Bikers are reminded to use hand signals and when in doubt walk bikes through intersections. Users are warned to lock bikes (high incidence of theft in Amsterdam), walk bikes on crowded streets and pedestrian areas, obey traffic signs (police will pull bikers over for running a red light), and beware of tram tracks. Visiting cyclists are warned to watch for pedestrians who don't understand local bike rules — in other words, "drive defensively." Never stop in a bike lane; move to the side of the lane.

Despite this campaign, common errors observed in Amsterdam, Haarlem, and Utrecht include infrequent use of hand signals and chatting on mobile phones, sometimes while transporting a child. Bikes are generally equipped with lights for after-dark travel, and bikers tend to comply with special traffic lights for bikers. No one wearing a bike safety helmet was observed. Few seem to obey the signs intended to bar bike parking; they lock their bikes anywhere it seems convenient.

Saturday shopping via bicycles is popular in Utrecht. While Dutch cyclists proceed at a moderate pace, the protected lanes and controls mean that bikers and drivers complete their journeys at about the same time. Bikers probably have an edge; bikes are usually stored closer to the intended origins and destinations than cars.

The Dutch are biking more, owning more and more elaborate bikes, and using their bikes for commuting (46 percent), recreation (40 percent), and other purposes such as shopping. There has been a recent increase in sales of bikes with small motors.

Amsterdam tried bike sharing — pick it up and drop it off without a charge — but discontinued the program when an unacceptable number were stolen. Washington, D.C., has started a sharing program with support from its department of transportation. Some costs will be met by advertising on bus shelters.

Freedom from Fear

Writing of "The Problem of Biking in America" in the *Bygone Bureau* journal, biking advocate Nick Martens says, "Of the many complaints an American cyclist can make, a concern over his or her safety is the most serious. It is also the best reason to stick with a car." Martens describes the common and disastrous consequences of the unexpected opening of a car door in the face of a biker properly staying in the designated bike lane on the right side of the street. Without question, fear of bike-auto conflict is the most pervasive factor limiting bike use for commuting in the United States. In the United States, the driver-side door opens into the bike lane; in European streets designed for bikes it does not.

In cities, the Dutch have invested heavily in dedicated bike lanes with special safety controls, essentially a separate set of red, yellow, and green lights for cyclists. The most elaborate arrangement of segregated lanes includes the following features that facilitate four different modes. Sideways from the center of a city street:

1. The first lane (in the center) is for cars, trucks, trams, and buses.
2. The next lane is devoted to auto parking; the driver's door does not open toward bikers.
3. The next lane — at the curb — is the bike lane.
4. Next to the buildings is the pedestrian lane, the sidewalk.

Making streets multimodal and widely used by bike commuters depends on the degree to which the guideways are reassuring. To produce comfortable conditions for bikers requires clarity: What are the rules, how must bikers and drivers behave, what is our turf and what is theirs? Ambiguity breeds uncertainty, which in turn contributes to accidents and discourages potential cyclists. Reassurance about clarity includes separate traffic signals for cyclists and obvious signs signaling where bikes may go and where they should not.

The broad popularity of biking in Continental cities at peak user periods has resulted from the infrastructure investments that have produced a comfort level almost unimaginable in the United States. If there were a comfort scale reflecting concerns regarding possible injuries, high scores would go to cities where both sexes, all age groups, commuters, and shoppers

bike regularly; where use of child carriers is common, few wear helmets, and use of mobile phones in traffic are indicators of biker comfort. Biking conditions in northern Europe would generally rate an eight or nine out of a possible 10. Typical U.S. conditions would rate a two, evidenced by how few wear helmets and how many ride on pavements. Cyclists in the United States feel most comfortable when breaking the rules.

Prospects for American Conversion

Martens notes the political impasse associated with encouraging public investment to produce bike-friendly cities when so little daily biking is actually occurring; there are so few commuting bikers that they do not represent a sufficient pressure group to influence capital improvement, a situation resulting from not having bike-friendly conditions. American bikers are predominantly young, male, and urban — not a powerful constituency. Most Americans are car owning, happy with that condition, and sometimes antagonistic to bikers.

Any jurisdiction contemplating a serious modification of streets to reduce fear of injury and to expand the use of bikes for commuting and shopping should study the research from Copenhagen. Important options have already been tested. Starting with specified goals would avoid some expensive missteps in the United States. Copenhagen, for example, seeks to increase to 80 percent the share of bikers who feel comfortable or "secure" when biking, and the city is well along toward that goal.

The successful shift from cars to bikes in Europe can be traced to the steady, persistent, decades-long pace followed by governments there in adapting streets to produce bike-friendly transportation routes. Cheap won't do it. An inexpensive stripe next to the parking lane does not produce comfortable biking conditions; in many cases it is a recipe for collisions with car doors. It is hard to imagine U.S. local governments following a commitment to two or three decades of block-by-block reconstruction and continued bike-oriented education and enforcement of rules. How often would one hear the threat of litigation raised at hearings when officials propose to move car parking toward the center of the street and to install special traffic controls and curbs designed to protect bicyclists?

And, of course, other competitors for America's infrastructure funding are stronger and more influential. The highway lobby has a notorious 50-year lock on gasoline tax revenues. Other claimants—subways, buses, and commuter rail—may receive a larger share of these funds as the United States for the first time gets serious about reducing its petroleum dependency. Then there is the newly recognized need to repair and upgrade thousands of bridges and tunnels that elected officials pray will not collapse on their watch.

Probably the best prospects for financing conversions would imitate the system used for appropriating monies for a larger public cause, such as reducing global warming or employing jobless workers. Two or three good examples in American cities might influence others. New York City is modifying a few streets to favor biking. Philadelphia and other local governments might start in such limited areas as university neighborhoods where substantial use can be expected. Requiring bike storage facilities and fewer car parking spaces in residential projects would help. Five-dollar-a-gallon gasoline would boost bike usage but do little for cyclists' comfort level in peak hour traffic.

In a nation attuned to quick solutions, the widespread replacement of cars by bikes as in European cities must be seen as a long-range and expensive objective.

CHAPTER 37

Portland Advances Green Stormwater Management Practices
Glenn Reinhardt

The City of Portland is a recognized leader in green stormwater management. The City is home to several award-wining BMP project designs, and its municipal program is highly regarded worldwide. Since the early 1990s, Portland's Bureau of Environmental Services (BES) has created a multi-faceted, highly successful program that achieves not only regulatory compliance, but also education, outreach, and community greening and beautification.

Stormwater Program Origins

Portland's stormwater program began in the early 1990s in response to the National Pollutant Discharge Elimination System (NPDES) Municipal Separate Storm Sewer System (MS4) Discharge Permit issued by the state to address water quality regulations. Portland began developing a stormwater management plan. As part of the process of developing the plan, the team at BES examined the City's procedures and practices to identify activities the City already performed that met the new regulations. They also began implementing and monitoring new techniques to determine BMP feasibility and effectiveness. Armed with this

information, they created a matrix of regulatory requirements and current practices to highlight where the practices met, exceeded, or failed to address the regulations. They then collaborated with other departments to identify new BMPs that were needed to meet the regulations, and in doing so established a "to-do" list and time-line.

The stormwater management plan that resulted outlines how stormwater will be addressed by the City and includes a specification that BMPs, including sustainable stormwater management systems, will be implemented to reduce pollutants in stormwater. To ensure that private property owners implemented the BMP requirements, the City needed to amend codes governing new and redevelopment. Because there were a number of possible approaches that could be adopted to require BMPs, in 1996 the City created a Stormwater Policy Advisory Committee (SPAC), which included a diverse group of stakeholders from landscape architecture, architecture, engineering, institutional organizations, and the stormwater treatment industry, to provide input to the City on stormwater matters.

Over the next three years, the SPAC developed policy and code statements, which were developed into the city's stormwater

Originally published as "Portland, Oregon: Building a Nationally Recognized Program Through Innovation and Research," *Best Practices Report*, July 2008, by the Water Environment Research Foundation, Alexandria, VA. Reprinted with permission of the publisher.

management manual; it describes City requirements for stormwater management and specific BMP design approaches. The manual is designed to ease calculations, streamlining formulas with simple coefficients, allowing users to plug in their numbers and get straightforward results. A chapter of the manual details simplified stormwater management BMPs designed to mimic natural systems using plants and soil. The manual is updated every two years based on stakeholder input and knowledge obtained from monitoring demonstration projects.

Early on, Portland developed the Combined Sewer Overflow (CSO) Facilities Plan under the CSO Abatement Program. They looked at BMPs for flow control to address CSO events in the Columbia Slough and Willamette River. In the Plan, downspout disconnection was recognized as one of four Cornerstone Projects, which are relatively low-cost projects that reduce CSOs by keeping stormwater runoff out of the combined sewer system. (Other Cornerstone Projects were sewer separation, sump installation, and stream diversion.) As a direct result of the Plan, Portland created the Downspout Disconnection Program in 1993, in which the City provides outreach and incentives for residents of selected neighborhoods to disconnect downspouts from the combined sewer system and to redirect roof water to gardens and lawns. More than 50,000 homeowners have disconnected downspouts, removing nearly one billion gallons of stormwater per year from the combined sewer system.

Since 1977 Portland has charged a separate stormwater utility fee to help pay for stormwater management costs. In 2000 the City Council established a reward system for ratepayers who keep stormwater from leaving their property. This program, called Clean River Rewards, came into effect in October 2006 after the City launched a new utility billing system. Clean River Rewards offers residential ratepayers up to a 30 percent discount based on the extent to which they can manage runoff from roof areas. Commercial customers can claim a discount for managing runoff from both roof and paved areas. Credits are offered for having a small impervious footprint (less than 1,000

square feet), creating or maintaining tree coverage, disconnecting downspouts, installing rain gardens or drywells, and other low impact development BMPs. The City processes applications without site visits and conducts oversight via spot checks to ensure that BMPs are in effect and maintained properly. To assist ratepayers with stormwater retrofit options, BES hosts an online technical assistance page and offers workshops tailored to residential and commercial customers.

Sustainable Stormwater Management Program

The City recognized a need for both internal coordination and promotion of sustainable stormwater management systems Citywide. In 2001 the Sustainable Infrastructure Committee was formed to coordinate efforts by City staff to investigate such options as porous pavement, enhanced street landscape, and stormwater reuse to limit the impacts of City projects on water quality. Shortly thereafter the Sustainable Stormwater Management Program was formed within BES. The group's functions are many. They monitor and test the performance and design of pilot stormwater BMPs, and they provide technical assistance to developers and designers who are incorporating stormwater measures into site designs. They partner with property owners (commercial, industrial, and institutional), other local public agencies, and the federal government with project design, funding and implementation. They develop supporting policy and implement specific program areas, including Green Streets, ecoroofs, and monitoring. The group also provides project documentation, outreach, and public education. Staff receive many calls from outside Portland as other communities strive to match Portland's success with stormwater BMPs.

Portland's stormwater management program has seen success after success as new programs are developed and as BMP projects are implemented throughout the City. Below are a few examples of Portland's multi-faceted and highly successful initiatives.

PROGRAM HIGHLIGHTS AND SUCCESSES

Green Streets. Portland has retrofitted a number of streets with landscaped curb extensions, swales, planter strips, pervious pavement, and street trees to intercept and infiltrate stormwater. These Green Street projects demonstrate ways to address street runoff, which is an important source of stormwater as streets comprise 35 percent of the City's impervious surface. In April 2007, the City Council approved a resolution, report, and policy to officially promote and incorporate the use of Green Street facilities in both public and private development. Green Streets are recognized as an important in-flow control strategy to address combined sewer overflows, sewer backups, and other system deficiencies as well as watershed health needs.

A number of green street projects have been installed throughout Portland, and more are being planned as retrofits for existing neighborhoods. One project, the SW 12th Ave Green Street Planters on the Portland State University campus, won an American Society of Landscape Architects Design Award in 2006. This project, built in 2005, includes four stormwater planters arranged in sequence that capture and treat runoff from 8,000 square feet of street surface. Water flows along the curb and enters the first planter via a channel cut into the curb. Depending on flows, water will pond to a depth of 6 inches, promoting infiltration and biological uptake of pollutants. If flows exceed this capacity, water will exit the first planter through a second curb cut and be routed into the subsequent planters, either infiltrating to groundwater or, during intense storms, eventually entering the storm drain system. The planters themselves are designed to be long and narrow to fit into the existing sidewalk space, and they contain a mix of rushes, trees, and shrubs that provide attractive landscaping year-round. To address access and safety concerns in the pedestrian right-of-way, the designers used metal grates to cover the curb cut channels, incorporated exposed curbs to warn pedestrians of the difference in grade, and set the planters back from the edge of the street by three feet to allow passengers to exit their cars.

Ecoroofs. A number of buildings and structures in Portland have living, vegetated roof systems that decrease runoff and offer aesthetic, air quality, habitat, and energy benefits. The City offers developers proposing buildings in Portland's Central City Plan District the possibility for floor area bonuses if an ecoroof is installed, allowing for additional building space than would otherwise be allowed. The City is considering expanding this bonus Citywide. Additionally, Portland adopted a policy that directs City bureaus to incorporate green building practices into all facilities constructed, owned, or managed by the City. The policy specifically requires ecoroof design and construction on all new City-owned facilities and all roof replacement projects.

Sustainable Stormwater BMP Monitoring. The Sustainable Stormwater Management Program monitors and reports the results of a variety of BMP demonstration projects throughout the City. They use these data to quantify benefits of sustainable stormwater practices, improve the design and function of BMPs for existing and future applications, and lower maintenance costs by tracking performance and addressing maintenance needs as they arise. The Sustainable Stormwater Management Program produces regular reports of monitoring efforts, including project-specific results, on their website.

BMPs at Schools. In addition to a wealth of BMP projects implemented at new development, redevelopment, and capital improvement projects throughout the City, Portland schools has partnered with the City to install facilities that can manage up to 90 percent of the stormwater on site. Schoolyards have been turned into educational facilities to inform students about watershed health, and the practices have helped to prevent sewer back-ups in neighboring houses by providing a safe outlet for stormwater. One such project, at Mt. Tabor Middle School in Southeast Portland, won a 2006 Design Award from the American Society of Landscape Architects. Neighboring residents had experienced sewer back-ups during heavy rains as a result of excess stormwater, so a rain garden, landscaped curb extension, and sump were installed on and surrounding the school grounds.

The rain garden drains three-quarters of an acre of roof area and asphalt, and it contains a variety of shrubs, grasses, and trees to slow runoff and promote infiltration. The design was intended to appear open while at the same time providing shade. A fence and shrubs were used to limit access to the feature, and the garden was designed to drain within a day with a maximum ponding depth of 6 inches. The design incorporated a variety of playful elements that allow passersby to watch the water flow through the system during rainstorms.

Funding Mechanisms. The Sustainable Stormwater Management Program provides funding for stormwater management projects through various grant and matching grant programs. Federal grants are used for Innovative Wet Weather Projects, the BES Watershed Services Division administers Community Watershed Stewardship Program grants for community-proposed projects as well as Watershed Investment Funds, and the Office of Sustainable Development offers Green Investment Funds, all of which can be used to implement sustainable stormwater management practices.

City Programs Supportive of Sustainable Stormwater Management

Other City programs and initiatives that promote natural system approaches to stormwater management supported the efforts of the Sustainable Stormwater Management Program, particularly with respect to watershed planning efforts. For example in 2004 Portland proposed the Clean and Healthy River Strategy as a comprehensive effort under the River Renaissance Strategy to clean up the Willamette River. The strategy includes creating healthier tributaries and watersheds, improving habitat for endangered fish, and creating a livable, sustainable community. Reducing CSOs is a key part of the strategy. The Clean and Healthy River Strategy also includes expanding Portland's program to disconnect residential downspouts from the combined sewer system; encouraging commercial landowners to install swales and other facilities to store and filter stormwater

runoff; planting more street and landscape trees to absorb rainfall, filter stormwater runoff, and shade streams; and offering incentives to homeowners to reduce stormwater runoff from private property.

Portland considered larger, watershed-scale issues through its 2005 Watershed Plan. The basis for the plan is the Portland Watershed Management Plan (PWMP), which integrates the activities of many City bureaus. The PWMP maximizes the use of limited resources by looking for solutions that meet multiple objectives, and it focuses on addressing environmental problems at their source. This comprehensive approach to watershed management also coordinates compliance with multiple environmental regulations, including MS4 permit requirements; the stormwater management plan is recognized as one part of the overall effort to improve watershed health.

Part of the Sustainable Stormwater Management Program's success is the fact that it is integrated with other stormwater-related programs within BES. Each staff member in the Program is also involved in other initiatives or regulatory programs, such as sewer backups, combined sewer overflow control, the NPDES municipal stormwater permit, and others. Also, each activity is tied to Portland's larger watershed objectives. Finally, the Program is made up of a mix of engineers, environmental specialists, and landscape architects who offer unique approaches and perspectives to stormwater management challenges.

SSMP staff credit some of the Program's successful innovations to a provision BES included in their original NPDES permit application that required the City to conduct research on better ways to manage stormwater. As a result, in the early 1990s the City began implementing and monitoring BMPs, referred to as Early Action Projects, to determine their feasibility and effectiveness. These projects were implemented mainly on publicly held properties, and they have formed the basis of Portland's experience with green technologies. Based in part on their success, the City has expanded its application of green technologies in its capital improvement projects and in its requirements for new development. The Sustainable

Stormwater Management Program continues to act as a "research and development" arm of BES, testing out new designs in a variety of settings, and they pass on their experience on to others who design Portland's capital improvement projects.

Lessons for Other Communities

Outreach to other jurisdictions is helpful early in the process to find out what other communities are doing to manage stormwater and what lessons they have already learned, particularly overseas. Now the Internet and conferences offer opportunities to interact and share with other communities and professionals at large. That said, Portland emphasizes the importance of using what can be learned from other communities to develop a unique strategy that is tailored to meet the particular needs of the community.

One of the lessons Portland staff want to emphasize is that the right-of-way is already within a city's authority, making projects like Green Streets fairly easy to do. Stormwater managers and planners still want to consult with homeowners about their aesthetic preferences and expectations to ensure community acceptance. The City has received a wealth of positive feedback about the green street installations because of their beauty — they are valued by residents as an amenity, and this is one of the most important and rewarding reasons to use green approaches wherever possible.

They also want to stress that a successful sustainable stormwater program requires a multi-disciplinary approach that involves landscape architects, engineers, planners, reviewers, department heads, and watershed managers. They knew they needed the participation of all these groups in discussions and planning for individual projects as well as Citywide initiatives. This type of collaboration can also bring more resources to the table where funding for a project or initiative might be limited.

Members of the community should be credited for recognizing the value of sustainable stormwater management and for serving as advocates for projects and initiatives. For example, a number of citizens have requested that the City install Green Streets in front of their homes or businesses and have asked how they can get more involved.

Portland has seen the value in starting small with demonstration projects. Implementing a few pilot projects allowed them to monitor the practices and modify the designs for improved function and effectiveness before being implemented more widely. Because of the supporting monitoring data, Green Streets and other BMPs are recognized as one solution to the City's CSO issues. In fact, up to 500 Green Streets are being included in the pre-design of a large drainage basin to alleviate CSO and sewer back-up challenges.

Finally, sustainable stormwater approaches are seen as an important watershed health strategy. As the Portland area continues to develop and urbanize, Green Streets, ecoroofs, rain gardens, and simple impervious area disconnection help to transform the landscape and achieve multiple objectives, from stormwater flow and water quality management to cooling the air, providing habitat, enhancing neighborhoods, and improving property values.

CHAPTER 38

Salt Lake City Turns Old Buildings into Green Buildings

Michael Glenn

As a measure for efficiency and "greenness," buildings that qualify under the U.S. Environmental Protection Agency's Energy Star Program leave a smaller impact on the environment while reducing operating costs, maintaining affordability, and improving occupant comfort. The more widely accepted "green" certifications include points for enhanced levels of energy efficiency equating to Energy Star qualification.[1] Energy Star is commonly associated only with new construction. On average, Energy Star qualifying new buildings operate 15 percent more energy efficiently compared with peer buildings constructed to current energy code. The incremental cost averages $1–$2 per square foot.

Energy Star is often overlooked for older buildings because of retrofit costs. However, Energy Star for older buildings can be achievable and cost effective. The historic Stratford Hotel in Salt Lake City is an excellent example. The old hotel was gutted by fire in June 2005. It was subsequently purchased by a for-profit developer, LaPorte Group, for renovation as a mixed-use project with 46 affordable housing units serving a very low income population. Energy Star qualification was deemed necessary to keep units affordable and because Ben Logue, President of LaPorte Group, believes it as, "the right thing to do."

When old buildings like the Stratford Apartments are retrofitted to Energy Star quali-fying levels, energy performance can improve by 25–30 percent. To achieve an Energy Star qualifying score, this project is retrofitted with better insulation (including walls), air sealing techniques for the building envelop and HVAC system's ducts, areas of new Low E glass, Energy Star appliances, and compact fluorescent lighting. Beyond the Energy Star threshold, the Stratford Apartments are equipped with rooftop solar photovoltaic panels to produce up to 1000 watts of electricity for each unit. HVAC for each unit is all electric to take advantage of the solar energy produced. Residents of the Stratford Apartments are benefiting from Energy Star and the photovoltaic system with average utility bills at only $21 per unit per month.

Like the developer/owner of the Stratford Apartments, other developer/owners have a prime opportunity to upgrade their older building's energy using equipment to Energy Star when the building energy using systems (heating, air conditioning, appliances, lighting fixtures, building control systems, and etc.) reach the end of their useful life (18 to 20 years old). As the replacement equipment is specified, it makes economic sense to ratchet up efficiencies. And, in some cases, there is no choice — replacement systems and equipment are now being manufactured at higher levels of efficiency than the old equipment when originally installed. In the case of replacing old air conditioning units with seasonal energy efficiency ratings (SEER) of 10.0 or less, manufacturers now produce units well above that rating at SEER 17.0.

Besides ratcheting up equipment efficiency, it is important to resize equipment. In the past, contractors have oversized building equipment as their "rule of thumb." Properly sized furnaces, air conditioners, chillers, boilers, and pumps operate much more efficiently. HVAC contractors and engineers should recalculate building heating and cooling loads as they develop specifications for replacement equipment.

The necessary replacement of aging equipment often gives building owners the impetus to make other substantial energy upgrades. Depending on the extent of that remodeling, there may be opportunities to tear into the building envelope and upgrade the building's thermal characteristics (windows, attic and wall insulations, and doors) and upgrade difficult to access systems (duct sealing, insulation of hot water lines, and enhanced ventilation/exhaust systems). As in the case of the Stratford Apartments, the more extensive these upgrades, the better the HERS rating.

For residential buildings of three-story and under, Energy Star qualifications are established by independent Home Energy Performance System (HERS) raters who are certified by and utilize rating standards provided by the national Residential Energy Services Network (RESNET). The raters determine a building's energy baseline and project long-term post retrofit savings using HERS software. From the baseline, the raters recommend cost-effective measures with estimates for achievable energy savings. Although not a guarantee of savings, the raters provide valuable information for allocating capital improvement dollars among energy retrofit measures and insuring that scarce funds are allocated to those upgrades more likely to create the greatest long-term savings.

When residential buildings are 4 stories or higher and for other commercially-sized buildings, the process for Energy Star qualification involves benchmarking directly through the U.S. Environmental Protection Agency's Portfolio Manager[2] rather than using a HERS rater. Using the EPA website, these buildings must rank in the top 75 percent of similar buildings to be Energy Star qualified. Because the Energy Star qualifying for larger buildings focuses on a ranking rather than scoring threshold, it is harder to achieve Energy Star for older compared to newer buildings. And, since larger residential and other commercially-sized buildings often possess more complex energy-using central systems (including central boilers, central energy controls, chiller, air handlers, and domestic hot water systems), benchmarking and specifying retrofits to achieve Energy Star may require assistance from a mechanical engineer.

Financing Energy Efficiency for Older Buildings

The bulk of costs for "going green" in new construction or older buildings is related to the energy features — taking a building to Energy Star levels of efficiency or beyond. Depending on a building's current use, age, and location; financing options range from utility demand-side rebates, the federal Weatherization Assistance Program, federal HOME and Community Development Block Grant (CDBG) programs, state and federal tax credits, and other federal and local initiatives. A listing of some financing options is posted by the U.S. Department of Housing and Urban Development[3] and the National Renewable Energy Laboratory supported DSIRE database of renewable and energy efficiency incentives.[4] More popular financing options include:

Utility Rebates. In most areas of the United States, utility companies offer incentives and rebates for energy efficiency upgrades as well as technical assistance, making Energy Star qualification an attractive investment as well as economic driver for other "green" upgrades. As an energy retrofit project is contemplated, it is important to readily enlist representatives from utility companies. In most cases, utilities require preapproval of projects to reserve utility rebates. Because utilities may require new equipment to meet certain energy efficiency specifications, it is important to partner early before equipment is ordered or contractors begin work. In the case of the Stratford Apartments, energy efficiency rebates from Rocky Mountain Power total over $20,000.

Weatherization Assistance Program. When an old building includes residential units for lower income populations, some Energy Star improvements can be provided under the U.S. Department of Energy's Weatherization Assistance (WAP) Program. The program funds upgrades for existing units, and does not participate in construction of new units. Units must serve households with incomes at less than 200 percent of federal poverty levels, but some states establish a lower income threshold. Retrofits provided through the Weatherization Assistance Program are considered "grants" and help keep utility payments affordable. As with utility rebates, it is crucial to involve the local WAP program coordinator up-front during a remodel project's planning phase. To locate a local WAP coordinator in your area, see: www.eere.energy.gov/wip/projectmap/. There is a maximum average funding threshold per unit of $6,500. And, depending on each state's Weatherization Assistance State Plan, there may be a cost share requirement for property owners. The energy audit instrument used by the local WAP agencies provides a customized printout that lists recommended energy measures. Local agencies implement the most cost effective measures first, proceeding down the list until the average funding threshold per unit is met. Based upon the audits, the most common WAP retrofits include: furnace repairs and tune-up, furnace replacement (to 90 to 95 percent AFUE), duct sealing, set-back thermostats, air testing and sealing building envelop, wall and ceiling insulation, an Energy Star refrigerator, and compact fluorescent lamps.

Federal HOME Program. If a project includes affordable rental housing units, retrofits to achieve Energy Star as well as other green improvements can also be funded using U.S. Department of Housing and Urban Development (HUD)'s HOME Program. HOME funds are administered and distributed by local and state government jurisdictions as low interest loans or grants. In conjunction with other financing, the HOME funds work for new construction or retrofit of existing units to HUD standards. The funds can be used in conjunction with assistance from utility companies and the Weatherization Assistance Program. But, HOME funds for Energy Star retrofits may be used to fund retrofit upgrades not otherwise eligible for utility and WAP assistance funding. For instance, WAP funding thresholds often preclude window restorations or replacements or renewable energy features. Yet, that window work or renewable features are eligible using HOME funds and can be funded with HOME funds as part of an overall project. To locate a HOME participating jurisdiction for your project area, please refer to: www.portal.hud.gov/portal/page/portal/HUD/states. Unfortunately, HOME funds require adherence to HUD's policy on "recapture" and "resale." In other words, if a project or units are resold within the "affordability period" and the cognizant government agency has adopted "recapture" provisions, any HOME funds must be recaptured and repaid to that agency. If the government agency has established "resale" provisions in lieu of recapturing funds, the seller can only sell to another income-eligible household. When HOME funds support a project, other various federal requirements such as Davis Bacon construction wage requirements also may apply.

Energy Performance Contracting. For building owners who are "cash strapped" to complete energy upgrades, there is energy performance contracting. As a form of equipment leasing, a well managed performance contract can provide for immediate improvements while creating a project cash flow that insures sufficient energy saving to cover the lease terms. An Energy Service Company (ESCO) partner on a performance contract evaluates building needs, provides design and engineering services, arranges for long-term lease financing, oversees installation and construction, provides a guarantee (performance bond) for energy savings, can maintain and service equipment, and evaluates project savings. In most cases, the ESCO will also work with owners so that ownership of the equipment passes to the owner at the end of the financing term. By using a competitive process to select an ESCO partner, project costs, fees, and terms will be more favorable to the building owner. The U.S. Department of Housing and Urban Development reports that a $1.62 million performance contract for Albuquerque Housing Services along with $648,000 from the city and utilities has financed energy updates for 953 housing units. The energy and water savings is expected to be $334,000 per year and net savings after payments to the ESCO is $130,000. ESCOs can also participate on renewable energy projects for existing buildings. For more information on performance contracting including sample procurement documents, see: www.hud.gov/offices/pih/pro grams/ph/phecc/eperformance.cfm.

Federal Tax Credits. Tax credits exist for projects where occupancy is dedicated to affordable households over an affordability period. Credits include the Federal Low Income Housing Tax Credit or LIHTC), tax credits for historic rehabilitation, and credits for energy and renewable improvements. The popular LIHTC Program, which is based on Section 42 of the Internal Revenue Code, was enacted by Congress in 1986 to provide the private market with an incentive to invest in affordable rental housing. Federal housing tax credits are awarded to developers of qualified projects who sell credits to investors. This raises capital (or equity) for the projects which reduces the debt that the developer would otherwise have to borrow. Because the debt is lower, a tax credit property can offer lower, more affordable rents. Provided the property maintains compliance with the LIHTC program requirements throughout the affordability period (usually 15 years), investors receive a dollar-for-dollar credit against their Federal tax liability each year for 10 years.[6] The sunset on federal energy tax credits range from late 2010 to 2016. Historic, energy efficiency, and renewable tax credits operate similarly for owners. In the case of buildings owned by nonprofit agencies or a local government, the secondary market for these other tax credits can also provide necessary financing.

Community Development Block Grant Program. This HUD-funded program is administered by either a state agency that serves as the "participating jurisdiction" (PJ) for receipt and distribution of HUD funds to local governments or by a local government that is large enough to receive and administer their own CDBG funds. When projects fulfill certain community-defined goals and priorities, communities may be willing to allocate CDBG funding to the project.[7] The primary statutory objective of the CDBG program is to develop viable communities by providing decent housing and a suitable living environment and by expanding economic opportunities, principally for persons of low- and moderate-income. Thus, at least 70 percent of CDBG grant funds must be used for activities which benefit low and moderate income families or aid in the prevention or elimination of slums or blight. Communities receiving CDBG funds either directly from HUD or from a State government may allocate funds for the following types of activities: acquisition of property for public purposes; construction or reconstruction of streets, water and sewer facilities, neighborhood centers, recreation facilities, and other public works; demolition; rehabilitation of public and private buildings; public services; planning activities; assistance to nonprofit entities for community development activities; and assistance to private, for profit entities to carry out economic development activities.

Design Savings. During an integrated or whole building design process, a project's architects, engineers, and other design team members collaborate more closely throughout all design phases. The closer collaboration helps the team to better accommodate any additional energy-saving and "green" technologies within the existing project budget. As the design team is fully integrated early in the design process, it can better understand the interaction of site, energy, materials, indoor air quality, acoustics, and natural resources. For example, siting a building on a slightly different axis can maximize daylighting and winter sunshine while reducing the number of lights to be installed (reducing the overall, upfront equipment and installation costs). Those same design considerations can reduce sizing for HVAC equipment. This frees up additional dollars in the construction budget to accommodate other energy or "green" upgrades.

Other financing mechanisms that are unique to each state should also be considered.

These include various financing mechanisms through the USDA Rural Development programs[8] (loans, grants, and loan guarantees), private activity bonds (allocated to states under the Federal Tax Act of 1986), and CRA funding through area financial institutions (in compliance with the federal Community Reinvestment Act). Each state government also administers the U.S. Department of Energy State Energy Program (SEP) which may offer grants or loans to various public and private entities for energy conservation projects.[9]

Specifying Greenness

Some commonly recognized certifications for greenness in larger, mixed-use, and multifamily projects include the U.S. Green Building Council's[10] LEED certification and the Enterprise Foundation's[11] Green Communities certification. For smaller housing projects including single family detached, duplexes, and four-plexes, a certification is provided through the Rural Community Assistance Council (RCAC)[12] and the National Homebuilders Association.[13] Varying levels of independent, third-party verification and record keeping are required depending on which certification process is chosen. The costs for certifications also vary, so it is important to carefully research the merits and relative costs for each, and make certain that overall certification costs fit within the overall project budget.

From the beginning stages of project development, the developer or building owner must establish greenness as a primary goal. It cannot be an afterthought. The goal for greenness and the certification to be used for attaining that goal must be explicitly listed in the solicitation for professional architectural and engineering (A/E) services. Moreover, the selection criteria used to rate A/E proposals should provide weight to those firms with proven and credentialed green experience. In many cases, responding A/E firms may not possess that experience with their primary staff. These firms may list a secondary partner as "experienced" in order to bolster the A/E firm's ability to compete and receive a design award.

The review committee reviewing and scoring proposals submitted by A/E firms should prefer firms with proven and credentialed green experience in their primary staff. "Greening" a project involves new approaches to design, protocols, and products that may be contrary to "old ways." Retaining an A/E firm with staff who are well-founded in greenness is superior to the investment of time and energy necessary to school A/E firms with little or no direct experience.

One useful approach to greening involves hosting a design charrette. Not to be confused with value engineering where the focus is maintaining acceptable levels of project quality at least first cost and under budget, the design charrette focuses on desirable sustainable design features that have long-term or lifecycle benefits. The charrette usually occurs as the schematic design phase begins.

Charrettes integrate overall design goals with the physical environment of the proposed project site. The charrettes consider sustainable features, livability, durability, environmental and social impacts, and energy savings. Charrettes include not only the A/E team selected for a project, but peers from the A/E community, neighbors to the site, local officials, and future occupants — all can offer unique perspectives, background experience, and considerations. The U.S. Department of Energy's (DOE) website offers links to a guide produced by the National Renewable Energy Laboratory for organizing and conducting a design charrette. The guide also provides sample checklists, agendas, and supporting material.

Going Solar

Solar features are integral to qualifying a project as green. But, it is important for building owners and developers to differentiate between "active" and "passive" solar features. Active solar includes photovoltaics, panels for space heating, and solar domestic hot water systems. Passive solar includes positioning glass to optimize winter solar gain, shading to minimize summer solar gain, trombe walls, and other thermal mass for storage/dissipation of winter solar gain.

Passive measures may be too expensive for older buildings unless there is substantial or "gut" rehabilitation. For older buildings, passive measures also create historic preservation issues. For the Stratford Apartments, historic tax credits were used to finance the building retrofits, and no changes could occur to the exterior including historic windows. To avoid losing the historic tax credits, it was more practical to install an active solar photovoltaic system on the roof, hidden by the parapet.

When economically and historically feasible, passive measures usually possess a longer useful life than active solar measures. Because passive measures are integral to the basic building design and possess few moving parts (controls, fans, pumps, valves, and sensors), their useful life may approach 35 to 50 years. Whereas, the useful life of active measures with more moving parts possess a useful life averaging 15–20 years if there is regularly scheduled maintenance.

Choosing between active solar options can be difficult. There is often limited space for mounting collectors and a tight budget — these force developers to decide between two or three systems. In the case of the Stratford Apartments, the owner weighed the advantages of active solar hot water collectors and photovoltaics. Because of the particular population housed at the Stratford Apartments and their daily schedules, La Porte Group chose photovoltaic panels over solar domestic hot water panels. La Porte Group determined that solar hot water panels would produce more than enough hot water at the end of each day, but require overnight storage capacity to meet peak morning demand. Whereas, PV panels would continue to produce power for sale back to Rocky Mountain Power while residents are at work or out — there would be no storage issue.

The Stratford Apartment's photovoltaic system was designed with no battery storage. The PV system features 1000 watts of capacity per unit at $8 per watt.

Electricity is powered directly through the inverter to the 46 units. The system designer recognized batteries as the "weak link" in panel maintenance and the system's long-term performance. In the case of the Stratford Apartments, it made sense to sell excess power back to the electric utility company and avoid battery maintenance issues.

When a solar hot water or photovoltaic system is designed, it is also important to specify equipment that easily allows for seasonable adjustment of panel angles, equipment that is climate-hardy (especially for solar hot water systems), equipment that is warranted by a well established supplier, and equipment mounted and installed with maintenance personnel in mind. Solar domestic hot water systems should be designed with a heat exchanger and glycol loop to avoid problems with freezing temperature.

NOTES

1. See Enterprise Green Communities Checklist at http://www.greencommunitiesonline.org/tools/criteria/, the Rural Community Assistance Council's Green Building Checklist at http://www.rcac.org/assets/greenbuild/grn-bldg-guide4-20-09.pdf and the U.S Green Building Council's LEED checklist at www.usgbc.org/DisplayPage.aspx?CMSPageID=147.

2. The portfolio manager can be accessed through www.energystar.gov/index.cfm?c=evaluateperformancebusportfoliomanager#set.

3. See www.hud.gov/offices/pih/proqrams/ph/phecc/funding.cfm.

4. See http://www.dsireusa.org/.

5. The incremental costs include the SEER upgrade to air conditioning units.

6. See www.hud.gov/offices/cpd/affordablehousing/training/web/lihtc/basics/work.cfm.

7. See www.hud.gov/offices/cpd/communitydevelopment/programs/ for more information on the CDBG Program.

8. See www.rurdev.usda.gov/Home.html.

9. See www1.eere.energy.gov/wip/sep.html.

10. See www.usgbc.org/DisplayPage.aspx?CMSPageID=147.

11. See www.Greencommunitiesonline.org/tools/criteria/index.asp.

12. See www.rac.org/doc.aspx?211 and www.rcac.org/assets/greenbuild/grn-bldg-guide4-20-09.pdf.

13. See www.nahbgreen.org/Certification/homecertification.aspx, which applies only to single family projects and not multifamily units.

CHAPTER 39

San Francisco and Other Cities Reduce
Their Air Pollution by Building Bikeways

Kyle Boelte

My legs start to burn as I hit a hill, but the soft yellows of dawn are filtering through the city streets, and a cool breeze is brushing my cheeks. My mind is clear. At the end of my five-mile bike commute, my blood is flowing, I'm focused, and I'm excited for work. This is how I start my day: fully alive. How many Americans can say the same about their commute? I have a hunch: all the cyclists.

Until recently, bike commuting in the United States was something of a cult, mysterious to outsiders who assume it's only for the young, the superfit, and the spandex-clad. But that's rapidly changing, as urban planners are designing streets where bikes are as welcome as cars, and employers are offering bike facilities as a way to attract creative professionals.

"Quality of life today is the most important tool of economic development," says Gil Penalosa, the former parks commissioner of bike-friendly Bogota, Colombia. "People save all year to go on vacation to places that are walkable and bikable. Why not live in a place where it's walkable and bikable?"

If you already bike to work, consider yourself part of the vanguard that's pushing the country toward a postcarbon future of high-density, vibrant communities. If you haven't biked since childhood, it's not too late to re-kindle your passion for that most efficient of human inventions.

In Copenhagen, home to Danish urban planner Jan Gehl, 37 percent of all commuting is done by bike — partly thanks to Gehl's interest in "human scale" urban design. "You have to start with people," he says. "You can't add the people after you have made the cars happy. A city with a lot of bicyclists is a city with a lot of life. A city with a lot of cars is a city with a lot of metal and speed."

In 2008, according to the U.S. Census, 720,000 Americans commuted to work by bike — 43 percent more than in 2000. It would be nice to say that the growth was driven by a concern for the climate, but the main reason is economics. "People bike because it's fast, cheap, and easy to get around," says Penalosa, "not because it's good for the environment." Christopher Leinberger, a land-use strategist at the Brookings Institution, notes that people who are auto-dependent spend 25 percent of their income on transportation, compared with 9 percent for those who walk, bike, or take public transit.

Incentives like that change the way our cities look and work. As Leinberger says, "transportation infrastructure drives development." Builders and real estate developers take their cue from the roads, highways, and public trans-

Originally published as "Look Ma, No Car! Pedaling Toward a Postcarbon Future," *Sierra Magazine*, March/April 2010, by the Sierra Club, San Francisco, CA. Article appears with the permission of *Sierra*, the national magazine of the Sierra Club.

portation options available in an area. Since the 1950s, U.S. transportation policy has focused almost exclusively on the automobile. Sprawling suburbs were sold as freedom but ended up trapping their residents in traffic jams. "We should build cities that we want to live in," insists Penalosa, now executive director of the Canadian nonprofit 8–80 Cities. "Do we want to be stuck in cars?"

Building a new bicycle culture requires extensive infrastructure, he says. "And I don't just mean painted lines. Bicycle lanes are not enough — you need physically separated bikeways." In this country, we call them "cycle tracks" — lanes physically divided from vehicular traffic by islands. Although more expensive to install, they provide an extremely high level of safety for cyclists, both real and perceived. In October 2007, New York City unveiled the country's first cycle track on Ninth Avenue in Manhattan, something the advocacy group Transportation Alternatives had been pushing since 1993.

The city has also added 200 miles of standard bike lanes — even more than in bicycle-friendly Copenhagen. Cyclists have responded. "There has been a huge surge in the number of cyclists on our streets," says Wiley Norvell, communication director of Transportation Alternatives. "You find yourself waiting at a light with four or five cyclists behind you. And that makes for safety in numbers, because everyone else on the street is starting to anticipate cyclists being on the road."

Cities like Seattle take a cheaper approach, separating cyclists and cars with a wide painted lane, as opposed to a mere line in the road. "Safety is important, but so is perceived safety," says John Pucher, a professor of urban planning and public policy at Rutgers University.

Many other cities — including Syracuse, New York; St. Paul, Minnesota; and Salt Lake City — are taking another tack, rechristening streets through residential neighborhoods as "bike boulevards." Car traffic is still allowed but is "calmed" with reduced speed limits, engineering fixes like planters and sidewalks that bulge at intersections, and signage that makes it clear to motorists to expect lots of bikes. ("Traffic calming may be just as important as

bike lanes," Pucher says.) Bike boulevards adjacent to major traffic arteries provide crucial direct links between destinations. While bike paths sometimes meander, bicycle commuters need routes that connect them to workplaces, shops, and schools.

Another easy fix for cyclists seeking safety is adding "bike boxes." These large, green-painted zones extend the bike lane into the vehicle lane at intersections, alerting drivers to the presence of bikes and allowing cyclists to make safer left-hand turns. Simple changes like these can have an enormous effect, given that the main factor suppressing the number of regular cyclists In the United States is fear. This is especially true of women, who are generally more risk averse than men. Pucher has found, for instance, that three times as many men as women use bikes for transportation in the United States, while in Europe, where infrastructure is better, the numbers are equal. Penalosa evaluates infrastructure on the "8–80 Rule": "If you would not send an 8-year-old along with an 80-year-old on a walk or a bike ride on that infrastructure, then it is not safe enough."

My initiation into the world of bike commuting came after college. Five days a week, I enthusiastically pedaled 17 miles each way between my home in Boulder, Colorado, and my office in Longmont, on a highway that cut through golden prairie to the foot of the Rocky Mountains. Given the uncertainties of Front Range weather, a sunny morning could give way to snowflakes by noon. But I had a secret weapon: the bus. Since the Boulder buses had bike racks, I could always bring my bike home with me. Bike racks are crucial to a green transportation system because they enable people who live or work far from public transportation to build cycling into a multi-vehicle commute. They're good for bus systems too, upping the number of potential passengers.

Trains and light rail are also inviting bikes on board, although often, as on Chicago's Metra and the San Francisco Bay Area's BART, only folding bikes are allowed during rush hour. Pucher's research shows that U.S. cyclists prefer to bring their bike on the train with them, but the availability of secure bike parking could encourage them to ride to the train station and lock up their steed there. Enter Bikestation, a nonprofit that has created cycling hubs in seven cities. In Washington, D.C., for example, Bikestation provides 130 parking spaces and changing rooms for cyclists at Union Station in a modem glass-and-steel structure with secure, automated access — all for an annual membership fee of $20.

Of course, bicycle commuting isn't for everyone. And most people — cyclists included — need buses and trains and, yes, cars to get around at least some of the time. But cyclists can be a catalyst in the green-transportation revolution; they fight passionately for safer infrastructure because their lives depend on it. ("And by the way," Gehl adds, "if you bicycle to work every day you can live seven years longer.")

Here is a future we can choose to make: Towns and cities where the streets are full of cyclists pedaling to work and the sidewalks vibrant with pedestrians walking to cafes, movie theaters, and farmers' markets. Healthier communities connected by rail lines and bus routes. A low-carbon transportation system that helps us avert a climate catastrophe.

And there you are, in the middle of it all, pedaling, your legs burning a little, sure, but a smile creeping across your face.

CHAPTER 40

Santa Rosa Implements a Build-It-Green Program
Dell Tredinnick

Growth and environmental protection are often at odds, but not in the City of Santa Rosa, where city leaders decided three years ago to bring the two into balance. The result was the voluntary Santa Rosa Build It Green (SR BIG) program. At present, SR BIG has certified as "green" more than 75 dwelling units, and 850-plus additional dwelling units have applied for green status under the program. A voluntary program, SR BIG promotes building and re-modeling homes in a way that reduces energy demands, releases far fewer pollutants into the atmosphere, conserves water and reduces construction waste. The resulting structures are easier to maintain, less expensive to operate, produce less air pollution and are healthier to occupy. This may seem impossible or impossibly expensive for most people, but it is neither.

The program follows a set of simple but comprehensive Green Building Guidelines that provide a roadmap for building design and construction. These guidelines were hammered out by developers, environmentalists, bankers, planners, educators, architects, engineers, maintenance personnel, designers, government officials and city staff. The result is a consistent and flexible tool that can deliver significantly better results and a better bottom line than the conventional building process. The guidelines SR BIG

uses are adaptable to any geographic/climatic region or distinctive culture.

What Does a SR BIG Home Look Like?

The short answer is "like any other home." The SR BIG program has certified large custom homes, production subdivision homes, affordable homes (built by Habitat for Humanity) and municipal remodeled dwellings, such as the Santa Rosa Samuel Jones Hall Homeless Shelter.

SR BIG also embraces the very active remodeling market by reaching out to the public in workshops and educating local home improvement suppliers. Remodelers can gain SR BIG certification by adding more insulation, installing low-flow and energy efficient fixtures and appliances, using paints and coating that emit low or no volatile organic compounds, and basically following the same guidelines, where possible, that exist for new construction.

How Are SR BIG Homes Evaluated?

Green homes differ from most conventional dwellings in how they perform in four rated categories. These categories and the required minimum points needed in each are:

1. Energy Efficiency —11 points (107 possible);
2. Resource Conservation — 6 points (64 possible);
3. Indoor Air Quality — 5 points (45 possible); and
4. Water Efficiency — 3 points (31 possible).

An SR BIG home must achieve a total score of at least 50 points, which includes the minimum number of points in each of these four categories. A dwelling or project can get additional points to bring it up to the total minimum requirement of 50 points if it qualifies for community and/or innovation points.

How Does SR BIG Work?

The SR BIG program's success is attributed to several key elements:

It Is Voluntary. Mandatory programs can work but typically result in construction that achieves only the minimum requirements. A voluntary program allows the market to drive the standard, achieving better and better buildings as time goes by and builders find more efficient ways to do things. The competition to be "greener" is already manifesting in the city's building culture

It Has a Strong Marketing Component. Santa Rosa actively educates the public, suppliers, designers, contractors and everyone involved in the building process. This creates an informed public that demands greater performance from their homes.

The Program Uses Trained Personnel. Independent third party inspectors, who must pass a rigorous exam at Sonoma State University, perform the inspections. Currently, about 50 SR BIG inspectors have been trained and certified. Developers and builders hire the SR BIG inspectors to help them achieve and verify their project's green status. The city recommends that the inspector is involved in a project as early as possible so that green scores can be

maximized by better design and early integration of green elements.

The Program Provides Certification. Once the project has been "scored" by the inspector, the SR BIG Executive Committee reviews each application, verifies the points gathered and awards the certificate, which is a source of pride to homeowners and can be used to enhance resale.

The Program Is Dynamic and Flexible. Santa Rosa is constantly looking for ways to improve the process and program. Currently, it's focusing on ways to bring "green" to affordable housing projects. Green homes cost much less to operate and maintain and are healthier living environments. Individuals with low or fixed incomes have the greatest need for such savings.

Information Is Readily Shared. SR BIG owes much of its success to regional and national partners and shared knowledge. An example is the shared product data base, an online tool developed by the regional green partners that helps a supplier or do-it-yourselfer find locally available "green" products to meet their project needs (online at www.ciwmb.ca.gov/GreenBuilding/Materials).

Leadership in Energy and Environmental Design (LEED) standards were originally established for commercial and municipal buildings. LEED is an international rating mechanism that requires significantly more attention and inspections. LEED is in the process of developing standards for homes. Once those standards are complete, they will complement the SR BIG program. The upfront costs are typically much more for LEED than SR BIG.

Homes in California account for 31 percent of the states energy use. New homes built in California must meet Title 24 energy efficiency standards. SR BIG homes must exceed the Title 24 standards and get 1 point for every percentage point by which they exceed the required energy efficiency standards. An SR BIG home is at least 11 percent more energy efficient than a conventional new home and is commensurately less expensive to heat, cool and operate. That also means that the environmental impact of the home is reduced, which benefits everybody.

Water conservation is another area included in the SR BIG integrated approach. Choosing landscaping plants that are drought tolerant and installing high-efficiency irrigation systems can greatly reduce water use and create a beautiful space even during a drought. Highly efficient water devices inside the home are also important. Low-flow fixtures and Energy Star appliances are vital in saving water and reducing overall energy demands.

The initial cost of going green can be minimal, and the long-term savings can be significant. While there are many types and levels of green homes, research shows that for every $1 invested in a "green" home, a return of $10 is realized after the first year or two and thereafter for the life of the structure. Building green is building smart.

CHAPTER 41

Savannah and Other Cities Create Fused Grid Street Networks

Fanis Grammenos *and* Carl J. Stephani

A neighborhood development involves the design of a street network. As an element of a neighborhood's structure, it deserves to be examined closely for its effect on the environment and the neighborhood's quality of life.

Streets occupy land and consume resources for their emplacement, and municipal resources for their maintenance. Streets incorporate a dwindling resource (bitumen from oil). They add to the impermeable surface area with a negative impact on water absorption and water quality, and they contribute to the urban heat island effect that influences cooling energy demand. Street patterns can impede or enable walking and bicycling thereby influencing energy use for transport. They can restrict or accommodate the flow of traffic thereby affecting greenhouse and noxious gas generation. Local streets represent the bulk of the entire network mileage of a district and, consequently, their influence can be significant.

Street patterns also affect the quality of life of a neighborhood. They can reduce or increase the risk of fatal accidents or injuries; particularly to children and seniors (walking is currently the least safe mode of travel). They can help increase the level of tranquility in a neighborhood and support social networking, which in turn reinforces a sense of security. They can reduce the noise intrusion and improve local air quality by managing traffic. They can make walking and biking pleasant or undesirable thus favoring or discouraging an active lifestyle. Street patterns can support or undermine the viability of amenities required for daily needs by providing or denying convenient access to them.

The Quest for an Environmentally Benign Street Pattern

Since the onset of the environmental agenda in planning in the 1970s, neighborhood plans have been regularly scrutinized for the potential impact of a planned development on the natural environment both local and regional. Only recently, however, have there been systematic analyses of the actual elements of impact and their magnitude. A systematic list of impacts includes several direct, and many indirect impacts. Land consumption, infrastructure costs and water quality impacts include the direct effects. Elements of indirect impact are: extent of car travel and its influence on local air quality as well as its contribution to climate change through CO_2 generation. Further in the same chain of potential causality are the negative health effects of air pollution, which, though indisputable, must be cautiously attributed and apportioned.

LAND CONSUMPTION

Depending on the choice of street pattern and the cross section of the street space, streets can consume from 24 percent to nearly 50 percent of the land available for development. For example the Portland grid[1] consumes 41 percent of the development land in street Right-of-Ways (ROW) while the Savannah, GA, pattern uses 42 percent. At the low end of usage, a segment of the Manhattan Commissioner's plan consumes about 29 percent for ROW, and Stein's influential Radburn[2] plan uses up to about 24 percent of the total.

Many other known patterns occupy the middle ground of land consumption in that range. The environmental importance of land utilization calculation rests on the following grounds:

- Land taken up by streets becomes unavailable for development;
- For the same number of similar housing units a pattern that requires less land for streets would lower the pressure to consume more of it;
- More units on an identical piece of land mean higher development density, which improves the economics of transit, municipal services and of the project as a business venture.

In introducing a street network pattern for a neighborhood that either comes from city history books or from the drafting board, one must consider the environmental significance of land consumption attributed to the streets. This consideration becomes amplified in importance when knowing that local streets represent the bulk, about 70 percent, of all streets of a district.

INFRASTRUCTURE EMPLACEMENT AND MAINTENANCE

Streets today represent the single largest component of capital infrastructure outlays for building a neighborhood. Until the end of the 19th century most city streets were unpaved, had no storm drainage sewers, or lighting, and hardly any signage. Also, the majority of them were narrow by contemporary standards and a good number did not have raised sidewalks. Consequently, they consumed few resources. By contrast, current design standards require a large investment for street construction and sig-

nificant city budget allocations for their maintenance.

A 2008 engineering study[3] compared three network patterns for the same district and found that the traditional, familiar, grid network pattern had about 33 percent to 39 percent respectively higher lane meters than each of the alternatives, excluding rear lanes (alleys). Similarly, the capital costs for roads were 46 percent and 30 percent higher in traditional grid networks than in alternative networks. Clearly, the choice of layout can have a measurable effect on capital and maintenance costs.

WATER CYCLE AND QUALITY IMPACTS

All new development alters the pre-existing natural condition of a site and its ability to absorb and recycle rain water. Reduced absorption often necessitates additional irrigation that may stress a limited water resource. Roads are a major factor in limiting absorption first by the sheer amount of impermeable surface they introduce. They affect water recycling by the generation of road surface pollutants that end up in the downstream water making it unfit for direct use. Of the total amount of impermeable surfaces that cover a developed site, roads account for 48 to 65 percent.[4] Evidently, they are a major factor in reducing a site's capacity to absorb rainwater; and that which is not absorbed affects downstream water quality and aquatic life. This run off may also erode streams with sudden and occasionally catastrophic results. For all these rainwater related effects, optimizing the street network, its total length and surface area becomes important from an environmental perspective.

GREENHOUSE GAS EMISSIONS (GHG)

Emissions from all vehicles count for about 30 percent of the total from all sources and personal commuting amounts to about 30 to 40 percent of that share that translates to about 10 to 12 percent of the total GHG production. To the extent that a local street network affects the total vehicle miles traveled (VMTs) of personal commuting, it should be rationalized toward reducing them. Greater reductions can be achieved by improving traffic flow in a network as a whole and, at the neighborhood level, by replacing car trips with walking and bike trips. A network pattern that reduces delay and encourages walking deserves persistent exploration.

HEALTH IMPACTS OF REDUCED AIR QUALITY

The health burden of breathing impure air is enormous and well documented.[5] The health impacts are caused by the powering of most city and regional economic activity with coal, oil or natural gas, they are not just from transportation. Air contaminants that affect human health are produced by all combustion devices. A key difference among them is that transportation permeates the urban milieu and therefore its by-products can be immediate, proximate and intense. Though trip length relates proportionately to overall emissions, noxious gases tend to peak at low speeds. To reduce their production, a street network would ideally be designed to optimize speeds that match the lowest emission levels.[6] With such design, reductions in pollutants could be significant. In addition to design rationalization, more pronounced reductions may be achieved by displacing local car travel with active transportation. It appears that a network design that would achieve reductions in emissions is at least theoretically feasible and, consequently, worth investigating for its beneficial health impacts.

WHY A NEW STREET NETWORK PATTERN

The land and infrastructure efficiencies that may be possible with a rationalized street pattern network, as evidenced by the above statistics, would by themselves be sufficient justification to search for such a network. But the additional, and just as important, grounds for the search relates to the improvements mentioned above which can be linked to environmental and quality of life objectives.

During the second half of the 20th century, it has become increasingly apparent that inherited street patterns do not work well under the new constraints of multimodal travel. As the range of modes increased to include cars, trucks, buses, trolleys, trams, transport trucks, motorcycles, bicycles, and pedestrians, street space was in high demand and street design became more complicated and also controversial. Moreover, not only was unconstrained movement a prime consideration, but also a new and critical factor emerged — safety — for those driving and for pedestrians using the streets. Traffic accidents top the list of leading causes of premature death.[7]

Starting in the 1940s and intensifying in the 1970s, there were calls for physical changes to the pattern of street networks, and for new traffic management techniques to enable goods to flow while safeguarding the health of city dwellers. The range of techniques that have been developed, adopted, and applied since, have now become a discipline of its own — traffic calming.[8] New ideas, some of which became movements, such as "Homezones," "Woonerf Streets," "Naked Streets," "Complete Streets," Plus 15 level, Below Grade street systems, and large pedestrian-only zones in city centers, all pointed to the need for a radical rethinking of the inherited network patterns and their design.

Environmental priorities added more urgency to that need. Water permeability of a neighborhood or district, for example, is closely tied to the amount of hard surfaces of which asphalted roads are usually a major component. Greenhouse and noxious gas emissions have been shown to be dependent on amount of travel (VMTs), and the characteristics of travel (speed, frequency of stops, cold starts and congestion).[9] All these are linked either directly or indirectly to the street network layout. Current patterns appear ineffective in reducing emissions even with strong management measures.

The potential for a well-functioning system that satisfies the above range of objectives motivates the search for improved street network patterns. Another, perhaps stronger, motivator is the negative experiences derived from the systems in current use; their necessary, costly adaptations and transformations; and the sensible desire to pre-empt the application of concepts that have proven dysfunctional. Under this pressure for change, planners, architects and other professionals advanced solutions, specific or general, to the issues generated by the incompatibility of traditional network patterns and the contemporary multimodal transportation context. One such proposal is the Fused Grid model for local and district mobility.[10]

The Structure of the Fused Grid

The fused grid configuration is formed by using two generative elements:

- A framework of a district transportation network and
- Neighborhood unit cells that reside within the framework.

The district network geometry is based on two well recognized principles: the spacing of collectors and arterials and the need for "arteriality"[11] and traffic distribution. Traffic engineering guides suggest quarter mile (400 m) spacing of collectors, half a mile (800 m) for minor arterials, and 1600 m (one mile) for major arterials. Arteriality and traffic distribution suggest that for mid- and long distance travel, the connectors should be continuous and the network of these connectors should offer route choices for the chosen destinations. Both arteriality and traffic distribution imply an open grid that inherently satisfies these requirements.

The result of applying these principles is a recursive, fractal grid that starts at the quarter mile dimension and increases in size and complexity as its size doubles and the circumscribed area quadruples. Traffic studies have shown that, to facilitate flow, access to each higher level road facility should be progressively restricted to longer space intervals. This progressive restriction is possible when a fused grid is used in the layout of the local streets.

Neighborhood Unit network geometry is based on two generative principles, the comfortable walking distance and the "filtered permeability"[12] rule. The walking distance of 400 meters (quarter mile) has historically and through research been established as an acceptable maximum for the majority of people. Most early walled-in cities register a diameter of about 800 to 1000 meters. Currently, bus routes and rider catch basins in cities are planned using this well-established metric.

"Filtered permeability" implies that, in the layout of a neighborhood network, one mobility mode is given priority over another in terms of connectivity. Within a neighborhood quadrant, an area enclosed by the 400 m square (quarter-mile) pedestrians and bikes have priority and, consequently, their routes show the highest connectivity. The street geometry of the neighborhood "filters out" the car by making the network discontinuous for it only; the finer grain of the movement network is reserved for active transportation; i.e., walking and cycling.

Another important physical element is associated with the pedestrian network and forms a structural part of the neighborhood layout — open space. Each 16 ha (40 acre) neighborhood cell includes small parks strategically placed to enhance pedestrian movement and to become focal points for recreation and socializing.

A final, less obvious element of the neighborhood unit layout is its virtual, underlying grid. The streets and their path extensions all follow a grid which serves the need for clarity of orientation and for route directness even though the physical streets don't occupy all segments of the grid.

The combination of a clear, open grid for the district transportation network and the neighborhood virtual grid with its filtered permeability produces a robust and efficient movement system for all modes of transport. This system, which combines well-known geometries and street types for its structure (i.e. straight continuous streets, crescents and cul-de-sac streets, paths and open spaces) also may incorporate a new element — the twinned connector (or one-way couplet). At the scale of the minor and major arterial, the road splits to frame regular or larger building blocks, and traffic flow is in two separate one-way streams, anticipating future growth in volume and in commercial activity.

Almost without exception, large city and small town downtowns now include one way street adaptations. These are often linked to one-directional entries and exits to higher level connectors or highways that connect the city to intercity routes. This technique of one-way pairs for facilitating flow has also been occasionally adopted in new districts and towns.

The main design elements of the Fused

Grid network model such as the open grid, street types, one-way pairs and neighborhood units are all known and familiar, as is the rationale for them. It is their combination that constitutes advancement over the inherited models and conventional practice.

Benefits of the New Model

As previous efforts at creating models have shown, the acid test of any model is in a practical application, where its effects can be measured. This insight also applies to the Fused Grid of which a full built up district is under development but incomplete. However, contemporary computer-based modeling techniques allow not only life-like visual representations of neighborhoods, but also the computation of outcomes for certain chosen variables; traffic performance, for example. Planners and traffic engineers regularly use computer models such as CORSIM, VISSIM, CELLSIM and INTEGRATION to explore network alternatives and gauge their outcomes. In addition to modeling, careful inspection of existing city districts can identify areas with characteristics similar to the proposed, and enable cautiously drawn inferences about the alternatives. Inevitably, due to the great complexity and interaction among factors, some issues will remain ambiguous until an application of the fused grid model allows for detailed observation on the ground (in progress as of this writing). However, outcomes of the fused grid network that could be tested through analysis and inferences from analogous site plan configurations are listed below.

PERMEABILITY AND RAINWATER RUNOFF

In this regard, three site plan layouts for a 300 acre district were compared for their permeability.[13] In all cases, roads represented the largest proportion of the impermeable surface area from 48 to 65 percent followed by buildings at about 30 percent. The layout with the highest street density, the traditional, modified grid, had the highest level of overall site impervious area at 39 percent and most of it (65 percent) was attributable to roads. The Fused Grid

road system design consumed only 34 percent in impervious area, 52 percent of which was attributable to roads. This reduction constitutes a significant improvement in overall permeability that can be attributed to its optimized street network configuration.

TRANSPORTATION EFFICIENCY

When judged in terms of investment for an overall reduction in delays, or, conversely, flow improvement, the results from an analysis[14] that compared three alternative layouts showed the following:

Using the existing site layout of a built up district as a base (100 percent), on the grounds that it emerged as the least satisfactory performer, the study calculated the cost benefit of changing the network to achieve better performance. The results show that the traditional, modified grid yields a decrease in traffic flow delay between 4 and 20 percent for a 21 percent increase in investment. By comparison, the Fused Grid produces an 11 to 35 percent decrease in traffic flow delay for only a 6 percent increase in investment. In other words, for a less than a third of an increase in costs it achieves approximately a double decrease in traffic flow delay.

EMISSIONS REDUCTIONS

The 11 percent to 35 percent in travel delay mentioned above would contribute to measurable reductions in emissions as a significant portion of them is generated in idling and in slow speed movement.

That effect is accentuated with increasing residential densities.

In addition, the 23 percent reduction in local VMTs predicted by the research mentioned below would also make a significant contribution to the overall reduction in emissions.

ACTIVE TRANSPORT AND LIVING

A statistical analysis[15] of geo-coded trip diaries of residential areas in Seattle, Washington demonstrates that — other factors being equal — residential street networks with either more direct routing for pedestrians, or more pedestrian facilities relative to the vehicular network, are associated with improved odds of walking and reduced odds of driving. More specifically, a change from a pure small-block grid to a Fused Grid–like configuration can result in an 11.3 percent increase in odds of a home-based trip being walked.

The Fused Grid–like pattern is also associated with a 25.9 percent increase (over street patterns with equivalent route directness for walking and driving,) in the odds a person will get a sufficient level of physical activity. Finally, the Fused Grid's 10 percent increase in relative connectivity for pedestrians is associated with a 23 percent reduction in local vehicle travel distance (VMT); and, its improved continuity is associated with increased walking trips and distance.

A study in northern California[16] focusing on children's play found that children living in cul-de-sacs played outdoors 50 percent more frequently than those living on conventional grid network streets. Another study[17] looking at youth active transportation motivators found that the only common and strong predictor for children's walking to destinations was the presence of open spaces. The fused grid model incorporates both cul-de-sacs and open spaces as regular design elements in the neighborhood layout which would increase the probability of children's play and walking.

ROAD SAFETY IMPROVEMENTS

Using an advanced model for predicting collisions within a network,[18] five types of network configurations were tested in consecutively larger areas culminating in the size of an actual built neighborhood for which traffic data were available. Using the Fused Grid configuration as a base (100 percent) and the 256 Ha land area module for the analysis, results show that the traditional grid and the cul-de-sacs test networks produce 260 percent and 150 percent as many collisions, respectively, as the fused grid network.

Further, using a 90 percent confidence level to test for statistical significance, the fused grid network appeared to be significantly safer than all other networks. The cul-de-sac test network ranged from a ratio of 1.5 to 2.3 times higher in predicted collisions than the Fused Grid network. The grid networks ranged from

1.5 to 4 times higher in predicted collisions than the Fused Grid. These results are consistent with earlier studies[19] and recent studies of network safety.[20] The apparent improvement in safety deduced from these analyses is sufficiently large to substantiate the value of the new model.

HEALTH BENEFITS

The health benefits of the Fused Grid model are attributable to the encouragement of active transportation, and to the systematic inclusion of open spaces within the neighborhood layout. The study mentioned above predicts an 11.3 percent increase in the odds of a home-based trip being walked and a 25.9 percent increase in the odds of a person getting sufficient physical exercise. An epidemiological study found a strong correlation between general population health and lower levels of morbidity with an increasing presence of green spaces in a neighbourhood.[21] Other studies have shown many additional benefits for children, adults and seniors arising from the presence of green spaces.[22] The Fused Grid network incorporates open spaces as structural components of the neighborhood network and consequently is likely to reproduce these benefits.

CONCLUSION

The need for rethinking the inherited street network patterns, whether recent or old is clear and strong. Hints for a new direction can be found in the several adaptations and modifications that have been proposed and incorporated sporadically in city districts over the last 50 years. The quest for a contemporary street network pattern that synthesizes these precedents into a complete system has led to the development of the Fused Grid. Research so far indicates that it may result in positive outcomes on environmental and health issues faced by cities and their citizens.

NOTES

1. Douglas Pollard and Fanis Grammenos, "Beloved and Abandoned: A Platting Named Portland," Planetizen (October 2009), www.planetizen.com.

2. M. Southworth and E. Ben-Joseph, *Streets and the Shaping of Towns and Cities* (Washington, DC: Island, 2003).

3. IBI Group, Canada Mortgage and Housing Corporation, "Comparing Current and Fused Grid Neighbourhood

Layouts for Mobility, Infrastructure and Emissions Costs," 2007.

4. Canada Mortgage and Housing Corporation, "A Plan for Rainy Days: Water Runoff and Site Planning," October 2007.

5. Canadian Medical Association, "No Breathing Room: National Illness Costs of Air Pollution," 2008.

6. David Brzezinski, Constance Hart, Phil Enns, "Final Facility Specific Speed Correction Factors: M6.SPD.002," Assessment and Standards Division, Office of Transportation and Air Quality, U.S. EPA.

7. M. Ernst. "Mean Streets 2004: How Far Have We Come? Pedestrian Safety, 1994–2003," report (Washington, DC: Surface Transportation Policy Project, 2004).

8. R. Ewing, "Traffic Calming: State of the Practice" (Washington, DC: Institute of Transportation Engineers, 1999).

9. Lawrence Frank, Sarah Kavage and Todd Litman, *Promoting Public Health Through Smart Growth* (Vancouver, BC: Smart Growth British Columbia, 2006).

10. F. Grammeno, et al., "Hippodamus Rides to Radburn: A New Model for the 21 Century," *Journal of Urban Design* (2008); Canada Mortgage and Housing Corporation, www.cmhc.ca/en/inpr/su/sucopl/fugr/index.cfm.

11. S. Marshall. *Streets And Patterns: The Structure of Urban Geometry* (London and New York: Spon, 2005).

12. S. Melia, "Eco Town Mobility," *Town and Country Planning* (November 2007) and S. Melia, "Neigborhoods Should be Made Permeable for Walking and Cycling But Not Cars" *Local Transport Today* (2008).

13. Canada Mortgage and Housing Corporation, "Plan for Rainy Days."

14. IBI Group and Canada Mortgage and Housing Corporation, "Comparing Current and Fused Grid."

15. Lawrence Frank and Christopher Hawkins, "Giving Pedestrians an Edge: Using Street Layout to Influence Transportation Choice," Research Highlight, CMHC 2008.

16. Susan Handy et al., "Neighbourhood Design and Children's Outdoor Play: Evidence from Northern California," 2008.

17. Lawrence Frank, Jacqueline Kerr, Jim Chapman, and James Sallis, "Urban Form Relationships with Walk Trip Frequency and Distance Among Youth" *American Journal of Health Promotion* (2007): 21.

18. Gordon Lovegrove, P. Eng, and James Sun, "Evaluating the Safety of the Fused Grid Road Pattern," Canada Mortgage and Housing Corporation, 2009.

19. Gordon R. Lovegrove, "Sustainable Road Safety Models: New Empirical Tools for Engineering Safer Communities," School of Engineering, UBC, 2007.

20. Eric Dumbaugh and Robert Rae, "Safe Urban Form: Revisiting the Relationship Between Community Design and Traffic Safety," *Journal of the American Planning Association*, Vol. 75, No. 3 (2009).

21. Richard Mitchell and Frank Popham, "Effect of Exposure to Natural Environment on Health Inequalities: An Observational Population Study," I, Vol. 372, Issue 9650 (November 8, 2008): 1655–1660.

22. Stephen Kaplan, "Some Hidden Benefits of the Urban Forest," University of Michigan, 2003.

RESOURCES

For information, drawings, pictures and discussion on the Fused Grid visit:

www.fusedgrid.ca and blog
www.Wikepedia.org search for fused grid
www.flickr.com the fused grid gallery

CHAPTER 42

Seattle and Other Cities Approve
Green Building Design Standards
Christopher Hawthorne

For the better part of a decade, Ed Mazria was a lonely prophet.

Not long after turning 60 in 2001, the garrulous, six-foot-six-inch architect, who lives in a solar-powered house of his own design just outside Santa Fe, New Mexico, came to a dismaying conclusion about his profession: It was more responsible than any other field for global warming and the planetary woes that go with it. Cobbling together statistics from scientific, government, and industry sources, Mazria calculated that U.S. buildings are responsible for almost half the country's global greenhouse-gas emissions every year and account for about the same proportion of total energy consumption. All our cars, trucks, trains, and planes, by contrast, have a smaller impact on global warming.

By 2003, Mazria had turned his data on the relationship between architecture and climate change into a slide show. He made the case that while environmental activists demonized coal-fired power plants and gas-guzzling SUVs, it was really architects and builders who deserved to wear a scarlet letter.

There was only one problem: Nobody seemed to care. Banking on his notoriety in the small solar energy community — Mazria wrote one of the earliest and most popular tomes in the genre, 1979's Passive Solar Energy Book —

he convinced Solar Today magazine to run a version of his argument. (It appeared with the headline "It's the Architecture, Stupid!") But his frustration with the slow response from his peers and the general public was palpable when I sat with him then at his dining-room table.

"If architects don't attack this," he said, the impatience in his voice rising, "the world doesn't stand a chance."

Whether the world stands a chance now, six years later, remains an open question, but for Mazria, at least, things have changed dramatically. At 67, he is a regular on the lecture circuit and in the mainstream media, having left his architecture practice to devote his attention to his nonprofit, Architecture 2030, which lays out a blueprint for making all new buildings and renovations carbon neutral by 2030.

Today the leaders of the sustainable architecture movement can no longer reasonably complain that they are not being given a hearing — not when Vanity Fair, Wired, and other mainstream magazines publish regular "green" issues or when the Sundance Channel offers environmental TV programs seven days a week.

Politicians and policymakers seem to be listening too: In the past two years, the three biggest cities in the United States — New York,

Originally published as "Building Better Emerald Cities: A Blueprint for Greener Living," *Sierra Magazine*, January/February 2009, by the Sierra Club, San Francisco, CA. Article appears with permission of *Sierra*, the national magazine of the Sierra Club.

Los Angeles, and Chicago — have announced programs requiring new buildings to meet basic green design standards, joining smaller cities that have already put such guidelines in place. (Seattle was the first large U.S. city to do so, in 2000.) L.A. now requires all new buildings larger than 50,000 square feet to satisfy a basic eco-checklist. Features that win points with the city include low-flow toilets, solar panels, and daylighting, which floods building interiors with natural light to reduce electricity use.

The measuring stick those cities rely on in their green building programs is the LEED ratings system, short for Leadership in Energy and Environmental Design, begun ten years ago by the U.S. Green Building Council, a non-profit based in Washington, D.C. Versions of LEED address new construction, renovation, residential design, interiors, and even neighborhood planning. According to the council, 16,000 U.S. buildings have received or are seeking LEED certification.

Some of the world's most influential architects, having long ignored green design, are now embracing it with the zeal of the newly converted. Santa Monica's Thom Mayne, winner of the 2005 Pritzker Architecture Prize, the field's top individual honor, has made sustainability a central focus of his high-profile practice. Other well-known architects working green include Norman Foster, Renzo Piano, Richard Rogers, and the venerable firm Skidmore, Owings & Merrill.

Still, the details and larger implications of green architecture remain hazy for much of the general public. Americans have parsed the ecological differences between a Prius and a Hummer. But the gap between an efficient 2,000-square-foot house and a McMansion — or between a wasteful, glass-wrapped office tower and a geothermal-heated warehouse — remains relatively opaque.

The growing prominence of green design has also opened it up to charges that it focuses more on marketing than substance. LEED ratings have been the subject of blistering critiques from some architects who find them inflexible and the point system in need of fine-tuning, if not a complete overhaul. (Mayne has essentially called LEED useless.) Others complain that the

larger sustainable architecture movement has been reduced to sales pitches. "I hate green architecture," design critic Cathleen McGuigan wrote in Newsweek recently. "I can't stand the hype, the marketing claims, the smug lists of green features that supposedly transform a garden-variety building into a structure fit for Eden." To be sure, in high-end real-estate markets, pitches for solar panels and recycled fly-ash countertops have become nearly indistinguishable from those for water views and chef's-style Viking ranges.

No matter what kind of success green architecture can achieve in the United States, it may ultimately mean very little if China, India, and other developing nations can't find a way to build more sustainably. Many of the most advanced experiments in green architecture and city planning are happening in those countries, but for every model eco-city in China, a dozen others pursue growth with a headlong, soot-covered ambition right out of Dickensian England.

Within the next decade or two, cities may begin constructing buildings that go beyond mere carbon-neutral status and — thanks to highly efficient windows, solar panels, geothermal pumps, wind turbines, and other features — actually produce more energy than they consume. But such buildings remain in the planning stages, hovering in the architectural imagination. For now, a fundamental contradiction lies at the heart of green architecture. Buildings remain, by definition, harmful to the environment, and choosing to construct one is still a decision to consume resources and tip the balance of planetary health, however modestly, in the wrong direction.

Too often that contradiction is underexposed. Imagine that a developer buys a swath of farmland or an undeveloped patch on the far suburban edge of a U.S. city, then proposes filling it with a collection of roomy single-family houses decked out with solar panels and recycled floorboards. Should environmentalists and local officials hail the houses' green features? Or should they explore the larger ecological implications of chewing up undeveloped land and producing a group of stand-alone homes with no connections to mass transit? It is in wrestling with the broader issues of land use, transit, and the scale of cities that green architects and their backers will really earn their stripes in the next decade.

Green architecture will never truly succeed as an ecological movement without setting its sights on the macro level, here and in the developing world. Instead of looking just at energy efficiency, it also needs to look at community. (The new LEED ratings for neighborhood development are a welcome start.) We need fewer green houses on half-acre parcels and more green apartment buildings that facilitate dense living near transit. More to the point, we need city planning and land-use policies that tie individual houses to a larger urban fabric. The most promising green projects are no longer stand-alone buildings; they are master plans, like the Dutch firm MVRDV's design for the Logrono Montecorvo Eco City near Rioja, Spain, which will knit 3,000 housing units into a parklike, carbon-neutral development

In the United States, we still tend to lose sight of the fact that green design and building is more about accepting the need for compromise and efficiency — about doing more with less — than it is about adding flashy features to a house or skyscraper. But with some modest retooling, it could begin to bring Americans' lives, which have in so many ways become bloated during the boom years of the past two decades, closer to achieving real balance.

CHAPTER 43

South Amboy Revitalizes
Its Aging Waterfront
Alan Hope

South Amboy gets it. The city is transforming itself from a dying urban center with
a run down waterfront that literally exploded
in flames in the 1950s into a forward looking,
exciting community. This Middlesex county
city is the new benchmark for what smart
growth, smart change and urban living can be
and, indeed, should be.

The success of South Amboy's revitalization has been so dramatic, that it has even
caught the eye of Professor Mario Gandelsonas
from the Princeton University School of Architecture, who is using the South Amboy model
as a classroom for the students who will build
and design the cities of tomorrow.

According to Gandelsonas, "The city of
South Amboy occupies a special place in New
Jersey, a state that enters the 21 century with
renewed energy. South Amboy as a future
transportation node within the proximity of
Manhattan, presents a unique opportunity to
create a new type of city that takes advantage
of unique conditions: a solid and stable community, a waterfront with exceptional views,
unspoiled natural preserves and large but dor-
mant industrial structures that offer an exciting
potential for jumpstarting future development.
In the last few years, ambitious plans of a scale
that very few large cities would envision have
materialized in the form of a new neighborhood

and the beginning of a new waterfront that
starts to create a new image for South Amboy."

But make no mistake about it, the South
Amboy phoenix is not the result of a massive
urban renewal effort where city blocks are destroyed and residents are displaced. It is instead,
a moderated, well thought-out, carefully planned
and finely executed integration of the old and
the new. In one area the reclaimed waterfront
is dotted with new homes; in another part older
neighborhoods have received the coveted national "Main Street USA" designation for their
beauty.

In South Amboy, the infrastructure has
been carefully rebuilt without destroying the
bends in the roads and the bumps in the sidewalks that give a community its sense of character and maturity. The city's planners have
given as much thought to new bridges' aesthetics as they do to traffic. Elsewhere in South
Amboy, quality builders are creating commercial ratables that will increase tax revenues without quality of life disruption.

The city's location, nestled on the water
but literally within walking distance of many
of New Jersey's major roadways, makes it an
ideal location for what will become one of New
Jersey's major data centers. "South Amboy is
uniquely suited to positively and proactively
take advantage of the major transportation im-

Originally published as "How to Succeed: South Amboy Gets It!," *New Jersey Municipalities*, Vol. 83, No. 4, April 2006, by
the New Jersey State League of Municipalities Trenton, NJ. Reprinted with permission of the publisher.

provements in which NJDOT is engaged," said NJDOT spokesperson, Erin Phalon.

But how did they do it? And where do they plan to go next?

It all starts with a vision, which grew out of long-time Mayor Jack O'Leary's love of his hometown and dreams for what it can become. O'Leary has never wavered from achieving the goals he set for himself and his city.

Today, South Amboy's renaissance continues under his leadership. Now in his 18th year as mayor, O'Leary's smart growth, smart change plan is paying huge dividends after nearly a decade of planning, analysis and management. The new South Amboy is a blend of family-oriented neighborhoods thriving side by side with a modern transportation village, new waterfront residences, and business and professional enterprise zones. In South Amboy smart change works hand in hand with family values, civic responsibility and fiscal conservatism.

Jack O'Leary knew when he began the South Amboy rebirth that it would take years to achieve his vision. But he never wavered. "It was clear to me that the city needed to undergo not only smart growth but smart change. We had to adapt to the changing times in New Jersey," O'Leary said. But he is quick to add, "I was absolutely committed to insuring that our city did not lose its special character and that it remained affordable for the diverse and vibrant family-based community that we are."

In order to succeed, O'Leary knew that South Amboy needed a redevelopment partner qualified to resolve significant up-front infrastructure and cleanup problems long before the development phase began. Faced with this unique redevelopment challenge, the city turned to Joseph Jingoli and Son to perform as the Master Developer for the Northern Waterfront Redevelopment Area. The location of the city and its assets dictated the selection of a partner with the expertise in engineering, infrastructure, power plants, technology and environmental cleanup. Jingoli has proven to be a crucial element in tackling the first commercial phase of the city's plan.

Joseph P. Baumann, Jr., of McManimon and Scotland LLC has been watching the redevelopment process evolve in South Amboy and had this to say: "Redevelopment is not for the faint of heart or the shortsighted. It requires vision, long range planning, leadership, diligence, and patience. It requires a leader willing to work hard and make hard decisions — decisions that may not bear fruit for many years. As such, redevelopment does not work well with many political cycles where instant gratification is often the real goal."

As a life long South Amboyan, O'Leary had seen his beloved city decline as so many others in New Jersey. "I intuitively understood that change was inevitable," O'Leary said. "However, I was going to commit myself to insuring that the change in South Amboy evolved in a positive direction, away from the darkness of decay and blight and toward the light of a future designed around combining the best of all worlds into a working city that served the needs of both its residents and its businesses."

New Homes

Today, the signature piece of O'Leary's dream is the transforming of the once underutilized waterfront of South Amboy into a beautiful environment of upscale homes, a bayfront brick paver walkway, surf fishing beach, marina, gorgeous waterfront park along with water ferry transportation, new public library, Community School and a state-of-the-art 600-plus seat Community Theater.

But long before these homes and amenities became a reality, O'Leary and his team needed to provide tens of millions of dollars in infrastructure repairs and rebuilding of the city's core business sector. Said O'Leary, "Broadway has always been the gathering spot for our community. Without that we've lost our heart."

Business

A walk through South Amboy's downtown shows the old and the new happily blend together in a vibrant business community.

Jim Moutsadatos, the owner of Jimmy's Broadway Diner, agrees "It's great to watch the changes that are taking place on Broadway. It took years of hard work and planning to bring it about and now there is definitely a difference."

The city has already been the beneficiary of well more than $100 million in re-development funds that the Mayor and the City Council have been directly responsible for bringing into our city.

Just ask Bob Dato, an attorney in town, who had a choice of where he wanted to locate his business, why he came to the city. He says, "Locating my business in South Amboy was an easy decision. The town is growing, the business potential is increasing and it is all due to the smart growth tools being used by the Mayor and Council."

The local government team is also committed to its Neighborhood Preservation Program, which provides grant money to improve the visual appearances of older homes in a targeted area of a community, and the surrounding entranceways including sidewalks and landscape plantings.

Community gatherings and festivals also enrich life in South Amboy. The annual St. Patrick's Day Parade fills the streets with onlookers as the city celebrates its Irish heritage. Each year, the highlight of the parade is the city's volunteer fire department, which has won the top honors in the statewide parade competition in Wildwood three times in a row. The city also hosts the Annual Raritan Bay Seafood Festival which draws anywhere from 8,000 to 12,000. And at its Annual Tree Lighting in December, South Amboy's youngest citizens are treated to a visit from Santa Claus who arrives on his own fire truck accompanied by other decorated fire equipment.

In South Amboy, no one is left behind. The city's elderly population, many of whom have lived and worked here for a lifetime are well cared for and housed in the senior citizen complex, known as McCarthy Towers. Under O'Leary's leadership, that facility has also enjoyed more than $1 million in renovations and upgrades in just the last year. The city and the South Amboy Housing Authority are poised to add another tower to its Senior Citizen housing inventory.

O'Leary believes that the community life of the city is a tribute to the strength and character of its citizens. He says the culture of the city attracts people who want to live and work together, sharing their common interests and protecting the middle class life style and unique quality of life that South Amboy provides.

According to Phil Green, a South Amboy native who has recently returned to the city, "South Amboy is not only the best kept secret in Middlesex County, it's the best kept secret in the state."

Redevelopment Tools

Mayor O'Leary and the South Amboy City Council have consistently used redevelopment tools made available by the State of New Jersey to reinvigorate their city. The positive impact of successful redevelopment can be seen readily in this mile square city. And nowhere is this more visible than where the city meets the bay. Here you will find residents strolling the waterfront walkway, and families enjoying the Karitan Bay waterfront park's panoramic views.

"The Raritan Bay Environmental Education Center and Nature Preserve in South Amboy is one of the regions most exciting and publicly beneficial new projects," noted Greg Remaud, the Preservation Director and NY/NJ Baykeeper for the Bi-State Harbor Estuary Program. "It combines natural land preservation, ecosystem restoration and environmental education in an urban setting. It also serves as a key component of South Amboy's model community redevelopment that links environmental preservation with mass transportation, main street revitalization and economic growth. The Nature Center and Preserve located along Raritan Bay at the mouth of the Raritan River will provide hands on research opportunities and nature education to school children and residents throughout the area."

The resurgence of Broadway, and jobs that will be produced by Raritan Landings, the planned Hotel, Conference and Office Park and Data Center are all positives that have resulted from the careful implementation of the city redevelopment plans.

A Transportation Village

Key to the overall business success of South Amboy has been its embracing and understanding of the benefits of its location and working with the major transportation players in the state.

For example, NJ TRANSIT has worked closely with the city for a number of years to both improve its rail station and implement transit-oriented development according to Jack M. Kanarek, NJ TRANSIT's Senior Director of Project Development. NJ TRANSIT assisted South Amboy in the development of a vision plan for transit-oriented redevelopment and new development using the rail station as the focal point. With the vision in place, South Amboy was among the first five Transit Villages designated under the State of New Jersey's Transit Village Program. This has enabled South Amboy to receive assistance from several state agencies. The result is that the rail station is being improved, roadway access is being upgraded, ferry service to Manhattan is operating and the city's Broadway area is being revitalized. In addition, new transit-oriented development is also planned along South Amboy's waterfront.

South Amboy can provide bus, rail, commuter and ferry service from within its borders for those that need it. Few, if any, other cities can compete with that convenience. For South Amboyans to have the lifestyle we provide without having to significantly extend their daily commute makes all the difference in the world to our residents. And finally, the design of our transportation village is such that we do not adversely impact our residential areas while maximizing opportunities for our commercial enterprises. That planning forethought makes a huge difference in the character and feel of South Amboy.

And for those that do not live in the city but want to take advantage of the transportation village, the direct benefits to the downtown business community are readily visible. Where once there were vacant storefronts and empty buildings, there are now few, if any, "for rent" signs.

In just the last three years, O'Leary's South Amboy has also seen the reclamation of its waterfront, the creation of beautiful new housing, the rise of an intermodal transportation village and business center and a new office park along with additional acreage for his open space inventory and so much more.

Mayor O'Leary wants to see the completion of the Community Recreation Center/ YMCA for his residents and their children. There are road improvement projects on the horizon and he pledges to continue the search for quality businesses that enhance the city while simultaneously providing the critical tax ratables that are the economic engine of the South Amboy miracle.

Asked about his success, O'Leary takes a moment or two to reflect before answering.

"We are a great city," he says, "and our people are our greatest asset. Because of that, I believe together we have a great future."

CHAPTER 44

Syracuse and Other Cities Encourage Watershed Education and Restoration

Mat Webber

In tight economic times, efficiency is important, especially for watershed organizations. One upstate New York–based Izaak Walton League of America (IWLA) program has developed protocols that serve multiple purposes and audiences at a relatively low cost. The group has combined education, monitoring and restoration programs into one package that appeals to teachers, benefits students and provides a platform for high quality data collection.

Called Project Watershed (http://project-watershed.org), the effort is an outgrowth of the IWLA's Save Our Stream program, a national watershed education and outreach program. (For more information, see www.iwla.org/sos, or read "Forty Years Later — and Still Saving Our Streams" in *Nonpoint Source News-Notes* issue 87, available at www.epa.gov/News-Notes/pdf/87issue.pdf.) "Project Watershed was started in the early 1990s by educators looking for ways to get their students outdoors," explained Mat Webber, Project Watershed Coordinator. Today, Project Watershed brings together adult volunteers with central New York middle school, high school and college students to monitor water quality and protect local streams. The program engages students in classroom instruction, stream data collection, data analysis, and in some cases, stream restoration projects.

How Does It Work?

Teachers use Project Watershed curricula in the classroom to introduce the students to water quality, nonpoint source pollution, and stream hydrology, biology and chemistry. All curricula meet New York state learning standards for science, math and technology.

Once the students are exposed to the curricula in class, Project Watershed staff members or volunteers meet the teacher and students at a local stream. Most of the participating schools have streams either on-site or within reasonable walking distance.

On the field day, Project Watershed leaders arrive at the site about an hour earlier than the students are expected. During this time, leaders set up for the students' arrival and collect data using sophisticated probes and other equipment that record dissolved oxygen, biochemical oxygen demand, pH, nitrate and phosphate levels, chloride, turbidity, total dissolved solids, temperature and other parameters. These data meet quality assurance requirements and therefore are considered valid by local and state agencies.

Once the students arrive, the leaders teach them how to properly collect the various types of stream data. Students carry out U.S. Environmental Protection Agency–certified Save

Originally published as "Project Watershed — Collecting and Sharing Information," *Nonpoint Source News-Notes*, Issue 89, February 2010, by the U.S. Environmental Protection Agency, Washington, D.C. Reprinted with permission of the publisher.

Our Streams biological survey protocols using kick seine nets to collect, sort and characterize benthic macroinvertebrate populations. They also conduct physical measurements of the stream and engage in simple water chemistry tests such as using pH strips. The students do not use the more complicated probes, as this "would take too much valuable time for the students to master... and that technical mastery would be of little educational value," adds Webber.

The leaders help the students understand what their data indicate about stream health. The students also compare their chemistry data with the quality-assured data collected by Project Watershed leaders prior to the students' arrival. "When the student's test results are different from those we got using the more sophisticated equipment, we use it as a teaching moment," explains Webber. "We ask the students what might have caused the discrepancy — such as human error, changed conditions between samplings, the area in the stream that samples were obtained, or equipment limitations, etc." Because the students' hands-on tests are conducted by several individuals or small groups, the students usually have several data points to consider. When averaged, the final number is usually very close to the quality assured result collected by the Project Watershed leaders. "If not, then we promise to redo the test after they leave, using our equipment — just to be sure of our initial readings," explains Webber. "And we promise that any error, if there is one, will be corrected."

After returning to the office, Project Watershed leaders upload the quality-assured data to Project Watershed's online database — the largest publicly accessible volunteer stream monitoring database in New York. Back in the classroom, teachers access the Project Watershed database to continue the students' stream education. Students hone their science and math skills as they compare their monitoring data with the results from previous years at that same site, as well as with data from other area streams.

Project Watershed provides the teachers with additional follow-up activities to reinforce the learning experience.

Success Stories

Many schools have participated in the program for numerous consecutive years conducting stream surveys every spring and fall. This provides a long-term data set that students, IWLA, and other groups can review and analyze. Sometimes the data will show the unexpected. One group of students in a school along Syracuse's Beartrap Creek noticed that the chemistry scores had dropped significantly compared to previous years. Project Watershed leaders alerted county and state authorities to a potential problem. The authorities collected samples to confirm the problem, investigated and discovered that de-icing chemicals from nearby Syracuse International Airport were reaching the creek. The airport has since installed a water filtration system that has dramatically improved water quality.

This event set into motion numerous additional water quality protection efforts along Beartrap Creek. An annual creek clean-up is held by students, neighbors, county officials and members of the Central New York IWLA. Additionally, a Project Watershed school installed in-stream structures to enhance aquatic habitat. Over the past 18 months of monitoring since the restoration effort, Project Watershed leaders and students have seen a significant improvement in the numbers and variety of insects, crustaceans and fish found in that section of the stream. "In fact, the stream improved to the point where we thought it could sustain trout again," notes Webber. "A local school raised trout as part of its aquaculture program and brought them to Beartrap Creek for release, after getting permission from the proper authorities."

At Corcoran High School, students' multi-year data showed consistently good water quality in Furnace Brook, a stream that flows wholly within the city of Syracuse's borders. In the 1990s, students learned of a proposed upstream development that would have filled in a wetland that feeds the stream. The students took their concerns to the local government and newspapers. They used their monitoring data to help convince local zoning officials not to permit new development that could degrade water quality. Project Watershed has continued to work with students along the stream. Now, almost twenty years later, "the stream is still in good shape," adds Webber.

Program Expands Reach

Project Watershed provides many students with their first opportunity to learn about and experience their local waterways. Thanks to positive feedback from teachers and school administrators, Project Watershed is currently expanding its target area. In just the past year, the program has doubled the number of students it reaches to more than 2,700 students from 42 schools, including 36 middle schools. To accommodate the expansion, IWLA is training a series of undergraduates and graduate school interns from local colleges, along with new volunteers, to take the program to additional schools.

IWLA has compiled a detailed list of equipment and materials needed to assemble a kit to successfully run a Project Watershed program. Each completed kit costs approximately $1500, and includes 20 pairs of slip-on waterproof boots, multiple kick seine nets, water quality measuring equipment and other items. "We currently have four sets of equipment that serve around 50 schools and 10 adult survey teams," explains Webber. Once assembled, the kits are relatively inexpensive to maintain, he adds. "Replacing worn boots would be the major annual resupplying expense. The boots and replacement chemicals, plus incidentals, would be in the $300 range. This would support an entire year of multi-school activities."

IWLA hopes to expand Project Watershed further—first across New York, then throughout the Northeast, and, eventually, nationwide. In the meantime, "other groups could adapt our program design to their needs fairly easily. We've worked hard at making this program an easy sell—even to teachers or group leaders who have very little knowledge of watersheds or stream life," notes Webber.

Program Expands Focus

In addition to its regular school outreach and monitoring program, Project Watershed staff and teachers worked together to develop a self-contained, two- to three-week-long, full-time summer school program revolving around science and environmental studies. The program, first held in 2009, included both intensive classroom learning and in-stream monitoring. Teachers easily incorporated required science and math elements into the curriculum. Teachers met the English requirements by asking the students to write about their experiences in the stream. For social studies, teachers asked the students to consider who had used the watershed in the past and for what purpose, and what human activities might be affecting the stream today. Students met art requirements by sketching macroinvertebrates and other stream-related subjects. "The students had a great time—and learned a lot," notes Webber. He anticipates repeating and expanding the summer school program to meet future needs in this and other schools.

IWLA has also expanded the focus of Project Watershed to include restoration activities. "Incorporating restoration elements was a natural progression of our stream monitoring program," explains Webber. The group has begun to offer its services to help people identify and manage potential stream restoration activities. Restoration activities might include stabilizing streambanks, removing invasive species, helping landowners restore riparian areas, and other efforts. Webber hopes that restoration will become an integral part of their education and monitoring program. "We have submitted several grant requests," he says, "one of which would involve awarding mini-grants to qualified projects run by students."

Program Design Benefits Many

Project Watershed offers immeasurable benefits to youth and local schools through education and outdoor water quality monitoring experiences. By using consistent protocols in the Project Watershed program, the IWLA also offers the unique benefit of an ever-growing, quality-assured, wide-scale monitoring dataset. This dataset, in turn, can help IWLA, watershed organizations and government agencies pinpoint trouble spots and target potential on-the-ground restoration projects. Unlike some restoration projects where the scale and duration of associated monitoring efforts is limited by a funding window, Project Watershed offers a wide-scale, long term dataset that often already contains years of baseline data for many streams.

Once a restoration project is implemented, Project Watershed leaders and students plan to collect years of follow-up data as an integral part of the education experience. "Far too often, restoration projects, though well intended, fail because there is no follow-up monitoring to catch and correct things that may not be working as expected," says Webber. "Continued monitoring and tweaking of the original restoration plan helps a project succeed, which gives everyone involved a great feeling of accomplishment — and lessons that last a lifetime."

NOTE

A key element of Project Watershed is the Save Our Streams water quality monitoring method — an inexpensive, low-tech, hands-on technique that works well for schools and other groups with limited budgets. The Save Our Streams biological monitoring method relies on the presence of benthic macroinvertebrates to indicate water quality. Macroinvertebrates are large enough to see with the naked eye (macro) and have no backbone (invertebrate). Benthic macroinvertebrates live in the benthos, or stream bottom, and include insect larvae, adult insects and crustaceans. A group can use the Save Our Stream method to assess water quality with just a few inexpensive supplies including a kick seine net, macroinvertebrate identification chart and a notebook. See www.iwla.org/sos.

CHAPTER 45

Tacoma and Other Cities
Redesign Their Roadways for People

Barbara McCann

When tiny University Place outside of Tacoma, Wash., incorporated in the mid–1990s, one of the first priorities was adding sidewalks to the former county roads. From there, the town made an early commitment to what is now called "complete streets" — the idea that all future road projects would integrate the needs of everyone using the road — not just motorists, but also people walking, riding bicycles or catching the bus. The town started by cajoling the gas company to split costs for transforming gravel shoulders into sidewalks during gas line replacements. They looked for opportunities to install bike lanes during repaving projects and to put in pads to provide space for county bus shelters. Then they started making more radical changes.

"People from outside University Place comment about how much they love driving down Bridgeport Way," says Steve Sugg, deputy city manager, of one of the first streets to get a full Complete Streets treatment. "There is a sense of calm."

The redesigned road features a landscaped median, new pedestrian crossings, bicycle lanes, a multi-use path and improved sidewalks. Sugg notes that when Trader Joe's was looking for a place to locate a store in the Tacoma region, they picked a site on Bridgeport Way, perhaps because of the extensive street improvements. University Place has added 23 miles of sidewalks to their streets since incorporation and has installed several modern roundabouts, the first in Washington State. Now the town is working with citizens on planning a Town Center to realize broader smart growth principles.

University Place is not alone. Across the country, a growing number of communities are using the deceptively simple tool of complete streets policies to change the way they approach transportation. Adopted as a state law, local ordinance or even as a city council resolution, these policies set a new vision for transportation investments. More than 85 states, regions and cities have adopted such policies, including new state laws passed in California and Illinois and policy resolutions or ordinances in major cities including St. Paul, Miami, Chicago, Seattle, Sacramento and Charlotte. And the pace is accelerating.

In Jefferson City, Mo., in March, disability advocates, trail-building organizations, bicycle advocates, health groups and even a realtor spoke at a state House hearing or wrote letters in support of a complete streets bill. In Hawaii, bicycle advocates and the state AARP chapter made common cause this spring to push for a similar bill with a particularly Hawaiian twist

Originally published as "Pedestrian and Bike-friendly Street Successes," *On Common Ground*, Summer 2009, by the Community and Political Affairs Division, National Association of Realtors, Washington, D.C. Reprinted with permission of the publisher.

they've linked it to a Hawaiian tradition known as "the splintered paddle"— a native myth that asserts everyone's right to travel safely. State legislators in Connecticut, Texas, West Virginia and Maine have also introduced complete streets bills.

Complete streets policies are also getting federal attention. Sen. Tom Harkin and Rep. Doris Matsui have introduced the Complete Streets Act of 2009 into the U.S. House and Senate (S.584, H.R.1443).

"We need to ensure streets, intersections and trails are designed to make them easier to use and maximize their safety," said Sen. Harkin upon introduction of the bill. "This legislation will encourage Americans to be more active, while also providing more travel options and cutting down on traffic congestion."

The bill would require states and metropolitan planning organizations to adopt complete streets policies to be applied to federally funded road projects, and it is expected to become part of the upcoming authorization of the federal transportation bill.

The success of a complete streets approach is starting to show up in research that shows fewer crashes on redesigned roads, as well as increased physical activity. A recently released study of a new pedestrian pathway along a major bridge in Charleston, S.C., found that two-thirds of the users of the bridge said the new facility had led them to get more exercise.

Promoting physical activity as a part of daily life has been at the center of a strong move in Minnesota toward complete streets, with three jurisdictions adopting policies in the first months of 2009: Hennepin County (Minneapolis), Saint Paul and Rochester. Rochester's city council passed the policy unanimously after hearing a variety of supportive testimony.

"Really it was the result of a lot of different people speaking and testifying at the public hearing and sending e-mails and letters in advance," says Mitzi Baker, senior transportation planner for the city of Rochester. "It was the power of civic engagement."

The insurer BlueCross BlueShield (BCBS) of Minnesota has been supporting "active living" initiatives across the state, based on research that shows that people who live in walkable environments, or who regularly take public transportation, are more likely to be active enough to ward off chronic disease. BCBS sponsored three Complete Streets Workshops in December to help planners and engineers understand how to broaden their scope when planning road projects to take into account the needs of pedestrians, bicyclists and public transportation users.

"It is probably a good deal, as it will make a residential development a little more attractive to people who are going to move in," says Ward Opitz of Bigelow Homes in Rochester, who met with city planners to see if the proposed policy would affect an upcoming subdivision. "I'm a little leery of what fees they may conjure up next time."

In University Place, realtors and appraisers are unsure if the improvements have made much difference to property values. But for some supporters, the economic impact is a primary reason to support a complete streets approach. Chris Leinberger, author of "The Option of Urbanism: Investing in a New American Dream," has been watching the downward trajectory of home prices and notes that most of the dive has been in places built for "drivable suburbanism," places where the road network features high speed arterials designed only for cars.

"Places that are walkable urban neighborhoods have held their value over the last two years," says Leinberger.

An indicator of the potential importance of a multimodal transportation network to property values is the new real estate tool, Walk Score. Walk Score uses the magic of Google Maps to give every address in the nation a score from 0 to 100, based on the number and variety of destinations within walking distance. The Walk Score website is enormously popular, but it isn't just a parlor game. Front Seat, the firm behind Walk Score, has commissioned research to determine if a higher Walk Score correlates to a higher home value. Economist Joe Cortright says the preliminary results show that each additional point on the Walk Score scale correlates with increased housing values on the order of $1,000 or more, depending on the regional market. Two major real estate websites,

Zip Realty and Zillo, now feature Walk Score on property listings.

Walk Score is based on the crow-fly distance to nearby destinations, so it doesn't take into account the disconnected street network common in many newer developments, or the lack of sidewalks and crosswalks that can make walking unpleasant, impractical or plain dangerous. But connected, complete streets are a prerequisite to true walkable urbanism, according to Leinberger.

"If you have an eight-lane arterial without complete streets infrastructure, you will never see high-density walkable urbanism take place along that corridor. Complete streets will be a precondition before you can get walkable urban development that will help meet the pent-up demand for this type of neighborhood."

He notes that the beauty of complete streets is being able to begin changing the street infrastructure right away, as transportation projects come up.

Health, economic development and sustainability are behind many complete streets efforts. The bill in Maine's legislature is part of a broader strategy to fight climate change. But complete streets policies are gaining ground for more fundamental reasons of simple demographics and safety. By 2023, nearly one in five Americans will be over the age of 65, and they will make up one-quarter of the driving population. As they age, many will face disabilities that will force them to give up driving during the last decade of their lives. Yet they may be reluctant to give up the keys when they face neighborhoods with infrequent and inadequate crosswalks, no sidewalks, poorly designed bus stops and inadequate speed control.

A recent AARP poll found that 47 percent of older adults said they did not feel safe crossing a major street near their home. In another large survey, AARP found that nearly two-thirds of the more than 1,000 planners and engineers surveyed have not yet begun considering the needs of older users in their multimodal planning. AARP recently issued a report based on this research, "Complete Streets for an Aging America," that makes three broad recommendations for transforming road design to better cope with an aging population, summarized as "Slow Down, Make it Easy, and Enjoy the View." It recommends re-engineering streets for slower travel speeds, making intersections less complex while providing lower-speed routes and reducing visual clutter.

It is no coincidence that the recent push for complete streets comes against a backdrop of a steady decline in the amount of driving and a rise in the use of public transportation even as more people take part in Bike to Work Day activities every year. Communities are responding by making a commitment to complete their streets.

CHAPTER 46

Tallahassee Approves and Enforces Clean Water Quality Regulations

John Abendroth

Developing a total maximum daily load (TMDL) for an impaired waterbody is one thing—implementing the TMDL and successfully restoring that waterbody can be much more difficult, especially if the waterbody is large with multiple pollutants and pollution sources. Florida is hoping to overcome these difficulties through its Basin Management Action Plan (BMAP) effort. By securing stakeholder participation and consensus, requiring scientific investigations and establishing opportunity for enforcement action, BMAPs arm the state with the tools and partners it needs to carry the TMDL process seamlessly through to its final result—cleaner water.

Development of BMAPs and implementation of TMDLs are the last steps in Florida's five phase watershed approach to water management in the state. Florida Department of Environmental Protection (FDEP) uses BMAPs as a tool to implement the pollutant reductions required by TMDLs. In a nutshell, a BMAP aims to improve water quality by bringing FDEP together with local stakeholders to collaboratively reduce pollution from wastewater facilities and "municipal separate storm sewer systems" (MS4) communities, implement urban and agricultural best management practices and implement conservation programs. The plan must establish a schedule for implementing strategies, develop a basis for evaluating the plan's effectiveness, and identify funding strategies. Phased implementation of management strategies can be used to promote timely, cost-effective actions.

To date, FDEP has completed and adopted 180 TMDLs but has only finalized four BMAPs. Each BMAP may include more than one TMDL area or pollutant. FDEP and local stakeholders are in various phases of BMAP development in several basins throughout the state. Progress is slow because the BMAP process can be extremely time consuming. FDEP and the watershed stakeholders must work very closely to study available data and reach a consensus on BMAP requirements, explains FDEP's John Abendroth. "Our group considers any new data that have become available since the TMDL for that waterbody was developed. We collaboratively agree on pollutant allocations for each group. Then we work together to develop a list of projects that help each participant achieve their necessary pollutant reductions. The development process can take several years, but we end up with a valuable product. By the time we have finished, people accept what their responsibilities are and they commit to moving ahead." Once finalized, BMAPs are adopted by

Originally published as "Florida Combines Local Buy-in with Enforceability to Improve Water Quality," *Nonpoint Source News-Notes*, Issue 86, February 2009, by the U.S. Environmental Protection Agency, Washington, D.C. Reprinted with permission of the publisher.

Secretarial Order to allow FDEP to enforce BMAP requirements. Examples of completed BMAPs and associated project schedules are available at: www.dep.state.fl.us/water/water sheds/bmap.htm.

Incorporating BMAPs into an Enforcement Structure

Once the interested parties agree on allocations and projects, FDEP takes the next step of working with these groups to integrate projects into any existing permits. For example, if an industry has agreed to lower its pollutant load discharge, FDEP will add that new requirement to its wastewater discharge permit the next time the permit is up for review. Likewise, a MS4 community will incorporate new BMAP requirements for specific pollution-reducing projects — such as a new street sweeping program — by referencing it into the MS4 permit.

BMAP participants prefer to have requirements made a part of their permits, notes Abendroth. "They have it in writing, which protects them from outside influences that might try to force them to do more." It also helps in the quest for funding. For example, since a MS4 is required to implement the BMAP projects as part of its permit, it can ask the state for money, increase taxes or establish a utilities fee to help meet requirements. "Having the projects as part of the permit gives the MS4 a leg to stand on," adds Abendroth.

Although having project requirements incorporated into existing permits enables FDEP to enforce the BMAP, Abendroth doesn't foresee enforcement actions becoming necessary. "By the time we get through the BMAP process, everyone is committed to seeing the process through," he says. This commitment holds true for stakeholders in areas with non-permitted nonpoint source pollution sources in urban areas as well as agricultural areas. "The state's Department of Agriculture and Consumer Services is responsible for working with agricultural interests to implement agricultural BMPs," adds Abendroth. "Everyone must commit to reducing their nonpoint source load or demonstrate that they are not a source."

Abendroth expects that landowners with non-permitted nonpoint source pollution sources will find ways to reduce pollutants by taking advantage of available technical and financial assistance. For example, since a BMAP qualifies as a comprehensive watershed management plan, the watershed becomes eligible for Clean Water Act section 319 grant funds. These funds are distributed through states from the U.S. Environmental Protection Agency and are specifically designated to help reduce nonpoint source pollution. Projects included in BMAPs will also be given priority for funding through the State Revolving Fund loan program and other state TMDL program funding.

Once a BMAP is in place, FDEP reviews it annually. The review process includes noting which projects were completed and whether monitoring data show any water quality changes. Every five years FDEP will completely reassess the BMAP and make changes or collect additional data. In some cases, existing data could suggest that implementing a different project might achieve better results. Or, in other cases, the funding might not be available to allow a particular project to progress on schedule — and the schedule will be adjusted. Like other states, Florida is currently facing a budget shortfall. "We recognize the financial reality. As long as we see, for example, that a MS4 is trying to get things done, we will work with them. On the other hand, if we find that a MS4 has made absolutely no effort after five years, there is enforcement action that can be taken." This five-year BMAP review cycle will repeat indefinitely — allowing each BMAP to be continually adjusted and adapted until the TMDL pollutant load reduction requirements are met and FDEP no longer considers the waterbody impaired.

Abendroth views the BMAP effort as a key to the state's economic future. "Our state relies on water-based recreation and tourism as a big part of the economy — as residents, we all know that we need to do what we can to protect and improve our waterways," he explains. "The BMAP provides us with the tools we need." The BMAP program's emphasis and reliance on stakeholder involvement at every stage, combined with the possibility of enforcement as needed, makes the program a recipe for success.

Florida to Develop Numeric Nutrient Water Quality Criteria

In the waning days of the recent Bush administration, the U.S. Environmental Protection Agency (EPA) issued a formal determination under the Clean Water Act that Florida needs to have "numeric" nutrient water quality criteria. As a result, Florida is accelerating its efforts to adopt numeric nutrient criteria into state regulations. EPA expects that Florida will have criteria for lakes and flowing waters in place by early 2010, and for estuaries and coastal waters by early 2011. Anticipating the need for such criteria, Florida just released a Numeric Nutrient Criteria Development Plan (www. dep.state.fl.us/water/wqssp/nutrients). To read EPA's decision letter, which details why these criteria are needed, see www.epa.gov/watersci ence/standards/rules/#det.

Fortunately, Florida has already invested substantial resources to collect and analyze nutrient data and involve stakeholders. The federal determination will build upon this investment. The new numeric nutrient water quality standards will help Florida improve the efficiency and effectiveness of its water quality management tools, identify waters impaired because of nutrient pollution, establish TMDLs and BMAPs and derive NPDES permit limits. Overall, numeric nutrient criteria will significantly improve Florida's ability to address nutrient pollution in a timely and effective manner.

Why are numeric nutrient water quality criteria necessary? Water quality degradation from nutrient pollution is a significant environmental issue in Florida. Excess nitrogen and phosphorus levels (nutrient pollution) in water-bodies can harm aquatic ecosystems and threaten public health. Nutrient pollution can lead to water quality problems such as harmful algal blooms, low-oxygen "dead zones" in water bodies and declines in wildlife and wildlife habitat. These effects also disrupt recreational activities and pose threats to public health.

How bad is the Florida nutrient problem? The state's 2008 Integrated Water Quality Assessment (www.dep.state.fl.us/water/docs/ 2008_Integrated_Report.pdf) revealed that nutrients impair approximately 1,000 miles of rivers and streams, 350,000 acres of lakes, and 900 square miles of estuaries. The actual number of miles and acres of waters impaired for nutrients is likely higher, since many waters have not yet been assessed and might also be impaired.

NOTES

Florida's Watershed Management Program is based on the following five-phase cycle that rotates through Florida's basins every five years:

Phase 1. Initial Basin Assessment.
Phase 2. Coordinated Monitoring.
Phase 3. Data Analysis and TMDL Development.
Phase 4. Basin Management Plan Development.
Phase 5. Begin Implementation of Basin Management Plan.

For more information, see www.dep.state.fl.us/water/tmdl /cycle.htm.

When water bodies do not meet water quality standards, states identify these waters as impaired for the particular pollutants of concern (e.g., nutrients, pathogens, mercury, etc.) The states must then develop a total maximum daily load (TMDL) for that water body. A TMDL is essentially a pollution budget. It calculates the maximum amount of a pollutant allowed to enter a water body, also known as the loading capacity, so that the water body will meet and continue to meet water quality standards for that particular pollutant. The TMDL allocates that load to point sources and nonpoint sources which include both human-caused and natural background sources of the pollutant. States use the TMDL to develop and implement plans to reduce pollution so the waterbody can meet standards.

CHAPTER 47

Washington, D.C., Encourages and Promotes Eco-Friendly Neighborhoods

Greg Plotkin

This may come as a surprise to some, but for the future of the American food system, there's no city more important than Washington, D.C. And, no, it's not because we pass laws here.

What makes Washington so influential is an educated and activist citizenry who is acutely aware of the need to transform both the nation's agricultural policy and the way food is produced, transported and consumed.

These food-focused advocates represent every sector, from government agencies to nonprofit organizations. Many are directly engaged in a range of agricultural sustainability issues — including organic production, smart growth development and infrastructure expansion — and are on the cutting edge of new research and demonstration projects that show the nation our future is paved through innovation, not the status quo.

Washington isn't satisfied with just theorizing solutions to our nation's food and farming problems. either. It's a city that embraces its position as the nation's sustainable compass and works hard to lead by example.

With a new organic vegetable garden planted on the front lawn of the White House and the launch of First Lady Michelle Obama's healthy-eating campaign dubbed "Lets Move," Washington has become the epicenter of a new dialog

on the future of food and sustainable living — something the majority of tourists don't realize.

Most visitors to Washington head straight to the Smithsonian museums and famous monuments that dot the landscape of the National Mall and rarely explore the heart of our nation's capital. If they were to venture out into the surrounding neighborhoods, they'd find a vibrant local-food and farming culture bursting from all four quadrants of the city.

D.C.'s sustainability road trip highlights the people, businesses and organizations leading the movement toward a more sustainable capital city and more eco-friendly nation. These people demonstrate a growing community that is committed to working on Washington rather than simply working in it.

People's Garden

Last summer, the United States Department of Agriculture launched its "Know Your Farmer, Know Your Food" campaign to encourage Americans to become reacquainted with their foods' origins. At that time, secretary of agriculture Tom Vilsack encouraged USDA employees from across the country to begin rethinking the way they use urban spaces in order to begin planting gardens of their own.

As of November 2009, there were 124

Originally published as "Urban Farm Road Trip: Washington, DC," *Urban Farm*, Vol. 2, No. 2, Summer 2010, by BowTie, Inc., Los Angeles, CA. Reprinted with permission of the publisher.

USDA People's Gardens throughout the country, including one at the USDA's Whitten Building in Washington that eliminated 1,250 feet of passé pavement and is being used by the agency as a demonstration in sustainable gardening practices. Each plant for the garden was chosen for its compatibility with Washington's climate and is designed to serve double-duty as elusive urban habitat for wildlife.

Visitors are welcome to tour the People's Garden any day of the week, and if they happen to stroll through on a Tuesday, they can also enjoy a variety of local treats at the USDA farmers' market, just steps from the garden.

Information: 1400 Independence Avenue, S.W., Washington, D.C.; www.usda.gov.

Common Good City Farm

Urban farming has recently emerged as a key resource in the drive toward a more sustainable food system and, more importantly, as an effective way to meet the food needs of many low-income city neighborhoods.

Common Good City Farm, recognizing this dual potential, embarked three years ago with the mission to grow healthy food for members of the LeDroit Park community. Located in the center of a dynamic neighborhood in transition (boasting residents like the Rev. Jesse Jackson), the farm helps strengthen the city's food security. Since 2007, the farm has obtained its 501(c)(3) nonprofit status, provided hundreds of pounds of food to local families and educated many District of Columbia residents about growing their own food.

Don't expect to see them operating as a nonprofit for long, though. Founder Liz Falk believes that urban farms must increase the level of food production to have a greater impact on food security. "The more food we grow in urban settings, the more that urban agriculture operations will be relied on to feed communities," she predicts. "Hopefully, these urban farms can start to develop as social and sustainable businesses rather than nonprofit organizations."

Information: 3rd and V Streets, N.W., Washington, D.C.; 202-330-5945; www. Commongoodcityfarm.org.

FreshFarm Markets

In many cities across America, farmers' markets have come to represent the center of urban food culture. This fact is especially evident in the nation's capital, where FreshFarm Markets coordinates two of the most famous markets in the country — the Dupont Circle farmers' market founded in 1993 and the brand-new White House farmers' market that opened with a visit from Michelle Obama in fall 2009.

Although the first lady may be the most noteworthy market visitor, it's not uncommon to see some of the city's most talented chefs shopping for chiogga beets or fresh mozzarella cheese at one of FreshFarm's nine locations in the metro area. Both Nora Poillan of Restaurant Nora (America's first certified-organic restaurant) and Jose Andres of Cafe Atlantico (home of the gastronomic adventure that is MiniBar) are regular market shoppers.

More than anything else, FreshFarm Markets is dedicated to presenting consumers with an alternative view of where food comes from and how it's produced. "If farmers' markets did not exist," explains FreshFarm's co-director Ann Yonkers, "people would not be able to imagine food outside of what they see on grocery-store shelves. Farmers' markets are so valuable because they serve as a place for farmers to sell food they believe in and are proud of and where customers can come to discover a different way of eating and thinking about food. And instead of having to imagine a new way of eating, the market lets customers see it, taste it, touch it and feel it for themselves."

For all FreshFarm Markets locations: 202-362-8889; www.freshfarmmarkets.org.

Miriam's Kitchen

Judging by the plates of creamy tomato risotto and venison potpie coming from this kitchen, you'd think that chefs Steve Badt and John Murphy cater to an upscale crowd of Capitol Hill politicians and lobbyists. Instead of using their vast culinary knowledge to satisfy the city's elite, Badt and Murphy are devoted to feeding local and healthy food to the hungry and homeless of Washington through one of the city's most well-known charities: Miriam's Kitchen.

"This is something we really view as a win-win situation for both the farmers and our guests," says Murphy. "We are able to serve our guests local food, and the farmers are able to sell products that would otherwise go to waste."

With experienced chefs who think quickly on their feet, Miriam's buys excess produce, meat and cheese from local producers at a discounted price and turns the disparate ingredients into delicious, coherent meals. During the summer months, the chefs source about 35 percent of their produce from local farmers.

The addition of Badt, and more recently Murphy, has transformed Miriam's from an ordinary soup kitchen into an establishment that provides its guests with nourishing food from local suppliers. Located on the fringe of The George Washington University, Miriam's Kitchen has been committed to serving the neighborhood's needy since 1983.

Information: 2401 Virginia Avenue, N.W., Washington, D.C.; 202-452-8926; www.miriamskitchen.org.

Sweetgreen

At this Dupont Circle eatery, crowds of professionals line up, sometimes around the block during weekday lunch hours, to grab a Guac Greens salad or cup of Sweet Flo frozen yogurt.

While Sweetgreen certainly isn't the only salad shop in town, their dedication to sustainability sets them apart from their competition. Their efforts have garnered them the nation's first three-star Green Restaurant Certification from the Green Restaurant Association.

Powered by wind energy, Sweetgreen's six Washington locations use reclaimed wood from a barn in Virginia for its walls and floors; and its tabletops and chairs are made from items found at bowling alleys that have been around since the 1980s. They've also taken great strides to source as many of their ingredients as possible from local producers, says their new "sourceress," Erin Littlestar.

This isn't just another priority within Sweetgreen's business plan either; it's something that many staff members are personally dedicated to. "We are redefining 'good food,'" says Littlestar. "For Sweetgreen, 'good' isn't just about tasty food or even just healthy food, it's also about ethical food. I want to feel comfortable telling people where every single thing on our menu comes from and how it was grown and by whom."

For all Sweetgreen locations: www.sweetgreen.com.

Green Festival

The seventh annual D.C. Green Festival, held in October 2010, will connect Washingtonians to celebrities and products from the world of sustainable living. In a city where "green" doesn't always refer to sustainability, this event brings out the city's (and the nation's) most extraordinary eco-friendly ideas.

A joint project of Global Exchange and Green America, the D.C. Green Festival features hundreds of business products along the lines of rainwater-collection barrels and designer reusable grocery bags. In addition to an organic beer and wine garden, the festival will host a variety of how-to classes for would-be urban gardeners.

Last year, the event featured more than 125 esteemed speakers — including former presidential candidate Ralph Nader, Polyface owner and sustainable-agriculture advocate Joel Salatin, and Earth Policy Institute president Lester Brown — and more than 350 green businesses.

Information: Walter E. Washington Convention Center, 801 Mount Vernon Place, N.W., Washington, D.C; 202-872-5332; www.greenfestivals.org/washington-dc.

Maine Avenue Fish Market

Hidden just a few blocks from the Capitol Building is a Washington landmark known by many locals as simply, "The Wharf." Although the aroma of fresh fish can be detected by drivers along the highway above, the Maine Avenue

Fish Market is virtually unknown to tourists and transplants alike (at least before its debut on Anthony Bourdain's No Reservations).

The not-so-secret market is the oldest continually operating outdoor fish market in the U.S. and has been serving residents of D.C. for nearly 200 years. More than being a place for the city's residents to access fresh fish, crustaceans and cephalopods, it is a place where the community comes together to enjoy great conversation and food, much of it from the nearby Chesapeake Bay.

The Maine Avenue Fish Market is one of the last remaining open-air fish markets on the East Coast and stands as one of the last remnants of the rich waterman culture that once dominated the food scene throughout the Chesapeake Bay region.

Information: 1100 Maine Ave., S.W., Washington, D.C; 202-484-2722.

Solar Decathlon

If you're looking for an energy-efficient home with a touch of modern style, there's no better place to find it than at the U.S. Department of Energy's Solar Decathlon. Held every two years on the National Mall, the 20-team competition challenges college students from around the globe to design, build and operate houses that are powered completely by solar and renewable energy.

While teams compete to win, the real purpose of the event is to draw attention to the issue of efficient energy usage. By developing innovative and applicable solutions to meet the growing global demand for energy, students are able to demonstrate how renewable and sustainable technologies can make homes more eco-friendly.

In addition to making houses that are aesthetically pleasing, the teams also build structures that are economically viable in an increasingly competitive construction market. Desirable features in the homes include living green walls, LED lights and even flat-screen televisions powered exclusively by the sun.

This event is a showcase of the most eco-friendly houses on Earth, but the real benefit may be obtained in educating and empowering the next generation of green engineers and builders. Through this competition, students demonstrate not only what can be done in the world of green building today, but also what's possible in the future.

The next Solar Decathlon will be held in the fall of 2011 between 10th Street and 14th Street and between Madison Drive and Jefferson Drive, Washington, D.C.; www.solardecathlon.gov. All of the houses in the competition are open to the public.

PART III : THE FUTURE

CHAPTER 48

Communities of the Future

Robert McIntyre

The U.S. Department of Agriculture has noted a remarkable demographic trend: In the 1990s, more Americans moved to rural areas than moved out. Why are so many Americans moving to exurban areas beyond the range of easy commuting and shopping?

Urban problems such as traffic congestion, crime, pollution, and high housing costs are driving people not only out of the city but also beyond the suburbs in search of a pleasant, relaxed environment that's closer to nature. This trend is likely to continue. As rural America braces for a surge of home-based workers and retired baby boomers, land planners face a difficult challenge. They must design new communities that appeal to homebuyers and allow small developers to make a profit, but minimize any adverse social, economic, and environmental impacts.

The need for creative solutions is greatest in parts of the South and West, where rapid growth is expected in areas lacking countywide zoning necessary to corral future development within existing cities and towns.

During the 1990s, the population of non-metropolitan counties grew by 5.3 million, or 10.3 percent. The majority of this growth occurred in counties near large urban areas, but the most rapid increase was (and continues to be) in scenic, mountainous counties of the western United States. This trend is consistent with surveys from such sources as the Gallup Organization and *American Demographics* magazine that show most Americans would prefer to live in a small town or rural area. Those making the move are usually college-educated people seeking a detached home on a large lot (one-half acre or larger) with adequate privacy. This rural revival will likely accelerate over the next two decades when some 85 million baby boomers retire. The highest percentage growth of people 65 or older will probably occur in the mountain states of the West, followed by the South.

To meet the surging demand for rural housing, the United States will likely depend on existing small towns and new residential subdivisions. But disenchantment with subdivision life may give rise to another alternative: moderately self-sufficient rural communities that I call "New Villages." In recent years, the rapid increase in home-based businesses (common in rural areas), farmers' markets, and mini-farms has enhanced the potential for these tiny new communities.

Satellite networks have made television and high-speed Internet service available at almost any rural site. The continued movement of retiring baby boomers into rural areas will transform rural America over the next two decades, and traditional villages may again become common.

Originally published as "New Villages for a New Era," *The Futurist*, Vol. 40, No. 1, January-February 2006. Used with permission from the World Future Society, www.wfs.org.

The New Village

For thousands of years, people in rural areas around the world have created villages for the safety, sociability, economic specialization, and agricultural cooperation they provide. Today, many of the world's traditional villages are nearly self-sufficient.

In the United States, a village is usually defined as a community that's larger than a hamlet (50 people or fewer) but smaller than a town (1,000 people or more). Like conventional rural subdivisions, New Villages would range in size. Some would consist of a few houses clustered at a crossroads, while others would be bustling communities with up to 1,000 residents. Each state has its own laws governing the creation of incorporated communities.

Unlike traditional neighborhood developments modeled after the compact American cities developed in the early 1900s, New Villages are inspired by earlier settlements — the scattered New England villages that were common in the 1700s. As one prominent geographer pointed out, colonial settlements in New England had a strong sense of community even though they were usually dispersed agricultural villages centered around a meetinghouse. Conventional subdivisions designed for commuters often have bucolic names including the word "village," but they lack the self-reliance of a traditional village. In a New Village, however, more than half of the jobs, food, and water could be produced within the community.

Today's New Villages are small, freestanding settlements with limited authority. In most cases, they cannot enact zoning laws or create taxes to fund new community services. However, a small, unincorporated village seldom needs these powers. A New Village is designed to help residents work at home, protect the natural environment, socialize with each other, and develop a sense of community.

The heart of the community would be the village center, which would reflect the character of the villagers and their reasons for congregating. A village center might feature a tiny meetinghouse and a chapel or temple depending on the importance or prevalence of a single faith among the villagers, or it could be a small park, green, or square with sculptures as well as outdoor tables for meals. In addition, a cluster of mailboxes would draw the community together each day, encouraging the social interaction that's often missing in today's impersonal suburbs.

In most cases, this walkable village would be 30 to 80 miles from the outskirts of a city having an airport and any necessary retail, entertainment, and professional services lacking in the village. Some New Villages near public-transit stations could be even further from cities.

Enabling Energy Self-Sufficiency

A modest level of energy self-sufficiency avoids much of the air pollution, traffic congestion, and other urban problems created by parasitic bedroom communities, where transportation can account for half of the total energy use. Like today's suburbanites, residents of a New Village would also drive to the closest city, but they would do so less often and usually not at rush hour.

The design of each New Village would vary considerably, depending on environmental conditions at the site, housing preferences of the intended buyers, the potential for mini-farms, and other factors. The design might also have characteristics of historic villages within the region. Examples include the use of country lanes with natural drainage systems and houses that face south toward the sun.

Theoretically, a New Village could use any conventional or unconventional energy source that was locally abundant. One of the exciting aspects of building a New Village from scratch is that it can serve as a laboratory for innovative ideas in fields like energy conservation, as well as building construction, telecommunications, social and health planning, and education. For example, if the village is several miles from the nearest power pole, each homeowner could generate electricity using some combination of photovoltaic panels and a wind generator or microhydroelectric unit.

Encouraging Agricultural Self-Sufficiency

In a typical New Village, several large "estate lots" would surround the community, or residents could use the help of a nonprofit land trust to create a conservation easement around the village. The easement would protect critical wildlife, prevent unwanted development near the community, yield tax benefits for the developer, and increase the value of adjacent lots.

In addition, the easement could supply villagers with fresh organic produce. In a New Village with an agricultural economy, a small parking lot could also be designed as an outdoor farmers' market on weekends. Here, residents could sell a variety of high-quality and specialty products directly to people from the nearby city who enjoy a pleasant weekend outing in the country. These products might include fresh organic vegetables, nuts and tree-ripened fruits, specialty mushrooms, herbs and herb vinegars, honey and maple syrup, and dozens of other items. A traditional grocery store would be impractical in a small village unless it draws shoppers from outside the community. Fortunately, a New Village is likely to attract residents who would grow some of their own food and sell or preserve the surplus. Villagers lacking an interest in vegetable gardening could buy some of their food at the farmers' market or barter with neighbors.

Another alternative is to create a Community Supported Agriculture (CSA) program where residents could buy "shares" of the next season's harvest from a small farm within or near the village. Shareholders would receive fresh organic produce at a reasonable price, while the advance payments would give the farmer a guaranteed market for all of his or her crop. Since 1995, the number of CSA farms in the United States and Canada has grown from 450 to more than 1,000. If some of the soil in the village is arable, part of the economy could be based on the production of high-value specialty crops. For example, while writing the master plans for several mini-farms, I compiled information on more than 40 specialized crops producing gross returns of $4,000 to $100,000 per acre per year for some experienced growers working small tracts.

The New Village could even be designed with smaller lots on nonproductive hillsides overlooking mini-farms on rich bottom land soils. If the farms are fenced, located downwind, and use organic growing methods, the neighbors should have few complaints. In fact, hundreds of subdivisions in the United States lure buyers who gladly pay premium prices for lots overlooking green areas in the form of manicured golf courses and parks.

Ensuring Economic Sustainability

Unlike many existing communities with zoning and deed restrictions impeding home-based businesses, the New Village would create a diversified economy by actively promoting home enterprises and cottage industries. Unless a small village serves a larger trade area, the population would be insufficient to support retail shops and municipal services such as a library or a neighborhood school. However, the Internet provides new options for the way these products and services are delivered.

Additionally, many of the residents could use the Internet to avoid commuting to work. According to the recent AARP *Working in Retirement* study, most retiring baby boomers want to do consulting or other part-time work, but do so from home — or at least not from an office. Improvements in teleconferencing and other changes will increase the number of teleworkers in the United States to 50 million within five years; according to some estimates. Interactive video would also allow villagers to participate in classes taught at distant locations and to receive expert medical diagnosis and treatment. Thirty states now have telemedicine programs serving rural clinics.

The increasing availability and affordability of highspeed Internet is making the New Village concept a more viable and attractive option not only for retirees but for young people as well. Without leaving home, people can shop, bank, earn a living, worship, access world libraries, earn college degrees, and educate their children. There would probably be less crime in communities where most of the residents work from home; there is also less need for day care (for both children and the growing number of elderly), and there is more social interaction within and between households. Such interaction is vital to creating a sense of community among the residents.

Some home businesses, however, may cause social and environmental conflicts in a residential community. For this reason, all properties in the village would be subject to deed restrictions controlling advertising signs, direct sales, and noise, fumes, odors, or other potential problems for neighbors.

Recycled Villages

New Villages need not be built from scratch. I've explored ways for non-developers to "recycle" some of the thousands of small, unmarked rural subdivisions that are mostly vacant and undervalued. In my experience, using existing subdivisions can greatly reduce the environmental impact, government red tape, and financial capital required to build a New Village. In recreational subdivisions alone, the United States has an estimated 15 million vacant lots, mostly in Florida and southwestern states.

It is also possible to create a New Village from, of all things, a ghost town. The landscape of America is littered with skeletons of towns that died because of various economic and political changes. In fact, I've identified more than 5,700 ghost towns across the United States and Canada that are less than 300 years old. There are advantages to reviving a ghost town instead of building a community from scratch. The lots are already platted, and some of the buildings and other improvements may be usable. Also, many ghost towns were located near prime farmland and a year-round source of drinking water. Finally, there's the satisfaction of breathing life into an abandoned community full of history and character. These same characteristics can also attract enough tourists to sustain the economy of a small town. Some of the rehabilitated ghost towns in the western United States attract over 300,000 tourists each year.

Another creative alternative is to use existing houseboats to form a floating New Village. In Asia, houseboat communities have existed for hundreds of years. The economy of a floating village might include commercial fishing, aquaculture, and fishing guide services.

Final Thoughts

Sometimes the future resembles the distant past. As digital interconnectedness, a growing retirement population, and a rising need for more communal and sustainable living transform rural America over the next two decades, traditional villages in the style of our ancestors may again become common. Like all land developments, New Villages have some negative effects. But these tiny new communities may offer a benign alternative to some of the thousands of new rural subdivisions that will otherwise be built.

CHAPTER 49

Cities and Sustainability

Michael Willis

With each passing day, the issue of sustainability becomes more prominent in debates on the future of our planet. Nowhere is this more apparent than in the example of climate change. The wide and divisive debate of a few years ago is now rapidly narrowing, according to Dr. R.K. Pachuri, chairman of the Intergovernmental Panel on Climate Change.

At Pachuri's presentation, made in Montreal in December 2005 at the 11th conference of the Parties to the United Nations Framework Convention on Climate Change, he showed how the earth's climate system has demonstrably changed on both global and regional scales since pre-industrial times. He noted that strong evidence exists that most of the warming observed over the past 50 years is attributable to human activities.

The past 20 years have seen record surface temperatures across the world. For people living in the Northern Hemisphere, 2005 was the hottest year on record since 1880.[1] A consensus is emerging that global warming is going to have a dramatic effect environmentally, economically, and socially on future generations and, in such cases as low-lying cities and islands, it will be doing this soon.

"Global warming" refers to increases in global temperatures resulting from an accumulation of greenhouse gases in the atmosphere. These gases, including carbon dioxide, methane, and chlorofluorocarbons, trap the sun's heat as it is radiated from the earth and prevent it from going back into space.

You may be thinking, "What's all this have to do with local government management?" A simple answer is at hand. Many years ago, the Speaker of the U.S. House of Representatives famously declared: "All politics is local." Assume for the moment that he was right. This also suggests that the answers to the issues of our age do not come solely from the global political arena but also from the very things we do at the local level. For nowhere is change more achievable than at the individual and local levels. In so many ways, it's the things we do locally that really count.

No one would idly pretend that global warming will be solved by neighborhood environmental programs. But equally, social attitudes and values are often forged in the heat of the projects and ideals that neighborhoods passionately commit themselves to in their own communities. It doesn't require a large leap of faith to see that the greater the awareness of environmental issues on the local level, the greater the awareness and readiness for action on the national and international levels.

Think of the "broken windows" analogy. It's the little tasks we do at the "micro" level, like fixing a broken window, that influence how we value our neighborhoods.

Originally published as "Sustainability: The Issue of Our Age, and a Concern for Local Government," *Public Management*, Vol. 88, No. 7, August 2006, published and copyrighted by the ICMA (International City/County Management Association), Washington, D.C. Reprinted with permission of the publisher.

So what are we, as local government managers and as a professional body, doing to address issues of environmental sustainability in our own communities? After all, we are very much in the legacy business, that is, the business of creating and nurturing things that can be used and enjoyed by generations to come.

Shouldn't sustainable communities be among these legacies? Are we doing enough to get sustainability onto our local agendas? This article explores some of these issues and briefly considers what local governments are doing to address sustainability.

The Meaning of Sustainability

One of the goals is to engage appointed and elected officials on the issue of sustainability. So, what do we mean by the term "sustainability"? I once heard it described as "a vortex for woolly thinking" (as someone originally hailing from a land renowned for its sheep, this author finds that this definition does have a certain appeal). Sustainability certainly is a term that is capable of widely disparate meanings, so it's worth taking space to describe it.

Sustainability is most often considered in the context of improving the health and welfare of the planet and its people into the future. There are numerous definitions, but the following notions capture the essence of the word:

- Meeting the needs of the present without compromising the ability of future generations to meet their own needs.
- Improving the quality of life while living within the carrying capacity of the supporting environment.

In local government terms, this concept has been described by one commentator as involving creating sustainable cities and counties, where we reduce the use of local natural resources and the production of waste while also improving human livability.[2] The idea of sustainability is generally viewed as having environmental, social, and economic components.

Current thinking on sustainability recognizes that human society is totally dependent on the natural environment. Thus, it follows that the integration of ecological thinking into all social and economic decision making is required.

Think Globally, Act Locally

The motto "Think globally, act locally" is well known and closely linked to the notion of sustainability. Its importance was highlighted at the United Nations Conference on Environment and Development held in Rio de Janeiro in 1992, where 179 governments took stock of the state of the world and decided to adopt the global action plan for sustainable development that we now know as Agenda 21.

Agenda 21 called on local authorities in every country to undertake a consultative process with their populations to achieve consensus on action plans for their communities. It recognized the need to work out local agendas (and ways of doing things) to achieve sustainable living in the 21st century.

In many ways, local government can be viewed as the glue that sticks together the "Think globally" component with the "Act locally" element. The call to action made by Agenda 21 in 1992 is still relevant today because it is about meeting the three most pressing needs of our times:

- The need for environmental protection of the air, water, soil, and biodiversity upon which life depends.
- The need for economic development to overcome poverty.
- The need for social justice and cultural diversity to enable local communities to express their values in addressing issues.

There is, however, an inherent contradiction in addressing these needs, as there is in the term "sustainable development" itself. As author W. Rees, in his 1995 *Journal of Planning Literature* article "Achieving Sustainability: Reform or Transformation?" put it: "How can we produce the growth necessary to 'improve living standards for all' and provide a 'more prosperous future' while at the same time protecting the environment, particularly when historic patterns of economic and material growth appear responsible for much environmental degradation?"

How can we foster economic and social growth (a major driver in many, if not most, of our communities) while also protecting and enhancing the environment? How can we promote and achieve community expectations and at the same time protect individual property rights? Our profession is very much at the interface of these apparently divergent concerns.

You see, in all of these things, managers are called upon to manage apparent opposites. And managing opposites is about more than finding a balance between them. It's about being able to achieve both objectives.

What is it that we can do, as citizens and local leaders, to address the environmental challenges that clearly confront us? How can we help local people and communities exercise power over what they can control, in the face of so many forces that seem beyond both control and comprehension itself?

These are important questions because, as much as sustainability is about making things better environmentally, it's also about intensifying the process of civic engagement, which is surely at the heart of the local governing process and at the heart of our profession.

There are no easy answers to these questions; indeed, different answers will be required for different localities. The following section outlines briefly how some local governments have taken the initiative in responding to sustainability issues in their local areas.

Sustainability Initiatives

A growing number of local governments have decided to take a leadership role in addressing sustainability issues in their local areas. Some, including my own council in the city of Blue Mountains, New South Wales, Australia, have worked in partnership with the community and its citizens to develop long-term visions and action plans that will guide the achievement of more sustainable outcomes, not only in the future but also now.[3]

Such community-owned visions and plans can build frameworks for helping citizens and local leaders to understand these values, chart a way forward, and reconcile seemingly competing needs. In the case of Blue Mountains, having a sustainability vision and action plan has also given us a platform for launching a range of related initiatives in partnership with other stakeholders, as outlined below.

Blue Mountains City is enclosed within a World Heritage Park on the edge of the Sydney metropolitan area. Serving 75,000 residents, it has placed sustainability at the core of its planning and operational programs. We have undertaken a number of programs that we hope will bring this ideal to our local government doorstep. More information on these programs is available on the website at www.bmcc.nsw.gov.au.

- Catchment restoration. We have launched partnership programs among residents, agencies, community groups, and schools to carry out local works to restore catchment facilities (reservoirs, dams, stormwater channels, and so on) that have suffered degradation.
- Bushcare programs. A bushcare group will go out into its patch of bush each month and carry out bush regeneration, removing exotic weeds to allow native plants to germinate and flourish. Other activities include stormwater control and erosion control works in the patch, track maintenance and improvement, seed collection, plant propagation, public education, and other bushland management projects.
- There are more than 50 groups in action and more than 400 active volunteers. The council has four bushcare officers employed to supply, train, and coordinate the groups. For every hour that the council puts into this program, the community puts in more than three. Each year, 6,000+ volunteer hours have been worked on bushcare projects.
- Energy use reduction. Since 2004, the Blue Mountains Council has significantly reduced energy consumption and greenhouse gas emissions in its buildings by implementing an innovative energy performance contract. We have joined the Cities

for Climate Protection(tm) program and completed an audit of our energy consumption. Currently, an action plan is being developed to reduce the city's energy consumption.

- Curbside chipping of garden waste. In 2001, the city began a curbside chipping service to process garden waste on-site at residents' homes. Each year, 22,000 services are provided that result in the chipping of 46,000 cubic meters of garden waste for reuse on residents' properties; otherwise, this material would be disposed into landfill. Significantly, as a result of this and other initiatives, since 2004 there has been a 20 percent reduction in the volume of waste being delivered to the council's two waste management facilities.
- Teaching our children. In partnership with local schools, the city has established a Blue Mountain School Environment Network, which supports teachers in their efforts to engage children and the community in learning about the environment and developing sustainable schools.
- Earthworks courses. The city is implementing earthworks courses to support residents in gaining such skills in sustainable living as composting, worm farming, "no-dig" gardening, and recycling. Through community workshops, more than 400 residents have enrolled in these courses.
- Sustainable tourism. The city has entered into partnerships with the state government to develop sustainable tourism destinations and other facilities.
- Business sustainability. The Blue Mountains Business Advantage Program offers local businesses the opportunity to become accredited in sustainable business practices through attendance at a training course at a local educational institution. More than 120 businesses have participated in the program.
- Sustainability research. In 2004, the Blue Mountains World Heritage Institute was founded with the support of the Blue Mountains City Council. The institute is a nonprofit organization promoting the conservation of the cultural and natural heritage of the Greater Blue Mountains World Heritage Park. It has attracted about $1 million in research funding for a range of such sustainable research projects as sustainable options for business and industry in a Blue Mountains town, Mapping Country (an indigenous cultural heritage project), and fire and climate change research.

Quite apart from the great good that such programs achieve for the environment, taken collectively they also arguably have a significant impact in shaping values and beliefs about environmental issues beyond the local level. They cannot help but make people think about sustainability issues on the national and international stage. Thus, not only are we doing good things for our local environment, but we are also giving expression to a set of values that will be played out as more people come to grips with such larger issues as climate change.

Obviously, what we do at the Blue Mountains City Council is by no means unique or unusual. Similar programs go on in many local governments around the world. In the area of climate change alone, substantial progress is being made at the local level, particularly through the Cities for Climate Protection (CCP) campaign, mentioned above under "Energy use reduction." This campaign enlists cities to adopt policies and measures that achieve quantifiable reductions in local greenhouse gas emissions, improve air quality, and enhance urban livability and sustainability.[4]

This campaign is run by the International Centre for Local Environmental Initiatives (ICLEI-Local Governments for Sustainability) in Australia, Canada, Europe, Japan, Latin America, Mexico, New Zealand, South Africa, South Asia, Southeast Asia, and the United States. More than 650 local governments currently participate in CCP, including 160 in the United States and more than 200 in Australia.

Action around environmental sustainability is clearly gaining national traction in the United States. For example, Portland, Oregon, continues to be a leader in a range of sustainability initiatives, as the first local government in the States to adopt a plan to address global warming.[5,6]

Last June in California, Governor Schwarzenegger declared the debate on climate change over and directed a "Climate Action Team," made up of representatives of various state agencies, to devise a plan to cut the state's greenhouse gas emissions. According to this plan, emissions need to be cut to 2000 levels by 2010, to 1990 levels by 2020, and to 80 percent below 1990 levels by 2050. Also in June of last year, 166 U.S. mayors signed up to approve a U.S. Mayors' Climate Protection Agreement.

Kent Portney's 2005 *Public Administration Review* article "Civic Engagement and Sustainable Cities in the United States" shows that, over the past decade, at least 42 U.S. cities have elected to pursue sustainable-cities programs to improve their livability.

ICMA, as a local government organization, has also been active in supporting sustainability activities, although that term has not always been used. Such activities have comprised a focus on best-practice environmental management, planning, smart growth, and brownfields redevelopment. The ICMA University offered its first formal workshop with a focus on sustainability at ICMA's 2005 annual conference.

Conclusion

We hold positions of great importance and influence in community decision making. Is our profession to be leaders or followers in creating more sustainable cities and counties? Should we be working harder to adopt more sustainable practices in the way we manage, following the examples of those who are leading the way?

This article has referred earlier to the dilemma faced by communities in resolving apparent opposites: fostering economic and social growth at the local level while at the same time protecting the environment. Local governance requires attention to such dilemmas. For, in truth, local governments are in the business of allocating community values in making decisions that directly affect the sustainability of our communities — socially, economically, and environmentally. There is no better place to start.

Surely, all administrators have an abiding and unswerving belief in the value and practice of local democracy. And local democracy does have a critical and pivotal role to play in addressing sustainability — the issue of our age. If we adhere to the adage that "all politics is local," then there can be no more powerful force than the democratic process, acting in concert with the community and the people within it, to produce sustainable outcomes.

In a sense, the future resides in the moment. For it is the things we do now that shape the future, for good or ill. If managers believe that we are in the legacy business, we need to think now about the things that must be done to develop more sustainable communities for those who will follow us. What greater calling can there be?

NOTES

1. U.S. National Aeronautics and Space Administration, "Global Temperature Trends: 2005 Summation" (New York: NASA Goddard Institute for Space Studies [GISS], 2005). Available at http://data.giss.nasa.gov/gistemp/2005/.

2. P. Newman and J. Kenworthy, *Sustainability and Cities: Overcoming Automobile Dependence* (Washington, DC: Island, 1999). The full quotation is: "The goal of sustainability in a city is the reduction of the city's use of natural resources and production of wastes, while simultaneously improving its livability, so that it can better fit within the capacities of local, regional, and global ecosystems."

3. See, for example, "Towards a More Sustainable Blue Mountains: A Map for Action, 2000–2025," on the Blue Mountains City Council web site at www.Bmcc.nsw.gov.au. Follow the links to "Our Future Blue Mountains."

4. See www.iclei.org. The CCP campaign is based on an innovative performance framework structured around five "milestones" that local governments commit themselves to reaching. The milestones allow local governments to understand how their decisions affect energy use and how these decisions can mitigate global climate change while improving a community's quality of life. The CCP methodology is a simple, standardized way of acting to reduce greenhouse gas emissions and of monitoring, measuring, and reporting performance.

5. City of Portland, "A Progress Report on the City of Portland and Multnomah County Local Action Plan on Global Warming" (Portland, OR: Author, 2005).

6. Visit www.sustainableportland.com for the range of sustainability initiatives being implemented by Portland, Oregon.

CHAPTER 50

Cars and Transportation

Ryan Chin

How can you design a city by designing a car? Today's automobiles are driven by an increasing number of users who live in cities. The United Nations reported in 2007 that migration patterns and population growth have created an equal split between inhabitants of cities and rural areas for the first time in human history. This general trend will continue for the next several decades and will produce a very urbanized world.

In 1950, New York City was the only megacity on the planet, with 10 million occupants. Today, there are 25 megacities that are mostly in developing countries. To verify this trend, we need only to look at the rapid urbanization in China to see the mass migration of the rural poor to urban areas for economic opportunity. Population experts project that most of the urban growth will occur in Asia and Africa for the next several decades. Simultaneously, humanity's thirst for personal mobility will continue to grow. History shows that, as countries develop economically, so does their use of four-wheeled motorized transportation.

The world's automobile fleet is currently estimated at 800 million cars that serve the 7.8 billion people living on Planet Earth. In the developed world, roughly seven out of 10 people own a car, whereas in the developing world, it's two out of 10. The continued economic development of Brazil, Russia, India, and China will fuel the growth of this fleet to more than 1 bil-

lion cars by 2020. The continued use of this personal transportation model is simply unsustainable given the combination of energy inefficiency, environmental consequences of fossil-fuel usage, potential disruptions to fuel supplies, urban sprawl created by automobile reliance, and congestion caused by inadequate alternative modes of transport. What we need is to radically rethink the problem by examining not only the automobile itself, but also how it is used in cities (where most of us are currently living).

Size and Weight

2010: Today's automobiles weigh an average of nearly 4,000 lb, approximately 20 times the weight of the driver. Today's automobiles also have a footprint of approximately 100 square feet, which is nearly 15 times the amount of space required for a comfortable office chair. But the size requirements don't stop at the footprint of the vehicle, if we consider the space that cars occupy on the road, in parking at home, work, and other destinations; add to that the space for maintenance and repair and it quickly grows to approximately 1,200 sq. ft. per vehicle. In midtown Manhattan, a 1,200 sq. ft. condominium would cost you upwards of $2 million to own.

2020: Tomorrow's automobiles will be

Originally published as "Sustainable Urban Mobility in 2020," *The Futurist*, Vol. 44, No. 4, July-August 2010. Used with permission from the World Future Society, www.wfs.org.

more lightweight and smaller. Size, weight, and energy efficiency are three factors that intimately interconnect in the design and engineering of automobiles. The lighter the vehicle, the more energy efficient it will be to move the mass of the car. The smaller the vehicle, the less mass you have. This set of relations forms a set of positive and negative feedback loops that ultimately affect the design of the vehicle. It will be imperative to incorporate technological improvements in lightweight materials, and composites will certainly help to make vehicles leaner, but this is not enough. Vehicles must also become more compact. These changes will not only improve energy efficiency, but also the vehicles' overall footprint.

Range and Speed

2010: Today's automobiles have a fuel range of about 300 miles (meaning they can travel 300 miles or so on one tank) can go from 0 to 60 mph in less than 10 seconds, and top out at more than 110 mph. This is great for intercity travel, but most Americans don't travel that far. More than 80 percent of daily commutes in America are less than 40 miles (round trip). With more than 81 percent of Americans living in metropolitan areas, you simply don't need to go 100 miles an hour down a city street. If you travel to Shanghai today, the average speed in the city is 9 mph. Bangalore, India, has achieved 24-hour congestion. Today's vehicle is simply over-engineered for most practical purposes in cities.

2020: Tomorrow's automobiles will not need that much refueling autonomy. BMW recently finished a series of user experiments to examine "range anxiety"—the fear of running out of electricity in electric cars—and discovered that their new electric mini (with 100 miles of range) has two to three times the range required for practically all trips. Users don't need to have five to six times the range, and they quickly learned to adapt to the constraints (and benefits) of this new vehicle type. The introduction of electric charging infra-structure in the upcoming decade will virtually eliminate range issues in urban areas. Cities like San Fran-

cisco, Portland, Paris, Madrid, and Barcelona all have initiatives to bring a network of charging stations in their respective metropolitan areas. Car makers are introducing plug-in options for many models that enable the electrical charging from a common 110V household outlet.

Gasoline Versus Electric

2010: Today's vehicles are predominantly powered by petroleum-based fuels. An internal combustion engine is terribly inefficient (approximately 15 percent) in converting, chemical energy into mechanical work to drive the wheels of your car. Hybrid vehicles are better at conserving energy at the cost of a more complex power-train, but projections for the next five years call for less than 12 percent of the total new car market. The remaining alternative fuels, like compressed natural gas, hydrogen, compressed air, and biofuels, have varying levels of efficiency, but are utilized in even fewer numbers than hybrids. Battery electric vehicles utilize electric motors that are more than 90 percent energy efficient, but these have not taken over mainstream markets because of limitations of battery technology.

2020: Tomorrow's automobiles will be increasingly electrified. The emergence of new battery chemistries such as lithium ion nanophosphate have allowed battery manufacturers to produce cells that have higher energy density and lower internal resistance, thus allowing rapid charging in less than 30 minutes. In fact, my colleagues at the MIT Electric Vehicle Team have been able to rapid-charge these new cells in less than 7 minutes with just a 10 percent degradation in capacity after 1,500 cycles. For comparison, lithium ion cells in your laptop today have roughly 1,000 cycles of usable life. The ability to rapid-charge will enable users to top-off their batteries in about the time it will take to order and drink an espresso, thus opening up new opportunities to create a ubiquitous charging network distributed throughout cities. No longer do we need to charge only at home or the workplace where our cars sit waiting for six to 10 hours.

Driver-Controlled Versus Autonomous Driving

2010: Today's cars are driven by human operators. Drivers have a number of telematic devices that aid in driving, such as antilock brakes for safe stopping, adaptive cruise control for the highway, parking sensors to help avoid scratches to the bumpers, and GPS for navigating unfamiliar places. However, we still have more than 50,000 deaths a year in the United States under the current driving paradigm. Today's drivers sit in traffic for more than 50 hours a year and endure the stop-and-go driving experience.

2020: Tomorrow's cars will be increasingly autonomous. The annual DARPA Urban Challenge has consistently proven to be a tremendously useful catalyst for innovations in autonomous driving. The most recent challenge shows that autonomously driven vehicles can navigate in busy city streets without incident. The potential of autonomous vehicles to self-drive and coordinate with other autonomous, vehicles is to smooth, traffic flows. In urban environments, top speed is not necessary; it is the orchestrated movement of vehicles within a speed regime that will improve congestion. The introduction of semi-autonomous systems such as self-parking and automated highway systems has provided useful lessons in the benefits and challenges of autonomous driving. Continued federally funded research in this area, combined with improvements in computational power, will enable the miniaturization of autonomous technologies, thus making autonomous driving commercially viable for mass markets in the coming decade.

Private Versus Shared Ownership

2010: Today's automobiles are designed for private ownership. The burden of ownership includes the cost of the vehicle, depreciation, tires, licensure, taxes, registration, insurance, maintenance, fuel, and parking. These individual direct costs are compounded by what economists call "negative externalities," which include congestion and pollution leading to global warming—that is, costs to society not immediately felt by the individual user. Privately owned commuter vehicles that may drive two hours a day (round trip) will sit doing nothing useful for 92 percent of the day. During, this state, the car takes up valuable real estate and doesn't move people around. Single passenger occupancy also doesn't help in this situation; if I stand on Memorial Drive in Cambridge, Massachusetts, I could wait up to 20 minutes before seeing a vehicle with two occupants. In that same city, approximately one-third of the land area is devoted to the servicing of automobiles (this includes roads and parking for cars) that are principally used by private individuals. This is not an atypical land-use percentage devoted to the automobile throughout the United States.

2020: Tomorrow's automobiles will be increasingly utilized in cooperative or shared-use models. The emergence of car-sharing and bike-sharing schemes in urban areas in both the United States and Europe have established alternative models and markets for fractional or on-demand mobility. Zipcar, the world's largest car-share program, has grown from just a handful of cars to a fleet of 6,000 cars and 275,000 drivers in 49 cities in just under 10 years, It's very difficult to own one quarter or one-tenth of a car with traditional ownership, and let's not even talk about fractional insurance; Shared ownership provides users fractional ownership that allows them access to any vehicle in the fleet whenever they please and for as long as they need, just like video on demand or print on demand.

Radical Rethinking Required

Since 2003, the Smart Cities group at the MIT Media Lab has developed solutions to directly tackle these problems. We have designed an electric two-passenger vehicle called the CityCar, which utilizes in-wheel electric motors called Wheel Robots that have incorporated drive, suspension, and braking directly inside the wheel. Each wheel is independently controlled with by-wire controls (no mechanical linkages) and is capable of 120 degrees of steering, which provides very high maneuverability. The CityCar can turn on its own axis (zero turn radius) and can make sideways turns by turning the wheels perpendicular to the primary driving axis.

The Wheel Robots eliminate the need for traditional components like drivelines, transmissions, and gearboxes. We have taken advantage of this freedom by rethinking the architecture of the vehicle. Since there is no driveline, we can make the vehicle very compact by folding the chassis. The CityCar can fold up to half its length to just under the width of a traditional parking space. The CityCar, when folded, is less than 60 inches in length and 100 inches when unfolded (comparable to the Smart Car). Three CityCars, when parked, can fit into one traditional parking space. It weighs just 1,000 lbs., thus making it very lightweight and energy efficient, and the new architecture allows us to rethink entry and exit. We have designed a front ingress solution that easily allows the driver and passenger to safely exit the vehicle onto the curb rather than the street. The folding mechanism complements this feature by articulating the seats so that the user can ergonomically and elegantly exit at an elevated position. CityCars are designed to park nose-in to the curb, which allows the users to use the sidewalk rather than the street. Finally, the in-wheel motors will provide plenty of low-end torque, thus making the CityCar fun to drive in urban areas.

Simply redesigning the vehicle is only one part of the solution. We have also created a new use model, called "Mobility on Demand" (MoD), which utilizes a fleet of lightweight electric vehicles (LEVs) that are distributed at electric charging stations throughout a metropolitan area. The LEVs are designed for shared use, which enable high utilization rates for the vehicles and the parking spaces they occupy. The use model mimics the bike sharing systems made popular in Europe, whereby users simply walk up to the closest charging station, swipe a credit card pick up a vehicle, drive to the station closest to their destination, and drop off the vehicle.

Our group has designed our CityCar to fit into these MoD systems, thus creating a complementary network that can solve what transportation planners call the "First Mile Last Mile" problem of public transit — that is, how to bridge the distance between your real origin (i.e., your home) to the transit station and from the transit station to your real final destination (i.e., your work-place). Often these distances are too long to walk, thus encouraging private automobile use.

The expansion of MoD into a sustainable urban ecosystem can be achieved by introducing additional shared-use vehicle types like electric bicycles and scooters. (Smart Cities has also designed an electric folding scooter called the "RoboScooter" and an electric bike called the "GreenWheel.") This will offer flexibility and convenience while allowing for asymmetric trips. For example, a user can drive a Green-Wheel to the supermarket, then go home with a CityCar that can carry groceries.

We believe that MoD systems will work better than private automobiles in cities because you never have to worry about storing the vehicle. In many cases, a MoD charging station will be closer to your final destination than if you had to park in a private lot. A typical urban trip is short; however, much of the time spent is not actually driving but rather walking to the vehicle and finding parking once you get there. A recent study by the Imperial College in London showed that, during congested hours, more than 40 percent of total gasoline use is by cars looking for a parking space!

In 2020, I expect the shift from private gasoline powered use to shared electric vehicles will be on its way. There are three primary factors that accelerate this trend:

1. Economic and environmental pressure to transition away from petroleum fuels.
2. Technological innovations.
3. Political leadership to promote new regulations and policies for this type of innovation.

In 2010, China has become the world's number-one automobile market, surpassing the United States in the number of cars purchased. The increased consumption of fossil fuels and the emissions of CO_2 will be part and parcel of this economic development. This will all but guarantee increased demand for petroleum and set the stage for political responsiveness.

Luckily, most of the technologies required to make the CityCar real already exist today, such as highly efficient electric motors, computational horsepower, new battery technologies, wireless network communications, lightweight composite materials, advanced sensing, and GPS. The only thing that limits us is the inherent difficulty of breaking away from our pre-conceived notions and embracing this radical rethinking.

NOTE

Industrial research has been conducted in the last decade on the benefits of Vehicle-to-Grid (V2G) charging. This enables cars to charge from renewable power sources and also feed power back into the grid, which can be sold at a premium back to the utility. Utilities will be able to load level the electric grid by "peak shaving" during the hottest days when everyone has the air conditioning running.

CHAPTER 51

Cities and Nature

Kevin Fletcher

"I want to protect our community's natural environment. I think most of our Town Board and a significant number of government staff thinks it's important... but taking that interest beyond mere words continues to be a challenge."—Town Planner, Upstate New York

I recently spoke at a local planning association meeting on techniques for creating a more sustainable future for small cities and towns. After the talk, one of the local planners from a rural community outside Albany, New York made this statement (above) to me. Clearly frustrated, he expressed something that green champions in communities across the country are expressing—a type of green fatigue. Elected officials and professional staff in communities from New York to Florida and beyond are struggling with a passion for environmentally-focused governance, without a means to make it "the way we do things around here."

Addressing Common Elements of Failure

It's important to recognize that you and others like you are "change agents" within your local government, and your goal is to create an environmental culture within your community — starting with the local government as a role model. Where to begin? Start by addressing eight common failures for environmental orga-

nizational change (adapted from John Kotler, *Leading Change*, Harvard Business School Press, 1996):

1. **Failing to Create a Sense of Urgency.** Moving people, and entire organizations or communities, in a new direction can be a little like moving an iceberg. Effective environmental champions find ways to create a sense of urgency. Incorporating environmental stewardship into local government has to be viewed as a critical part of your community's long-term success, and a critical part of each persons job. It's also critical to secure top management support for your environmental efforts. If employees see upper management or elected leaders treating the environment as a side issue, then they will too.

2. **Not Creating a Guiding Coalition (Team).** You can't go it alone. Build a "green team," with people from all levels and departments — and ideally, include community residents who are not a part of the government structure. Be aware of who, throughout your local government, has an ability to help motivate staff and coordinate government opera-

Originally published as "Injecting Environmental Culture into Local Government," *New Jersey Municipalities*, Vol. 83, No. 4, April 2006, by the New Jersey State League of Municipalities, Trenton. Reprinted with permission of the publisher.

tions. Who in your community has knowledge and technical skills to help solve environmental problems? Who has the authority and respect to help you mobilize your entire community? Answers often lead to people not directly involved in local politics.

3. **Underestimating the Power of a Vision.** People want to feel as if they are a part of something bigger than themselves. Create a bigger vision for your community — starting with your government operations. Every town and city is located in a watershed. Every facility depends upon energy, water, and other natural resources in order to function. Every person on your staff has a family. Find the connection between the day-to-day actions that people take, and the effect that those actions can have on our natural environment and everyday quality of life. Make a connection between the financial health of your community and the money wasted on eco-inefficiency (i.e., lights left on, leaking water pipes, waste that could have been recycled).

4. **Under Communicating the Vision.** Once you've developed a "vision message," make sure that vision is communicated to staff, and to town and city residents. You may think that people have heard or read what you're saying, but most environmental messages are under-communicated. Use posters, regular departmental and public meetings, and perhaps even bonuses or other incentives to reinforce the vision and the role that each individual plays in achieving that vision.

5. **Not Addressing Obstacles.** Most environmental efforts fail in organizations — public and private alike — because they are viewed as side issues. Remove these obstacles along the way. The City of Eufaula, Alabama — the first community designated a Certified Audubon Sustainable Community — made environmental protection and sustainability the driving force for their comprehensive planning process, but only after generating a great deal of buy-in from the entire community. By the time citizens gathered to talk details about the vision for their community, many of the potential obstacles had already been addressed.

6. **Failing to Create Short-Term Wins.** Keep you and your staff motivated throughout any culture-building process. Have a long-term vision, but set short-term goals. Meet them. Publicize and celebrate those shorter term successes. Then, set new goals.

7. **Declaring Victory Too Soon.** At the same time, don't settle on limited results. Remember that the longer term goal is to create an environmental culture throughout your community, starting with the local government itself. One or two recycling success stories do not lead to changed culture. Culture change takes years to accomplish. And the bigger the organization or community, the longer it takes. That's why rural and small communities have an advantage over larger communities to become more sustainable.

8. **Not Anchoring Changes in the Culture.** Use projects and performance goals to change behavior, but use management systems, rewards programs and training programs to reinforce and embed that behavior in staff. As an environmental champion, part of your job for ensuring success is managing the environmental culture that you've created.

Final Thoughts

With top management and elected officials' support, a team of staff from all levels and departments, a well-communicated vision, a set of achievable short-term goals, and mechanisms to make environmental stewardship "the way we do things around here," you will be on your way to improving the overall environmental performance of your community. Be willing to start small while thinking big. Remember that any positive environmental action you and your staff take brings us that much closer to a more sustainable world.

CHAPTER 52

Revitalizing America's Downtowns
Roger L. Kemp *and* Carl J. Stephani

Many citizens have left downtown areas for the suburbs over the years. Also, many businesses have moved to the shopping mall over the years. Much of this was brought about by the development and expansion of our nation's Interstate Highway System, a product of the mid–1950s, which is still evolving today! Traditionally, a family wanted to raise its children in a single-family house with a yard, away from the traffic and noise of the downtowns. This seemed like the "American Dream" for many years, and is now changing.

A quick overview of history would reveal that, as our highway system expanded, many residential subdivisions were developed in the suburbs. Families moved there for the reasons noted above. This trend went on for several decades! When our parents were young, there was typically one car in a family. As mothers went to work over the years, they acquired cars too. Nowadays, it seems like many children over the legal driving age in every state have cars. Older citizens recall seeing old homes with single car garages, newer homes with two-car garages, and more recent homes with three-car garages. A colleague was recently visiting one of our nation's growth states, and saw some new homes with four-car garages. Wow!

Things are now changing! There are families where the children have grown, and they would like to relocate in urban downtown areas. There are young professionals that would like to focus on their respective jobs before starting a family. They wish to locate in inner-city areas and relocate to the suburbs later in life. There's also another group, consisting of those folks that would like to live their lives without having a vehicle. Hence the new type of residential developments around public transit stations called Transit Oriented Developments (TOD's). There is also a rapidly developing market for condominiums and townhouses that are located next to light-rail public transit systems.

There is a national need, a community one too, to make downtowns attractive, which requires a redevelopment effort to make them more livable. Such positive movements require states, and their local governments, and especially those folks who are responsible for managing downtowns, to advocate for changes that will benefit downtown areas. We think history has gone, or is going, full circle in this regard. We were recently looking at a picture of a high-rise residential area in the Lower East Side of New York City from a century ago. Individuals and families lived in several story residential structures, with an assortment of commercial businesses located on the ground floor. All of the restaurants, markets, and other types of commercial activity, took place at street level. Then over the years we separated our land uses as we imposed pyramidal zoning on our cities. After all, you would not want citizens living in commercial or industrial areas. This way of thinking is now rapidly changing.

If communities want to revitalize their downtown areas, they must change their zoning laws to allow for mixed-uses of commercial (on the ground floor) and residential (on the floors above that). Also, arts, entertainment, and culture are coming back to downtown areas. Lately, citizens have seen their city officials using libraries and museums as tools to stimulate economic development. Also, cities are trying to lure educational institutions and nonprofit organizations back downtown. We recently read where some states are even relocating some of their offices from the suburbs back into their downtown areas.

There's also a big trend to preserve what's left of nature in our downtown areas, as well as to restore what's been removed over the decades, as well as to expand various aspects of nature. This includes parks, wetlands, waterways, as well as ways to enhance pedestrian access and movement through the use of walkways, bikeways, plazas, and the widening of public areas to accommodate people as opposed to cars.

Many citizens have thought that their downtowns were designed by cars. It seems like people were a secondary consideration. Times have changed! Streets are now getting narrower, as well as are the number of lanes used to accommodate traffic. Sidewalks are now getting wider — as well as greener. This trend has facilitated the movement of people back to our downtown areas! It's also great for those commercial businesses established on the ground level to have their market built-in around and above them. No need for those one story commercial centers and block after block of retail buildings of the past. Rezoning them and placing residential units above them is the wave of the future. If you build them, people will come, especially if there's public transit in the area.

Some of our nation's major evolving downtown trends are highlighted below:

- Restoration and enhancement of all aspects of nature.
- Buildings that have mixed-uses, and are multi-story in their height.
- Making public transit available, usually light-rail systems.
- Restoration of the public infrastructure to favor people over cars.
- Combine landscaping with the restoration of all aspects of the public infrastructure.

- Conversion of surface parking to parks, gardens, and open spaces.
- Attraction of culture, the arts, and entertainment amenities and facilities.
- Attraction of educational institutions and nonprofit organizations.
- While many businesses have located to shopping malls, smaller specialized ones are locating downtown.
- Focus downtown on ethnic and niche stores, such as markets, delicatessens, bakeries, and restaurants.
- Restoration of a sense of "public place" in the core of our "new" downtowns.

Above all, these trends make our downtowns more "people friendly" rather than favoring the movement and parking of vehicles. Many of the items on this list, if accomplished by a city government, would stimulate the local economy, and attract the type of businesses, educational institutions, and nonprofit organizations that would benefit the rebirth and growth of our downtown areas. Additional incentives would further facilitate the attraction of desirable private, educational, and nonprofit sector additions in our downtowns. These incentives typically include:

- Low-interest loans.
- Grants for "high priority" projects.
- The construction of certain "on-site" improvements, such as parking garages.
- The construction of certain "off-site" improvements, such as utilities, roadways, and signalized intersections.
- Facade improvement programs.
- Provision of a "user-friendly" development process.
- Property tax incentives, usually in the form of reductions or rebates.
- Agreed upon Sales Tax rebates.
- Zoning to accommodate "mixed" land-use developments.
- Public investments in downtown improvements.
- Programs to market the "new image" of your downtown.

As we all know, to sell economic development incentives to local public officials, they must be reasonable as well as have a long-term benefit to the taxpayers.

More importantly, those public officials elected by the citizens must feel comfortable with such incentives, as well as feel that they will improve their downtown. They must also benefit all of the citizens within the community. A nice downtown should not only serve as a great public place for those citizens who live there, but for other individuals and families in the community as well. They should not only be attracted to "their" downtown, but they should also feel comfortable within the entire inner-city area, including the surrounding neighborhoods. The various trends outlined above, when facilitated by local public officials, will make these trends a common reality!

Public officials, both elected and appointed, should always keep in mind that prudent economic development incentives are a wise way to increase a local government's revenues without raising its taxes. During these difficult eco-nomic times, the above practices should be embraced and facilitated by politicians, downtown professionals, and citizens alike, since they will assist in balancing their community's budget with the increased revenues that result from renewing a community's downtown.

Most cities evolved piecemeal over the years, and now need to be retrofitted and redesigned for the future. Planning, zoning, and building laws and regulations should be in place to accommodate mixed land-uses, infill development, and redevelopment projects. Call it New Urbanism, Sustainability, Smart Growth, Pedestrian Cities, Healthy Cities, Livable Cities, Inner-City Renewal, or the Green Cities Movement, whatever you wish! We must all work together to get our respective downtowns moving in these positive directions.

The practices facilitated by these downtown revitalization trends can be increasingly applied to projects of all sizes — from a single building, to a full block, to a neighborhood, and even to an entire community.

Appendices

Containing **A.** *Periodicals Bibliography;* **B.** *Glossary;* **C.** *Acronyms and Abbreviations;*
D. *Regional Resource Directory;* **E.** *National Resource Directory;* **F.** *State Municipal*
League Directory; **G.** *State Library Directory*

A. Periodicals Bibliography

The following list consists of periodicals that are dedicated to planning or that often address related subjects:

California Planner, monthly: subscription included with membership in the California Chapter of the American Planning Association, c/o S/G Assoc., 1333 36th St., Sacramento. CA 95865. This is the official newsletter of the CCAPA. It contains articles on current planning activities around the state, an update on state legislation relating to planning, and information on workshops on planning.

The Commissioner, quarterly; subscription included with "planning commissioner" membership in the American Planning Association, 122 S. Michigan Ave., Suite 1600, Chicago, IL 60603-6107, (312) 786-6344.

This periodical features expanded coverage on contemporary planning issues, and land use practices, and planning commission trends throughout the country. This is a non-technical publication written for citizens who serve as planning commissioners in their community.

GreenSource, bimonthly, from the McGraw Hill Construction Company, Two Penn Plaza, New York, New York 10121-2298, (515) 237-3681.

This magazine publishes successful green case studies, the latest trends in green construction, and technology issues facing designers and contractors. This publication also focuses on new products in the green building field, recent developments in green design legislation, and new policies established by private owners in this field.

Journal of the American Planning Association; quarterly; from the American Planning Association Planners Book Service, 122 S. Michigan Ave., Suite 1600, Chicago, IL 60603-6107, (312) 786-6344.

A collection of academic articles relating to current physical, economic, and social planning research. Recent topics include infrastructure finance, homelessness, strategic planning, and economic development. In addition, it contains detailed reviews of new literature in the field.

New Urban News, 8 issues per year, from the New Urban Network News Publications, 202 East State Street, Suite 303, Ithaca, New York 14850, (607) 275-3087.

This publication is the source of the latest news on emerging issues, trends, and developments in the fields of urban planning, walkable communities, and smart growth. This was one of the first publications of its type in America, starting in 1966, on these important and timely planning and development topics.

PAS (*Planning Advisory Service*) *Memo*; published six times a year for subscribers to the American Planning Association's Planning Advisory Service, 122 S. Michigan Ave., Suite 1600, Chicago. IL. 60603-6107, (312) 786-6344.

The PAS *Memo* highlights new planning programs, identifies and examines planning trends, and analyzes escalating problems relative to land use planning throughout the nation. It offers expert commentary on timely topics like immigration, Internet resources for planners, and using remote sensing technology for planning.

Planning; monthly; from the American Planning Association Planners Book Service, 122 S. Michigan Ave. Suite 1600, Chicago. IL 60603-6107, (312) 786-6344.

The magazine of the American Planning Association, *Planning* focuses on solutions to common planning problems, reviews new planning techniques, and highlights successful planning programs. It is written by practitioners for practitioners.

Planning and Environmental Law; monthly; from the American Planning Association Planners Book Service, 122 S. Michigan Ave., Suite 1600, Chicago, IL. 60603-6107, (312) 786-6344.

This periodical summarizes recent litigation occurring in state and federal courts around the country. Other topics include recently enacted state legislation affecting planning and expert commentary on subjects relating to land use regulation.

Urban Land; monthly; subscription included with membership in the Urban Land Institute, 1090 Vermont Ave., N.W., Washington, D.C. 20005, (202) 289-3381.

This is the magazine of the Urban Land Institute, an independent education and research organization primarily made up of developers and private sector planners. It profiles successful development projects around the country as well as discussing current planning topics such as transportation funding and mixed use development.

Western City; monthly; from the League of California Cities, 1400 "K" St., Sacramento, CA 95814, (916) 444-5790.

This is the League of California Cities' magazine. Its articles concentrate on innovative programs in city administration, funding, and other topics such as fire and police protection. Although it does not concentrate on planning, it usually contains news of local planning-related programs.

Zoning and Planning Law Report; 11 issues per year; from Clark Boardman, Co., Ltd., 435 Hudson St., New York, NY 10014.

In each issue, this report carefully examines some aspect of planning law. Recent topics have included vested rights, exaction ordinances and "takings" theory. This periodical is valuable to both those considering new land use regulations and those interested in keeping current regulations up to date.

Zoning News; monthly; from the American Planning Association Planners Book Service, 122 S. Michigan Ave., Suite 1600, Chicago, IL 60603-6107, (312) 786-6344.

This is a four-page newsletter devoted to monitoring trends in local land use controls. It discusses innovative development regulations, code amendments, development projects, development incentives, and design standards. Each issue usually concentrates on a particular subject.

B. Glossary

The following terms relate to the fields of municipal and regional planning and development.

Acre: 43,560 square feet of area. For example, a residential parcel of land that is 52' × 100' is 5,200 square feet which is 0.12 acres. The term gross acres means all land within a given boundary. The term net acres means all land measured to remove certain features such as roads, utilities, and open space.

Blight: Physical and economic conditions within an area that cause a reduction of or lack of proper utilization of that area. A blighted area is one that has deteriorated or has been arrested in its development by physical, economic, or social forces.

Brownfield: Abandoned industrial site likely to have groundwater or soil pollution that is deterrent to redevelopment.

Buffer Zone: A strip of land created to separate and protect one type of land use from another; for example, as a screen of planting or fencing to insulate the surroundings from the noise, smoke, or visual aspects of an industrial zone or junkyard.

Building Area: The total square footage of a lot covered by a building, measured on a horizontal plane, exclusive of uncovered porches, terraces, and steps.

Building Envelope: The net cubic space that remains for placing a structure on a site after setbacks and height/bulk regulations are observed.

Bulk Regulations: Zoning or other regulations that control height, mass, density, and location of buildings. The purpose of bulk regulations is to provide proper light, air, and open space. Some bulk regulations also are intended to reflect context-sensitive design.

Carrying Capacity: The level of land use or human activity that can be permanently accommodated without an irreversible change in the quality of air, water, land, or plant and animal habitats. In human settlements, this term also refers to the upper limits beyond which the quality of life, community character, or human health, welfare, and safety will be impaired. The estimated maximum number of persons that can be served by existing and planned infrastructure systems; the maximum number of vehicles that can be accommodated on a roadway.

Cluster Development (zoning): A type of development pattern for residential, commercial, or other uses in which the uses are grouped, or clustered through density transfer, rather than spread evenly throughout a parcel. Cluster development is more efficient because it requires building fewer streets and utility lines.

Community Plan: A portion of the local general plan that focuses on a particular area or community within the city or county. Community plans supplement the policies of the general plan.

Conservation Easement: A tool for acquiring open space with less than full-fee purchase; the public agency or not-for-profit corporation buys only certain specific rights from the landowner to restrict the development, management or use of the land. The landowner may be allowed to continue using the property for agricultural purposes.

Context Sensitive Design: A collaborative, interdisciplinary approach that involves all stakeholders to develop a transportation facility that fits its physical setting and preserves scenic, aesthetic, historic, and environmental resources, while maintaining safety and mobility. CSD is an approach that considers the total context within which a transportation improvement project will exist.

Density: The average number of families, persons, or housing units per unit of land. Usually density is expressed "per acre." Gross density includes the area necessary for streets, schools and parks. Net density does not include land area for public facilities.

Density Bonus: An increase in the allowable number of dwelling units granted by the city or county in return for the project's providing low- or moderate-income housing.

Floor Area Ratio: Abbreviated as FAR, this is a measure of development intensity. FAR is the ratio of the amount of floor area of a building to the amount of area of its site. For instance, a one-story building that covers an entire lot has an FAR of 1. Similarly, a one-story building that covers ½ of a lot has an FAR of 0.5.

General Plan: A statement of policies, including text and diagrams setting forth objectives, principles, standards, and plan proposals, for the future physical development of the city or county.

Geographic Information System: Computer mapping system that produces multiple "layers" (coverages) of graphic information about a community or region. For example, one layer might show the parcels, another layer might show key habitat areas, another layer might show school sites, etc. Considered a tool for analysis and decision-making, it may be composed of maps, databases and point information.

"Granny" Housing: Typically, this refers to a second dwelling attached to or separate from the main residence that houses one or more elderly persons.

Grayfield: A blighted area that is ripe for redevelopment; the distinguishing characteristic between a grayfield and a brownfield is the absence of substantial groundwater or soil pollution.

Greenbelt: A wide band of countryside surrounding a city on which building is generally prohibited, usually large enough to form an adequate protection against objectionable uses of property or the intrusion of nearby development.

Gridiron Street Pattern: A pattern of streets that, from the air, looks like a gridiron (i.e., based on right-angle intersections and parallel sets of roadways). Grid street pattern usually refers to shorter, more frequent block patterns, as compared to "superblocks" or a streets system with cul-de-sacs predominant.

Historic District; An area or group of areas designated by a local agency as having aesthetic, architectural, historical, cultural, or archaeological significance that is worthy of protection and enhancement.

Imageability: The quality in a city or any of its districts that will evoke a strong image in the observer.

Improved Land: Raw land that has been improved with basic utilities such as roads, sewers, water lines, and other public infrastructure facilities. The term "developed land" usually means improved land that also has buildings.

Infill Development: The creative recycling of vacant or underutilized lands within cities and suburbs. (Congress of New Urbanism). Among the variables in the definitions of infill development are whether the property must be surrounded by existing development or just within existing urban boundaries, whether infill projects must have a higher density than surrounding properties, and whether individual infill projects must be mixed use.

Infrastructure: A general term describing public and quasi-public utilities and facilities such as roads, bridges, sewers and sewer plants, water lines, power lines, first stations, etc. necessary to the functioning of an urban area.

Intensity: The degree to which land is used.

While frequently used synonymously with density, intensity has a somewhat broader, though less clear meaning, referring to levels of concentration of activity in uses such as residential, commercial, industrial, recreation, or parking. Density usually refers to residential, while intensity usually refers to non-residential uses.

Jobs-Housing Ratio: The numeric relationship between the number of jobs (employment) divided by the number of housing units. A "jobs-housing balance" is the jobs-housing ratio that has a job for every member of households participating in the labor force. For example, if a typical housing unit has 3.0 people/housing unit, and ⅔ of those residents are in the workforce, then each housing unit generates 2 workers. In a "closed system," two jobs need to be available per housing unit within that system (e.g., a region).

Leapfrog Development: Development that occurs well beyond the existing urban limits of urban development, leaving intervening vacant land. The pattern of urbanization characterized by leapfrog development is sometimes referred to as "sprawl."

Livability Space: Open space used for people, planting, and visual appeal which does not include parking and driveway areas. It is a basic element of land-use-intensity ratings.

Lot Area: The total square footage of horizontal area included within the property lines. Zoning ordinances typically set a minimum required lot area for building in a particular zoning district.

Neighborhood: Residential area within a governmental unit that has some distinct identity to its inhabitants and observers.

Neighborhood Completeness: A land use indicator that attempts to define how well a neighborhood is served by specific land uses (e.g., affordable housing, fire/police station, grocery store, parks, library, school, post office).

New Urbanism: Similar to Traditional Neighborhood Development, this design philosophy is intended to create a strong sense of community by incorporating features of traditional small towns.

Open Space: That part of the countryside which has not been developed, and which is desirable for preservation in its natural state for ecological, historical, or recreational purposes, or in its cultivated state to preserve agricultural, forest, or urban greenbelt areas.

Overlay Zone: A set of zoning requirements that is superimposed upon a base zone. Overlay zones are generally used when a particular area requires special protection (as in a historic preservation district) or has a special problem (such as steep slopes,

flooding or earthquake faults). Development of land subject to overlay zoning requires compliance with the regulations of both the base and overlay zones.

Planned Unit Development: Land use zoning which allows the adoption of a set of development standards that are specific to the particular project being proposed. PUD zones usually do not contain detailed development standards; these are established during the process of considering the proposals and adopted by ordinance if the project is approved.

Quality of Life: Those aspects of the economic, social and physical environment that make a community a desirable place in which to live or do business. Quality of life factors include climate and natural features, access to schools, housing, employment opportunities, medical facilities, cultural and recreational amenities, and public services.

Rural: Areas generally characterized by agricultural, timberland, open space, and very low-density residential development (e.g., less than one dwelling unit per acre). A rural community is not generally served by community water or sewer services.

Setback: A minimum distance required by zoning to be maintained between two structures or between a structure and property lines.

Smart Growth: A contemporary phrase related to development that better serves the economic, environment and social needs of communities. The U.S. Environmental Protection Agency identifies the following 10 principles of smart growth:

1. Mix Land Uses
2. Take Advantage of Compact Building Design
3. Create a Range of Housing Opportunities and Choices
4. Create Walkable Neighborhoods
5. Foster Distinctive, Attractive Communities with a Strong Sense of Place
6. Preserve Open Space, Farmland, Natural Beauty, and Critical Environmental Areas
7. Strengthen and Direct Development Towards Existing Communities
8. Provide a Variety of Transportation Choices
9. Make Development Decisions Predictable, Fair and Cost Effective
10. Encourage Community and Stakeholder Collaboration in Development Decisions

Specific Plan: A plan addressing land use distribution, open space availability, infrastructure, and infrastructure financing for a portion of the community. Specific plans put the provisions of the local general plan into action.

Sphere-of-Influence: A planning area usually larger than, although sometimes contiguous with, a city's municipal limits.

Sprawl: The process in which the spread of development across the landscape far outpaces population growth. The landscape sprawl creates four dimensions: a population that is widely dispersed in low-density development; rigidly separated homes, shops, and workplaces; a network of roads marked by huge blocks and poor access; and a lack of well-defined, thriving activity centers, such as downtowns and town centers. Most of the other features usually associated with sprawl — the lack of transportation choices, relative uniformity of housing options or the difficulty of walking — are a result of these conditions. (Smart Growth America)

Subdivision: The process of laying out a parcel of raw land into lots, blocks, streets, and public areas. Its purpose is the transformation of raw land into building sites.

Suburban: Areas generally characterized by low-density residential development (e.g., 1 to 5 dwelling units per acre) and limited commercial uses.

Sustainability: A strategy by which communities seek economic development approaches that also benefit the local environment and quality of life. For a community to be truly sustainable, it must adopt a three-pronged approach that considers economic, environmental and cultural resources. Communities must consider these needs in the short term as well as the long term (Smart Communities Network).

Traditional Neighborhood Design: These neighborhoods encompass many modern land use strategies into one concept. Several cities across the nation (including Sacramento) have studied these models to improve the efficiency and facilitate the use of transit, pedestrian, and other alternatives to single-occupant motor vehicles. Public transportation and pedestrian use is encouraged through compact neighborhood development, where the distance from the center to the edge of a neighborhood can be walked at an easy pace in 10 minutes. Public interaction is fostered through the development of sidewalks, trees along streets, narrow roads that slow down cars, and parks or plazas that are located close to housing.

Universal Design: Various sources list the Seven Basic Principles of Universal Design:

1. Equitable Use (design is fair)
2. Flexibility in Use (design is adjustable)
3. Simple and Intuitive Use (design is elegant)
4. Perceptible Information (design is obvious)
5. Tolerance for Error (design is safe)
6. Low Physical Effort (design is easy)
7. Size and Space for Approach and Use (design is reasonable)

Urban: Areas generally characterized by moderate and higher density residential development (e.g., 5 or more dwelling units per acre), commercial development, and industrial development.

Urban Design: The attempt to give form, in terms of both beauty and function, to entire areas or to whole cities. The focus is on the massing and organization of buildings and on the spaces between them, rather than on the design of individual structures.

Urban Service Area: The area eligible to receive urban infrastructure (sewer and/or water service) in the short term.

Valued Environment: A place that holds personal meaning for a group of people, who may act to enhance or protect it.

Visual Preference Survey: An innovative and successful technique that enable citizens to evaluate physical images of natural and built environments. The process involves asking participants to view and evaluate a wide variety of slides depicting streetscapes, land use, site designs, building types, etc. Individual scores indicate whether the participant likes what they have seen and whether they feel it is appropriate for the community.

Zoning: Local codes regulating the use and development of property. The zoning ordinance divides the city or county into land use districts of "zones," represented on zoning maps, and specifies the allowable uses within each of those zones. It establishes development standards for each zone, such as minimum lot size, maximum height of structures, building setbacks, and yard size.

C. Acronyms and Abbreviations

The following acronyms and abbreviations relate to the fields of municipal and regional planning and development.

ACEC — area of critical environmental concern
ADT — Average Daily Traffic
APF — Adequate Public Facilities
ARPA — Archaeological Resources Protection Act
AUM — animal unit month
BA — Biological Assessment
BCC — Birds of Conservation Concern
BE — Biological Evaluation

BMP — Best Management Practices
BRT — Bus Rapid Transit
CCC — consult, cooperate, and coordinate
CEQ — Council of Environmental Quality
CIP — Capital Improvement Program
CO — carbon monoxide
CRD — Clustered Residential Development
CSD — Context Sensitive Design
CWA — Clean Water Act
DEIS — Draft Environmental Impact Statement
EA — Environmental Assessment
EIR — Environmental Impact Report
EIS — Environmental Impact Statement
EPA — Environmental Protection Agency
ESA — Endangered Species Act
FAR — Floor Area Ratio
FGT — Fixed Guideway Transit
GFA — Gross Floor Area
GIS — Geographic Information System
IGA — Intergovernmental Agreement
IMPLAN — Impact Analysis for Planning
LOS — Level of Service
LSS — Level of Service Standard
MPOT — Master Plan of Transportation
NAAQS — National Ambient Air Quality Standard
NEPA — National Environmental Policy Act
NHPA — National Historic Preservation Act
NLCS — National Landscape Conservation System
NOI — notice of intent
NOX — oxides of nitrogen
NRA — Natural Reserve Area
03 — Ozone
OHV — Off Highway Vehicle
PAB — Planning Area Boundary
PLC — Public Lands Council
PLF — Public Lands Foundation
PM — particulate matter
POD — Pedestrian-Oriented Development
PSD — prevention of significant deterioration
PUD — Planned United Development
RNAs — Research Natural Areas
SEF — Sensitive Environmental Features
SFR — Single Family Residential
SOI — Sphere of Influence
SOX — oxides of sulphur
SWL — Sustaining Working Landscapes
T&E — Threatened or Endangered
TCP — Tree Conservation Plan
TDR — Transfer of Development Rights
TIP — Transportation Improvement Program
TMP — Transit Master Plan
TNC — The Nature Conservancy
TND — Traditional Neighborhood Design
TNR — temporary, nonrenewable

TOD — Transit-Oriented Development
USA — Urban Service Area
USC — United States Code
USFS — U.S. Forest Service
USFWS — U.S. Fish and Wildlife Service
WSA — Wilderness Study Area

D. Regional Resource Directory

The local governments included in the best practices section are listed below alphabetically by their name.

Central City: co.somerset.pa.us/
Annapolis: http://www.ci.annapolis.md.us/
Asheville: http://www.ashevillenc.gov/
Atlanta: http://www.atlantaga.org/
Austin: http://www.austintexas.org/
Billings: http://www.billings.mt.us/
Blackwater: http://www.docogo.com/
Charleston: http://www.charleston-sc.gov/
Charlotte: http://charmeck.org/
Chattanooga: http://www.chattanooga.gov/
Chicago: http://www.ci.chi.il.us/
Columbus: http://www.cityofcolumbus.org/
Concord: http://www.ci.concord.nh.us/
Dallas: dallascityhall.com/
Daybreak: http://www.southjordancity.org/
Denver: http://www.denvergov.org/
Detroit: http://www.detroitmi.gov/
Eugene: http://www.eugene-or.gov/
Flagstaff: http://www.flagstaff.az.gov/
Gaithersburg: http://www.gaithersburgmd.gov/
Greensburg: http://www.greensburgks.org/
Hartford: http://www.hartford.gov/
Huntersville: http://www.huntersville.org/
Ithaca: http://www.ci.ithaca.ny.us/
Los Angeles: http://www.lacity.org/
Memphis: http://www.cityofmemphis.org/
Minneapolis: http://www.ci.minneapolis.mn.us/
North Fair Oaks: http://www.nfocouncil.org/
Oakland: http://www.oaklandnet.com/
Oregon City: http://www.orcity.org/
Philadelphia: http://www.phila.gov/
Portland: http://www.portlandonline.com/
Salt Lake City: http://www.ci.slc.ut.us/
San Francisco: http://www.sfgov.org/
Santa Rosa: http://www.ci.santa-rosa.ca.us/
Savannah: http://www.savannahga.gov/
Seattle: http://www.cityofseattle.net/
South Amboy: http://www.southamboynj.gov/
Syracuse: http://www.syracuse.ny.us/
Tacoma: http://www.cityoftacoma.org/
Tallahassee: http://www.talgov.com/
Washington, D.C.: http://www.dc.gov/

E. National Resource Directory

Major national professional associations, foundations, and research organizations serving local governments, as well as environmentally concerned professionals and citizens are listed here.

Advisory Council on Historic Preservation: http://www.achp.gov/

Air and Waste Management Association: http://www.awma.org/

Alliance for National Renewal: http://www.ncl.org/anr/

Alliance for Regional Stewardship: http://www.regionalstewardship.org/

America Walks: http://www.americawalks.org/

American Economic Development Council: http://www.aedc.org/

American Planning Association: http://www.planning.org/

American Public Works Association: http://www.apwa.net/

American Real Estate and Urban Economics Association: http://www.areuea.org/

American Society for Public Administration: http://www.aspanet.org/

American Water Resources Association: http://www.awra.org/

American Water Works Association: http://www.awwa.org/

Asset-Based Community Development Institute: http://www.nwu.edu/IPR/abcd.html/

Association for Enterprise Opportunity: http://www.microenterpriseworks.org/

Brownfields Technology Support Center: http://brownfieldssc.org/

Building Officials and Code Administrators International: http://www.bocai.org/

Canadian Mortgage and Housing Corporation: http://www.cmha.ca/

CEO's for Cities: http://www.ceosforcities.org/

Clean Cities: http://www.eere.energy.gov/

Community Associations Institute: http://www.caionline.org/

Community Development Society International: http://comm-dev.org/

Congress for New Urbanism: http://www.cnu.org/

Corporation for Enterprise Development: http://www.cfed.org/

Council for Urban Economic Development: http://www.cued.org/

Downtown Development and Research Center: http://www.DowntownDevelopment.com/

Ecological Society of America: http://www.esa.org/

Enterprise Green Communities: http://www.greencommunitiesonline.org/

Federal Transit Administration: http://fta.gov/

Environmental Assessment Association: http://www.iami.org/eaa.html/

Global Alliance for EcoMobility: http://us.mg203.mail.yahoo.com/

Government Finance Officers Association: http://www.gfoa.org/

Green Building Focus: http://www.greenbuildingfocus.com/

Green Cities California: http://www.greencitiescalifornia.org/

Green Corps: http://www.greencorps.org/

Green Job Corps: http://www.greenjobcorps.org/

Greenroofs.com: http://www.greenroofs.com/

Institute of Transportation Engineers: http://www.ite.org/

Insurance Institute for Highway Safety: http://www.iihs.org/

International City/County Management Association: http://www.icma.org/

International Conference of Building Officials: http://www.icbo.org/

International Downtown Association: http://ida-downtown.org/

Leadership in Energy & Environmental Design: http://www.leed.net/

Livable Streets Initiative: http://www.livablestreets.com/

Local Government Commission: http://www.lgc.org/

Local Government for Sustainability: http://www.iclei.org/

Low Impact Development Center, Inc.: http://www.lowimpactdevelopment.org/

National Association for Environmental Management: http://www.naem.org/

National Association of Counties: http://www.naco.org/

National Association of Development Organizations: http://www.nado.org/

National Association of Flood and Stormwater Management Agencies: http://www.nafsma.org/

National Association of Housing and Redevelopment Officials: http://www.nahro.org/

National Association of Local Government Environmental Professionals: http://www.nalgep.org/

National Association of Regional Councils: http://www.narc.org/

National Association of State Development Agencies: http://www.ids.net/nasda/

National Audubon Society: http://www.audubon.org/

National Center for Safe Routes to School: http://www.saferoutesinfo.org/

National Center for the Revitalization of Central Cities: http://www.uno.edu/~cupa/ncrcc/

National Civic League: http://www.ncl.org/

National Community Development Association: http://www.ncdaonline.org/

National Congress for Community Economic Development: http://www.ncced.org/

National Council for Urban Economic Development: http://www.ncued.org/

National Green Energy Council: http://www.greenenergycouncil.com/

National Ground Water Association: http://www.ngwa.org/

National League of Cities: http://www.nlc.org/

National Main Street Center: http://www.mainst.org/

National Resources Defense Council: http://www.nrdc.org/

National Rural Water Association: http://www.nrwa.org/

National Trust for Historic Preservation: http://www.mainst.org/

Nature Conservancy: http://www.nature.org/

New Urbanism: http://www.newurbanism.org/

Orton Family Foundation: http://www.orton.org/

Partners for Livable Communities: http://www.livable.com/

Partnership for a Walkable America: http://www.walkableamerica.org/

Pedestrian and Bicycle Safety: http://safety.dot.gov/

Preservation Initiatives: http://www.pi-inc.net/

Preservation Institute: http://www.preservennet.com/

Rails-to-Trails Conservancy: http://www.railtrails.org/

Rocky Mountain Institute: http://rmi.org/

Sierra Club: http://www.sierraclub.org/

Smart Growth America: http://www.smartgrowthamerica.org/

Society of Wetland Scientists: http://www.sws.org/

Sonoran Institute: http://www.sonoraninstitute.org/

Trust for Public Land: http://www.tpl.org/

U.S. Conference of Mayors: http://www.usmayors.org/

U.S. Department of Agriculture: http://www.nrcs.usda.gov/

U.S. Department of Energy: http://www.energy.gov/

U.S. Department of Housing and Urban Development: http://www.hud.gov/

U.S. Department of the Interior: http://www.doi.gov/

U.S. Department of Transportation: http://www.dot.gov/

U.S. Environmental Protection Agency: http://www.epa.gov/

U.S. Fish and Wildlife Service: http://www.rws.gov/

U.S. Green Building Council: http://www.usgbc.org/

Urban Design: http://www.urbandesign.org/

The Urban Institute: http://www.urban.org/

Urban Land Institute: http://www.uli.org/

Walk Score: http://www.walkscore.com/

Walkable Communities: http://www.walkable.org/

Walkable Streets: http://www.walkablestreets.com/

Water Environment Federation: http://www.wef.org/

Water Environment Research Foundation: http://www.werf.org/

Water Quality Association: http://www.wqa.org/

World Carfree Network: http://www.worldcarfree.net/

World Future Society: http://www.wfs.org/

F. State Municipal League Directory

Most states have a municipal league, which serves as a valuable source of information about municipal governments. State leagues frequently have copies of municipal laws and policies, as well as model practices available for public officials to review in their state. The contact information for the various leagues is shown below.

Alabama League of Municipalities: http://www.alalm.org/

Alaska Municipal League: http://www.akml.org/

League of Arizona Cities and Towns: http://www.azleague.org/

Arkansas Municipal League: http://www.arml.org/

League of California Cities: http://www.cacities.org/

Colorado Municipal League: http://www.www.cml.org/

Connecticut Conference of Municipalities: http://www.ccm-ct.org/

Delaware League of Local Governments: http://www.ipa.udel.edu/localgovt/dllg/

Florida League of Cities: http://www.flcitics.com/

Georgia Municipal Association: http://www.gma net.com/

Association of Idaho Cities: http://www.idaho cities.org/

Illinois Municipal League: http://www.iml.org/

Indiana Association of Cities and Towns: http://www.citiesandtowns.org/

Iowa League of Cities: http://www.iowaleague.org/

League of Kansas Municipalities: http://www.lkm.org/

Kentucky League of Cities: http://www.klc.org/

Louisiana Municipal Association: http://www.lamunis.org/

Maine Municipal Association: http://www.me mun.org/

Maryland Municipal League: http://www.md municipal.org/

Massachusetts Municipal Association: http://www.mma.org/

Michigan Municipal League: http://www.mml.org/

League of Minnesota Cities: http://www.lmnc.org/

Mississippi Municipal League: http://www.mml online.com/

Missouri Municipal League: http://www.mo cities.com/

Montana League of Cities: http://www.mlct.org/

League of Nebraska Municipalities: http://www.lonm.org/

Nevada League of Cities and Municipalities: http://www.nvleague.org/

New Hampshire Local Government Center: http://www.nhmunicipal.org/

New Jersey State League of Municipalities: http://www.njslom.com/

New Mexico Municipal League: http://www.nmml.org/

New York Conference of Mayors and Municipal Officials: http://www.nycom.org/

North Carolina League of Municipalities: http://www.nclm.org/

North Dakota League of Cities: http://www.ndlc.org/

Ohio Municipal League: http://www.omuni league.org/

Oklahoma Municipal League: http://www.oml.org/

League of Oregon Cities: http://www.orcities.org/

Pennsylvania League of Cities and Municipalities: http://www.plcm.org/

Rhode Island League of Cities and Towns: http://www.rileague.org/

Municipal Association of South Carolina: http://www.www.masc.sc/

South Dakota Municipal League: http://www.sdmunicipalleague.org/

Tennessee Municipal League: http://www.tmll.org/

Texas Municipal League: http://www.tml.org/

Utah League of Cities and Towns: http://ulct.ocg/

Vermont League of Cities and Towns: http://www.vlct.org/

Virginia Municipal League: http://vml.org/

Association of Washington Cities: http://www.awcnet.org/

West Virginia Municipal League: http://www.wvml.org/

League of Wisconsin Municipalities: http://www.lwm-info.org/

Wyoming Association of Municipalities: http://www.wyomuni.org/

G. State Library Directory

Most state libraries have copies of state laws, both proposed and adopted, in an online database. Many states also have copies of the various laws adopted in those cities and towns within their jurisdiction. They are an excellent resource. The contact information for the various state libraries is shown below.

Alabama: http://www.apls.state.la.us/

Alaska: http://www.library.state.ak.us/

Arizona: http://www.lib.az.us/

Arkansas: http://www.asl.lib.ar.us/

California: http://www.library.ca.gov/

Colorado: http://www.cde.state.co.us/

Connecticut: http://www.cslib.org/

Delaware: http://www.state.lib.de.us/

District of Columbia: http:/dclibrary.org/

Florida: http://dlis.dos.state.fl.us/

Georgia: http://www.georgialibraries.org/

Hawaii: http://www.librarieshawaii.org/

Idaho: http://www.lili.org/

Illinois: http://www.cyberdriveillinois.com/de partments/library/

Indiana: http://www.statelib.lib.in.us/

Iowa: http://www.silo.lib.ia.us/

Kansas: http://www.skyways.org/KSL/

Kentucky: http://www.kdla.ky.gov/

Louisiana: http://www.state.lib.la.us/

Maine: http://www.state.me.us/msl/

Maryland: http://www.sailor.lib.md.us/

Massachusetts: http://mass.gov/mblc/
Michigan: http://www.michigan.gov/hal/
Minnesota: http://www.state.mn.us/libraries/
Mississippi: http.//www.mlc.lib.ms.us/
Missouri: http://www.sos.mo.gov/library/
Montana: http://msl.state.mt.us/
Nebraska: http.7/www.nlc.statc.ne.us/
Nevada: http://dmla.clan.lib.nv.us/
New Hampshire: http://www.state.nh.us/nhls/
New Jersey: http://www.njstatelib.org/
New Mexico: http://www.stlib.state.nm.us/
New York: http://www.nysl.nysed.gov/
North Carolina: http://statelibrary.dcr.state.nc.us/
North Dakota: http://ndsl.lib.state.nd.us/
Ohio: http://winslo.state.oh.us/
Oklahoma: http://www.odl.state.ok.us/

Oregon: http://oregon.gov/OSL/
Pennsylvania: http://www.statelibrary.state.pa.us/libraries/
Rhode Island: http://www.olis.ri.gov/
South Carolina: http://www.statelibrary.sc.gov/
South Dakota: http://www.sdstatelibrary.com/
Tennessee: http://www.tennessee.gov/tsla/
Texas: http://www.tsl.state.tx.us/
Utah: http://library.ut.gov/index.html/
Vermont: http://dol.state.vt.us/
Virginia: http://www.lva.lib.va.us/
Washington: http://www.secstate.was.gov/library/
West Virginia: http://librarycommission/lib.wv.us/
Wisconsin: http://www.dpi.state.wi.us/dltcl/pld/
Wyoming: http://www-wsl.state.wy.us/

About the Editors and Contributors

Editors

Roger L. Kemp, ICMA-CM, has been a city manager of cities on the west and east coasts of the United States for more than 25 years. He holds the ICMA designations of Credentialed City Manager (since 2002) and Legacy Leader (since 2007). He has also been a visiting scholar, senior adjunct professor, professorial lecturer, and adjunct professor at leading universities during his city management career.

Carl J. Stephani, ICMA-CM, has a bachelor's degree from the University of California at Berkeley, and a master's of regional planning from the Maxwell School of Citizenship and Public Affairs of Syracuse University. He began his local government career in the Mayor's Office of Neighborhood Government in New York City, and has worked for cities, counties, and regional governments in California, Oregon, Colorado, Arizona, and Connecticut. He is the author of *Zoning 101* (National League of Cities).

Contributors

The affiliations of the contributors are as of the time the articles were written.

John Abendroth, administrator, Watershed Planning and Coordination Section, Division of Water Resource Management, Department of Environmental Protection, State of Florida, Tallahassee.

Thomas Arrandale, free-lance writer, Livingston, Montana.

Theresa Barger, staff writer and copy editor, *The Hartford Courant*, Hartford, Connecticut.

Gary Binger, director, California Smart Growth Initiative, Urban Land Institute, Regional District Office, San Francisco.

Kyle Boelte, communications specialist, Sierra Club, San Francisco, California.

Johanna Brickman, associate partner and director of sustainability, ZGF Architects LLP, Portland, Oregon.

Dan Burden, executive director, the Walkable and Livable Communities Institute, Port Townsend, Washington.

Ryan Chin, research specialist, Media Lab, Smart Car Research Group, School of Architecture and Planning, Massachusetts Institute of Technology, Cambridge.

Storm Cunningham, chief executive officer, RestorAbility Inc., Alexandria, Virginia.

Maurice Estes, Jr., environmental planner/program manager, Space Research Association, National Space Science and Technology Center, University of Alabama, Huntsville.

G.M. Filisko, attorney and free-lance writer, Chicago, Illinois.

Kevin Fletcher, executive director, Audubon International, Headquarters Office, Selkirk, New York.

Steve Garman, city manager, City of Decatur, Illinois.

Fanis Grammenos, principal, Urban Pattern Associates, Ottawa, Ontario, Canada.

Michael Glenn, director of housing programs, Division of Housing and Community Development, State of Utah, Salt Lake City.

Sharon Harkcom, secretary-treasurer, Borough of Central City, Pennsylvania.

Tracy Hatmaker, township administrator, Prairie Township, Franklin County, Ohio.

Christopher Hawthorne, architecture critic, *Los Angeles Times*, California.

Jim Heid, founder and president, UrbanGreen, LLC, San Francisco, California.

Allan Hope, executive director, Main Street Program, City of South Amboy, New Jersey.

Alan Horton, managing director, the Freshwater Trust, Portland, Oregon.

Lawrence Houstoun, redevelopment, public spaces, and improvement district consultant, Philadelphia, Pennsylvania.

Insurance Institute for Highway Safety, an independent, nonprofit, scientific, and educational organization, Arlington, Virginia.

Margaret C.H. Kelly, consultant, Public Finance Program, Trust for Public Land, San Francisco, California.

Miriam Landman, writer and green building advisor, City of San Rafael, California.

Cherie Langlois, free-lance writer, Graham, Washington.

John Laplante, chief transportation planning engineer, T.Y. Lin International Inc., Chicago, Illinois.

Glen Martin, environment writer, *San Francisco Chronicle*, California.

Jill Mazullo, free-lance writer and director of communications, 1000 Friends of Minnesota, St. Paul.

Barbara McCann, president, McCann Consulting, Washington, D.C.

Joe McElroy, founder and president, McElroy Associates, Naperville, Illinois.

Robert McIntyre, community planner and landscape architect, Austin, Texas.

Edward T. McMahon, senior resident fellow and Charles E. Fraser Chair for Sustainable Development and Environmental Policy, Urban Land Institute, Washington, D.C.

Leah Miller, director of clean water programs, Izaak Walton League of America, Inc., Gaithersburg, Maryland.

Tucker Mitchell, free-lance writer and editor, Huntersville, North Carolina.

Josh Murphy, digital coast manager, Coastal Services Center, National Oceanic and Atmospheric Administration, U. S. Department of Commerce, Charleston, South Carolina.

Sam Newberg, founder and president, Joe Urban, Inc., Minneapolis, Minnesota.

Zach Patton, staff writer, *Governing Magazine*, eRepublic Inc., Washington, D.C.

Greg Plotkin, free-lance writer, Washington, D.C.

Dale Quattrochi, geographer/senior research scientist, Marshall Space Flight Center, National Aeronautics and Space Administration, Huntsville, Alabama.

Glenn Reinhardt, executive director, Water Environment Research Foundation, Alexandria, Virginia.

Anthony Sasson, freshwater conservation manager, The Nature Conservancy, Ohio Chapter, Dublin.

Paul Sedway, principal, Sedway Consulting, San Francisco, California.

Erin Sherer, supervisor for compliance and enforcement, Environmental Protection Agency, State of Ohio, Columbus.

Elizabeth Stasiak, project manager, International City/County Management Association, Washington, D.C.

Matt Stransberry, freelance writer, Needham, Massachusetts.

Dell Tredinnick, project development manager, Build It Green Program, City of Santa Rosa, California.

Paul Tullis, free-lance writer, Los Angeles, California.

John Van Gieson, free-lance writer, Tallahassee, Florida.

Chad Vander Veen, contributor, *Governing*, Washington, D.C.; and associate editor, *Government Technology*, Folsom, California.

A. Elizabeth Watson, principal, Heritage Strategies LLC, Sugarloaf, Pennsylvania.

Don Waye, outreach coordinator, Nonpoint Source Control Branch, Office of Wetlands, Oceans and Watersheds, U.S. Environmental Protection Agency, Washington, D.C.

Mat Webber, project watershed coordinator, Izaak Walton League of America, Inc., Cazenovia, New York.

Michael Willis, general manager, City of Blue Mountains, New South Wales, Australia.

Jay Womack, director of sustainable design, Wight and Company, Darien, Illinois.

Heather Wooten, senior planning and policy associate, Planning for Healthy Places Program, Public Health Law and Policy, Oakland, California.

Matthew Zieper, research director, Public Finance Program, Trust for Public Land, San Francisco, California.

Index